DISCIPLINE of POWER

JEFFREY SIMPSON
DISCIPLINE of POWER

THE CONSERVATIVE INTERLUDE AND THE LIBERAL RESTORATION

Macmillan of Canada
A Division of Gage Publishing Limited
Toronto, Canada

Copyright © 1980, 1984, Jeffrey Simpson
All rights reserved. The use of any part of this publication
reproduced, transmitted in any form or by any means,
electronic, mechanical, photocopying, recording, or otherwise, or stored in a retrieval system, without the prior
consent of the publisher is an infringement of copyright
law.

Originally published by Personal Library

Macmillan of Canada
A Division of Gage Publishing Limited

Canadian Cataloguing in Publication Data
Simpson, Jeffrey, 1949-
    Discipline of power

Includes index.
ISBN 0-7715-9875-0

1. Canada - Politics and government - 1979-1980.*
I. Title

FC630.S55 1984   971.064'5   C84-098193-7
F1034.2.S55 1984

Printed in Canada

For RLS, ECS, and WEB

Acknowledgements

This book could not have been written without the cooperation of many members of Canada's three political parties who patiently answered my inquiries and gave me their impressions about the events discussed in these pages. Since our conversations were all "off-the-record," I cannot name them individually, but they will know in reading the book my debt to them. I would especially like to thank the Right Honourable Joe Clark, who re-lived these events with me without ever asking what I might write about him or his Government.

Four friends and fellow-journalists read parts of the manuscript and made many valuable suggestions for which I am grateful: Bill Fox of the Ottawa bureau of *The Toronto Star*; Graham Fraser, Quebec bureau chief of *The Gazette* (Montreal); Colin MacKenzie, assistant national editor of *The Globe and Mail*; and Geoffrey Stevens, associate editor (Ottawa) of *The Globe and Mail*. My editor, Jennifer Glossop, was enormously efficient and considerate.

I owe a special debt to Richard J. Doyle, editor-in-chief of *The Globe and Mail*, and to Edward Moser, the paper's managing editor, who graciously granted me a leave-of-absence to complete the manuscript.

Finally the writing of this book was inspired by my wife, Wendy Bryans, *sine qua non*.

Ottawa, 1980

Contents

Introduction

They had worked so hard for this day that no one could begrudge them their smiles. After sixteen years in Opposition, the cream of the Conservative Party rose up the steps of Government House, past the waiting crush of reporters, to take their seats in the white and gold ballroom. There, in turn, they swore their loyalties to Queen and country as members of Prime Minister Joe Clark's Cabinet.

It was June 4, 1979, one of those sweet days of sunshine and the smell of cut grass that come late in the capital's brief spring. Earlier that day, Pierre Trudeau had handed his resignation to Governor General Edward Schreyer, jumped into his sportscar and sped down the curving driveway towards apparent retirement. His parting words were "I'm free." When the Conservatives arrived several hours later, all handshakes and backslaps and smiles, it appeared that the Trudeau era in Canadian politics was over.

The Conservatives, after eleven years of heartbreaking failure against Trudeau, had finally defeated their nemesis. They had not routed him, because their overwhelming triumph in English Canada had been partially blunted by Quebec's unshakable devotion to the Liberals and to Trudeau. As a result the election left the Conservatives six seats short of a majority government. But their minority position did not seem to bother them; they all but put it out of their minds, for they imagined that the election of 1979 was not an isolated event, but the harbinger of a prolonged period of Conservative rule in Canada.

The Conservatives had won the election with fewer votes than the Liberals had received and the PCs remained a minority party, but such a sour reflection seemed out of place now as Cabinet ministers, clutching their family Bibles and curbing their joy in order to look suitably dignified for the ceremony, took their oaths of office. Each was introduced to the Governor General by the new Prime Minister. Joe Clark was in many ways an improbable national leader, but he had given his party the internal cohesion it needed to win. Clark, who would turn forty the next day, had not captured the hearts of Canadians; but he had won enough of their votes to defeat Trudeau. The Conservatives were finally in power after five consecutive electoral defeats. For those who watched the new ministers congratulate each other and willingly answer reporters' questions that day, it was hard not to be touched by their infectious enthusiasm and beaming countenances.

Two hundred fifty-nine days later, the Conservative interlude was over, and the Liberals were restored to power. This book is one observer's account of that extraordinary period in Canadian politics. It analyzes the tragically erroneous assumptions of the men and women of the Conservative Party who, conditioned by an extended spell in Opposition, could not wield effectively the political power they had finally won. It would be easy to write their story with cynicism, or even with sarcasm. It would be simple to explain the Conservative Government's troubled life and premature death, as some have already done, by dismissing Clark and his Cabinet as bumbling incompetents. It might be satisfying to say that the Conservatives simply met the fate they deserved, and none too soon, at that. But such simplistic explanations will not suffice for what befell the Conservatives.

Blunders there were aplenty. Some were crass and took a deserved political toll. Others were born of misplaced confidences and faulty assumptions, for which sympathy can be offered but no credit can be extended to the party. Still others were the product of inexperience in governing; for how can a long-standing minority party ever grasp the nettle of governing when it finds itself so frequently in Opposition? Indeed, the assumptions upon which the Conservatives foundered could trip any party long removed from the discipline of power.

The Conservatives are Canada's party of the Official Opposition. Before winning the 1979 election, the Conservatives had been in Opposition for sixteen consecutive years, and for about thirty-eight of the forty-four years since the Conservative Government of Prime Minister R. B. Bennett was defeated in 1935. As a result, the Conservatives developed an Opposition-party mentality—an approach to problems born of reaction to the exercise of power rather than the wielding of it.

Any party is a coalition of interests bound together by certain common perceptions and the driving ambition to take power. Successful pursuit of that ambition is a party's surest cement; unrequited ambition produces doubt, quarrelling, and division. That is why the Conservatives have been the more fractious of Canada's two major political parties. Even in power under Prime Minister John Diefenbaker from 1957 to 1963, the party was racked by internal dissension. The bitterness surrounding Diefenbaker's electoral defeat and removal from the leadership in 1967 plagued efforts by his successor, Robert Stanfield, to give unity to the Conservatives and to win the country. To Joe Clark's credit, he succeeded as leader of the Opposition in bringing discipline and purpose to his ranks; but there was little he could do to overcome his own inexperience and that of his team. They were skilled in the politics of the Opposition, but were untutored in the defensive compromises of power.

The lifeblood of an Opposition party is rhetoric: the penetrating phrase, the daily portrayal of things as worse than they really are, the ongoing effort to exploit verbally the electorate's discontent with the Government of the day. Often imperceptibly, an Opposition party can begin to believe its own rhetoric; can believe that the nation teeters on the brink of catastrophe. This rhetoric usually deepens the determination of an Opposition party, especially if it has been long removed from power, to act in a fashion boldly different from that of the former ruling party, once given a chance to govern. This determination, in turn, leads an Opposition party to feel compelled to design comprehensive solutions to every problem. Repeated electoral defeat engenders an almost desperate desire to develop policies in order to answer every question and so persuade the electorate that the Opposition party is ready to govern. This desire is compounded when an Opposition party has a deep-seated nervousness about its ability to govern. A shelf full of comprehensive and ready policies eases this nervousness.

Problems inevitably arise for at least two reasons, as the Conservatives discovered. First, some Opposition policies, developed simply in order to be different from those of the Government, are more politically compelling than intellectually sound. Secondly, policies take on a liturgical quality through incessant repetition. Since these policies are not moulded by the discipline of power, they remain unchanged and can become political liabilities rather than assets. Thus, when a party such as the Conservatives arrives in power after a long march from Opposition, it can find itself with a sackful of weighty promises strung across its back, and it must soon decide just what to do with this burden.

This leads the party into a terrible predicament. An extended spell in Opposition has likely convinced the party that its rival in power is venal and unprincipled. How else to explain the other party's long stay in office while the country headed towards ruin? This conviction stiffens the Opposition party's determination not to shift positions, once in power, as cynically as its rival had done. The Opposition party convinces itself that the public is tired of half-measures and expediency. This supposition means that once in power the party wants to keep its promises, even at political cost, because in the long run voters will surely prefer honour to expediency. On the other hand, time has elapsed and circumstances may have changed since the policies were initially announced. Once in power, the civil service and interest groups start telling the party its policies are wrong. What was so pristine in Opposition becomes clouded by power. If the Opposition party won on a protest vote against its rival, as the Conservatives did in 1979, the policies probably counted for little in the election result. Some of the policies become political millstones, and the question arises: which are kept and which are jettisoned? The party is damned either way, just as the Conservatives were from their first day in office.

Ironically and sadly for them, the Conservatives knew how limited their mandate for change was when they won the 1979 election. They had based their campaign on an astute exploitation of the electorate's fatigue with Liberal Prime Minister Pierre Trudeau. They knew that Canadians had not voted enthusiastically for Joe Clark. The Conservatives' own survey data showed them how unstructured the electorate's desire for change was. Yet they forgot all these things after their triumph, and set about making changes for which insufficient popular support existed, without ever trying—until it was too late—to build a constituency for what they had in mind. And many voters, understandably, having echoed in 1979 the feelings about Trudeau that Henry II once expressed of Becket—"Who will rid me from this turbulent priest?"—were as surprised, angry and ultimately as full of doubt as Henry at the string of unexpected consequences that flowed from the initial outburst of rage.

The Liberals were astonished at the opportunity to return to power. Profoundly convinced that they were Canada's rightful rulers, they sat morosely in Opposition, disdainful of their adversaries but equivocal about their own party's leadership. Unwilling to reflect on their mistakes in office and ill-prepared for a searching examination of future plans, the Liberals were treading water. But familiarity with power had given them an instinct for survival that sustained the party long after principles had been abandoned and power had been lost. Never has this instinct served the Liberals better than in 1980, when they seized the chance offered by the Conservatives' braggadocio and recaptured power.

Politics is like an endless river winding its way through the nation's psychological terrain. Elections are the white-water passages, where political life froths and boils, hurtling the participants at accelerating speeds through a chute of perils towards calm waters at the end. This book is an account of our politicians' two most recent brushes with the white-water passages of politics: the election of 1979, which brought Joe Clark to power, and the election of 1980, in which he was defeated. Twice within eleven months, voters were confronted by the rich public spectacle of election campaigns: colourful and carefully staged rallies; parades of canvassers winding up city streets and down country roads; debates among candidates; and most obviously, by reports about the campaigns on television, that demanding mistress of modern politics whose attention it was the abiding purpose of every party to attract. What voters did not see behind this public spectacle were the machinations and private calculations of those who shaped the parties' campaigns. This book attempts to explain some of these calculations, and to describe how an election campaign is structured around them.

For all the money and effort, neither the campaign of 1979 nor that of 1980 was decisive. In both cases, the party entering the campaign ahead in the polls wound up the winner, although the Conservatives lost ground during their victorious campaign of 1979 and improved their position during their losing campaign of 1980.

Victory, however, has a way of misleading the triumphant. For the Conservatives, power numbed their political judgement and lulled them into a series of disastrous assumptions. As a result, they frittered away the power that has come their way about once a generation in this century. They were vanquished by power, their hopes blasted, their illusions shattered and their confidence shaken, with only the flickering and bittersweet remembrance of their months in power to warm them on the chill benches of the Opposition.

PART ONE: DEFEAT

~ 1 ~

The Collapse of the Government

By 10 p.m. on Wednesday, December 12, 1979, the four bars at the Liberal Party caucus Christmas party were doing a brisk business. An hour earlier, before the crowd arrived, it had taken only seconds to purchase a drink; now, a crush of people waited at each bar, sending bartenders scurrying for refills of scotch and gin. At one end of the huge, wood-panelled room on the second floor of Parliament's West Block, a band was playing Christmas carols that could barely be heard above the racket of talk and laughter. It was so crowded that people stood in the corridor to catch a breath of air. Some spilled prematurely into nearby committee rooms, transformed for the evening into places where Liberals and their guests could eat a late-night buffet.

An excitement was in the air that transcended the high spirits of the season. Liberal leader Pierre Trudeau had arrived at 9:15, but he stayed only twenty minutes, long enough for the caucus to present him with a Christmas-cum-retirement gift. Trudeau had announced just three weeks before, on November 21, that he was resigning as party leader. The party's national executive had already called a leadership convention for March 28-30 in Winnipeg, and the Liberal caucus was absorbed in the unfolding leadership race.

The only important public move in the leadership contest so far had been former Finance Minister John Turner's announcement two days earlier that he would not be a candidate. Pierre De Bané, a former Minister of Supply and Services and M.P. for Matapédia-Matane, had entered the race, but he was not a serious contender. The big names were yet to come.

Former Liberal Finance Minister Donald Macdonald, who had resigned his Commons seat in early 1978 and returned to practise law in Toronto, had already formed a campaign organization and planned to announce his candidacy formally after Christmas. Kathy Robinson, a Toronto lawyer and one of the best organizers in the Liberal Party, had agreed to serve as Macdonald's campaign manager. She arrived at the caucus Christmas party having spent the day prowling around Parliament Hill lobbying for Macdonald. Stephen Goudge, another Toronto lawyer who had volunteered to serve as Macdonald's executive assistant for the leadership campaign, was also circulating through the caucus party after spending the day in Ottawa on private business. Among those shaking hands and offering best wishes of the season to those at the party were other leadership aspirants, including former Agriculture Minister Eugene Whelan from Windsor, former Consumer and Corporate Affairs Minister Herb Gray from the same city, and former Finance Minister Jean Chrétien from Shawinigan. Lloyd Axworthy, the freshman M.P. from Winnipeg, was spending Wednesday in Toronto, scouting his own leadership chances. While his colleagues amused themselves in Ottawa on Wednesday night, he attended a reception of prominent Liberals in Toronto organized by Lorna Marsden, a vice-president of the Liberal Party's national executive and an enthusiastic backer of Axworthy for the leadership.

But, curiously perhaps, the talk at the party was not about the leadership race. Instead, the crowd erupted in a roar when Trudeau received his gift: a chainsaw "to cut down the government," said the master of ceremonies. Trudeau smiled at the reaction, offered a few words of appreciation, and made his way through the crowd towards the door.

"They're crazy. They'll never do it," Lynne Deniger, the wife of a young Liberal M.P. from Quebec, told a group of friends and reporters gathered in a corner of the room.

"Yes, we will. The Conservatives are nowhere in Quebec. That's obvious. There's no problem in my riding, of course, but even in other parts of the province, the Tories are in hopeless shape," interjected her husband, Pierre, M.P. for Laprairie riding on the south shore of Montreal.

Nearby, another group had been joined by Marc Lalonde, the godfather of the Quebec caucus and one of the few men in Ottawa close to Pierre Trudeau. Lalonde, a long-time minister under Trudeau and the Liberals' energy critic, was in splendid spirits, flashing a huge grin as he told his listeners about the Liberals' decision to vote against the Conservative budget brought down Tuesday night.

"People will never accept that eighteen-cent excise tax. We've got those two guys in hospital, but one is coming out tonight, I think, and the other is coming tomorrow night for sure. We'll have all our members there," he predicted.

"Do you want to bet on that?" someone asked sceptically.

"Sure, how about a hundred dollars?" Lalonde replied, his face growing tight.

For all his bonhomie, Lalonde was worried, as he later admitted, but the Liberals were caught up in a defiant mood, orchestrated by a few key men within the party. Public boasts about defeating the Government both reinforced their determination and assuaged their nervousness.

A few minutes later, Herb Gray and Eugene Whelan found themselves chatting with friends.

"We can't vote for that budget. It's too hard on low- and middle-income Canadians," said Gray with customary seriousness.

"Wait until the farmers hear about that excise tax," Whelan chimed in, his double chin quivering as he chuckled at the thought.

Similar talk was everywhere, and Stephen Goudge could not believe what he was hearing.

"They've gone crazy. I can't believe it. Why are they doing this?" he asked his dinner companions. None of them had attended the Wednesday morning meeting of the Liberal caucus and so groped for a reply.

Indeed, it did seem incredible, even to some Liberals, that the party might risk defeating the Conservative Government of Prime Minister Joe Clark, elected fewer than seven months before. True, the November Gallup Poll, published December 3, had shown a sharp drop in Conservative support. After hovering around 36 per cent in popular support for the summer and fall, the Conservatives tumbled to 28 per cent in the November Gallup Poll, nineteen points behind the Liberals. If the poll was accurate, the Conservatives were in serious political trouble. However, every so often the Gallup Poll reflects a wild swing in public opinion that is corrected in the next month's poll. Several powerful Liberals, including Jim Coutts, Trudeau's principal secretary, and Senator Keith Davey, the party's 1979 campaign chairman, had taken the November Gallup Poll seriously; it confirmed the Liberals' private polls showing the Conservatives in a perilous political position. But few of the rank-and-file Liberals thought the "blip" represented by the November Gallup Poll meant much. The Conservatives had also lost two by-elections in November, including former Prime Minister John Diefenbaker's riding of Prince Albert. But the Liberals had been expected to win former Minister Don Jamieson's Newfoundland seat of Burin-St. George's, and Diefenbaker's plurality, based more on loyalty to the Chief than to his party, had been sliced by nearly two-thirds in the 1979 election.

To fight an election campaign, the Liberals would need a committed leader. Trudeau had admitted that he was not the man to lead the renewal of the Liberal Party when he announced his intention to resign. He had bought a house in Montreal, where he intended to live with his three sons. Trudeau had been defeated in the May 22 election, and feelings against him were still running deep in English Canada, or so many Liberals believed. With a new leader, probably Donald Macdonald, the Liberals could regain lost ground in English Canada, retain a vise-grip on Quebec, and whip the Conservatives in a spring or fall campaign. It did not make sense to many English-speaking Liberals to court an election with Trudeau as the party leader when Macdonald was the alternative, even if the Conservatives were in political trouble. And the Liberal organization was not ready for a campaign; in fact, the party still had sizeable debts left over from the May campaign.

Speculating about an election seemed a titillating but academic exercise. After all, even if the Liberals threatened to vote to a man against Finance Minister John Crosbie's budget, the Conservatives would undoubtedly make a deal with the Créditistes, just as they had done on previous non-confidence votes since the beginning of the parliamentary session in early October. There were 136 Conservatives and five Créditistes in the Commons. Their combined strength totalled 141 votes, one vote more than the combined numbers of the Liberals with 113 (Speaker James Jerome, a Liberal, could vote only in the case of a tie) and the NDP with twenty-seven. There were a few Conservatives away from Ottawa, but if the vote looked close, the Conservative leadership would make certain that they returned. If the Liberals were pulling out all of their members, the Conservatives would see the danger and do likewise.

The Liberals could huff and puff all they liked about Crosbie's budget; they did not have the votes to bring the House down—or so it appeared to many rank-and-file Liberals on that Wednesday night in December as their tongues, loosened by liquor, wagged about the party's determination to vote against the budget and, if necessary, to campaign in the harsh Canadian winter.

Jim Coutts did not stay long at the Liberals' Christmas party. He was not much of a man for crowds, unless they were screaming for Trudeau at election rallies. He preferred smaller gatherings, where he could lower the veil that shrouded his private thoughts. Most of all, he liked to deal one-on-one, by telephone or at lunch, to piece together his assessment of a given political problem and begin to formulate his own plans for its solution. As he left the party, Coutts understood that the scenario he had been hoping for throughout the fall of 1979 was unfolding through a combination of careful planning, bizarre circumstances, and good luck.

Before joining Trudeau's permanent staff, Coutts had been above all a Liberal Party man, not tied to any particular Liberal, although he had served as appointments secretary to Liberal Prime Minister Lester Pearson from 1963 to 1966. In the 1974 campaign, Coutts had travelled the country with Trudeau, at Keith Davey's behest, keeping the media away from Trudeau and helping to orchestrate the Liberals' slashing attacks on the Conservatives' wage-and-price controls promise. He and Trudeau had hit it off immediately; Trudeau admired Coutts' clear, comprehensive and often cold-blooded assessment of political strategy. Coutts became Trudeau's principal secretary in 1976, developing a loyalty to his boss so deep that enhancing and protecting Pierre Trudeau's political career was the overriding preoccupation of Coutts' life. Trudeau reciprocated this loyalty; and although few Liberals knew their party as intimately as Coutts, he became known more for his loyalty to Trudeau than for his commitment to the policies of the Liberal Party. Coutts viewed policy from the exclusive perspective of its political utility in enhancing the Liberal Government's popularity; any Liberal policy could be changed, or any Conservative or NDP policy stolen, as long as it furthered the popularity of the Liberal Government.

The eighteen months prior to December 1979 had been difficult ones for Coutts and Trudeau. The party kept putting off an election in 1978 because the polls had gone sour. The Liberals lost thirteen of fifteen by-elections in October 1978. In the dying months of their five-year term, the Liberals were forced to call an election, which they lost—their first defeat in sixteen years. Much of the blame for the defeat and for the events leading up to it was placed on Coutts; the negative reaction within the party to him was fierce. He was accused of manipulating every event for political gain, of isolating Trudeau from the party, of keeping advice contrary to his own from Trudeau, and of having been the architect of the Liberals' election defeat. But he had stayed with Trudeau in the bountiful times, and he reaffirmed his loyalty to Trudeau in defeat by working just as hard in Opposition for his idol as he had in Government. His own influence derived from Trudeau's power as party leader, and when Trudeau reflected on his own future in the fall of 1979, Coutts urged him to stay on. He showed Trudeau private polls done by Martin Goldfarb, the party's Toronto polling expert, indicating that the Liberals could win an election. When Trudeau finally announced his decision to resign as Liberal leader on November 21, Coutts was downcast but determined to find some way of bringing Trudeau back to power. He asked Goldfarb for more polls, and these confirmed the Gallup Poll's finding that the Conservative Government was in political trouble. If the Liberals could push the Conservatives into an election, the Liberals could certainly win a minority Government and perhaps a majority. That was Goldfarb's advice, and Coutts took it to heart.

Coutts' next problem was to find an issue on which to defeat the Conservative Government. The Conservatives' bill to provide a tax credit for mortgage interest and property tax was a possibility, but the Conservatives had attracted many voters with that promise in the 1979 election; it might be too risky to force an election on that issue. Another issue was the Conservatives' intention to turn PetroCanada, the crown energy corporation, into a private company, a policy opposed by the Liberals and unpopular with the public. PetroCanada might offer the opening Coutts sought, but the PetroCanada bill would not be introduced in the Commons until late February or March, and that was too close to the Liberal leadership convention to think about precipitating an election. Some other piece of legislation or government action had to be found. When John Crosbie introduced his budget on Tuesday, December 11, Jim Coutts was quietly ecstatic.

On that Tuesday afternoon, Opposition M.P.s were given an advance text of the budget and their customary briefing by finance department officials. Among the Liberals at the Tuesday lock-up there was genuine distaste for portions of the budget, especially the additional 18-cents-per-gallon excise tax on transportation fuels that compounded sharply higher crude oil prices. That distaste surfaced again in a brief meeting of the party's finance committee in Trudeau's office after the lock-up. Trudeau, Coutts and the party's principal economic spokesmen were present: Jean Chrétien; Herb Gray; Marc Lalonde; John Evans, a young M.P. for Ottawa Centre; Robert Andras, the former president of the Treasury Board; Ed Lumley, M.P. for Stormont-Dundas; Donald Johnston, M.P. for Saint Henri-Westmount, and Allan MacEachen, the Liberal House leader. Those present concluded that the budget was so regressive that the Liberals had no alternative but to vote against it in a non-confidence motion Thursday night. The question was: should the party vote with a few members absent or in full force, even if this meant risking an election?

In October, the Conservatives had won a non-confidence vote on PetroCanada by 137 to 128, thanks to the support of the Créditistes and the absence of nine Liberal M.P.s. The Liberals were embarrassed when the press and the Conservatives chided them for lacking the courage of their convictions. If the Liberals were going to vote against the budget Thursday night, they would have to avoid a humiliating repetition of their October embarrassment. Lalonde and MacEachen insisted that the party's credibility was at stake. All Liberals must be made to vote against the budget, including the two Liberal M.P.s in hospital if possible, although the prevailing wisdom among senior Liberals Tuesday afternoon was that the Conservatives would muster the votes to win the non-confidence test or find a procedural way of delaying the vote until they were assured of victory. In the few minutes remaining before the budget speech itself, discussion turned to the tactical matter of how to reply that night to the budget. Herb Gray, the Liberals' finance critic, was ready to deliver his reply following Crosbie's address. Should Trudeau face the television cameras set up in the lobby outside the entrance to the Commons chamber and also criticize the budget? Coutts thought so, but Trudeau was ambivalent. He entered the chamber and listened to about half Crosbie's speech before reading a note sent by Coutts urging him to say something for television. With note in hand he went out to the lobby, criticized the budget, and returned to his seat.

After the budget speech, politicians milled about in the lobby outside the Commons talking to each other and to reporters. Trudeau returned to his office, where he met briefly with Coutts. Coutts, who always called Trudeau "sir" and adopted a deferential tone in Trudeau's presence, inquired if his boss realized the anomalous position the party was now in as it faced a possible election without a leader. Trudeau replied that he did understand. He would urge the caucus to vote against the budget, but he did not want to stay on as party leader and would say so at the Liberal caucus meeting the next morning. The Liberals should vote with their consciences against the budget, but if by some chance the Government fell, he was not inclined to reconsider his position.

On Tuesday night Allan MacEachen also began to sense that the Liberals could use the Crosbie budget as a reason for trying to topple the Government. MacEachen, a bachelor from Cape Breton who had been in Parliament, with only a four-year interruption, since 1953, had not shared Coutts' initial enthusiasm for an election. The Conservatives were a new Government, and throughout most of the fall MacEachen did not believe that the public would take kindly to an election so soon after the last one. Gradually, his opinion began to shift in late November and early December. He was not impressed with the way Walter Baker, the Government House leader, was conducting the Government's business in the Commons.

In the House of Commons especially if the Government is in a minority position, the House leader must sense the "mood" of the House, since without give-and-take between the Government and the Opposition parties, the Commons can degenerate into obstruction and bickering. The Government House leader meets formally with his opposite numbers in the Opposition parties at least once a week, and they chat each day in the Commons. The House leaders form their own small club, wherein the written rules of the Commons are adjusted by agreement among gentlemen.

Shortly after introducing the mortgage and property-tax credit bill, the Conservatives had moved to limit debate on second reading, a procedural initiative that enraged MacEachen. Baker was not dealing with the Commons as sensitively and adroitly as MacEachen had done as House leader during the Liberals' minority government of 1972 to 1974. MacEachen thought some Conservative ministers were performing poorly in Question Period, especially Energy Minister Ray Hnatyshyn and External Affairs Minister Flora MacDonald. The Conservatives would probably improve as they gained experience and confidence, but in mid-December, they struck MacEachen as vulnerable.

If MacEachen had any doubts about the Conservatives' vulnerability, they were erased Tuesday night after Crosbie's budget. Like other Liberals, MacEachen found the budget unacceptably regressive and he was confident that the country would think so, too. On Wednesday, MacEachen spoke to Martin Goldfarb by telephone, who related to MacEachen what he had been telling

Coutts for weeks: the Conservatives had slipped badly, the Liberals could win power, and Trudeau was the most popular leader the Liberals could find for an early campaign. Goldfarb's information blended with MacEachen's political intuition and his desire to keep Trudeau at the head of the Liberal Party.

At first blush, two men could hardly have been more dissimilar than Allan MacEachen and Pierre Trudeau. MacEachen, a brooding and publicly impassive man, had none of Trudeau's public flair. He dressed plainly, often looking slightly rumpled, and his long black hair was occasionally askew. He possessed none of Trudeau's marvellous body language, the ability to convey by gesture or facial expression a range of strong emotions; it was only the eyes that counted with MacEachen, as they darted around a room looking suspiciously for danger. He had never cut an impressive political figure outside of Nova Scotia. His home was the House of Commons, where he was regarded as the shrewdest parliamentarian on either side of the Commons, and as an indispensable ally for his leader.

In other ways, MacEachen and Trudeau were similar, and over the years they developed an enormous mutual respect. They were intensely private men who shared their innermost thoughts only with a handful of intimate friends. Although they were skilled public performers, they were shy men, preferring their own company to that of others. Their intellectual talents were complementary, Trudeau's philosophically structured ideas blending with MacEachen's grasp of tactics and timing. They both thought of themselves as liberals pressing for social reforms: MacEachen was proudest of Medicare, adopted when he was Minister of National Health and Welfare under Pearson; Trudeau of bilingualism, which flowed from the Official Languages Act of 1969. Most of all, MacEachen was reliable. Although he had fought many hard political battles, he never got himself or his party into trouble by carelessness or grievous error. He was Secretary of State for External Affairs, a job he loved, from August 1974 to September 1976, when Trudeau asked him to resume his former (1970 to 1974) job as Government House leader. He hated giving up the external affairs portfolio, but he did Trudeau's bidding and was rewarded with the title of Deputy Prime Minister a year later. When Trudeau needed a minister to steer Canada through negotiations with the United States for the Alaskan natural gas pipeline, he handed the task to MacEachen, who successfully completed the negotiations and defended the agreement skilfully in the Commons.

Of course, Trudeau held a fascination for the Canadian people that MacEachen could never dream of developing. By 1979, he had been too long in politics without etching a clear public profile to aspire to his party's leadership. He had run for the leadership in 1968, finishing seventh on the first ballot and throwing his support to Trudeau on subsequent ballots. MacEachen had taken many years to pay off his debts from the 1968 leadership campaign, and at fifty-eight years of age, he was not about to try again. When Trudeau announced his intention to resign in November, MacEachen made it known immediately that he would not contest the leadership. From the moment he began thinking about how the Conservatives might be defeated and began manoeuvring the Liberals towards that end, MacEachen never doubted who should lead the party in the campaign. It had to be Trudeau.

On Wednesday morning, Trudeau told the Liberal caucus members that they should not count on him to lead the party if the Government fell Thursday night. He agreed that the party should vote against the budget, but the caucus must know that he preferred to retire. With that, he left the caucus meeting and returned to his Centre Block office.

MacEachen was at the top of his form when he took the floor at the caucus meeting after Trudeau left and began criticizing the Crosbie budget. MacEachen in the full flight of his oratory was an impressive sight to behold. He usually started slowly, stumbling over his early phrases as if unsure of what he would like to say. He would repeat his initial phrases, rolling them over to get the cadence just right. He was an oratorical hustler, inviting his opponents to believe early in his speech that he will be easy pickings when their turn comes to reply. Then, gradually, the hesitation would cease, the repetition would end and out would pour a cascade of homilies, history, and arguments all wrapped in a logical and emotional package until, towards the end of his remarks, he was delivering his message with a synthesis no one could have believed possible at the start.

MacEachen told his caucus colleagues that the budget was regressive and unfair. It would hurt low-income Canadians. Liberals had no choice but to vote against it. If they wavered, they would be the laughing stock of the country. The Conservatives were weak in the Commons. They were politically vulnerable in the country and could be defeated. Finishing with a flourish, he asked them to stand by their principles and be counted Thursday night.

It was a masterful speech, calculated to appeal to a party that was convinced that it had principles, but was a bit uncertain about where they had been hiding in recent years. For eighteen months before their election defeat in May, the Liberals had thrown overboard many of their stated principles. For example, so worried had the Liberals been by negative public reaction to excessive government spending that Trudeau had unilaterally announced $2 billion in expenditure cuts without informing his Minister of Finance. Liberal Justice Minister Otto Lang had floated the idea of a referendum on capital punishment and had not been upbraided for doing so by Trudeau, who seemed to toy with the referendum idea himself after years of firm opposition to capital punishment. And after stoutly defending the need to resist provincial demands for more power, Trudeau had convened a constitutional conference in February 1979 at which he offered more concessions to the provinces than had any Prime Minister in Canadian history.

In Opposition, the party was restless and bored. Former ministers were frustrated sitting in Opposition; they yearned for the action and power of their former posts. The party was wasting time and energy wondering when Trudeau would retire, and once he announced that he was leaving, the party threw itself into the leadership race. The Liberals deeply disdained Prime Minister Joe Clark, believing him incapable of handling the responsibilities of his job; Clark and his Cabinet ministers were pleasant individuals, but they just did not know how to govern. Many Liberals admitted privately that their party had grown tired in power, and several reform-minded groups had called conferences to spark a debate about where the party should go in the 1980s, implying that the Liberals had long ago used up their creative ideas.

Now, at that Wednesday morning meeting, MacEachen, telling his caucus that the Liberals had principles that were worth fighting for, summoned them to a parliamentary battle of uncertain outcome but just cause.

Speaker after speaker rose to support the House leader. Swept up by the enthusiasm of the moment, the Liberals dedicated themselves to vote *en masse* against the budget. Whip Thomas Lefebvre was instructed to ensure that all 112 Liberals were in their seats Thursday night, even if the two Liberal M.P.s in hospital had to be brought to the Commons on stretchers. There would not be any pairing with absent Conservatives. Pairing was customary Commons courtesy, by which one party held back one of its members when a member of the other side was unavoidably away; but this was not to be an ordinary vote.

The caucus adjourned, and the Liberal communications committee met over lunch. Coutts and MacEachen, of course, were increasingly eager for a showdown and were alert to the possibility of an election. Roméo LeBlanc, the former Minister of Fisheries and one of the most reform-minded members of the caucus, was angry at the Crosbie budget. Deniger, the young M.P. from Laprairie, was certain that the strategy of voting to a man against the budget was politically wise and intellectually sound. Jim Fleming, M.P. for York West, hesitated. He worried about lingering anti-Trudeau feeling in Toronto, but he agreed that the party could not be seen voting at less than full strength against the budget.

The Liberals, however, could not topple the Government alone. Unless the Créditistes abandoned the Conservatives and the NDP and Liberals voted together, the Government would survive. Until Wednesday afternoon, both parts of the equation were unclear, but shortly after Question Period that afternoon, the Liberals began to realize that their determination to vote against the budget might bring down the Government.

On Tuesday night, Fabien Roy, leader of the five Créditistes, had told reporters that he did not like the budget, especially the excise tax. Roy was a Quebec nationalist, the closest politician to the Parti Québécois in the House of Commons. As soon as the budget was read, Quebec Finance Minister Jacques Parizeau and other PQ Cabinet ministers denounced the excise tax, claiming it fell within provincial jurisdiction. Roy took his lead from the PQ attacks when speaking to reporters after his party's Wednesday caucus meeting. He blended the jurisdictional argument with complaints about the budget's heavy impact on farmers, small merchants, and non-unionized workers who formed the core of the Créditistes' dwindling support in Quebec. Roy did not, however, say how the Créditistes would vote Thursday night on the non-confidence motion. They were playing for time, waiting to see what the Conservatives would offer for their support. When Roy went downstairs after Question Period to what is known as the "hot room," where politicians give quick press conferences, he repeated his criticisms of the budget. But when pressed to say how his rump group would vote, Roy replied: "My personal preference would be to abstain." Roy said that the Créditistes would meet Thursday morning to consider their position.

By chance, Allan MacEachen had also appeared in the hot room to give a press conference of his own. He stood waiting for

Roy to finish talking to the French-speaking reporters and for Eudore Allard, Créditiste M.P. for Rimouski, to state the party's position for the English-speaking reporters. Allard was less categorical than Roy in denouncing the budget; but then Allard was less emotional than Roy and more accustomed to the shifting currents of Commons' negotiations that might yet produce a glittering catch for the Créditistes, if they were patient for long enough with the Conservatives. The Créditistes departed, and MacEachen answered questions, repeating the now-familiar Liberal position that the party would vote against the budget. He left the room knowing that the Créditistes were thinking of abstaining, which meant that the Liberals now stood a better than fifty-fifty chance of defeating the Government.

Minutes earlier, the odds had shortened on the Government's defeat when MacEachen met NDP leader Ed Broadbent in the lobby outside the Commons. There, Broadbent showed MacEachen a piece of paper on which was written the wording of the NDP sub-amendment to the Liberals' non-confidence motion. The NDP could have drafted this sub-amendment to reflect pure party dogma, in order to make the motion unacceptable to the Liberals, as they had done earlier in the parliamentary session. This time, however, the motion was deliberately bland. It read:

> This House unreservedly condemns the Government for its outright betrayal of its election promises to lower interest rates, to cut taxes and to stimulate the growth of the Canadian economy without a mandate from the Canadian people for such a reversal.

MacEachen glanced at the piece of paper Broadbent held out to him, studied the wording of the sub-amendment, and replied tersely: "I think we can live with that." Broadbent was delighted. Ever since Trudeau's resignation, Broadbent had been hoping for an election, and MacEachen's answer confirmed that an election might now be at hand.

Ironically, Broadbent wanted Trudeau to lead the Liberals in the election almost as much as Coutts and MacEachen did. He had been caught off-guard by Trudeau's November 21 resignation. Broadbent had been attending the opening session of the NDP's national convention in Toronto when he heard the news of Trudeau's decision. He invited a group of NDP officials to come to his hotel suite that evening for a strategy meeting. Trudeau's departure obviously changed the country's political landscape, and

Broadbent wanted the party brass to consider how the NDP should react. In addition to members of his personal staff, Broadbent invited Terry Grier, NDP campaign chairman; Robin Sears, NDP federal secretary; Cliff Scotton, the former federal secretary, and several NDP organizers, including Penny Dickens from Toronto, Bill Knight from Saskatchewan, and Joyce Nash from British Columbia.

Broadbent opened the informal discussion by saying that the party should seek an early election before the Liberals replaced Trudeau. He had consulted Saskatchewan NDP Premier Allan Blakeney, and both agreed that an English-speaking leader of the Liberal Party would hurt the NDP in Ontario and western Canada. A new Liberal leader might also move the party slightly to the political left, and without a track record to defend, the leader could appeal directly to NDP voters. Broadbent thought the party would be in fighting form after the national convention, so the NDP caucus should look for an election opening as soon as possible.

Some of those listening to Broadbent could scarcely believe their ears. At first they thought Broadbent might be joking, but it soon became apparent that he was not. Scotton and Grier, who had fought the 1974 campaign when the NDP lost fifteen seats, protested that the party lacked an issue on which to force an election. The NDP would be blamed and punished if it helped to precipitate an election, just as it was in 1974 when the NDP withdrew its support for the minority Liberal Government. No one in the room knew what the December budget would bring; so the Conservatives' confusion over the fate of PetroCanada seemed the only available issue, and it was not striking enough to justify an election seven months after the last one. Since the Liberals would be busy searching for a successor to Trudeau, they would resist an election. If the NDP started braying for an election, the party would be labelled a bunch of opportunists.

The organizers complained that they were not ready for an election. Dickens, for example, predicted with considerable prescience that an early election would produce a sweep for the Liberals among ethnic groups in Toronto, Liberal gains at the NDP's expense in northern Ontario, and increased Liberal strength in middle-class suburban ridings. Only Sears and several members of Broadbent's personal staff supported the leader. The meeting broke up inconclusively. Broadbent felt that he had at least opened a few minds, and his party officials were fearful that the NDP caucus might do something rash back in Ottawa.

When the Conservatives brought down their budget on December 11, there was never a doubt that the NDP would vote against the 18-cents-per-gallon excise tax, higher energy prices, and the failure to provide tax relief for low-income Canadians. The energy tax credit looked appealing, but the NDP dismissed it as a pittance in the context of the overall budget. When the caucus gathered for its regular Wednesday meeting, everyone quickly agreed that the NDP could not support the budget. But, under parliamentary rules, the Commons would vote first on the NDP sub-amendment to the Liberals' motion of non-confidence. Unless the Conservatives changed the order of business, that vote would be held Thursday night. Several caucus members, notably John Rodriguez, M.P. for Nickel Belt and the self-appointed leader of the so-called Left Caucus within the party, demanded that the NDP sub-amendment reflect NDP party dogma. If the NDP wanted to put the Liberals in a tight corner, then it should give the Liberals the dilemma of voting on a motion of pure NDP principles. The vast majority of the caucus, however, figured that such a strategy would offer the Liberals too easy an excuse for voting against the NDP sub-amendment. By proposing a broadly worded motion, the NDP could put more heat on the Liberals. If the Liberals voted against a motherhood motion, then the NDP would shout that the Liberals were tough talkers who backed off their principles. Nothing pleased the NDP more than lumping the Liberals and Conservatives together as the "old-line parties," and a Liberal refusal to support a broadly worded motion would allow the NDP to trot out its favourite accusation. If, however, the Liberals voted for the NDP motion, that was equally acceptable in strategic terms, because the NDP could claim that they had taken the initiative and the Liberals had followed. The possibility of an election was barely discussed. An election remained Broadbent's objective, but he kept quiet about the possibility at Wednesday's caucus meeting, where NDP M.P.s assumed that either the Conservatives would secure Créditiste support or the Liberals would hold back some of their M.P.s. Either way, it seemed to the NDP caucus that the Conservatives would survive. But later, when MacEachen said, "I think we can live with that," Broadbent knew that the election he had been hoping for was a distinct possibility.

By 4 p.m. on Wednesday, Jim Coutts had heard about the Créditistes' position and the NDP's sub-amendment. He took this information to Trudeau, and the two men talked for about thirty minutes in Trudeau's third-floor office just above the lobby in front of the Commons chamber. Coutts gave Trudeau as accurate a picture as he could piece together, concluding that the Government would probably be defeated Thursday night. Coutts suggested that they needed to think about Trudeau's future, but the leader replied that he had already done so. He had told the caucus that his preference was to leave politics, but he recognized the opportunity now emerging for his return.

On Wednesday afternoon, Parliament Hill was full of excited, whispered conversations as reporters, politicians, and their staffs sought the latest shred of gossip or information. Events were moving so rapidly that rumours flew up and down the corridors. The Opposition parties had declared their intentions: defiantly, in the case of the Liberals and NDP; tentatively, in the case of the Créditistes. Everyone—including many Conservative M.P.s— now wondered what the Conservatives were doing.

As it turned out, not much. Like the tsar's army on the eve of Tannenberg, the Conservatives were plunging forward, apparently oblivious to the mounting danger and convinced that right was on their side. They were confident that if a battle developed they would win it. While the other parties laid plans for a parliamentary ambush, the Conservatives were congratulating themselves on Finance Minister John Crosbie's budget.

Since the election, the Conservative Government had been accused of "flip-flopping" and indecision. In the face of overwhelming domestic and international opposition, Prime Minister Joe Clark had reversed his position on the shifting of the Canadian Embassy in Israel from Tel Aviv to Jerusalem. The Government's PetroCanada policy seemed confused; a task force had submitted a report on the future of the crown corporation recommending that PetroCanada be turned into a private company, but the Government was still studying the report. On the economic front, interest rates had jumped four times since the Conservatives took power, an embarrassing state of affairs for a party that had criticized high interest rates before the election. The Government had also disavowed its election promises to cut taxes and provide a short-term "stimulative deficit."

At last, the Conservatives had taken bold action, and in John Crosbie, a tart-tongued Newfoundlander, the party felt it had the right salesman for the budget's tough economic message. "Short-term pain for long-term gain" was the way Crosbie summarized his budget. He made the Commons laugh with him twice during the budget speech when he read several sentences in terrible French, grinning as M.P.s from all sides of the House saluted his effort. Even his English set Crosbie apart; the Commons had never before heard a thick Newfoundland accent from a Minister of Finance. Conservative M.P.s were delighted when he departed from his budget text to deliver partisan sallies at the Liberals. Budget night is usually a stately, serious occasion, but Crosbie was irrepressibly partisan, and his Conservative colleagues admired him for it.

"[This] is the first budget of a new era in the economic and financial affairs of this country—an era of new realism and an economic climate to provide improved opportunities and incentives for Canadians," Crosbie said in his budget address. Indeed, Crosbie's budget certainly heralded a change in economic thinking from those of previous Liberal governments. The budget's "fundamental objective" was the reduction in the federal deficit. To bring about this reduction, Crosbie chose to increase revenues rather than slash expenditures, which he forecast would rise by 10 per cent. He slapped a 5 per cent surtax on corporate profits and added new taxes on tobacco and alcoholic beverages.

His largest sources of new revenue were an additional excise tax on transportation fuels and an increased federal levy on higher crude oil prices. The excise tax, raised from seven to twenty-five cents per gallon on transportation fuels would bring Ottawa an additional $2.1 billion a year. A new energy tax would allow the federal treasury to take half the revenues from yearly increases in the price of crude oil above $2 per barrel. Since the budget forecast a $4-per-barrel increase in 1980 and $4.50-per-barrel increases thereafter (with a clause tying Canadian prices to 85 per cent of the benchmark U.S. price on January 1, 1984), this new energy tax would bring the federal government $3.6 billion by the 1983–1984 fiscal year. Crosbie said that these dramatic increases in energy prices would be offset by an energy tax credit of $220 a year for families earning less than $21,380. However, the tax credit would not be fully in effect until 1981; the excise tax increase was effective immediately.

This was tough medicine all right, but the budget also contained politically attractive measures that pleased Conservative backbenchers. In particular, Crosbie allowed the deductibility of a wife's salary paid by an unincorporated small business. He allowed farmers to put $100,000 of capital gains from the sale of their farm into a Registered Retirement Savings Plan. There were also tax changes to help small businessmen and incentives for investment in common stock issued by Canadian companies.

This "face-the-facts" budget, as Crosbie called it, was generally well received by the Conservative caucus, whose members appreciated the incentives for small businessmen, farmers, and women. They especially liked the attack on the deficit, since many of the new Conservative M.P.s had entered politics in protest against excessive government spending. The higher energy prices posed a political problem, but that could be addressed over time and sold in concert with the energy-tax credit to low- and moderate-income Canadians. At Crosbie's post-budget party Tuesday night and at the Conservative caucus meeting Wednesday morning, the Conservatives' mood was confident, almost cocky.

At 8:45 a.m. on Wednesday, slightly more than an hour before the Conservative caucus meeting, Prime Minister Joe Clark held his daily staff meeting with his closest advisers. Crosbie and other Conservative ministers had handled themselves well on budget night. Editorial reaction to the budget in the morning newspapers had been generally positive. There was no cause for alarm, even when Nancy Jamieson, Clark's legislative assistant, reported that both the Liberals and the NDP had said Tuesday night that they would vote against the budget. It was too early to tell what the Créditistes might do, she reported, and the meeting passed on to other routine matters. Clark left the staff meeting for a brief meeting with officers of the Conservative caucus before attending the caucus itself. He stayed in the Commons for a while after Question Period, presided over an "inner Cabinet" meeting until supper and went home, apparently oblivious to the unfolding disaster.

Nancy Jamieson awoke early Thursday morning. She hurried down to Parliament Hill for a 7:30 a.m. breakfast meeting with middle-ranking staff from Clark's office in a private dining room adjacent to the parliamentary dining room. William Neville, Clark's chief-of-staff, had called the meeting to allow members of Clark's staff to talk about the Government's priorities for the coming weeks with Conservative Party officials such as national director Paul Curley, communications director Jodi White, and Walter Gray, head of the party's research bureau. Midway through the meeting, Neville turned to Jamieson and asked her to outline the parliamentary timetable for the period until Christmas.

"I think you're a little premature," she replied. She explained to her startled audience that she now believed the Government would probably be defeated that night. Throughout Wednesday, Jamieson had been observing the disturbing signs from the Opposition parties. Jock Osler, Clark's press secretary, had called her Wednesday night after hearing reports from the Liberal Christmas party. Maybe the Liberals were serious after all, Osler said. On Wednesday night, Jamieson made several other calls and satisfied herself that the Government was headed for defeat. No one at the breakfast table believed her. Her warning was treated as a minor joke, an excessively skittish reaction to a tight but manageable parliamentary crisis.

At 8:30 a.m., Jamieson walked over to Conservative whip Bill Kempling's office. Kempling had not yet arrived, but Jamieson learned after talking to an assistant and making several phone calls that six Conservative M.P.s were out of town, sulking, or ill. She could scarcely believe it: six Conservative M.P.s missing on the day of a non-confidence vote in a minority Parliament!

Fifteen minutes later, Jamieson took her seat at one end of a U-shaped table in Clark's office for the Prime Minister's daily staff meeting. Beside her sat Senator Lowell Murray, Clark's closest political confidant and chairman of the Conservatives' 1979 campaign. He did not always attend the morning staff meeting, but he had risen that morning and watched a television program on which Liberal and NDP spokesmen repeated their intention to vote against the budget and Créditiste Eudore Allard said his party would abstain. With that jolt, Murray hustled down to Clark's office for the staff meeting. As usual, Clark called on Marcel Massé, Clerk of the Privy Council, to open the meeting. For about twenty minutes, Massé ran through a list of items of routine government business. When he finished, Clark went slowly around the table, asking those present if they had anything to raise. Jim Gillies, Clark's policy advisor; Neville, chief-of-staff; Ian Green, Clark's executive assistant; Donald Doyle, assistant chief-of-staff; Jock Osler, press secretary; André Payette, director of communications; Bev Dewar, a senior official with the Privy Council—some raised routine matters, others passed. No one mentioned the budget vote. With about ten minutes left in the meeting, Clark turned to Jamieson.

"Sir, the Government is going to be defeated tonight," she said.

"Why?" Clark asked.

Jamieson bluntly replied: "Because we don't have the numbers." Clark's face tightened. "What do you mean?"

Briefly, Jamieson sketched the scenario of defeat. The Liberals and NDP were going to pull out all of their members to vote against the budget. The Créditistes would abstain. And the Conservatives were missing six M.P.s. Secretary of State for External Affairs Flora MacDonald was in Brussels at a ministerial meeting of the North Atlantic Treaty Organization. Calgary North M.P. Eldon Woolliams was the defence lawyer at a trial in progress in Calgary. Lloyd Crouse, M.P. for South Shore, was somewhere in the South Pacific. Stan Korchinski, M.P. for Mackenzie, had been in a sour mood for weeks; he was probably in his riding, but his office could not reach him. Paul Yewchuk, M.P. for Athabaska, was in Ottawa, but he was still angry with Clark for not being included in the Cabinet. He had stayed away from previous important votes and might do so again. Alvin Hamilton, M.P. for Qu'Appelle-Moose Mountain, was extremely ill and undergoing treatment for a kidney ailment; he could not be moved. With six M.P.s missing, the Conservatives could count on only 130 votes. Even if the Créditistes changed their minds and supported the Government, that would bring the count to 135. The combined Liberal-NDP strength was 140. The numbers said defeat was inevitable.

William Neville did not believe it. Asked by Clark for his reaction, Neville, who prided himself on being a hard-nosed political analyst, said the Liberals would crack. The party was without a leader. If an election was called, Trudeau would probably lead the Liberals, and the party would hardly want to enter a campaign with a leader whom Canadians had rejected fewer than seven months before. The Liberals were talking a brave game, but their resolve would break if the Conservatives let it be known that they did not fear an election. It was a game of chicken, both parties hurtling towards a clash. If the Conservatives kept their nerve, the Liberals would lose theirs. As for the Créditistes, how could they not fail to support the Government? The Créditistes' organization in Quebec was falling apart. The party was broke and needed time to regroup and rebuild. Abstention would be suicidal, and the Créditistes were not fools, Neville concluded.

Lowell Murray had listened carefully to what Jamieson had to say. Clark had rewarded Murray with a Senate post after the election, but between his party responsibilities and his outside interests such as reading and travelling, Murray had not been closely monitoring developments in the Commons. He remembered a Cabinet meeting on the budget at which Walter Baker had remarked that the budget's chances of acceptance in a minority

Parliament were "extremely slim," but he had put Baker's warning out of his mind. Now, he contemplated the Government's defeat with equanimity, believing that the Conservatives would win the ensuing election. He agreed that the Conservatives should not flinch. Moreover, signals that the Conservatives were standing firm should be sent that day to the Liberals. Clark's office should request television time and reserve the press conference theatre in case both were needed. The press office should announce both moves during the day so that the Liberals would understand that the Conservatives were ready to fight an election. Someone should contact the Governor General's office and find out when Clark could see Schreyer if the Government fell. Party headquarters should check on the availability of a plane for the campaign, and party organizers should be alerted that a campaign was imminent.

Clark was leaving after the staff meeting for a luncheon speech in Burlington and an evening speech in Kitchener. It was snowing lightly in Toronto and Murray suggested that Clark should cancel the Kitchener portion of his trip, since it would look ridiculous for the Prime Minister to be away from Ottawa when his Government fell. Everyone agreed, and Green was dispatched to tell the party's advance men of the change in Clark's itinerary. Finally, Clark said every effort must be made to get the six Conservative M.P.s back to Ottawa, especially Flora MacDonald in Brussels.

The staff meeting ran half an hour longer than scheduled. Clark was already late for his departure for Burlington. He huddled quickly with Baker and Jamieson, making in those brief minutes a ruinous tactical error based on a set of monumental political miscalculations.

On Wednesday, strictly as a matter of routine in preparation for a non-confidence vote, Jamieson had asked the Privy Council office to prepare a memorandum outlining the Government's options in the event of a defeat. The memorandum reviewed the historical precedents of defeat on non-confidence motions, including the Liberals' surprise defeat on a tax bill in 1968, which the Liberals subsequently ignored by passing a motion saying the defeat did not constitute a vote of non-confidence. A covering letter from Marcel Massé summarized Clark's options. It read, in part:

> Although any defeat during the budget debate would be regarded generally as a major defeat for the Government, technically at least dissolution is not your only option.

First, since the NDP motion is only a sub-amendment of
the main motion, you could choose to continue the
budget debate and try to defeat the Liberal amendment
(as amended), then carry the main motion. Second, you
could attempt to follow the 1968 precedent by moving a
motion declaring that the defeat is not a declaration of
non-confidence. Procedurally, though, such a motion
might be flawed because the vote on the Liberal amendment would not yet have taken place. . . . These two
alternatives to dissolution may be somewhat theoretical.
Any defeat on the budget would seriously undermine the
Government's position. An election might then be the
only real cure.

Clark had not seen the Privy Council memorandum, but when the
options were sketched briefly for him, he dismissed these technical
alternatives, believing properly that a Government defeated on a
non-confidence vote on a budget should resign. Clark had a deep
respect for parliament and its traditions, and he was not about to
keep governing on a technicality.

There was, however, another reason for Clark's quick dismissal of the technical option, a reason that became clear when
Jamieson and Baker suggested that the Government could postpone the budget vote. It was entirely within the Government's
power to change the orders of the day after Question Period at
3 p.m. The Opposition parties would undoubtedly cry foul, but the
Government sets the parliamentary timetable. Baker could explain
to the Commons that the Government had changed its mind and
wanted debate on another bill. The change could be justified by an
appeal to fair play; after all, circumstances had kept six Conservative M.P.s away, and it was only fair that the Government face a
non-confidence vote at full strength if the Opposition parties were
insisting on a showdown.

There was nothing illegal or even offensive to parliamentary
tradition in suggesting that the vote be delayed. In fact, during the
previous week the inner Cabinet had approved a schedule for
House business that called for the budget debate to begin on
Friday, December 14, with the first vote on Monday, December 17.
That schedule had been subsequently changed, but no rule required
the budget debate to start the day after the budget speech. Delay
would offer the Liberals more time for second-guessing themselves and would give the Conservatives more time to negotiate
with the Créditistes and to ensure that a full complement of

Conservative M.P.s was on hand for the non-confidence vote.

Baker, however, did not press that option on Clark; he merely raised the possibility and did not argue with the Prime Minister's refusal to consider it. A man with a stronger personality would have persisted, explaining that the Government was taking an avoidable risk in insisting on having the vote that night. Baker might have lost the argument, but he did not even try. An affable man who looked like a big teddy bear, Baker abhorred personal confrontations. He was not a strong enough House leader to argue with the Prime Minister.

Joe Clark did not want his Government to be labelled a lame duck, even for a few days, while Parliament awaited a showdown. Any delay in the budget vote would be interpreted as a sign of weakness; from his first day in office, Clark had tried to confound those who said he was unfit for the job of Prime Minister by show-ing how firm and decisive he could be. He had reaffirmed his party's election promise to move the Canadian Embassy in Israel from Tel Aviv to Jerusalem the day after he became Prime Minister. He had stared down most of his inner Cabinet and insisted that PetroCanada be turned into a private company. He had dismissed warnings about the political impact of the excise tax, believing the party needed to fulfil its election promise to reduce the federal deficit. Now he would show the Liberals and the country that he was not about to be pushed around in the Commons.

Most of all, Joe Clark thought the Conservatives would win the election. He did not want his Government to fall, but if that happened, then Clark believed the Conservatives would win a majority Government. Trudeau would probably lead the Liberals, and Canadians could never bring themselves to support him again. It was safer politically for the Conservatives to face the Liberals led by Trudeau than by Donald Macdonald or John Turner. True, the Conservatives had suffered from a few decisions—the Jerusa-lem Embassy, PetroCanada, the long delay in calling Parliament after the election—but they could now show the country a prin-cipled budget, a new PetroCanada policy that was ready for release, and an energy package with Alberta that awaited resolution of only minor details. The Gallup Poll of November showed the Conservatives trailing the Liberals by nineteen points, an insur-mountable lead for any party entering a campaign, but Clark was convinced that the Conservatives could overcome that disadvan-tage. The Conservatives had been in power for fewer than twenty-eight weeks; surely the Canadian people would recognize that the Conservatives had not been given a fair chance to govern? The Liberals and New Democrats would be perceived as opportunists; the Conservatives as honest, hard-working politicians.

Jim Coutts, Allan MacEachen, Senator Keith Davey, and Martin Goldfarb knew better; they had been keeping a constant check on public opinion through Goldfarb's polls. But Joe Clark and his Conservatives had not commissioned a single poll since August. It was incredible that a party in a minority situation in Parliament had been governing without private polls that prudent parties always use to check their course. The Conservatives had carefully monitored public opinion in Opposition; in power, the party had conducted just one poll in twenty-eight weeks.

The November Gallup Poll was just one of many signs the Conservatives were ignoring. The party had lost two by-elections in November: one in a safe Liberal seat in Newfoundland and the other in John Diefenbaker's former riding of Prince Albert. The last three Conservative caucus meetings before the budget were filled with backbenchers' criticisms of the Cabinet's performance. Conservative M.P.s complained about appointments—such as that of Professor John Meisel of Queen's University as chairman of the Canadian Radio-Television and Telecommunications Commission—because they were not being made fast enough nor given to loyal Conservatives. High interest rates were hurting farmers, fishermen, small businessmen, homeowners, and other groups, and the Conservative M.P.s were hearing plenty about the Bank of Canada's policy when they returned to their constituencies for the weekends. The inner Cabinet did not seem to be producing any politically enticing legislation, and the backbenchers were getting impatient. They had waited all summer while the inner Cabinet prepared legislation; and by late fall, when little had been made public, the backbenchers were restless.

These were all unmistakable signals that the Government was unpopular, but Joe Clark reasoned that an unjustified election and the return of Trudeau would quickly put things right for the Conservatives. The Liberals would probably crack, but if not, then the Conservatives had nothing to fear from an election. So said Lowell Murray, William Neville, and Joe Clark. The vote would be held as scheduled, Clark informed Jamieson and Baker before departing for Burlington.

The challenge now facing Jamieson and Baker was to get the six missing Conservatives to Ottawa in time for the 9:45 p.m. vote. Lloyd Crouse was in the South Pacific, but no one knew where.* Alvin Hamilton was too sick to be moved. Clark spoke to the sulking Paul Yewchuk, who agreed to vote. Eldon Woolliams was reached in Calgary, and he rushed to the airport still wearing his court attire. Stan Korchinski could not be found in his riding, but he unexpectedly called his office from Ottawa later in the afternoon and was told to turn up. And Flora MacDonald was in Brussels.

MacDonald had left Canada the previous weekend, assuming that the budget vote would not take place on Thursday, December 13, but on Monday, December 17. At her last inner Cabinet meeting on Thursday, December 6, the Government's parliamentary schedule showed the vote on Monday the 17th. She had checked before leaving about securing a Liberal pair, although a pair is usually granted automatically to an external affairs minister representing Canada at an international meeting. She was told by Baker and Kempling that she need not worry. On Wednesday night, her office in Ottawa, hearing the rumours about the Liberals' and NDP's intentions, asked the whip's office about bringing her back for the vote. Again her staff was told not to worry, and a message was sent to her in Brussels from the Prime Minister's office: "Despite Bold Talk We Believe Diplomatic Flu Will Hit Liberal Benches"—in other words, some Liberals would be absent for the vote, struck by "flu."

At 4 p.m. Brussels time (10 a.m. in Ottawa) on Thursday, Hugh Hanson, MacDonald's executive assistant, was called out of the NATO ministerial meeting to take a call from Ottawa. MacDonald was needed in Ottawa for the vote, Hanson was told. A few minutes later, MacDonald herself left the meeting to talk to Clark, who had just completed his meeting with Baker and Jamieson. Clark said he was leaving for Burlington and put Baker on the line. The Government needed her vote; could she get back? MacDonald was flabbergasted. She did not even know that the date for the vote had been changed. For the next three hours in Brussels, MacDonald and her staff tried frantically to find a way to get back

---

*Crouse was severely and justly criticized after the election for having missed the vote. He had been attending a meeting of the Commonwealth Parliamentary Association in New Zealand and decided before he left to spend ten days in Australia after the CPA meeting to study trade between Canada and Australia. He insisted that he told Clark that he would be away without a pair and that Clark agreed that he could go. Clark and Kempling denied that Crouse had permission to be away. Crouse, of course, was angry at having been passed over for the Cabinet.

to Ottawa by 9:45 p.m. The Concorde had already left for New York. So had most of the transatlantic flights that leave Europe for North America early in the morning and return to Europe overnight. The only available flights would get her to Ottawa too late for the vote. She tried to charter a plane, but none was available. She was stuck in Brussels.

The parliamentary timetable had been changed because the Conservative House strategists were more concerned about getting the mortgage and property-tax credit bill and the main estimates passed before Christmas than they were about the timing of the budget debate. They felt the Liberals were stalling on both. To induce the Liberals and New Democrats to co-operate, Baker had proposed three different schedules for the allocation of parliamentary time until Christmas to the other House leaders at a meeting on Tuesday morning, the day of the budget. Baker said that any of the schedules were acceptable to the Government, because each required the Opposition parties to pass the mortgage bill and the main estimates before Christmas. MacEachen and NDP House leader Stanley Knowles chose the schedule that put the budget debate on Wednesday and Thursday, with the first vote on Thursday night, thus selecting the day for the Government's execution themselves.

Without Crouse, Hamilton, and MacDonald, all now certain to be absent, the Conservatives could count on only 133 votes. But if a couple of Liberals defied their whip, and by Thursday afternoon there were plenty of nervous Liberals, then the Conservatives could be saved if Fabien Roy and the Créditistes voted with the Conservatives. After the special Créditiste caucus session Thursday morning, Fabien Roy emerged to say the party would abstain. When the Commons met at 2 p.m., Armand Caouette, Créditiste M.P. for Abitibi, confirmed the party's intention to his seatmate David Kilgour, a Conservative M.P. for Edmonton-Strathcona whom Baker had placed next to the Créditistes to act as a liaison with the group throughout the session because of his ability to speak French. Kilgour asked to see Roy, but the Créditiste leader was busy preparing a speech for the Commons debate that afternoon and giving interviews to reporters outside the Commons. It was not until about 4:45 p.m. that Kilgour and Roy met in the corner of the government lobby. They spoke for about ten minutes, during which time Roy said his party would vote with the Conservatives only if the Government committed all the revenues from the 18-cents-per-gallon excise-tax increase to the Government of Quebec or to energy projects in Quebec. Earlier in the day, Roy had demanded the doubling of the energy tax credit. The same message had reached William Neville in a roundabout way, after Eudore Allard telephoned an acquaintance in the Saskatchewan legislature, Conservative MLA Paul Rousseau, who in turn phoned Neville with the Créditiste demand. The Créditiste headquarters in Montreal called Walter Baker's office Thursday afternoon requesting a briefing for the party's M.P.s on the budget's impact on Quebec. The information was provided by the finance department and given to the Créditistes in writing by Ron Ritchie, Conservative M.P. for York East and Crosbie's parliamentary secretary, just before the Commons rose at 6 p.m.

The Créditistes were demanding a high price for their support, a price Joe Clark deemed excessive on his return from Burlington in the late afternoon on Thursday. In such a critical parliamentary situation, it might have seemed prudent, if not essential, for either Clark or Baker to talk directly to Roy to see if a compromise could be found. But Joe Clark was not afraid of an election, and he had decided before the parliamentary session that he would neither form a coalition with the Créditistes to secure a parliamentary majority nor even develop a close working relationship with them.

In mid-November, Kilgour had suggested a Conservative-Créditiste coalition to Armand Caouette, who, to Kilgour's surprise, greeted the suggestion enthusiastically, offering to take it to the Créditiste caucus. Several days later, Caouette told Kilgour that the Créditistes were prepared to enter into an informal coalition with the Conservatives to guarantee the Government's survival for eighteen months. There were no strings attached to the offer, although the Créditistes would have undoubtedly expected subsequent recompense and recognition from the Conservatives. But when Kilgour and Caouette discussed the idea with Clark after a Question Period in late November, and suggested a meeting between Clark and Fabien Roy, the Prime Minister seemed indifferent to the idea.

Despite his minority position, Clark had decided that he would govern as much as possible without the Créditistes. More than that, he was determined to crush the Créditistes in order to improve his own party's miserable fortunes in Quebec. Clark worried that the Créditistes might constantly hold the Conservative Government to ransom and then brag about their booty in Quebec. Like Lowell Murray, Clark believed in the erroneous proposition that if the Créditistes faded in Quebec their supporters would find a new political home with the Conservatives. There was much evidence that disaffected Créditistes actually headed for the Liberals, a party more deeply rooted in French-Canadian society than the Conservatives. By putting constant pressure on the Créditistes and by refusing to bend Commons rules that require parties to elect eleven members to qualify for official-party status, Clark thought he could induce Créditiste M.P.s to join the Conservatives. Just before Parliament opened, Richard Janelle, Créditiste M.P. for Lotbinière, bolted his party to join the Conservatives. Clark took heart from Janelle's defection, believing that other Créditiste M.P.s would follow if the Conservatives demonstrated that the Créditiste Party was powerless in Ottawa. Walter Baker thought Clark's policy was reckless in a minority Parliament, but he did not press his objections with Clark— although he occasionally found ways as House leader to provide the Créditistes with small favours.

The Créditiste M.P.s, despite their party's slow decline in Quebec, were proud men, well liked by those of their parliamentary colleagues who could speak with them in French. The Commons had no warmer gentleman than Adrien Lambert, a farmer with a booming voice and a theatrical speaking style who was first elected Créditiste M.P. for Bellechasse in 1968. He was popular in Ottawa for his smiling, backslapping ways, and in his rural constituency, with which he kept in contact through weekend trips and weekly hot-line programs conducted from his Commons office. He did not care much about economic theory, except the Social Credit monetary gospel he had learned, nor about external affairs, defence, immigration, science policy, foreign investment, or anything else that did not directly touch the lives of his constituents. But let the Minister of Agriculture announce a new milk-subsidy program for dairy farmers, or let the Minister of Employment and Immigration talk about changing the unemployment insurance program, and Adrien would be on his feet in the corner of the Commons, his voice shaking the stained-glass windows, his arms waving, and his face quivering as he poured out his heart about the issue at hand.

Lambert's Créditiste colleagues were quieter versions in the same mould: tireless workers for their constituents; simple, honest, and decent men who found that not speaking much, if any, English was a serious impediment to their effectiveness despite the bilingual functioning of the federal government. Fabien Roy, of course, was not a Créditiste, nor did he know his caucus members well. He had been drafted to lead the Créditistes, giving up his seat in the Quebec Legislative Assembly to run in the 1979 election. He was an erratic, fiery man who never understood the traditions of the federal Parliament. He was also a proud man accustomed to fighting for the "little people" of the Beauce, an isolated corner of Quebec tucked against the Maine border. Like his caucus colleagues, he smarted under Joe Clark's constant humiliation of his party. He chafed against the restrictions under which the Créditistes laboured when denied official-party status, but there was little the Créditistes could do about their plight except complain, bargain as best they could with the Conservatives, and await the day when they could exact vengeance for their humiliation.

It was not, therefore, until Thursday, the day of the budget vote, that the Conservatives faced up to their probable defeat, only to dismiss all of the options that might have prevented that defeat—including postponing the vote and entering into negotiations with the Créditistes. The Liberals and NDP had made their critical decisions on Wednesday, while the Conservatives slumbered; but on Thursday key Liberals began to waver. The more it seemed that the Conservatives were unwilling to save themselves from defeat, the more a few Liberals wanted to do the job for them. On Wednesday morning, the Liberals did not believe that the Government would allow itself to be defeated. Now—on Thursday afternoon—with the non-confidence vote approaching, doubt spread through the Liberal ranks.

On Wednesday, Robert Andras, the veteran M.P. from Thunder Bay-Nipigon and a former senior Liberal Cabinet minister, had finally ruled himself out of the Liberal leadership race. He spent the day phoning potential supporters to tell them of his decision. So preoccupied had he been with that task that he had not paid attention to the developing parliamentary crisis. On Thursday morning, Paul McRae, Liberal M.P. for the neighbouring riding of Thunder Bay-Atikokan, walked into Andras' office and told him that a growing number of Liberal M.P.s were getting nervous because the Government seemed likely to fall. Andras verified McRae's information with other M.P.s. Before the Liberals toppled the Government, Andras wanted to know who would lead the party in the election. Donald Macdonald was ready to seek the leadership, and Andras had agreed on Wednesday to serve as one of four co-chairmen for Macdonald's leadership campaign.* Despite

---

*Macdonald was hoping to land Roméo LeBlanc, former Health and Welfare Minister Monique Begin, and Vancouver Centre M.P. Art Phillips as the other co-chairmen.

his long association with Trudeau, Andras felt the party needed a
new leader. He phoned Allan MacEachen at noon on Thursday to
say that it would be foolish for the party to enter a campaign
without a resolution of the leadership question. MacEachen replied
that he assumed Trudeau would lead. Throughout the afternoon,
Andras spoke to other nervous Liberals and to officials of the
Ontario and national caucuses, asking them to convene a special
meeting at which the party could reconsider its position in light of
the looming campaign. It was too late for caucus meetings, Andras
was told by caucus officers.

At 5:30 p.m. he phoned Trudeau's office asking for an urgent
meeting. He was told that the leader was busy but would call back.
When he did not hear from Trudeau by 7 p.m., Andras phoned
again. Trudeau had gone to Stornoway for dinner, but Andras was
told that if he came by Trudeau's office around 9 p.m., the two men
could chat then. Andras arrived at the appointed hour, but Trudeau
had not returned. So Andras took his seat in the Commons Thursday night believing he would be called up to Trudeau's office
before the vote.

The Andras-Trudeau meeting was not held Thursday night,
because shortly after his return from Stornoway, Trudeau was
accosted by Judd Buchanan, M.P. for London West since 1968 who
had held four Cabinet posts under Trudeau. After the Liberals'
defeat in May, Buchanan had been asked to head a "rebuilding
committee," a vague assignment that nevertheless kept Buchanan
in touch with the party organization in English Canada. He had
travelled across English Canada in late September and early October talking to party members and had reported his findings to
Trudeau in early November. First, Buchanan said the party felt
that Coutts had to go; his interest in political manoeuvring rather
than policy was hurting the party. Second, Liberals in English
Canada did not think the party could win again with Trudeau.
Buchanan himself shared both of these views and with only half an
hour remaining before the non-confidence vote at 9:45 p.m., he
wanted to know what Trudeau intended to do. The two men
talked for about twenty minutes, and Trudeau listed his preferences in order: accelerate the date for a leadership convention,
select an interim leader for the campaign, or carry on himself.

Andras and Buchanan were not the only Liberals who
thought the party was making a terrible mistake. Just before
Thursday's Question Period, Jean Chrétien stopped Ed Broadbent
in front of the blue curtain separating the Commons chamber

from the doors to the Opposition parties' lobby. Gesturing animatedly, Chrétien suggested that if the NDP kept two M.P.s away for the vote the Liberals would hold back enough additional M.P.s to allow the Government to survive. Chrétien, who was set for his own run for the Liberal leadership, had no authority to make such a deal on behalf of the Liberals, and Broadbent had the Conservatives at the edge of defeat, where he wanted them. He dismissed Chrétien's offer.

Lloyd Axworthy arrived in Ottawa on Thursday after tending to his own leadership chances on Wednesday in Toronto. An early election would kill any chance he had for the leadership, since he needed time to become better known within the party. With Trudeau leading the party, the Liberals would be crushed again in western Canada. "It's like a high school cheerleading section in there," he muttered as he left the Liberal lobby after Question Period.

Donald Macdonald was attending a business meeting in Montreal on Thursday when word of the Liberal strategy reached him. He tried to concentrate on his meeting, but his mind focused increasingly on the apparent foolishness of what was happening in Ottawa. He went up to his hotel room and began phoning supporters in the Liberal caucus, such as Charles Caccia, M.P. for Davenport, and Peter Stollery, M.P. for Spadina, to tell them that the Liberal strategy was crazy. He was ready to run for the leadership, and felt the party would do much better with him than with Trudeau, still thought to be widely disliked in English Canada. At the same time Kathy Robinson, his campaign manager, tried to deliver the same message from her office in Toronto. Both Macdonald and Robinson were told that the Liberal M.P.s were helplessly bound by the party's whip.

All Thursday afternoon, the Liberal lobby was full of agitated conversations, as clusters of M.P.s eager to defeat the Government gathered around their wavering colleagues, bucking up their courage. Coutts came down from his office to join the hand-holding sessions. He and MacEachen had eaten lunch together, and now they circulated through the Liberal lobby to make certain that nothing went awry at the last moment. Around them in the lobby, the party's instinct for power was doing its work. Only with discipline and loyalty could power be won in politics, and the Liberals possessed a larger measure of both than any other party in federal politics. To demonstrate disloyalty by breaking ranks in a critical vote would bring a heavy penalty—not necessarily immediately but most assuredly in the future—to any dissident. Certainly, Liberals often disagreed among themselves; but when the time came to act publicly, Liberals were united because they understood that the pursuit and retention of power demanded solidarity. By the 6 p.m. dinner break, Coutts and MacEachen knew that their ranks were solid.

Shortly after the Commons rose at 6 p.m., Joe Clark dined with Lowell Murray, William Neville, Jock Osler, and Paul Curley. Ian Green, Clark's executive assistant, had called Esmond Butler, the Governor General's secretary, to arrange for Clark and Schreyer to meet, if necessary, Friday morning. Butler had warned that Schreyer might need time to consider any request for dissolution, but those gathered in Clark's office believed Schreyer could not fail to grant Clark a dissolution after a defeat on a budget. Murray and Neville had spent part of the afternoon preparing a statement for Clark to make on television, in case the Government fell. Although Clark and Neville still clung to the belief that the Liberal ranks would break before 9:45 p.m., the five men spent most of their meeting discussing the party's strategy for the election campaign. The most obvious initial question was the date of the election. Neville and Murray both pressed for the earliest possible election date to give the Liberals less time to campaign if they were forced to hold a leadership convention. February 11, the earliest date under the law, had been ruled out by Chief Electoral Officer Jean-Marc Hamel. He had told Neville in the afternoon that the Christmas season would make it impossible to organize an election for that date. The other possible dates were February 18 and February 25, and Clark chose February 18. Paul Curley confirmed that party headquarters had secured an airplane from Air Canada for the following week and that the party organization was in excellent shape for a campaign. The group then turned its attention to the party's campaign themes, agreeing that the election should be blamed on the Liberals and NDP and that the Conservatives should claim they had been deprived of a fair chance to govern. Both themes were already included in the statement prepared for Clark by Murray and Neville.

At 9:30 p.m., Clark left his office and headed for the Government lobby, making his way past the reporters and politicians in the public lobby at the entrance to the Commons chamber. En route, he was stopped by Secretary of State David MacDonald, who had been in meetings all day. MacDonald asked Clark innocently if he had seen the proposed terms of reference for a new agreement with the Federation of Francophones outside Quebec. Clark looked blankly at his minister, mumbled something Mac-Donald could not understand and continued making for the Government lobby. As Clark passed, Green handed MacDonald a typewritten note: "In case of defeat, meet me in my office at 10:15." MacDonald, who had gone home at 9 p.m. and learned about news reports predicting the Government's defeat from his wife, wondered what was going on. So did other ministers who had been otherwise occupied throughout the day, such as Health and Welfare Minister David Crombie and Labour Minister Lincoln Alexander, who arrived in the Commons and promptly bet bottles of scotch with Jacques Olivier, Liberal M.P. for Longueuil, and Jean-Robert Gauthier, Liberal M.P. for Ottawa-Vanier, that the Liberals would not produce all of their members for the vote.

Once inside the Government lobby, Clark stood on a chair and delivered a brief pep talk to cheering Conservative M.P.s, saying that the party was ready for an election and would win a majority Government. When Clark took his seat in the Commons, Conservative whip Bill Kempling tapped him on the shoulder, Eldon Woolliams had arrived from Calgary, still wearing his court clothes. Yewchuk had turned up, but Kempling said the Government was still missing three M.P.s and would be defeated. Clark nodded. On the other side of the chamber, Liberal M.P.s were bursting into applause as the symbol of their determination arrived. Maurice Dionne, M.P. for Northumberland-Miramichi, shuffled towards his seat with a cane in his right hand, obviously in pain from a back operation that had confined him to hospital until shortly before the vote. David Kilgour, who had spoken to Fabien Roy as the division bells started ringing, came over to Clark's seat and repeated Roy's demands to the Prime Minister. It was far too late for negotiations. Clark shook his head and said no. The bells stopped ringing, and M.P.s hurried to their seats.

"Mr. Broadbent," cried Commons Clerk Beverley Koester, and the vote began, with NDP M.P.s rising one by one to support their motion. Senator Davey, Jim Coutts, and the rest of Trudeau's senior staff leaned forward in the Liberal Party gallery when Trudeau rose and bowed to the Speaker, leading his Liberals in support of the NDP motion. Only Serge Joyal, Liberal M.P. for Hochelaga-Maisonneuve, was absent, having defied the whip and remained in New York on private business. The Liberals and NDP had 139 votes.

Fabien Roy was not even in the Commons. He was waiting

outside for reporters who would besiege him after the vote. Adrien Lambert and Eudore Allard were the only Créditiste M.P.s present, and they remained seated after 133 Conservatives rose to oppose the NDP motion. Koester turned and read the count to Speaker James Jerome: "Yeas 139, Nays 133." The Conservative Government had fallen.

Then Clark spoke. "I rise on a point of order. The Government has lost a vote on a matter which we have no alternative but to regard as a question of confidence. I simply want to advise the House that I will be seeing His Excellency the Governor General tomorrow morning."

When Clark sat down, the Commons erupted. M.P.s threw paper in the air in the traditional salute to the end of a Parliament and the onset of an election. They shouted across the aisle at each other, laughing at the huge mistake the other side had just made.

Trudeau, however, remained in his seat for about ten seconds while those around him stood and headed for the door. His head rested on his hand and his shoulders were hunched forward. Throughout the roll call vote, he had gazed downward, lifting his head only to listen to Clark's announcement. Then he dropped his head again and kept it there. When he looked up again, he had a quizzical, thin smile on his face.

Secretary of State David MacDonald walked across the aisle to Trudeau's seat. He and Trudeau were members of the Class of 1965, having entered the Commons together in that year. MacDonald said simply that they both had been in Ottawa for nearly fifteen years and they might not see each other again. He wished Trudeau well. "Being in politics, Pierre, is a bit like eating peanuts. Once you start, it's hard to stop."

Trudeau smiled and replied: "Yes, and it's not very good for you, either."

Trudeau went to his office and spoke to Coutts. They decided that a special Liberal caucus should be held the next morning. Trudeau said he still wanted the caucus to choose someone else to lead the party in the campaign. He gave the same message to Senator Alasdair Graham, the party president, and left for Stornoway.

Clearly, Jim Coutts had a problem on his hands. Everything had gone perfectly, better than he had dared to hope. Now, Trudeau was hesitating. If he stood by his original decision to resign, Coutts would be gone, too, since his loyalty to Trudeau would make him a liability to any other leader. He needed to intensify his pressure on Trudeau, and for that, Coutts picked up the phone and reached Martin Goldfarb, who was skiing at a Utah resort where one of the most popular runs is called Election. Coutts needed a quick poll to use to convince Trudeau to stay. He wanted the results by Sunday. Could Goldfarb deliver? Goldfarb said yes, and Friday morning his polling began in six ridings in southern Ontario, British Columbia, and Nova Scotia.

While Coutts and Goldfarb were speaking, Joe Clark was meeting his inner Cabinet. Clark remains outwardly cool under pressure, and his face was impassive when he left the Commons after the vote. If he was churning inside, no one would have known it when he bounced up the stairs to meet his ministers. They seemed to be in a state of shock, except for Crosbie, who boasted that the Conservatives would knock the stuffing out of the unprincipled Grits in the campaign. Clark hurried through the signing of the official documents needed to request a dissolution of Parliament, told his ministers to meet again Friday morning, and left for the press conference theatre, where he tested his campaign themes for the first time:

> The Opposition parties have decided to disrupt the nation's business. That was not our choice; we wanted to get on with governing the country. But the decision has been made by the Liberals and the NDP. I, of course, accept it. I will be calling on the Governor General in the morning.
>
> Only six months ago, Canadians voted to change the Government of Canada because they wanted to change the direction of the country. By their action tonight, the Opposition parties are saying Canadians were wrong to make that decision.

Clark's statement then ran through some of his Government's initiatives, including a budget that "fairly and honestly" faced the nation's economic problems, an energy policy designed to make Canada self-sufficient by 1990, an improved climate in federal-provincial relations, and parliamentary reform.

Clark declined to take questions and returned to his office for a brief meeting with Senator Robert de Cotret, Minister of Industry, Trade and Commerce, about where de Cotret might run in the 1980 election, having been appointed to the Senate and named to the Cabinet after losing the riding of Ottawa Centre in the 1979 election. After talking inconclusively with de Cotret for fifteen minutes, Clark chatted with Neville and left for home.

Early Friday morning, Clark crossed the street from 24 Sussex Drive to Government House to ask the Governor General for a dissolution of Parliament. Clark had been warned that Schreyer's answer might not be given immediately, but he was taken aback when Schreyer inquired if Clark might consider forming a care-taker government for a few months so that the election would not be held in winter. Clark rejected the suggestion; it would be impractical, and anyway Clark wanted to confront the Liberals as soon as possible. The Governor General and the Prime Minister talked for about forty-five minutes. When Clark left, Schreyer had still not agreed to the dissolution, although he assured Clark that he would make a decision before the inner Cabinet met at 10:30 a.m. Clark left feeling that the Governor General was being unusually difficult. But he was confident that Schreyer would grant the dissolution, and at 9:50 a.m., Schreyer's office confirmed that February 18 would be an acceptable election date.

Not far from Government House, Pierre Trudeau was meet-ing at Stornoway that morning with Coutts, MacEachen, Lalonde, and Davey. Coutts, MacEachen, and Davey, of course, wanted an early commitment from Trudeau that he would lead the party in the campaign. Lalonde, Trudeau's long-time ally from Quebec, hesitated, to the surprise and consternation of the other three who had come to see Trudeau. Lalonde worried that a second elec-toral defeat would damage Trudeau's reputation in history and hurt the federalist cause in Quebec. Lalonde did not want Trudeau pressured into a hasty decision he might later regret. Trudeau himself repeated his desire to leave politics, but he agreed to return if the caucus and the party wanted him to fight the cam-paign. MacEachen was dismayed by Trudeau's attitude, realizing that he would now have to work hard to rally the caucus and the national executive for Trudeau. Didn't Trudeau realize it was his duty to lead the party after participating in the defeat of the Government? MacEachen complained to Davey when the two men drove away from Stornoway.

Just before noon, the Liberals' national caucus gathered to hear Trudeau, but he stayed only a few minutes, saying his pre-ference was to leave politics. He could be persuaded to return, but "the sovereign would have to ask me three times," an enigmatic statement that left the caucus perplexed about his wishes. Trudeau asked the caucus for a secret ballot vote on his leadership and left for Montreal.

After lunch, the Liberal M.P.s split into regional caucuses to ponder Trudeau's words and to begin deliberating what to do next. The Atlantic caucus, led by MacEachen and Alasdair Graham, was solidly for Trudeau; the western caucus was overwhelmingly opposed. The Quebec caucus, of course, lined up behind the leader, but Lalonde and André Ouellet, the most popular former minister from the Quebec caucus, cautioned their colleagues against imposing their will on the national caucus. Trudeau had been the party leader for eleven years; if the rest of the party thought an English-speaking leader would improve the party's chances in the rest of the country, then the Quebec caucus should accept that decision. Ouellet, in particular, worried about the Liberal Party's becoming only a Quebec-based party. It would help the referendum fight to have Trudeau re-elected Prime Minister, but the consequences for federalism in Quebec could be disastrous if Trudeau ran again and was beaten decisively in English Canada. The Quebec caucus wanted Trudeau, but its members wisely decided to mute their enthusiasm and await the reaction of the other regional caucuses.

The decision of the Ontario caucus was crucial. The election would be won or lost in that province, and when the debate began more than half the Ontario caucus wanted a new leader. Former ministers John Reid, Judd Buchanan, and Robert Andras all thought Trudeau should be replaced. Many Ontario M.P.s worried that a latent anti-Trudeau feeling in the province would overwhelm them in the election. The leading candidates to replace Trudeau—Donald Macdonald and John Turner, if he could be persuaded to change his mind—were from Ontario. Either would undoubtedly strengthen the party in Ontario, and both men had many admirers in the Ontario caucus.

When the regional caucuses came together for a national caucus in the late afternoon, the Ontario M.P.s were still sorely divided. Gradually, however, they began to swing to Trudeau: some feeling that an early leadership convention was impractical, others swayed by Senator Keith Davey, who had delivered an impassioned speech on Trudeau's behalf, and Allan MacEachen, whose speech on Friday was said later to be the best many M.P.s had heard in their lives.

Why was there such hesitation? MacEachen demanded of the M.P.s. When the caucus decided on Wednesday to vote against the budget, it must have known that the Government might fall. If that happened, then the party would have no alternative but to turn to Trudeau. Moreover, Trudeau was the best leader in the present circumstances and one of the greatest prime ministers the country had known. He deserved their support for the strong leadership he had given the party in the past and for the contribution he could still make to national unity. The alternatives to Trudeau's leadership—an early convention or an interim leader— were fraught with political danger. The party owed Trudeau this final testament of loyalty for all that he had done for the Liberal Party and for Canada, MacEachen concluded.

Shortly after MacEachen's speech, the M.P.s broke for dinner, his words ringing in their ears. Some had swung behind Trudeau before he spoke, but MacEachen's speech brought other wavering M.P.s to Trudeau's side. The more they looked at the logistical problems of a late January convention, held in the middle of an election campaign, the more Trudeau's detractors accepted the inevitable, especially after Alasdair Graham, the party's president, said the party's lawyers had concluded that an early convention would violate the party's constitution. At 11 p.m. the caucus broke up, having decided against a secret ballot, preferring instead to instruct officers of the caucus and the national executive to report the full range of feeling about Trudeau to the leader.

Trudeau had gone to dinner in Montreal Friday night and then driven to his property in the Laurentians. From there, he phoned Coutts for information about the caucus decision. Coutts, who never attends the Liberal caucus, was receiving reports from Davey and others throughout the day and evening. Coutts told Trudeau the caucus wanted him back, although the support had initially been far from unanimous.

Saturday morning, the Liberal Party's national executive, whose members are elected by provincial associations across Canada, met at the Chateau Laurier Hotel. The executive was in an abrasive mood, as MacEachen, Graham, Coutts and caucus chairman Jacques Guilbault soon discovered. The members of the executive quickly began peppering MacEachen with questions, complaining that the party organization had not been consulted about defeating the Government. The caucus had once again ignored the party organization, and the executive was angry at being taken for a mere rubber stamp. The party organization had repeatedly complained of being overlooked by Trudeau and the caucus, and here was further proof that the party was justified in its complaints.

Gradually, the steam left their arguments when MacEachen

explained that the caucus did not have any choice but to vote against the budget. The Liberals were in an excellent position to win the election. Under pressure from the executive, he promised that the party organization could contribute to the drafting of a platform for use during the campaign. Graham again reported that a January convention would be impractical and probably illegal. The executive was unhappy, but it was powerless under the circumstances. The Liberals were already in an election, and there was no sense struggling among themselves when the Conservatives were giving every sign of itching for a fight. The executive yielded and gave Trudeau a vote of confidence.

While the national executive debated the election and Trudeau's leadership in Ottawa on Saturday morning, another group of Liberals gathered in Toronto to consider their next move. Donald Macdonald had invited his key advisors to his home for a strategy session. The group included Kathy Robinson, Stephen Goudge, and Robert Prichard, a young law professor at the University of Toronto who taught a course in public policy formation with Macdonald and had agreed to serve as Macdonald's policy coordinator for the leadership race. Until Trudeau declared his intentions, the Macdonald forces were caught in maddening uncertainty made worse by the memory that a few days ago, after John Turner had withdrawn from the race but before the Conservative Government fell, Donald Macdonald had the leadership almost for the asking. Even before Turner's announcement, Macdonald believed he was going to win the convention. He had tried to stop the Liberals from defeating the Government on Thursday and now he waited anxiously while the man whom he had supported for the Liberal leadership in 1968 decided if he would stay on or throw open the leadership for Macdonald to win.

There was one question Macdonald and his advisors needed to answer immediately: If Trudeau decided to remain, should Macdonald run in the election? Robinson and Prichard urged him to contest a seat, arguing that he would solidify his position as the heir apparent to Trudeau if he won. But Macdonald's wife, Ruth, was adamantly opposed to her husband's running, and Macdonald himself did not want to return to Ottawa unless he could be leader. He had held five ministerial positions in Ottawa, ending his Cabinet career in 1977 as Minister of Finance. When he resigned, still on excellent personal terms with Trudeau, he drew the curtain on fifteen years in the House of Commons. He had seen all that Ottawa could offer, except the highest elected office in the land. Macdonald was earning a handsome salary as a partner at the Toronto law firm of McCarthy and McCarthy and as a director of several companies. He did not want to give all this up unless he could be party leader.

As they discussed the confusing political situation, Macdonald's advisors wondered if he should tell Trudeau directly that he was prepared to run. Presumably, Trudeau knew this already, because Coutts, Andras, and Davey, among others, had been in contact with Macdonald. There could be little doubt in Ottawa that Macdonald was available, but in any case Robinson arranged with Trudeau's office for the two men to speak on Sunday afternoon. When Trudeau came on the line, Macdonald explained that he had decided to run for the leadership. Trudeau replied that he was still unsure what he would do, but he was worried that a January convention might violate the constitution of the party. He asked Macdonald if he would seek election as an M.P. if Trudeau remained as leader. Macdonald said no.

Macdonald's advisors were alarmed that Trudeau was worried about the constitutional legality of a January convention. On Monday, Prichard consulted several colleagues at the University of Toronto law school, who contested the validity of the opinion given the national executive.

While the Macdonald forces waited in Toronto for a decision from Trudeau, the leader returned to Ottawa late on Sunday afternoon. That evening, he received a delegation from the national executive and the Liberal caucus, including Allan MacEachen, Alasdair Graham, Jacques Guilbault, Senator Gil Molgat, and Torrance Wylie, a member of the executive invited by Graham to meet the caucus' request that a cross-section of Liberal representatives report the outcome of the caucus and executive meetings to Trudeau. Trudeau listened to the reports, discussed with his guests the arguments for and against his staying on, but offered no hint of his intentions.

Trudeau was also made aware on Sunday night of the results of Goldfarb's quick polling done Friday and Saturday after Coutts' Thursday-night telephone request. The results from the six ridings—Vancouver Centre, Halifax, and four ridings in Ontario—showed that the Liberals could win the election with Trudeau.

On Monday, Trudeau closeted himself in his office, making telephone calls to friends and party organizers and receiving Liberal M.P.s and senators. He called his close friend Gérard Pelletier, who was in Paris, where Trudeau had sent him as ambassador in 1975 after seven years in Trudeau Cabinets. He phoned Boston and spoke to Michael Pitfield, in exile at Harvard after being dumped as Clerk of the Privy Council by Clark. Ed Lumley and Donald Johnston saw him for about forty-five minutes and urged him to remain leader of the party. Senator Alasdair Graham brought the same message.

Judd Buchanan had spent the weekend canvassing opinion among Liberal organizers in twenty-eight swing ridings in Ontario, thirteen in Metropolitan Toronto. He told Trudeau on Monday afternoon that Liberals in these ridings wanted him to retire.

Robert Andras finally got to see Trudeau on Monday afternoon and urged him to step down. Alasdair Graham had developed a contingency plan for a leadership convention based on a series of "mini-conventions" in cities across Canada. Andras felt the plan would give the Liberals important publicity in the first half of the election campaign and solve the logistical nightmares of organizing a massive leadership convention in one city on short notice. Andras suggested the plan to Trudeau as a way of overcoming the handicap of a leadership campaign in the middle of an election, but Trudeau seemed more concerned with the divisive impact of a leadership fight between Donald Macdonald and John Turner.

Turner had resigned as Minister of Finance in 1975, in disagreement with the emerging Liberal wage-and-price controls program. Turner and Trudeau had never been close in Ottawa; their ambitions and egos grated on each other. Their mutual suspicion deepened after Turner sent circulars to clients of his law firm criticizing the performance of the Trudeau Government. But Turner's stature in the party remained sufficiently high that, when Trudeau announced his intention to retire on November 21, many Liberals assumed that Turner would seek and win the leadership. Friends of Turner went to work immediately preparing his entry into the contest. Toronto lawyers David Smith, Jerry Grafstein, and Jim Peterson and his wife, Heather; Vancouver lawyers John Swift and Keith Mitchell; Montreal financier John Payne and M.P.s Jeanne Sauvé, André Ouellet, Robert Kaplan, and Mark MacGuigan formed the core of the Turner team. The last three presidents of the Ontario wing of the Liberal Party— Norman MacLeod, Jeff King, and Bruce Laird—were also in the Turner camp. But on Monday, December 10, the day before the Crosbie budget, Turner asked Smith, Heather Peterson, John Payne, John Swift, and Toronto advertising executive Hank Karpus to come to his plush office at the McMillan and Binch law firm. There, he told his friends that he was not going to run. He knew the race with Macdonald would be close; there was no guarantee he could win. He wanted financial security for his family, and he was not prepared to give up his $250,000 income in exchange for the uncertainties of politics. Several hours later, he held a press conference and made public his decision, before heading to the Windsor Arms Hotel for a party with two dozen friends and supporters.

Turner's public announcement was categorical, but as the week's bizarre events unfolded in Ottawa, some of his supporters, notably Jeanne Sauvé, began to wonder if a draft-Turner movement would get their man into the race. When Trudeau told the caucus on Wednesday morning that he did not want to fight an election, Ed Lumley, a Turner supporter, phoned Turner and told him that pressure might grow on him to reconsider his decision. André Ouellet passed on the same message, and the longer Trudeau hesitated, the more the draft-Turner movement looked intriguing to his supporters.

Trudeau had coupled his November 21 announcement with an assurance that he would remain neutral in the leadership contest. But it was widely and correctly assumed wherever Liberals gathered that Trudeau did not want Turner to lead the Liberal Party. Trudeau had given a long interview to two reporters during the fall, and their stories quoted him saying that Turner did not share his views on the future of Canada—an indirect way of indicating that Turner was not an acceptable replacement. While Trudeau pondered his decision about coming back, no one knew whether Turner would agree to rethink his previous decision not to run. The possibility that Turner might yet become Prime Minister of Canada was one of many factors weighing on Trudeau's mind when he retired to Stornoway to consider his decision on Monday night.

He considered his options alone. He had been Prime Minister of Canada for eleven years. He had recently suffered the first defeat of his political career. Goldfarb's polls, the Gallup Poll, and Coutts were telling him that he could win again. If so, he could erase the smudge that defeat had placed upon his political career. He had read the press notices after his resignation and had not liked what he had seen: the general impression was of a man and a Prime Minister who had failed to fulfil the promise expected of him when he took office in 1968. He was a proud, sensitive, and shy man, and the obituaries of his political career stung deeply.

The Quebec referendum was coming, and although he would play a secondary role in the federalist organization to fight the Parti Québécois, opposition to separatism had been the driving passion of his intellectual and political life. It would be tempting to remain in federal politics a while longer, to mould events to fit his view of Quebec in Canada. He could end his political career a winner and satisfy his need for history's approval by governing in a dynamic, even dramatic, fashion once returned to power. Above all, he had enjoyed the exercise of power, the constant struggle to match his intellect against events and circumstances. He did not deal well with people—that was among his greatest failings as a political leader—but he felt comfortable in power, believing that although others were capable of succeeding him, no one could do the job as well as he could.

Although his party had given him a public vote of confidence, he could not forget that western Liberals had been against his return. Within the Ontario caucus, former ministers such as Reid, Andras, and Buchanan had opposed him, and more than half the Ontario M.P.s had expressed misgivings about his continued leadership. Behind them stood the party organization, which Trudeau had never taken much time to think about—riding presidents and party workers who wanted him replaced. If he ran, they would probably work as hard as they always did for the party in an election, but would their support be given grudgingly? If he retired, could the party knit itself together quickly enough to defeat the Conservatives? Could John Turner be his successor?

Trudeau was two months past his sixtieth birthday. He was physically fit—he always made sure of that—and his three sons needed his time and attention. His wife Margaret could not be counted upon to guide them in their formative years, and she often irritated him with her interventions in their lives. In Montreal, they would be farther removed from her, and he would have more time for them. Most important of all, he had already made the decision to leave politics, after agonizing about his future for months. When he resigned in November, he knew that the national executive was probably going to vote in favour of holding a convention in the spring at which delegates would be asked if they wanted a leadership review. He did not have the votes to stop the national executive, but he might have beaten any challenge to his leadership at the convention if he worked hard enough on his own behalf. Instead he had decided to retire and he was making the difficult psychological withdrawal from politics.

He called Donald Macdonald in Toronto late on Monday night. Macdonald explained his advisors' view that a January convention would not offend the party constitution. Macdonald did not offer any advice; the decision was for Trudeau to make, without pressure from a potential successor. Trudeau briefly reviewed some of the factors weighing on his mind. He said he was going to take a walk and think things over. Macdonald put down the phone and told his advisors that Trudeau left the impression that he was probably going to quit.

Shortly thereafter, at midnight, Trudeau called Coutts, who was at his office working on a statement explaining Trudeau's decision to remain as party leader for a press conference Tuesday morning. He told Coutts, too, that he was going for a walk. An hour later he phoned back, saying he was probably not going to run.

At 8:30 Tuesday morning, Trudeau called Coutts again to say he did not think he would run. Coutts said he was coming right over. Coutts stopped by his office to dictate a short statement just in case he could not change Trudeau's mind, and at 9:30 he arrived at Stornoway. For an hour, he and Trudeau reviewed again all the arguments. They had reached this point because Coutts, more than anyone else, seized the opportunity created by the Conservatives' incredible strategic errors. Trudeau had known what was happening at every step of the week's events. Coutts pressed him a final time, and Trudeau agreed. The chance for a last crack at power was too tempting to resist. Trudeau called Macdonald and Alasdair Graham to tell them of his decision. He told Macdonald how sorry he was for all the disruption he had brought to Macdonald's life.

On November 21, Trudeau had said in explaining his resignation: "Liberals are in the process of rethinking the party's policies and of rebuilding its organization to be ready to return to office. In my view, one element of that renewal should be a change in leadership."

Now, on December 17, he sat in the press conference theatre ready to tell the nation why he had changed his mind. He barely looked up from Coutts' text as he spoke:

> I have accepted the strong appeal of the National Liberal Caucus and the National Liberal Executive and I will lead our party in the current election campaign. If we are elected, I will form a new Liberal Government to govern our country.
>
> This was the single most difficult decision I have ever

made. You know my reasons for wanting to step down from public life. My strongest desire was to leave politics and raise my family in Montreal.

I decided last night, after two days of long consultation with friends and colleagues in the caucus and the party, that because Canada faces most serious problems, because the Government has been defeated and because our party faces an election, my duty is to accept the draft of my party—that duty was stronger even than my desire to continue with my plan to re-enter private life.

In London, Ontario, where he was already campaigning, Prime Minister Joe Clark watched Trudeau's press conference on television. Clark was delighted. He would have Trudeau to kick around again. It would be a repeat of the 1979 campaign—only this time the Conservatives would win a majority Government.

PART TWO: POWER

~ 2 ~

Roots of Policy

The Conservative Government that fell in its twenty-seventh week in office was more than three years in the making. During the long march from Opposition to Government, the Conservatives prepared themselves assiduously to govern, but along the way they picked up so much intellectual baggage that they began to stagger as soon as they attained their goal. More than anything else, except perhaps for the public's perception of Joe Clark himself, the Conservatives were undone in office by their inability to fulfil the vast and untidy assortment of promises made in Opposition.

The promises grew from the Conservatives' desperate desire to appear united and competent to govern. Having been so infrequently in power, the Conservatives could not recommend themselves by pointing to accomplishments in office; they could only present promises to persuade the electorate of the party's readiness for office. Despite the effort the Conservatives poured into developing policy, their promises were of only marginal help in winning the election, and they became a burden when the party took power.

When he captured the party leadership in February 1976, Joe Clark understood political scientist George Perlin's observation that "the history of the Conservative Party has been profoundly influenced by conflicts over its leadership."* Clark had spent most of his adult life working in a variety of party jobs, emerging as a

---

*George Perlin, *The Tory Syndrome* (McGill-Queens, 1980), p. 28.

backbencher, brash of voice and awkward of appearance, after his election as M.P. for Rocky Mountain in 1972. He had watched the Conservatives' disintegration under John Diefenbaker; and while working for Robert Stanfield, Clark had observed the party struggling to throw off Diefenbaker's querulous legacy. Nothing preoccupied Clark more as Conservative leader than his attempts to bring cohesion and discipline to the ranks of his party. Without them, Clark knew that the Conservatives would continue to pursue power as Quixote had searched for Dulcinea.

The Conservative Party had greatly changed under Robert Stanfield. In the 1968 election, Stanfield had assembled an impressive list of candidates—Duff Roblin, Premier of Manitoba; Marcel Faribault, constitutional advisor to Quebec Premier Daniel Johnson; Dalton Camp, former president of the party; Earl Brownridge, president of American Motors (Canada) Ltd.; Julien Chouinard, Quebec's Deputy Minister of Justice; André Gagnon, president of the Montreal Catholic School Board. More significant perhaps than their defeat was their willingness to run. For the first time since the late 1950s, when Diefenbaker excited the imagination of the party and the country, the Conservatives had undergone an infusion of new blood. Gradually, the Conservatives under Stanfield reached out to the young, the upwardly-mobile and voters in large urban centres, nearly taking power in 1972 with 107 seats before falling back to ninety-five seats in 1974.

Stanfield never led the Conservatives to victory, but he dispelled some of the bogeys left from the Diefenbaker era. The Conservatives became more tolerant of French-language rights, although that scarcely eroded Quebeckers' image of the Conservatives as the party of *les anglais*. The Diefenbaker "cowboys," western Conservatives who worshipped the aging chieftain, were moved aside by Stanfield, not without hard feelings and public squawks, to make room for such M.P.s as Jim Gillies, Flora MacDonald, Ron Atkey, Sinclair Stevens, John Fraser, John Wise, Walter Baker, Jack Murta, Allan Lawrence, Jake Epp, Allan McKinnon, and Elmer MacKay. Stanfield, although he could never match Trudeau's public allure, at least made the Conservative Party a more modern institution than it had been under Diefenbaker, receptive to fresh ideas and more interested than before in future problems than past battles.

Still, as Stanfield learned, the Conservatives were a difficult group to lead. Conservative M.P.s from rural or small-town Canada rubbed shoulders uneasily with colleagues from Toronto and Vancouver. Western and Ontario M.P.s clashed over issues such as energy; in fact, the party never developed a coherent response to the energy crisis of 1973 because of the differences between the western and Ontario caucuses, a failure that Stanfield always believed was more damaging to the party in the 1974 election than the promise of a wage-and-price freeze followed by controls. The party also had more M.P.s whose careers dated from the early Diefenbaker years—twenty of them entering the 1979 election—than the Liberals, and these M.P.s co-existed uneasily with younger members whose influence within the party had grown while theirs' waned. The party's repeated setbacks in Quebec created a vicious circle of ignorance: the lack of Quebec M.P.s led the party to misunderstand Quebec's concerns, which weakened the party still further in that province.

The Conservative Party also stretched across a wide band of the Canadian political spectrum, from so-called Red Tories, who saw the state as a necessary vehicle for solving social problems, to hard-line free enterprisers, who believed that the state's excessive growth must be curbed. While the federal Conservatives were in Opposition, their provincial cousins were in power in more than half of the provinces, and this set up a debate within the federal party about federal-provincial relations. M.P.s were torn between aligning themselves with the demands of their provincial cousins and defending the national role of the federal government. Unlike the Liberals, therefore, the Conservatives were usually struggling to define the appropriate role for the federal government in Canadian society.

It did not take Joe Clark long to discover how fractious the Conservatives can be. Clark won the Conservative leadership by only sixty-five votes out of 2,309 on the fourth ballot, simply because he was an acceptable second choice to more delegates than any of his rivals were. Two of the defeated candidates—Claude Wagner and Jack Horner—never reconciled themselves to his victory. Wagner, a brooding and prickly man, seldom participated in either party or parliamentary work. Clark and Wagner sat beside each other like Bolingbroke and Mortimer, suspicious of each other's every move, until Wagner withdrew into sullen silence after Clark's candidate, Roch LaSalle, M.P. for Joliette, wrested control of the Quebec wing of the party from Wagner. Stripped of everything but his overbearing pride, Wagner accepted an appointment to the Senate offered by the Liberals in 1978. Wagner then wreaked his final vengeance on the Conservatives by refusing to campaign in the ensuing by-election, won by the Liberals. Jack Horner displayed his contempt for Clark during the leadership campaign, belittling Clark's abilities and suggesting none too subtly that Clark was not a true Albertan, with all the political and personal machismo that statement implied for Horner. After fourteen months spent chafing under Clark's leadership, Horner succumbed to Jim Coutts' blandishments and joined the Liberals.

As if these defections were not sufficient to cause the public to wonder if Clark controlled his party, John Diefenbaker was never above making mischief. Clark made every effort to treat Diefenbaker with respect, and relations between the two men were less frosty than those between Diefenbaker and Stanfield. Diefenbaker even attended a Conservative caucus meeting, an event so rare since his removal from the leadership in 1967 that the Conservatives extracted from it every conceivable ounce of publicity, arranging for a photographer to record the event and deliver the pictures to Canadian Press for nation-wide distribution. But Diefenbaker, even in his eighties, could not reconcile himself to someone else leading *his* party; or if he accepted the fact publicly, he could never believe that his hold on the Canadian imagination did not surpass his successors'. In this he may not have been entirely mistaken. About a year after Clark won the leadership, the party conducted a poll asking who was the best-known Conservative in Canada, and the response was Diefenbaker.

When he was asked how Clark was performing as Opposition leader, Diefenbaker's answers overflowed with disingenuousness. Diefenbaker never criticized Clark directly, but he usually left the impression, by word or facial expression, that Clark was not up to the job. On his eightieth birthday, Diefenbaker received a rare public rebuke from Stanfield for his belittling of Clark. After expressing satisfaction that so many people had wished Diefenbaker well on his eightieth birthday, Stanfield added: "I regret, however, that Mr. Diefenbaker does not express the same generous sentiments towards our leader." Stanfield said Diefenbaker should "stop sticking a knife into Mr. Clark," an astonishingly blunt remark from the discreet Stanfield. Once asked how Clark might perform as Prime Minister, Diefenbaker replied with customary malice that the job of Prime Minister was not for any "passing Joe."*

---

*Diefenbaker's office denied the quotation, but *La Presse* reprinted the sentence in full: *"Le leadership c'est qu'il y a de plus important dans un pays. On ne peut pas laisser le gouvernement à n'importe quel 'passing Joe.'"*

Even in his own constituency, Clark could not be assured of
unity. Following the 1974 election, redistribution changed the
boundaries for most of the ridings in Canada. Clark's Rocky
Mountain constituency disappeared from the electoral map, and
Clark decided to run in the riding of Bow River, which included his
home town of High River. Unfortunately, Stan Schumacher,
Conservative M.P. for Palliser, argued that he should be the
Conservative candidate in Bow River since the new constituency
overlapped considerably with Palliser. Schumacher was an undistinguished M.P., most noted for his passionate love of the
monarchy, his admiration for John Diefenbaker, his opposition to
bilingualism, and his intellectual limitations. Like most men of
prejudice, he had an unshakable belief in the justice of his cause.
And he was stubborn. So was Joe Clark, who demonstrated in the
Bow River imbroglio the same approach to leadership that hurt
him when he was Prime Minister of Canada. "To be known as 'the
man from High River' is a source of personal pride to me and is of
very real importance to our party's chances of forming the national
government because of the general affinity it gives me for the
smaller communities across Canada which remain the bedrock of
this country," Clark wrote in a letter to the *Lethbridge Herald*.*
Clark staked out his position assuming that Schumacher would
back down. When Schumacher refused to yield, Clark faced the
prospect of choosing another riding or fighting for the nomination,
which he thought would be humiliating for a party leader. After
saying he would stand firm, Clark relented and jumped to Yellowhead riding in northern Alberta. Clark thus avoided an internecine
squabble, but at the price of looking weak as party leader.

Aware of the fractiousness of the Conservative Party, Joe
Clark set about trying to give the Conservatives unity and self-
confidence before the 1979 election, which the Liberals had delayed
calling twice in 1978 while waiting for an improvement in their
standing in public opinion. In 1976, Clark established an elaborate
structure of caucus committees, distributing the responsibility for
leading these committees to a large number of Conservative M.P.s.
By keeping his M.P.s busy formulating policies, Clark hoped that
they would have less time to bicker among themselves. The
committees would force the Red Tories, the free enterprisers, the
veterans, the inexperienced M.P.s, and the regional caucuses to
work together. The most important of the caucus committees

---

*Quoted in David Humphreys, *Joe Clark: A Portrait* (Deneau and Greenberg,
1978), p. 244.

were led by Conservative M.P.s elected in 1968 or 1972: only a few M.P.s from the Diefenbaker years, like Walter Dinsdale from Brandon-Souris, George Hees from Prince Edward-Hastings, and Eldon Woolliams from Calgary North, were given major responsibilities—an indication that Clark, like Stanfield, wanted to give the party a contemporary image.

The development of new policies became one of Clark's passions in the first two years of his leadership. The Conservatives' last two sorties into policy under Stanfield had proven disastrous for the party. The first occurred in 1973, when the Conservatives could not develop a consistent energy policy; oil and natural gas prices were under pressure from leapfrogging world oil prices after the OPEC price increases. The oil-producing provinces in western Canada wanted Canadian prices to move towards world levels, but the consuming provinces resisted higher prices, and Conservative M.P.s aligned themselves with the interests of their respective provincial interests, thus splitting the federal caucus.

Next, the party unveiled its wage-and-price controls promise during the 1974 election, a promise disavowed by some Conservative candidates during the campaign. When the Liberals imposed wage-and-price controls in 1975, the mixture of ironic laughter and anger within the Conservative Party was not sufficient to erase the memory of a politically unwise promise, hastily conceived and insufficiently explained before the campaign. If the Conservatives were to demonstrate to the Canadian public that the party was capable of governing, Clark felt the Conservatives needed to improve on their recent policy-making record.

In a parliamentary system, an Opposition party like the Conservatives can become easily typecast as simply the "critic" of the Government. Clark understood the institutional constraints on breaking free from this essentially negative public perception. He offered a lengthy and revealing analysis of the problem in his own master's thesis, pointing to policy conferences as a possible solution.

> Certain serious electoral disadvantages attach to the role of Official Opposition in the Canadian parliamentary system. There are undeniable advantages as well, involved in the status and visibility of some parliamentary leaders, but probably too little attention has been given to the institutional disabilities of that role, and their implications for the party in the role and for the system.
> It is, for example, difficult to cite a single case in any of the eleven jurisdictions of Canada where the perform-

ance by a party of its responsibilities as Official Opposition was the primary source of its success in forming the Government in a subsequent general election. So far as parliamentary performance is concerned, the truism holds that office has been often lost but seldom won. This is not to deny that campaigns conducted by former Opposition parties have sometimes been the critical factor in changing governments, but those have been campaigns in which the parliamentary performance of the challenger has been largely irrelevant. An inept performance in Opposition might prejudice a party seeking to mount a successful campaign outside Parliament, but there is little evidence to suggest that the effective performance of the role of Official Opposition has had any more than a marginal influence in campaigns which succeeded in changing governments.

This does not deny the importance of an effective Official Opposition in Parliament or legislature, but is simply to affirm that the importance of that role is institutional, not electoral; its effect is to criticize governments but not to change them. The important point is that the very effectiveness of the Official Opposition party in parliamentary politics can inhibit its effectiveness in electoral politics. Classically, the Official Opposition has two roles in Parliament, as critic and alternative. In practice in Parliament, the role of critic is paramount. . . . The limitations inherent in the role of the critic are two, one traditional and one emerging. The traditional limitation is that the party is habitually off-balance, responding and bound to the initiatives and priorities of the Government. It can occasionally flush a hare and chase it, but that is more diverting than decisive. Not only is the Official Opposition party precluded from making its own issues, it is often so preoccupied with Parliament that it fails to see issues developing in the country.

The other limitation is that the stance of a critic is essentially negative. This is a particular burden in modern circumstances, when developments in education, information and the scope and complexity of public business have changed public perceptions and expectations of Parliament and parties. There is reason to believe that an increasing proportion of the Canadian electorate perceives the function of Parliament to be legislative and the function of parties to be the proposal of "positive" policy for public consideration. That change, from classical perceptions of Parliament as a place of debate and parties as the

> major participants in debate, creates particular problems
> for Opposition parties, whose institutional role is to be
> critical or "negative."*

Clark also needed policies for his own purposes. He had sought the
leadership without many clearly defined notions of where he
wanted to take the country. Like the other leadership candidates,
he spoke in generalities about the future. He wanted the party to
encourage the entrepreneurial spirit in Canadians by reducing the
interference of government in their lives, but he was supportive of
the major government programs of social assistance introduced
since World War II. He argued in favour of parliamentary reform.
He thought that Canada should rejoice in its regional and ethnic
diversity, even if that meant giving more power to provincial
governments. "Canada is too big for any one identity or ideology,
and the attempts to make us all the same serve only to frustrate
and divide. We should recognize that a respect for diversity is itself
a form of Canadian identity. Let us build a sense of community
rather than a central bureaucracy," Clark said in announcing his
candidacy for the leadership. These ideas were too anodyne to
withstand daily scrutiny in the House of Commons or in the media.
Clark needed specific policies to fit within the superstructure of
his ideas. He knew a great deal about politics, a little about social
policy, but next to nothing of substance about economics, international relations and defence, and cultural policy.

The caucus committees went to work, some travelling across
the country on fact-finding missions. Clark established a policy
advisory council under the leadership of Toronto businesswoman
Reva Gerstein, but the council produced disappointingly little. The
party also sponsored conferences on industrial strategy at Monte-
bello, on Quebec's economic future at Sherbrooke, and on foreign
affairs at Toronto. Unfortunately, the policies the party developed
often contradicted one another or fit uncomfortably together.
Although the committee structure gave the responsibility for co-
ordinating policies to Jim Gillies, M.P. for Don Valley West, it
often seemed that no one was in charge of assembling the policies
into a coherent package.

The problem, however, went much deeper than the committee
structure within the Conservative caucus. Quite often, the Conservatives developed policy in a vacuum. Because they had not been

---

*Joe Clark, *Policy Conferences of Major Parties in Canada as Innovating Agencies* (Master's
thesis, University of Alberta, 1973), pgs. 173-176.

in power for many years, the Conservatives did not undergo the daily discipline of considering the consequences of their policies, of asking themselves: what will happen if we do this or that? Only five Conservative M.P.s had served in a federal Cabinet and four others in a provincial Cabinet, so the bulk of the caucus had never personally experienced the constraints imposed on those who wield power. Interest groups, provincial governments, private institutions, and ordinary citizens, all of whom keep watch on the Government, paid less attention to what the Conservatives were saying than to what the Liberals were—or were not—doing. Some of the civil service's information was available to the Conservatives, but the civil service's advice was reserved for the Government. Unchecked by outsiders, inexperienced themselves, and deprived of the civil service's advice, the Conservatives fell back on themselves to design policy.

The Conservatives had resident experts in specialized policy areas like defence, which was the special domain of Allan McKinnon, M.P. for Victoria. He knew his subject intimately and performed splendidly as the party's critic. The Conservatives were well served in drafting a policy for small businessmen by a number of M.P.s who had worked in small businesses and understood the difficulties of financing, marketing, and government red tape. The transportation and agricultural policies of the party were detailed and thoughtful because the Conservative M.P.s from the Prairies came from a milieu where political survival partially depends on talking sensibly about freight rates, rail line abandonment, and grain.

The Conservatives' limitations were most evident in fields such as foreign affairs, federal-provincial relations, energy, and economic policy. In foreign affairs, Claude Wagner never even tried to point the party in a coherent policy direction. But since foreign policy does not tickle the electorate's fancy, the Conservatives' fuzziness went unnoticed. In federal-provincial relations, the party was handicapped by not having run the federal government since the provincial premiers began ganging up on Ottawa in the early 1970s. This lack of experience, coupled with a shared political affiliation with five or six provincial governments, led the Conservatives to believe that the provincial premiers were more benevolent than they in fact were. The Conservatives assumed that by making specific concessions to provincial demands for more power, they could "put a fresh face on federalism" and bring a new spirit of harmony to federal-provincial relations—a misapprehension under which the Conservatives might not have laboured after dealing with the provinces as the Government of Canada. In energy, the party skated around the difficult question of oil and natural gas prices by concentrating its attention on increasing domestic supplies. This preoccupation with supply reflected the analysis of Harvie Andre, M.P. for Calgary Centre, and Jim Gillies. It also prevented an internecine debate on oil pricing between M.P.s from producing and consuming provinces such as the one that racked the party in 1973. (See Chapter 7.)

Nothing, however, more clearly demonstrated the lack of co-ordination than the party's economic policies. (See Chapter 8.) Sinclair Stevens, M.P. for York-Simcoe (York-Peel after the 1979 election), spoke for many in the party when he attacked the burgeoning size of the federal deficit and called for a substantial reduction in government expenditures. How did the Conservatives propose to cut spending? First, by reducing consulting and advertising contracts—which amounted to a pittance in the federal government's $49-billion budget in 1978-79. Second, by eliminating waste and duplication—a promise parties often make during election campaigns. Third, by reducing the size of the federal civil service by 60,000 persons through attrition over three years—a harebrained scheme that originated with Sinclair Stevens. Its sole basis in reality seemed to be that each year about 20,000 civil servants left the government's employ. Neither Stevens nor anyone else in the party ever satisfactorily answered the questions this policy provoked: What would be the effect of such cuts on government programs and on morale within the public service? How would a department or agency fill gaps if hit by an abnormally high rate of attrition? Since women and francophones left the civil service more frequently than other groups, how could the party make good on its pledge to promote women and encourage francophones to join the public service? Who would organize the massive readjustment within the civil service and arbitrate among departments? What was the definition of a civil servant? Did employees of crown corporations count? Did the military?

A few of these questions, notably the definition of a civil servant, were answered after the 1979 election; but before the writs were issued the confusion was comical, except to Conservative candidates Jean Pigott and Robert de Cotret, who lost their Ottawa seats when their constituents, many of whom were civil servants, voted for other candidates.

Clark and his political advisors, however, knew that restraint is everyone's favourite chestnut as long as it falls on someone else's head. When Prime Minister Pierre Trudeau announced $2 billion in expenditure cuts in August 1978, Conservative spokesmen denounced the exercise as a death-bed repentance from a politician approaching electoral defeat. Conservative backbenchers echoed the criticism that the expenditure cuts were politically motivated—until the reductions threatened to hit their constituencies; then they hopped up in the Commons to cry for mercy and justice. Like good politicians, they understood that although restraint sounds good, largesse looks better. To satisfy this political requirement, the Conservatives' 1979 platform was littered with promises to which the party attached its own cost estimates: incentives for tar-sands plants in Alberta ($125 million); a fisheries development fund to loan money for ship construction ($10 million); more manpower and an increased capital budget for the military ($125 million); a new youth training program ($5.5 million); widened eligibility for spouses' allowances ($15 million); increased funding for the Medical Research Council ($15 million); training programs and research for treatment of the elderly ($5 million); enriched veterans' pensions ($34.5 million); freight rate subsidies ($175 million), and these were just the half of the package of promises. The Conservatives estimated the cost of all their new spending programs at about $520 million, a figure most observers— and of course the Opposition parties—thought flagrantly underestimated the likely cost of the total package.

The expenditure side of the Conservatives' economic policy was muddled enough, but the revenue side was worse. First, the party committed itself to partial deductibility of mortgage interest and property taxes, a socially regressive scheme designed to appeal to homeowners. The Conservatives estimated that the program would cost the treasury $400 million in the first year and about $1.6 billion four years later, when the program was in full operation. Second, the party pledged to cut personal income taxes by $2 billion for low- and moderate-income Canadians. The Conservatives reckoned that the mortgage plan and the tax cut, coupled with several less grandiose taxation incentives, would reduce federal revenues by $2.8 billion in their first year in office. This from a party pledged to bring the budget closer to balance by the end of its four-year term!

These tax cuts rested on a shaky economic foundation. Normally, a large tax cut is occasioned by one of three circumstances: a recession, a budgetary surplus, or a reduction in expenditures.

None of these applied. The economy was experiencing slow growth, but it had neither entered a recession nor was likely to do so. The budget was certainly not in surplus; it was more than $12 billion in deficit in 1978-1979. And expenditure reductions, even when vigorously pursued, make only a small dent in government spending in the short run because so little of the government's budget is discretionary. But the Conservative economic theorists— notably Jim Gillies and Robert de Cotret after his election to the Commons in an October 1978 by-election—believed that U.S. President John F. Kennedy had demonstrated with his $10-billion tax cut of 1963 that a deep tax cut could quickly stimulate the economy and produce new revenues for the federal government, which would in turn make up for the revenue lost initially from the tax cut. But economic analysis of the Kennedy tax cut has demonstrated that at the time of the stimulus the American economy was coming out of a recession and heading for strong economic growth. The tax cut itself did not create the stimulus, although it encouraged the already accelerating economy. The Kennedy analogy also ignored Canadians' propensity to save a larger portion of their income than Americans. The Liberals discovered in 1978 when they reduced sales taxes that Canadians socked away more money in savings than the Government had hoped; all of the new disposable income from the tax cuts did not find its way quickly into the economy.

Whatever the merits of their economic theories, the Conservatives were forced to admit that combining all of the elements of their package produced a short-run increase, not a decrease, in the federal deficit. "Stimulative deficit" was the phrase Clark, Gillies, Stevens, de Cotret, and other Conservatives used to explain their position. But it all sounded rather strange coming from a party that pledged to bring the budget closer to balance, and, as a result, Clark and his economic team were mercilessly badgered to define their policy with greater precision. Clark finally issued what he prayed would be the last word on the subject six weeks before the 1979 election. In a long letter to *The Globe and Mail*, he explained:

> There is always a "lag" of a few months between the introduction of tax reductions and their stimulative effect on an economy; it takes time for their benefits to work through the system.
>
> But as the experience of the Kennedy administration, among others, showed, effective tax reductions do pro-

vide significant stimulus and so net the Government increasing revenues from an expanding economy. It was in the context of this rather elementary economic reality that I acknowledged during a recent television interview that our program might produce a temporary short-term increase in the deficit until the offsetting effects of our restraint program and increased economic growth take full effect over a fiscal year.

In addition to controversial fiscal policies, the Conservatives committed themselves to unrealistic economic targets: 5 per cent inflation by 1985 (inflation was 10.8 per cent in 1975; 7.5 per cent in 1976; 8 per cent in 1977, and 9 per cent in 1978); 5.5 per cent unemployment by 1985 (unemployment ranged from 6.9 per cent in 1975 to 8.4 per cent in 1978), and an average growth rate of 5.25 per cent between 1980 and 1985 (growth had not been above 5.5 per cent in any year since 1975).

This unlikely amalgam of policies and goals might never have been forged had Joe Clark known more about economics. As it was, he left the formulation of economic policies to others, particularly to Stevens, Gillies, and de Cotret. They defined the government's most pressing priorities as reducing the federal deficit and stimulating private-sector growth, but they suggested different solutions to these challenges. Stevens was obsessed with slashing government expenditures; Gillies and de Cotret favoured the use of fiscal tools to put more money in the hands of consumers. Rather than forcing a synthesis between these two approaches, Clark allowed them to be stitched together into a patchwork garment he called the Conservatives' economic policy. He memorized the component parts of the policy, so that when questioned about the Conservatives' solutions for inflation, unemployment, slow growth, or the current account deficit, he could point to the appropriate part of the policy to demonstrate that he knew something about economics and that his party was ready to govern.

Everyone in the Conservative Party, whatever their thinking, could find a part of the policy to admire. The party also hoped that the electorate would find something enticing in the policy and concentrate on that aspect, rather than examining the entire structure, because the party's economic policy, with all of its contradictions, was part of a broad political strategy the Conservatives developed in the run-up to the 1979 campaign, in order to counter the party's political predicament.

The Conservatives are decidedly a minority party in Canada.* The number of Canadians who think of themselves as Conservatives is much smaller than the number who call themselves Liberals; in other words, the Conservative Party's core vote is smaller than the Liberals'. The Conservatives' own research before the 1979 election put the party's core vote at about 18 per cent of the electorate, compared with about 30 per cent for the Liberals. As a rule of thumb, the Conservatives need about 38 per cent of the votes in a general election to win a majority Government and the Liberals need about 43 per cent, the difference being accounted for by votes the Liberals waste in sweeping Quebec with huge majorities. To form a majority Government, therefore, the Conservatives must add many more voters to their core vote than the Liberals, which explains in large measure why the Conservatives have so seldom been in power since World War I. Of course, defeat feeds on itself: the more the Conservatives are out of power, the fewer the opportunities to enlarge their core vote through wise governing. The Conservatives also have a smaller pool of potential voters in which to fish than the Liberals. The party's research showed that only about 60 per cent of the Canadian electorate would ever consider supporting the Conservatives compared with about 75 per cent for the Liberals. That means that to win a majority Government, the Conservatives must attract almost two-thirds of all the voters who would ever think of voting for the party, an exceedingly tall order for any party.

A Canadian political party has seldom prepared itself as thoroughly for an election as the Conservatives did in the two years preceeding the 1979 campaign. The Conservatives knew that to win a majority they needed at least to double their 18-per-cent core vote. For this, the party chose three tactics: tying Trudeau to all Canada's problems, identifying the Conservatives with an underlying mood of optimism they detected in the electorate from their research, and making specific promises designed to appeal to particular segments of the Canadian population. The most spectacular example of the latter approach was mortgage-interest and property-tax deductibility, unveiled on the eve of the campaign for fifteen by-elections in October 1978. Whatever its economic merits, the promise was directed at voters in the suburban areas

---

*This observation is documented in many academic works, including John Meisel, *Working Papers in Canadian Politics* (2nd enlarged edition, McGill-Queen's Press, 1975); and Harold Clark et. al., *Political Choice in Canada* (McGraw-Hill Ryerson, abridged edition, 1980), especially chapters 5-8.

that the Conservatives desperately needed to win in several of the by-elections and in the general election. The promise to move the Canadian Embassy in Israel from Tel Aviv to Jerusalem was aimed at Jewish voters in five Metropolitan Toronto ridings. (See Chapter 6.) And throughout the party platform there were specific promises for fishermen, farmers, small businessmen, women, young people, and industries such as mining, shipbuilding, construction, and transportation.

These promises were also designed to create a favourable image for the Conservative Party among voters who were not interested in the specifics of the promises themselves. This use of promises was outlined by Allan Gregg, the Conservatives' polling expert, in a memorandum on campaign strategy in December, 1977:

> While many would disagree, I tend to concur with early voting studies that issues have little positive influence on voting behavior. Due to the low salience of politics in the day-to-day life of the average voter and due to the sophistication of policy, the electorate is fundamentally unequipped to understand the substance of policy. Other studies, however, have demonstrated that while the details of policy may have little impact on election results, the emphasis on policy may. In this view, issues and policy reflect two important elements in voting behavior: a) the perception of competence and b) the perception of concern. These perceptions influence voting in a positive and negative manner. While the detail of policy in itself is not important, the absence of detail creates the perception of incompetence. Similarly, if a party articulates policy (in the broadest sense of the word) that parallels the concern of a portion of the electorate then the empathy towards the party increases accordingly ("they represent people like me," "they're talking about the right issues").
>
> In terms of strategy, then, the issues can cut both ways for us. We can deal with the problematic aspects of policy and issues to underline the Government's incompetence in this area—their record. On the other hand, we can deal with the "goals" of policy in order to reinforce the fact that our party has not only the right concerns but also the right answers. In this sense, we would not say . . . that "this party stands for wage and price controls" but rather "this party will and is committed to bringing the level of inflation down to 5 per cent by 1981." When asked how we might retort "by implementing wage and price controls . . . or whatever." The difference is that when

> dealing with issues we should speak in terms of goals and
> only when queried and for purposes of enhancing our
> perception of competence vis-à-vis that goal, should we
> bring up the detail of policy.

Seldom has a party leader put forward so many promises as Joe
Clark did in the 1979 campaign. To show that the Conservatives
were ready to govern, he offered a dizzying array of goodies, most
based on policies developed by the Conservative caucus, hoping
that individual policies would appeal to particular segments of the
population and produce a majority Conservative Government.
During the campaign, the Canadian Real Estate Association circulated to its members an outline of the Conservative platform
listing 211 general or specific promises made by the party in
Opposition and in the campaign. The "Conservatives' Speaker's
Manual," briefing notes on party policy sent to candidates in
preparation for an election, was the size of a telephone book in a
city of 250,000 people. If the Conservatives could demonstrate
their competence to govern by the sheer volume of their policies,
the election was a foregone conclusion.

At his major campaign speech of the 1979 election in Kitchener,
Clark promised mortgage-interest and property-tax deductibility,
exemption from capital gains tax for shares of Canadian-owned
companies, a plan to encourage employees to buy shares in their
company, privatization of crown corporations, and a Small Business
Act. Before the first week was finished, he had promised a fisheries
development fund, a $2-billion tax cut, lower inflation and unem-
ployment, higher productivity and growth, $125 million in research
money for the tar sands plants, parliamentary reform, tax incentives for the mining industry, deferment of rail-line abandonment
in western Canada, a freeze on public service hiring, zero-based
budgeting in the federal government, and government expenditure restraint.

If the first week of the campaign was laden with promises, the
next ten days were even more bountiful. He promised provincial
control of Loto Canada and more money for amateur sport, a new
national defence policy with an increase in manpower for the
military, purchase of a fighter aircraft, a 12-per-cent increase in
the military's capital budget, a re-equipment program for the navy
and an extended search and rescue capability, a 50-per-cent increase in the country's grain-handling capability, the shift of the
Canadian Embassy in Israel from Tel Aviv to Jerusalem, a youth-
employment secretariat and other youth-oriented programs,

decriminalization of marijuana, tax incentives for businesses investing in slow-growth regions, and a national conference on Medicare, which he said "very clearly isn't working." And so it went for the remainder of the campaign: promises for women, seniors, native people, the RCMP, Yukoners, charitable organizations, French Canadians, civil servants.

Clark and those organizing the Conservative campaign believed that these promises served three immediate purposes: they appealed to selected groups, demonstrated that the party was ready to govern, and identified the party with the underlying mood of optimism the Conservatives detected in the country. Two men more than any others shaped the party's campaign to identify with this optimism: Lowell Murray, the national campaign chairman, and Allan Gregg, the party's research expert. Together, they monitored public opinion in the eighteen months preceding the 1979 election, designing a strategy that put the Conservatives in power for the first time in sixteen years. Murray and Gregg made the Conservatives better-prepared for an election than the party had been since the late 1950s.

Lowell Murray ran unsuccessfully for the Nova Scotia legislature in 1960. Thus chastened, he resolved never to ask the voters directly for a favour. Instead, he applied his talents to furthering the political careers of a string of Conservative politicians: Davie Fulton, Wallace McCutcheon, Robert Stanfield, Richard Hatfield, and Joe Clark. Somehow, Murray never lost his sense of humour or his candour: two qualities in scarce supply in the backrooms of politics. Nor did he succumb to the occupational hazards of excessive smoking and dishevelled attire: he was always fastidious about his appearance and his health, although he was not above a long night of carousing with friends. A bachelor who once studied for the priesthood, Murray had about him an aura of orderliness that reflected his intellectual discipline and his determination to structure his life so that politics did not crowd out time for reading, travelling, and reflection.

Murray was born in the mining town of New Waterford on Cape Breton Island, where politics was a serious vocation for some and of interest to many. By the late 1950s, he was working in Conservative M.P. Donald MacInnis' election campaigns. Defeated in the 1960 provincial election, Murray arrived in Ottawa as executive assistant to Justice Minister Davie Fulton. Humiliated by Diefenbaker's affronts to his pride, Fulton resigned in November 1962 and moved to British Columbia to lead the moribund

Conservative Party. Murray followed Fulton to British Columbia, returning to Ottawa in the employ of Senator Wallace McCutcheon, when Fulton's hopeless venture in British Columbia collapsed. From McCutcheon's office, Murray watched the storm clouds gathering over Diefenbaker's leadership. Murray supported party president Dalton Camp's call for a leadership review, winding up as Fulton's campaign manager for the leadership race eventually won by Robert Stanfield.

Just as he later did the day after Joe Clark won the 1979 election, Murray left immediately after the 1967 leadership convention for an extended holiday. He was in Tokyo when Stanfield called asking Murray to join his staff. Murray got as far as Saigon when Stanfield and other Conservatives reached him again and implored him to return. Murray, who likes to be coaxed into doing something, agreed to cut short his around-the-world tour after three and a half weeks to return to Canada. After three years with Stanfield, it was time for another break from politics. This time he travelled extensively in Europe and took a job with Canadian National on his return. That job did not last long, because New Brunswick Premier Richard Hatfield wanted Murray as his chief-of-staff.

In the fall of 1976, Murray was at Queen's University taking a Master's degree in public administration—a daunting prospect for his professors, some of whom knew less about the subject than he did. In November of that year, the Parti Québécois won the Quebec election, and the new Conservative leader, Joe Clark, began to worry that the federal Liberals might call a snap election to capitalize on the sense of crisis about national unity in English Canada. On Christmas Eve 1976, Clark asked Murray to serve as the Conservatives' national campaign chairman. The offer came while Murray was attending the christening of his godchild, Joe Clark's daughter Catherine.

Clark and Murray first met in the early 1960s when Murray was Davie Fulton's executive assistant and Clark was working at Conservative Party headquarters. They met again when Clark surfaced in Fulton's British Columbia campaign, which offered a welcome diversion for Clark from his studies at the University of British Columbia law school, where he failed his second year. The two men worked together again on Fulton's leadership campaign. A few months later, both joined party leader Robert Stanfield's office, sharing an apartment not far from Stornoway, the Opposition leader's official residence. They left Stanfield's office within three months of each other in 1970, Murray winding up in Hatfield's office and Clark in the House of Commons.

Murray was a key organizer in Flora MacDonald's leadership bid, but that did not inhibit Clark from persuading Murray to form what Murray called a "planning committee of one," using his spare time at Queen's to discover what people the Conservatives could rely on in an election. After the academic year, Murray moved to Ottawa and began putting together the Conservatives' 1979 election machine.

Lowell Murray was Joe Clark's closest political advisor. Clark, no mean political tactician himself, listened respectfully to everything Murray said; after all, Murray had been Clark's boss in all of their previous professional relationships. Murray was the only man in Clark's entourage who could tell the leader that he was wrong without coating the admonition with deference. At one point during the 1979 campaign, he told Clark to stop worrying so much about details of organization in ridings and spend more time mastering his briefing notes on policy. Murray had Clark's complete trust, and Clark seldom made a political move without first consulting Murray. When others would bemoan Murray's absences in Europe or Cape Breton, Clark would defend his friend, saying, "That's just Lowell." Every day in the 1979 campaign, the two men spoke by telephone, often late at night: Murray at Conservative Party headquarters and Clark in a hotel room on the road. In setting the overall strategy for the campaign, in allocating the leader's time, in controlling Clark's access to the media, in designing the party's media strategy, and in preparing Clark for the televised debate among the party leaders, Murray's influence was enormous.

Murray was a Napoleonic political strategist: the grand design was what he cared about; the execution of his plan was left to talented assistants. He appreciated research, especially polling data, and was loathe to make a decision without it. Thus, he brought Allan Gregg to Conservative headquarters. Gregg, a PhD student at Carleton University, was a most unlikely-looking Conservative: he sported a beard, often wore a ring in one ear, and talked rapid-fire about salience, deviation indices, variables, scenarios, and a host of other psephological ideas. He was extremely bright and provided Murray with regular reports on the state of public opinion in the country. He also helped with campaign organization and attended to many details Murray could not be bothered with.

Gregg's polling data showed that Canadians believed that the country's problems—inflation, unemployment, slow growth, energy, national unity—could be solved. The data demonstrated that Canadians saw Trudeau as not only indifferent to the problems but unable to solve them. From the same research, the Conservatives knew that Trudeau was more highly regarded than Clark on most counts of leadership. The key to the Conservatives' campaign, therefore, was twofold: to reinforce the voters' belief that Trudeau, much as he might be admired, could not solve the country's problems, and to present the Conservatives as a party with solutions to the problems, thereby identifying themselves with the voters' underlying optimism.

Eighteen months before the campaign began, Murray and Gregg began drafting the approach Clark used in the 1979 campaign, as shown by a memorandum Gregg sent Murray on December 19, 1977.

> We must make the voter ask: "What kind of country is Trudeau going to make for us?" We can tie this future-oriented question to the past. Make the electorate remember the broken promises and the shams Trudeau has perpetrated on them ('The Land Is Strong') and let them know that more and worse will be coming if [he is] re-elected. . . .
>
> We should tie inflation directly to the Government, but we can also use inflation to emphasize the human side of Clark and the PC Party by emphasizing our concern over the influence of inflation on eroding the income of the aged, the poor; how it deepens the income disparity between the wealthiest and the poorest. Inflation can also be tied to the fear of rising uncertainties—"Your children will never be able to own a home," "Rising prices cause increased wage demands, labor unrest and social conflict etc." Finally, lowering expectations, implicit in Trudeau's position on the issue and accepting the inevitability of inflation, is repugnant to many of the aggressive, upwardly-mobile voters we are trying to attract.

In his opening press conference of the 1979 campaign, Clark put the Conservatives' strategy into play, and he never lost sight of that strategy for the next eight weeks.

> That is where the campaign begins—with the record of the Trudeau Government. Mr. Trudeau obviously wants to avoid that subject. . . . Mr. Trudeau may talk of a decade

of development, but Canadians will know what a Trudeau decade already has done to their country.

It has been a decade in which separatism in Quebec has gone from a fringe movement to a provincial government. A decade in which living costs have doubled and unemployment tripled. A decade in which the Canadian dollar has gone from strong to weak. Above all, it has been a decade of a Prime Minister and a Government who sell Canada short. . . .

Unlike Mr. Trudeau, we do not sell Canada short. . . . We are determined to restore a sense of building to Canada and to give Canadians a stake in the development of their country. This is and will remain the major thrust of our policies for Canada—to help Canadians own a home, expand a business and participate in the ownership of their resources.

The choice facing Canadians on May 22nd is clear. They can have four more years like the past eleven; or they can make a fresh start with a new government which truly represents Canada and which is committed to its potential and its future.

A month later, Clark's message had not changed. On April 25, he said,

At this mid-way point in the election campaign, I want to emphasize how important it is that a new government restore Ottawa's credibility with the people of Canada. Mr. Trudeau is wrong when he tells Canadians to lower our expectations. This nation needs a government that shares the people's confidence in Canada. The Trudeau Government has wasted Canada's economic potential.

In a memorandum written after the 1979 campaign, Gregg reviewed the reasons for the Conservatives' election victory.

The public . . . displayed a virtually unanimous view that the country was worse off than it had been four or five years ago, that we were not living up to our potential and, indeed, that it was time for a change. These beliefs, while most intense among our partisans, cut across partisan lines. That is, even Liberals and those who were prepared to concede that Trudeau was more fit to lead the country than Clark, were also prepared to maintain that it was time for a change.

The key for us, then, was to play to our strengths. That is, to address those beliefs that were most readily agreed upon and, at the same time, to provide the linkage that would join these beliefs to our greatest advantage. We therefore attempted to tie the Trudeau record and the notion that things had gotten worse over the last four or five years directly to Trudeau.

Moreover, and probably most importantly, we attempted, through the use of our media campaign, to demonstrate that Trudeau as 'P.M.' and 'change' were mutually exclusive. In other words, if the public wanted change, they could not have Trudeau and vice versa. This was necessary because, quite clearly, if the voter believed that they could have a change with Trudeau, they found this a much less bitter pill than change with Clark. This basic finding was, in my opinion, the underpinning of our "attack" phase. . . .

The key for us, then, was to make sure that the average voter went into the ballot box with the "right" question in their mind. If they thought the question they were answering through their vote was . . . "Do I want Pierre Trudeau or Joe Clark for Prime Minister?" . . . we would have lost because Trudeau was perceived to be more capable of leading the country. If the question was . . . "Do I want candidate X or Y?" . . . we would have lost [because] by and large Liberal incumbents were far more visible and positively perceived than PC challengers. If the question was . . . "Do I want a Liberal Government or a PC Government?" . . . we would have lost because a significant plurality of voters continued to consider themselves as "Liberals" throughout the course of the campaign.

The reason we won was because we recognized that asking any of these questions was not to our advantage. The question we begged, based on the data and through our campaign efforts, was . . . "Do you want four more years like the last eleven?"

For all of Clark's efforts to identify the Conservatives with the public belief that problems could be solved—the promises of action, the uplifting rhetoric about "building" and "potential"— the Conservatives scored a protest victory, more than anything else because of an unstructured desire for change in the Canadian electorate. The Conservatives' own data showed voters crossing to them, not because of promises made during the campaign, but because they were tired of Trudeau and wanted a change. The Conservatives' biggest mistake in power lay in assuming that the electorate had given them a mandate for sweeping change. Instead, the Conservatives received a tenuous mandate in May 1979 based on a desire to replace Trudeau. Allan Gregg pointed out the precariousness of the Conservatives' position in a memorandum three months after the campaign.

> All indicators were that, with the exception of Quebec, factors influencing vote behavior were entirely national. . . . The reason for the nation-wide impact on voting behavior undoubtedly stemmed from the almost unanimous belief that it was simply time for a change. *The research showed again and again that the reasons for voting PC were negative six to one over positive.* Equally, our core support—that is, 1979 voters who identify with the PC Party and claimed that they always voted PC—comprised a mere 18% of the electorate, or about one-half of our May 22nd support. *There was nothing in the data to suggest that our forming the Government would do anything to change this, which would lead me to the conclusion, based on two years of research, that the PC electoral position was weaker on May 23rd as a consequence of forming the Government than it was on May 22nd as a consequence of being in Opposition.* (italics mine)

Such an alarming analysis—that the Conservatives were in a weaker political position for having won the election—ought to have induced caution throughout Clark's Government. Every policy should have been designed to keep together the Conservatives' fragile coalition of core supporters and disaffected Liberals and New Democrats. Every move in the Commons needed to be tempered by a recognition of the Conservatives' minority position. The discipline of power requires prudent compromises, especially for a party in a minority position with a fragile mandate—but Joe Clark had other ideas in mind for his Government.

~ 3 ~

Leader As Liability

The fragility of their election mandate was not the Conservatives' most serious problem after the 1979 election. Rather, it was the public perception of Joe Clark, who, despite winning the election, neither improved his standing during the campaign nor left his party hoping that much could be done in office to enhance his unfortunate public image in the eyes of the Canadian electorate.

"Joe Who?" read the headline in *The Toronto Star* the morning after he won the Conservative leadership in February 1976. Three years later, Clark was certainly better known but less appreciated than in the months following his convention victory. Clark's fundamental problem was stark: few people could see him as Prime Minister of Canada. Try as he might, he could not persuade Canadians that he possessed the qualities necessary to lead the nation. After a six-month honeymoon with the electorate following his leadership victory, Clark's stock plummeted, never to recover. Indeed, it is not an exaggeration to say that the Conservatives won the 1979 election in spite of Clark. Throughout the campaign, he trailed Trudeau in popularity. Asked by the Conservatives' research team to rate the leadership qualities of the two men, voters across Canada consistently gave higher marks to Trudeau than to Clark. The Conservatives also conducted extensive polling in selected ridings during the campaign, and results showed considerable unhappiness with Clark, even among Conservatives.

Part of Clark's problem was the inevitable comparison drawn between him and Pierre Trudeau. Trudeau possessed a raw intellectual power that Clark could never hope to match. Asked a

72

question on an unfamiliar subject, Trudeau would deflect the question with an impressive, if occasionally irrelevant, display of logic or abstract philosophy. Clark, asked a similar question, would stumble for a reply, his sentences losing their grammatical shape as he scrambled to hide his ignorance of the subject. Trudeau was a dashing character, with a rose in his lapel, superb body language, elegantly tailored clothes, and a fascinating background. Clark, by contrast, displayed no interest in athletics, wore clothes that made him appear stuffy, carried himself awkwardly, and brought an undistinguished curriculum vitae to the Prime Minister's office.

Clark's four predecessors as Prime Minister brought to the office an understanding of Canada developed largely outside of politics, but most of what Joe Clark knew about Canada came from politics, especially from experience in political organization. The essential ingredient in successful political organization is team-work, and Clark as leader of the Opposition applied the lessons he had learned in an assortment of political jobs, encouraging M.P.s to believe that their contributions were valued by him and indispensable for the party. His door was always open to an M.P. with a grievance or a point of view different from his own. He worked tirelessly with Murray to build an impressive organization for the 1979 campaign, spending days recruiting candidates and reviewing party strategy with them. Political organization, however, is more about tactics and strategy than goals and visions, and Joe Clark was never able to convince Canadians that he possessed a sure sense of where Canada should be headed.

Clark grew up in the small Alberta town of High River, about thirty miles south of Calgary. His family lived in a rambling, white clapboard house not far from the newspaper offices of the *High River Times*, the paper owned by Clark's grandfather and father. High River was so small that everyone in town knew everyone else, and this warm community spirit was part of Clark's childhood. Although he left High River at eighteen years of age, Clark returned there frequently for brief visits and often referred to High River as a symbol of values he held dear: respect for individuals and a sense of community. He liked to say that his ancestors in southern Alberta had "dreamed big" when he talked about his party's plans to encourage individual initiative. When he returned to High River in the opening week of the 1979 campaign, he delivered his finest speech of the campaign, urging the students gathered at Senator Riley High School to learn French "not only to unite but also to understand the country" and to think beyond

High River to the challenges of a "country where people who believe in their own possibilities can realize those possibilities." He believed High River represented the capacity of people of different means and ethnic backgrounds to work together to build a proud community. He applied the same analysis to Canada writ large. In a speech to the Empire Club designed to give Clark an opportunity to outline his vision of Canada, he said:

> Our diversity in this country is both utterly inescapable and immensely valuable.
>
> It is typical, I think, of this country that our official emblem—the maple leaf—is not indigenous to two of our provinces and to two of our territories and that there are thousands of happy and successful Canadian citizens who are most at ease in neither of our two official languages.
>
> We are a nation that is too big for simple symbols. Indeed, our preoccupation with the symbol of a single national identity has, in my judgement, obscured the great wealth we have in several local identities which are rich in themselves and which are skilled in getting along with others. . . .
>
> In an immense country, you live on a local scale, and governments make the nation work together by recognizing that we are fundamentally a community of communities.

"Community of communities" had a pleasant ring to it, and Clark used the phrase so often during the campaign that it became a slogan. But the phrase rang hollow because Clark never defined what political acts should flow from this conception of Canada—apart from a promise to get along better with provincial governments than Trudeau had. A Cabinet committee spent a day after the 1979 election trying to put flesh on the skeletal concept of "community of communities," but it was only after his defeat in 1980 that Clark asked some advisors to draw practical policy conclusions from the phrase.

The same problem plagued his references to the "building spirit" within Canada: Clark had never been an entrepreneur himself and had accomplished nothing outside politics to demonstrate that he knew what his phraseology meant. It was important politically for the Conservatives to identify with the anger against Big Government and the spirit of fundamental optimism that Murray and Gregg had identified in their research, but Clark seemed an inappropriate embodiment of the message. In his Empire Club speech, he said:

> We can all think, all of us in this room, of Canadian innovators who have moved successfully into the world. But they have been left to do that on their own, and they have often succeeded in spite of unco-ordinated federal policy concerning taxes, concerning trade, concerning research and development, and in spite of an indifference in Ottawa to Canada's industrial future.
>
> We intend to remove those specific obstacles. Even more important, we intend to change the attitude in Ottawa. We intend to create an atmosphere in Canada in which the innovator and the entrepreneur are encouraged to go out and build in the world.
>
> No one who travels in this country, no one who knows it can escape being impressed with the great potential that is here. . . . This is a time for Canadians to raise our expectations, because only if our expectations are high will we go out and go to work and go out and build, and there is a great deal in this country to be confident about.

This was a laudable enough goal, but it was articulated with such a large collection of clichés that it hung limp even by the hackneyed standards of campaign rhetoric. Coming from a man who had never personally experienced any of the emotions associated with entrepreneurial enterprise, the rhetoric sounded empty rather than inspiring.

The lack of experience outside politics deprived Clark of an intangible but indispensable element of effective political leadership: the assumption by those who follow that their leader has untapped sources of strength on which to draw in times of difficulty. This strength can be the product of reading and reflection, of religion, of tasks accomplished outside politics, of past battles won or lost, or simply of lessons learned from long experience in politics. There was never a sense about Clark that he possessed such sources of strength.

Asked in the 1979 campaign to describe any extraordinary talents he possessed, Clark replied:

> I think that I have demonstrated an unusual ability to attract strong people from various parts of the country to make them work together as a team in a national context within a national party. We've brought some unity and

direction to a national party that has been generally disorganized. I think that the particular need for Canada
right now is for a Prime Minister who can reconcile
differences, who can draw on the strengths of different
people in different regions.

I might not have been a particularly appropriate
Prime Minister for a time like 1967 when everyone was
going in the same direction. But when there is now that
sense of division, that sense of divergence, I think what
the nation needs is someone with the talents to recognize
strength, to draw it together into a common purpose.
And I think that's my extraordinary skill.

Drawing people together in politics is important, but this skill
hardly represents more than might be reasonably expected of a
competent manager. It certainly does not create an aura of
untapped strength that a successful political leader needs to
establish trust and respect between himself and his followers.

"The charismatic leader is a man who demands obedience on
the basis of the mission he feels called upon to perform," the
German sociologist Max Weber wrote in *Wirtschaft und Gesellschaft*.
"He dominates men by virtue of qualities inaccessible to others
and incompatible with the rules of thought and action that govern
everyday life." By that definition, Clark was the antithesis of the
charismatic leader. It may well have been, as Clark believed, that
the country was tired of Trudeau's charisma, but without a touch
of charisma himself, Clark was not seen as leadership material.
When Mayor Lucille Dougherty of High River sent Joe Clark on
his way in the 1979 campaign saying, "When he becomes Prime
Minister of Canada, he'll still be Joe to me," she was expressing a
touching but politically lethal sentiment.

Political appeal, especially in the television age, also partly
depends on a politician's demeanour. In this, Joe Clark was cursed
by nature. Unfair though it was to think about such matters in
judging his qualifications for high office, the Conservatives' own
research showed that Clark's personal mannerisms irritated many
of those who observed him on television or in the flesh. Clark
looked uncomfortable with his own body. He carried himself
awkwardly, his arms pendulating in unnaturally long swings.
When he ran, which was seldom, he looked like a wounded heron.
The cruellest piece of television footage in the 1979 campaign
caught Clark running gracelessly across the sand of the Beaches in
east-end Toronto towards a woman sunbathing in a bikini. The
camera soaked up Clark's running style and the woman's embar-

rassed reaction as the stranger in the carefully pressed suit, a trifle breathless after his effort, stuck out his hand while the woman's hand recoiled to cover the upper half of her body. Indeed, Clark's hands were always busy in uncommon gesticulations, as if they were uncertain of their proper role at the end of his arms. Clark had long, bony fingers, and his most instinctive mannerism— thrusting his left hand forward with fingers outstretched but slightly crooked—make the hand look like a chicken's foot scratching aimlessly at the air. When he waved to a crowd, his arms and hands wiggled unnaturally. Towards the end of the 1979 campaign, he unconsciously began using U.S. President Richard Nixon's distasteful pose: both arms raised above the head, each hand flashing a "V" sign.

Clark's speaking style was appropriate for the House of Commons, but was excessively stilted in other settings. He spoke the layered language of Parliament, repeating phrases and using convoluted sentences that gave his points an unwarranted portentousness. This style, combined with a resonant voice and a talent for repartee, put him at ease in the Commons. But the same combination sounded pompous in less formal places, especially if he was speaking on unfamiliar subjects. A Clark speech often sounded better on radio than on television, where people could see the mannerisms that accompanied the delivery. Clark would have failed the test devised by Joe Napolitan, a polling expert and media consultant for the Democratic Party in the U.S.: his litmus test was to turn off the sound and watch only the picture to discover a politician's effectiveness on television. What's more, even though Clark often wrote his own material, his words still sounded as if they were written by someone else. The Conservatives once showed sample films of Clark to selected panels of Canadians and Americans. The party found that the panels thought Clark was mouthing words prepared for him even when Clark was reading from his own text.

This concentration on Clark's physical characteristics was grossly unfair to him; it was irrelevant to his fitness for office. In fact, it created a largely erroneous impression of his personality. Clark looked pompous and stiff in public, but in private he was warm-hearted to his friends and generous to his enemies. No group was more critical of Clark than the Ottawa press corps was, but he seldom lashed back at what he considered to be unfair reporting. During his two campaigns or on long trips, he would wander into the media section of his plane and exchange pleasantries or sing songs with reporters. He was unfailingly polite and tried hard to understand the other person's point of view. For example, he wrote a note of appreciation to John Crosbie's wife, Jane, when she reluctantly agreed to sell shares in a company to comply with conflict-of-interest guidelines for Cabinet ministers that were made to apply to spouses. He often sent similar notes to individuals who had done him a good turn. He read sparingly, dipping into a pulp novel such as *Shogun* en route to Japan or into a detective novel while on holidays, but he absorbed briefings quickly and impressed those who had not seen him before with his ability to focus quickly on the crux of an issue. He had considerable grace under pressure and possessed a remarkable stamina for a man who paid so little heed to physical fitness.

The inability to communicate the more attractive sides of Clark's personality frustrated his advisors, who were always searching for ways of simultaneously making Clark look both prime ministerial and human. Allan Gregg summed up the problem in a memorandum written May 16, 1978, after the Liberals backed off an election call:

> 4. The objective of our pre-writ campaign is emphatically *not to portray the leader as a campaigning politician*. On the contrary, we want him to come through as the emerging Prime Minister, more "intimate" with Canadians and their concerns, accepting his responsibility to act, determined to act, learning and preparing to govern and increasingly credible in the Prime Ministerial role. *His public initiatives must therefore be carefully selected, planned and executed.*
>
> 5. At the same time, we should take advantage of this 2-3 month interval to work on something that is related to, but not completely subsumed by (4) above: that is, to work on the "imagery" task of conveying more of Joe Clark as a person so that Canadians feel they *know him personally.* . . .
>
> One of our biggest problems with leadership perception is that there is so little sense among the people that they "know" Joe Clark as a person. Again, we have a couple of months of grace to do something about getting a "personal image" (The People Magazine Syndrome) across. We need ideas.

More than two years after Clark's election as Conservative leader, his advisors were searching for "ideas" to improve his image, which had begun to lose its lustre within a few months of assuming the leadership.

After a leadership convention, the winner is usually given what political journalists call a "honeymoon period." The recipient enjoys the most blissful days of his political career: the newspapers carry effusive profiles about the winner and his family, his party offers congratulations and pays homage, and the public suspends scepticism, indulging its natural curiosity to learn more about the new man. A wise politician seizes this unique time in his career to imprint as favourable an impression of himself as possible upon the public, but the temptation to attend to other matters is great. There are often broken hearts and wounded egos following a convention, and the new leader wants these to heal under his care and attention. There are organizational details such as hiring staff, assigning new responsibilities within the party, and erasing campaign debts and personal obligations. The months can pass quickly under the pressure of attending to these tasks, and no one notices the loss of a precious opportunity because the polls continue to show the new leader enjoying his honeymoon with the voters.

Joe Clark let his own honeymoon slip by succumbing to the understandable temptation of a new leader. He took a trip to western Europe, for which he was insufficiently prepared, and he suffered from the poor impression he created overseas. He established his caucus committees, and explained that he did not want to enunciate party policy before they reported. Instead of turning the public's curiosity into affection or respect, Clark gave a series of bland speeches and interviews that left many voters wondering what all the fuss was about when Clark won the leadership convention. The Conservatives' popularity began to slide before the election of the Parti Québécois on November 15, 1976. Three months after the PQ victory, when the significance of the threat to national unity took hold, the polls showed the Conservatives trailing the Liberals for the first time since Clark's leadership triumph.

The seven months from March to October of 1977 were the most discomforting in Clark's leadership of the Conservative Party in Opposition. Jack Horner's public sniping and public dalliances with the Liberals caused Clark to give him an ultimatum to stop his public bitching or get out. Horner, upset that Clark would not support his claim to Crowfoot riding against another Conservative M.P., bolted to the Liberal Cabinet. David MacDonald, M.P. for Egmont, defied the Conservative whip in voting against the Government's immigration bill and was dropped by Clark from the caucus' twenty-member political strategy committee. Clark campaigned in five Quebec by-elections in May 1977, foolishly putting his prestige on the line for a lost cause. His stature was diminished and his judgement called into question when the Liberals swept all five Quebec by-elections and added a further humiliation by taking a Conservative seat in Prince Edward Island. Jacques Lavoie, M.P. for Hochelaga, watched the results in the five Quebec by-elections and decided that his political life was threatened with the Conservatives. He jumped to the Liberals, depriving the Conservatives of one of their four Quebec seats. Three other Conservative M.P.s resigned for personal reasons—Gordon Fairweather, Sean O'Sullivan, and John Reynolds. The Liberals benefited from the national-unity crisis because Trudeau appeared more capable of persuading Quebeckers to remain in Confederation. By the fall of 1977, Conservatives quietly discussed among themselves The Clark Problem, fearing that the Liberals might call a snap election to capitalize on the national unity crisis. Trudeau's political advisors, notably Coutts and Davey, pressed him to take advantage of the Liberals' popularity, but Trudeau declined.

The winter of 1977 to 1978, however, doomed the Liberals. The economic news was unremittingly discouraging. Inflation and unemployment worsened appreciably and the Canadian dollar tumbled on world markets. English Canada gladly returned to its customary somnolence about the national-unity crisis, believing that Trudeau's talk about constitutional and language reform was designed to draw attention from the Government's economic record. A weariness with Trudeau had taken hold before the Parti Québécois' victory. Once the shock of November 15, 1976, faded, the weariness returned. After all Trudeau's preaching and pontificating and after all the sacrifices English Canadians believed they had made to keep Quebec happy, the "ingrates" in Quebec had turned around and slapped the country in the face. Once this mood returned in English Canada, Trudeau was like a man trapped in a confessional box, condemned to repent for his every sin and to suffer a humiliating defeat in order to secure his release.

By the fall of 1977, Lowell Murray had taken up residence as the Conservatives' campaign chairman. Clark knew that he needed to compensate for time lost during his first year in the leadership. He began to speak more aggressively, backed by some of the policies developed in his caucus. He met the Conservative premiers in Kingston, and the meeting produced a document outlining the party's approach to federal-provincial relations. The document was itself of less significance than the symbolic support given Clark by the premiers through it. As long as economics dominated political debate, as it did throughout 1978, Clark profited from voter dissatisfaction with Trudeau. Clark's appearances became more tightly scripted and carefully planned, as evidenced by a memorandum Lowell Murray sent Clark on October 31, 1978. It set forth a political program that contained the germ of many events subsequently organized by the Conservative Party.

I think we should have a major national political event in the first week of April. . . .

With regard to Quebec, I think we must have a Quebec policy conference at which our Quebec candidates, together with a limited number of resource people and Quebec party people, come up with an economic program for Quebec. Participation from the federal caucus should be minimal, consisting of yourself as a keynote or windup speaker and one or two others such as de Cotret as interested participants.

I continue to think that the best card we have to play in Quebec is the fact that we have the government of six provinces. We have to persuade Quebeckers that a vote for us is a vote for Canada. I rather doubt that we could pull off another Kingston Conference because I doubt that we could achieve agreement on many important specific items over and above the matters enumerated in the Kingston Communique. Furthermore, we have made so much of the Kingston Conference that to announce another would generate considerable comment and expectations and in the event would probably fall short of the publicity. It occurs to me however that we might begin trying to get all the premiers to attend, say, a fundraising dinner in Montreal. Arrangements could be made quietly for a private meeting of the seven of you during the afternoon devoted to matters of mutual political interest. Meanwhile, we could quietly explore through Flora [MacDonald], Michael Meighen [the former party president] et. al. whether there might exist a basis for some significant communique which would [be] issued at the end of the afternoon, or even at the dinner. The important thing is to show that the Conservative Party and Conservative Governments in six provinces want to work with Quebec in renewing Confederation.

I also want to consider a much smaller but I think important conference on foreign policy bringing together a dozen caucus people or candidates, a small number of party people and some resource people from universities, C.I.I.A. [Canadian Institute of International Affairs] and senior Canadian journalists who have worked abroad to discuss Canada's role in the world in general and two or three foreign policy topics. What I want to do is provide a forum for a strong critique of Trudeau's foreign policy without having the critique come exclusively from party spokesmen.

These suggestions—a conference on Quebec's economy, a fund-raising dinner attended by the premiers, and a conference on foreign policy—all took place in the run-up to the 1979 election.

When the Conservatives swept twelve of fifteen by-elections in October 1978, party officials began talking publicly about "pre-paring to govern." They tried to curb their partisan spirits by proposing alternative policies in the winter parliamentary session. The Liberals appeared in irredeemable political difficulty. If the Conservatives could avoid making a major error, they could win the election, whenever it was called. Then came Joe Clark's world tour.

Clark's advisors had discussed a lengthy foreign trip for nearly a year before Clark left for Japan, India, Israel, and Jordan on January 2, 1979. Clark acknowledged his inexperience in foreign affairs. A long trip was considered to be an essential part of his own "preparing to govern." Douglas Roche, M.P. for Edmonton South and the party's interim foreign affairs critic, had taken an extensive world trip at Clark's request in 1978 and recommended that Clark should see the developing world and the Middle East. Gradually, the trip's itinerary took shape: Clark would visit Japan because of its importance to Canadian trade; India as an example of a developing country; Israel for its political importance at home and its significance in Middle East politics; Jordan because Clark should visit an Arab country. The itinerary offered no coherent theme, except for the education of Joe Clark, whose party stood poised to form the Government of Canada. This fact alone allowed Clark to meet the leading political figures of the countries he visited, and it attracted more journalists than the Conservatives had reckoned might be interested in Clark's travels.

The trip was a public-relations disaster. Clark was exceptionally nervous and only met journalists at infrequent "scrums," at which he sounded ill-briefed. He looked uncomfortable throughout the trip: wearing an eggshell-blue suit and an ascot while side-stepping the cow patties on the earthen streets of an Indian village; asking ludicrous questions—"What is the totality of your land?"—or making ridiculous statements—"Jerusalem is a very holy city." King Hussein of Jordan kept Clark cooling his heels for seventy-five minutes, perhaps in retaliation for Clark's having spent twice as much time in Israel as in Jordan. Organizational foul-ups plagued the trip: Clark's Egypt Air flight from Tokyo to Bangkok arrived too late for Clark's luggage to be loaded on a connecting flight to New Delhi; his flight back to Canada was four hours late. Some of the accompanying journalists, devoid of "hard news," took to writing more about Clark's gaffes than about the rest of the trip. When Clark returned to Canada he was known as the man who could not keep track of his own luggage.

Some of the coverage degenerated into merciless satire. On the way out of Jerusalem, the press bus found itself behind a garbage truck. Seizing the opportunity, a television journalist instructed his film crew to record the event as a symbol of Clark's trip, causing another reporter to quip: "Christ was led out of Jerusalem on a donkey; Joe Clark was escorted by a garbage truck."

Heading into the 1979 election, Joe Clark's image was a serious liability for the Conservative Party. He had frittered away his chance to make a positive impression during his honeymoon period, raised doubts about his capabilities with his performance in Opposition, and harmed himself with an ill-conceived and poorly executed world tour.

Clark's performance in the 1979 campaign did not improve his image. Lowell Murray was determined that nothing should detract from the Conservatives' basic message that Trudeau and change were irreconcilable. If Clark's leadership became the issue, the Conservatives might lose the election. Stung by unfavourable publicity from the world tour, the Conservatives mounted a superb logistical campaign. They feared that a single piece of misplaced luggage would generate stories reminding voters that Clark could not properly organize his own trips.

In a series of commercials, the Conservatives' media campaign zeroed in on Trudeau's record. Clark attacked Trudeau for telling

Canadians to lower their expectations and for wasting the potential of Canada. But Clark kept making small mistakes. These were not fatal; as Lowell Murray once said: "When you're losing, you can't do anything right. When you're winning you can't do anything wrong."*

In the first week of the campaign, Clark suggested that the RCMP could break the law, provided that illegal acts were sanctioned by a Cabinet minister.

"It would be essential for us to have a system in place whereby any breach of the law that might be necessary would be authorized by a responsible official of Cabinet. And that responsible official would have to carry the can for any consequences that flowed," Clark said. He never satisfactorily explained how such a system would operate, saying near the end of the campaign that the minister should report to a closed parliamentary committee. "I have confidence that a committee that was composed of all parties and presumably would be composed in part of members who were there because of their very sharp concern for civil liberties would find some ways to let abuses be known," he said.

That seemed, at best, an odd response: a closed committee would either make information public or leak the information to the press. Clark's position generated considerable editorial comment, but the protection of civil liberties is unfortunately not a subject that excites Canadians in making political choices.

A few days later, in Halifax, Clark was asked the standard campaign question: how much would the party's promises cost? The Conservatives had prepared a reply—$2.8 billion—but Clark waffled. He said he did not have a "magic accountant" and could not answer the question with "specificity." Clark hoped that the issue would die, but the Liberals made certain that it did not, tagging Clark with the label "The Seven-Billion Dollar Man"—a reflection of the Liberals' calculation of the cost of Conservative promises.

In mid-campaign, Clark argued that he would neither negotiate sovereignty-association nor use force to prevent Quebec from leaving Confederation. He was hounded for a week to clarify his position. How else could the federal government keep Quebec in Confederation, if Quebeckers voted for sovereignty or opted for it after a refusal by English Canada to negotiate sovereignty-association? Clark would give only a non-answer: his Government

---

*Quoted in Geoffrey Stevens, *Stanfield* (Macmillan, 1973), p. 215.

would call together the premiers and make a few small changes in the federal system before the referendum to show Quebeckers that his Government was prepared to put a "fresh face on federalism."

The Liberals, of course, knew that Clark was their best and only hope for victory. None of the issues was running their way, except leadership, and even that issue required the isolation of Trudeau from his record. The Liberals did all they could. They placed advertisements that showed Trudeau in his "gunslinger" pose, standing behind a solitary microphone, speaking defiantly to his audience about national problems. "A Leader Must Be A Leader," boomed the Liberal advertisements. Every effort was made to divorce Trudeau from his record and to place him in direct contrast to Clark. The Liberals' strategy raised Clark's profile in the campaign, but eleven years had taken too large a toll on the Liberals' credibility, in spite of the fact that Trudeau defeated Clark decisively in the televised debate among the party leaders.

Television debates do not play nearly as important a role in determining the outcome of elections as an untutored observer might believe. The media assessment following the debate can have an effect, but debates themselves tend to reinforce the preconceived biases of the viewers. Since Trudeau was perceived to be a stronger leader than Clark, Trudeau had to annihilate Clark in their thirty-minute debate to score a decisive win. Trudeau, with his sure grasp of fact, battered Clark, who was constantly on the defensive.

Two days before the debate, the Conservatives interviewed 250 people to test their assumptions about the debate. After the debate, the Conservatives interviewed 150 of these people again and a new group of 100 voters. The Conservatives discovered that NDP leader Ed Broadbent had performed better than the press assumed. They also learned that Clark finished third among the leaders, but he still exceeded the expectations of many viewers. Those who ranked Clark third were most irritated by his mannerisms, especially his nervous laugh. When the results were compiled, the Conservatives breathed a collective sigh of relief: Clark lost but not badly enough to jeopardize the party's chances. It did not say much for the prospective Prime Minister of Canada that his advisors believed he had "won" the debate by remaining upright for thirty minutes with Trudeau.

Joe Clark assumed the highest elected office in the land on June 4, 1979, one day before his fortieth birthday. He faced a public that doubted his ability to handle the job he had just won. For three years, Clark had grappled unsuccessfully with his image problem. Nine days after the election, Allan Gregg wrote a long memorandum tracing the public perception of Clark, concluding with a sombre warning that hung over Joe Clark during his seven months in office:

The Clark Image

Perhaps the most direct way of describing the Clark image is simply to say it is "no image." Canadian voters, in the past, have had vague notions of what "Clark is," but these perceptual sets have shifted over time and usually have been defined in relation to other individuals (most specifically Trudeau) or "temporary" conditions.

Unlike Trudeau, Clark has never been able to engender unanimous concurrence as to his leadership qualities on any dimension, be it honesty, toughness, competence etc. This in itself is not that uncommon in as much as "style" over the last ten years has been defined by Trudeau himself and notions of what "Trudeau is" have taken root over ten years. Moreover, evaluative decisions concerning leadership (read Prime Ministerial) style are much more difficult cognitive processes for voters to reach when considering a leader out of power. For Clark and Broadbent, such evaluations must be made on two dimensions (one of which is more speculative than evaluative), while for Trudeau only one simple evaluation on well-understood criteria is required.

Notwithstanding the competitive disadvantage opposition leaders face in such comparisons, it should be noted that perceptions of Clark on election day were largely negative and that, on some dimensions of leadership, affective evaluations of him have deteriorated over time.

In the first study following his leadership victory, Clark led Trudeau on every salient measure of leadership except intelligence. There was also evidence at that time that a new coalition was beginning to gravitate towards the PC Party through Clark's leadership—44 per cent of labor support was directed towards the PC Party, well over 50 per cent of the female vote and the so-called ethnic vote was similarly turning to Joe Clark and the Conservatives. This "current" vote intention did not translate into partisan identification or feelings of "closeness" to the Progressive Conservatives and consequently, as we now know, this new support quickly gravitated back to more traditional partisan moorings. Even during this period, however, the high level of undecidedness concerning Clark's leadership qualities gives credence to the contention that positive assessments were a function of "newness," in contrast to a negatively-perceived incumbent and "benefit of the doubt" rather than successive judgments based on evaluative criteria of "who Clark is."

At any rate, by early 1977 the short-term advantage over our opponents was lost, both at a party and leadership level. The interesting thing during this period of time, however, was that while the party stood at an all-time low, Clark himself continued to lead Trudeau on some particularly important aspects of leadership. The strength of incumbency, the so-called "national unity crisis" and a marginal crystalization (sic) of opinion about Clark, gave Trudeau an advantage on dimensions such as experience, toughness and, most damagingly, competence. The spill-over from this re-alignment of perception was that Trudeau was once again perceived to be best able to govern the country. Notwithstanding this movement, Clark, by a significant margin, was still perceived to be the most principled, understanding and honest of the two national leaders.

In large measure, these trends continued, although on a less exaggerated basis until the spring of 1978. At that time, a major change was noted. Trudeau, for the first time, was being perceived by a key group of switchers as unable to deal with the national unity issue. Subsequent to this phenomenon, Trudeau also began to slip badly on various dimensions of issue competence. Overall assessments of the principals' leadership qualities, however, continued to hold, although the gap between the two leaders on their respective strengths was beginning to close—i.e., Clark was beginning to be perceived as marginally more competent and less principled etc. and the reverse was true for Trudeau. While these trends seemed to portend well for the PC Party and Leader, it was still clear that definitions of Clark were still being based on "Trudeau criteria." What was happening was that, for the first time, the problems of the country were becoming Trudeau's problems. The evaluative analysis of Trudeau's performance in the minds of the voters was changing from . . . "he's not doing it because he's wrong-headed or uncaring etc." to . . . "he's not doing it because he can't."

The problem for Trudeau was particularly acute

among voters who shared many of the demographic and attitudinal characteristics of PC identifiers but who supported the Liberal Party. As the Trudeau style began being associated with the problems of the country, the solutions for the country were beginning to be associated with an alternate (sic) style for this voting group. At this point, there was some evidence that a particular type of voter was changing the cognitive requisites of leadership. This is, these voters were beginning to change their definition of "what a leader is." At this point, Clark led Trudeau decisively on the question . . . "Who would you most trust to lead Canada into the 1980s."

By the eve of the election, one year later, there had been very little voter re-alignment. The Liberals went into the election with their traditional coalition of "minorities," and the Conservatives enjoyed the support of traditional Tory supporters and a group of higher-educated, PC-Liberal switchers who wanted change. Negative assessments of Trudeau were every bit as deep-rooted as a year earlier, although voters were not as able to articulate the reasons "why" they disliked him. Qualitative assessments of Clark, however, had slipped drastically over the year, although a significant portion of the electorate were still undecided about his ability. The typical Canadian voter did not particularly dislike Clark (although overall reaction to him was generally unfavorable), or disapprove of his performance as leader of the Opposition. In fact, the average, non-Liberal voter, found very little risk with Clark. Rather, voters could simply not envision Clark as the Prime Minister. As a consequence, Clark trailed Trudeau on virtually every qualitative dimension of leadership, including Prime Ministerial ability, although his issue competence (especially on economic issues) was perceived to be quite close to Trudeau's. Where Clark held a distinct advantage over Trudeau was in perceived attitudinal proximity to the voting public, especially among key switchers. In other words, our "target" voters felt Clark's belief in the potential of the country, role of government, solvability of problems etc. was much more closely aligned to their own value sets than were Trudeau's.

Generally speaking, these beliefs held throughout the course of the campaign. Clark's "favorable" rating increased incrementally but steadily throughout and with about two weeks remaining, exceeded unfavorable responses. In the dying days of the campaign, however, this trend began to reverse and, in some areas of Metro

Toronto, returned to the lows experienced at the start of the campaign. Negatives towards Trudeau tended to heighten somewhat as the election progressed and as our negative media campaign intensified, his "approval rating" hit the "Truman Bottom" of 27 per cent. This disapproval manifested itself in extremely low issue competence ratings to the point where he ran behind both Clark and Broadbent in perceived ability to handle the economy, bring prices down etc. This disapproval also translated into lower ratings of Prime Ministerial abilities compared to the other leaders. However, this trend never developed to the point where, nationally, Clark was perceived to be better equipped to handle the job of Prime Minister. Towards the end of the campaign, this trend also began to reverse and Trudeau, once again, held a significant leader over Clark on this last measure of ability. In fact, in the final days of polling, it was Broadbent who was perceived to be the most able to handle select issue management (e.g. inflation, creating jobs).

Clark's image problems at the end of the campaign, by and large, were the same as at the beginning. He suffered primarily from being perceived as unqualified to assume the senior office of government, as uninformed and lacking strength. *In fact, it may not be an exaggeration to suggest that a national leader has rarely, if ever, assumed office with lower expectations concerning his ability to govern.* (Italics mine.)

At each stage of his career, Clark had surprised those who held low expectations of him; his persistence, intelligence, and grasp of tactics carried him to victories none of his adversaries thought possible. He won the Conservative nomination in Rocky Mountain, although he knew few party members when he began his quest for the nomination, against two men who had long associations with the constituency. He captured the Conservative leadership because he was the most acceptable second choice to the largest number of delegates. He became Prime Minister of Canada despite the doubts his fellow citizens held about him. But the Prime Minister is unlike any other politician in the power he wields and the attention he commands. As such, he is judged by the most exacting of standards.

Clark understood the public perception of him when he took office, and he governed with it uppermost in his mind. He approached many choices as Prime Minister thinking about how his decision would affect that public perception. As a result, he staked out positions from which he refused to budge, fearing that retreat would be interpreted as a confirmation of his weakness. He had not gained confidence in himself nor familiarity with the responsibilities of the Prime Minister's office before his Government collapsed.

~ 4 ~

Setting a Course

The twenty-nine members of Joe Clark's Cabinet brought to their jobs an eagerness that had been missing in the twilight years of the Liberal Government. Instead of the weary cynicism of the Liberal Cabinet, most of the Conservative ministers crackled with enthusiasm to master their responsibilities. They were a friendly, gregarious group, and it was sad, even alarming, to see their ebullience fade when the pace of work and their own uncertainties rendered some of them brittle caricatures of their former selves.

They wanted so badly to succeed that they were afraid of making the smallest mistake; they cocooned themselves in their departments, emerging to issue tentative statements or to establish study groups to help them formulate policy. At the time of the Government's defeat, some of them were beginning to feel at ease with power, understanding how to cope with the insistent demands on their time. If they had been in office longer, more of them would have become national figures. As it was, only Finance Minister John Crosbie, External Affairs Minister Flora MacDonald, and Treasury Board President Sinclair Stevens imprinted their personalities on the national political consciousness; the rest of them were barely recognizable outside their own regions and areas of specialization.

Perhaps because of a surfeit of work and their own inexperience, but more likely because of a lack of sure direction from Joe Clark and his advisors, the Cabinet drifted into a series of disastrous assumptions that led to the Conservative Party's defeat in the 1980 election. It seemed inconceivable that such an intelligent and politically sensitive group of men and women could have ignored the many danger signals that loomed along the way. Indeed some ministers had tried to point them out. But Joe Clark and his advisors, whose job it was to keep a sharp watch out for such signals, were lulled into heedless overconfidence. They succumbed to the pressure of work, inexperience in governing, plain stupidity, and an uncritical acceptance of the party's Opposition rhetoric.

The formation of a Cabinet is always attended by broken hearts. Geography, religion, history, and exaggerated impressions of self-worth inevitably rule out many of those M.P.s who aspire to the Cabinet. In Joe Clark's case, two groups were sorely disappointed by their exclusion from the Cabinet. The first group were M.P.s who had lingered for ten or twenty years waiting for the Conservatives to return to power and who were considered either too old or too lacking in political appeal. Only three of the twenty M.P.s from the Diefenbaker era were chosen for the Cabinet—Erik Nielsen from the Yukon, Heward Grafftey from Missisquoi, and James McGrath from St. John's East. Former ministers from the Diefenbaker Government, like George Hees from Prince Edward-Hastings, Walter Dinsdale from Brandon-Souris, Marcel Lambert from Edmonton West, and Alvin Hamilton from Qu'Appelle-Moose Mountain, were all overlooked.

The second group left out of the Cabinet were M.P.s from Alberta, Saskatchewan, Manitoba, and Nova Scotia who were blocked because only one or two seats at the Cabinet table were available for each of those provinces. The selection of a Canadian Cabinet has always hinged on the balance of competing regional or provincial claims for representation. An abundance of talent from a given province forces the exclusion of worthy M.P.s; a paucity of seats in another province elevates men of limited ability but fortuitous geographical circumstances. The 1979 election left the Conservatives with an excess of Cabinet aspirants from the English-speaking provinces, but the election gave Clark only two seats in Quebec. That meant Clark had a handful of unhappy English-speaking M.P.s on his hands. M.P.s such as Jack Murta from Lisgar, Michael Forrestall from Dartmouth-Halifax East, and Douglas Roche from Edmonton South swallowed their disappointment; others—Paul Yewchuk from Athabaska, Lloyd Crouse from South Shore, and Robert Coates from Cumberland-Colchester, the party's national president—grumbled publicly or sulked. The election result also meant that both Conservative M.P.s from Quebec—Roch LaSalle from Joliette and Heward Grafftey—

automatically entered the Cabinet, although neither commanded respect in the party or in the province. LaSalle, appointed Minister of Supply and Services, was a friendly man whose preoccupation was to ensure that long-suffering Quebec Conservatives received a healthy slice of federal patronage. Grafftey, his mind floating above issues like a waterbug on a lake, was named Minister of State for Social Programs, a new portfolio of limited responsibility which matched his talents. But Grafftey groused so incessantly about his insignificant station that Clark gave him the science and technology portfolio during the first week of the parliamentary session.

Clark tried to tempt prominent Quebeckers to join his Cabinet by offering them Senate appointments, but the sorry state of the Conservative Party in Quebec frustrated his efforts. Quebeckers did not want to be associated with a party scorned by the vast majority of Quebec's population and by most of the province's elite. Clark was forced, therefore, to reach into the undistinguished ranks of Quebec Conservatives in the Senate to find Jacques Flynn and Martial Asselin, two ministers who served briefly in the Diefenbaker Government. He appointed Flynn Minister of Justice and Asselin Minister of State for the Canadian International Development Agency, appointments that rounded out his feeble Quebec contingent. Clark gave eight of his ministers two portfolios apiece, leaving some flexibility for later changes if he could find any prominent Quebeckers willing to serve.

Clark's paucity of French-speaking talent led him to make his most audacious Cabinet appointment—Robert de Cotret, a former president of the Conference Board in Canada and an economist who had dazzled Clark after winning the riding of Ottawa Centre in an October 1978 by-election. De Cotret should never have lost the riding in the 1979 election, but he did not spend enough time worrying about his constituency and ran an indifferent, almost lazy, campaign. De Cotret was undeniably bright, but he had the public personality of a cold fish. Rejected by the voters, de Cotret nevertheless found himself appointed to the Senate by Clark and then to the Cabinet as Minister of Industry, Trade and Commerce and Minister of State for Economic Development. Aspirants disappointed by their failure to enter the Cabinet were enraged at de Cotret's appointment; he had been defeated at the polls, but he had still been given two important portfolios and a place in the inner Cabinet.

Clark planned that the inner Cabinet would be the most

powerful body within the Cabinet structure. The full Cabinet, or "outer" Cabinet, was to meet less frequently and concern itself with the political direction of the Government. Much of the Cabinet's work would be done in committees of Cabinet—economic development, social and native affairs, external affairs and defence, federal-provincial relations, and economy in government. Each was to be chaired by a member of the inner Cabinet. These new committees, as well as three committees retained from the Liberal Cabinet structure—treasury board, legislation and House planning, and security and intelligence—would report to the inner Cabinet. Any minister who lost his case in a Cabinet committee could appeal to the inner Cabinet. In practice, however, appeals to the inner Cabinet were seldom successful. Although appeals to the full Cabinet were theoretically possible in some cases, Clark actively discouraged such appeals. The inner Cabinet became the court of last resort.

The Ontario and Quebec Governments had both tried variations on a two-tiered Cabinet system. In both cases, senior ministers were relieved of departmental responsibilities and given a broad policy area to think about. Ontario scrapped its system because the "super-ministers" found themselves acting in a vacuum, without a civil service to direct, and ignored by the media and the Opposition parties. A similar system worked better in Quebec under the Parti Québécois Government, because the super-ministers were busy overseeing the development of comprehensive policy papers on language and cultural policy, industrial strategy, and federal-provincial relations, all of which became controversial subjects for debate in Quebec.

The decision-making rationale for the inner Cabinet made good sense; a small group could more easily come to a decision than could a group of thirty or more. When John Diefenbaker formed his first ministry, the Cabinet had twenty-three ministers. By 1968, the Cabinet had grown to thirty-three members. Trudeau, like Clark, recognized that such a large group was too unwieldy to make expeditious decisions, so he structured his Cabinet around a central committee, the priorities and planning committee. It did not exercise as much power as Clark's inner Cabinet because its decisions could be thrashed over by the full Liberal Cabinet.

Structural problems with the inner and outer Cabinet system soon became apparent. The names *inner* and *outer* created two classes of ministers, and those excluded from the inner Cabinet were liable to feel slighted, as were regions denied representation in the inner Cabinet. Clark was forced to add John Fraser from Vancouver South to the inner Cabinet after party members, newspapers, and interest groups in British Columbia set up a howl against the exclusion of a British Columbian from the inner Cabinet. Although Clark's Cabinet system was modelled partly on the British system, it lacked the administrative rationale of the British Cabinet. In Great Britain, ministers sit in the equivalent of the inner Cabinet by virtue of the importance of their portfolios. They are given two, three, or four junior ministers, to whom responsibility is delegated for specific aspects of the ministry. Clark did appoint five ministers of state and assign them to senior ministers, but the senior-junior system was not as elaborately designed as in Great Britain. What's more, membership in Clark's inner Cabinet was not based on the importance of a minister's portfolio. Ministers for four of the five largest-spending departments in the federal government were excluded from the inner Cabinet: Health and Welfare ($13 billion budget in 1979), Defence ($4.1 billion), Employment and Immigration ($3 billion), and Transport ($1.6 billion). The $21.7 billion spent by these four departments represented about 45 per cent of federal budgetary expenditures in 1979.

The exclusion of these ministries deprived the inner Cabinet of two of the most attractive members of the Conservative Party: Health and Welfare Minister David Crombie and Transport Minister Don Mazankowski. Crombie had been one of the most popular mayors in the history of Toronto, winning re-election in 1974 and 1976 with more than 80 per cent of the votes. He had seriously considered seeking the leadership of the Conservative Party in 1976, while still mayor of Toronto. Clark may have suspected that Crombie's personal ambition outstripped his loyalty to the party or to Clark himself. In any event, the exclusion of Crombie robbed Clark of a minister with an excellent political sense and deprived more than two million people in Metropolitan Toronto of representation in the most powerful institution in the federal government.

Don Mazankowski was an outstanding Minister of Transport who quickly established a reputation for competence and sensitivity in dealing with the crushing responsibilities of his department. In short order, he set about fulfilling the party's campaign promise to increase Canada's grain-handling capacity by 50 per cent by 1985. He received Cabinet approval to build 2,000 hopper cars, negotiated an agreement with the three Prairie provinces for another

2,000 hopper cars, and signed a deal with Canadian National Railways to build another 1,000. He appointed a grain transportation co-ordinator with sweeping powers to clear away the bottlenecks in the rail transportation system in western Canada. He pledged $42.5 million for the development of a new grain-handling port at Prince Rupert, British Columbia. His achievements in air and water transportation were less spectacular, but still impressive. But both Mazankowski and Clark were Albertans, and that prevented Mazankowski from entering the inner Cabinet, an example of the excessive rigidity of the entire system.

The inner Cabinet also lacked the wide range of political insights that a full Cabinet can bring to bear on government policy. Politically sensitive decisions on PetroCanada and energy policy, for example, were not tempered by debate in the full Cabinet. In theory, the full Cabinet was the forum for discussing the political direction of the Government, but the full Cabinet met less often and exercised less power than did the inner Cabinet. In effect, the full Cabinet was left to consider the political ramifications of decisions already taken by the inner Cabinet.

Still, the members of the inner Cabinet, apart from LaSalle and Flynn, made an impressive group: Finance Minister John Crosbie from Newfoundland; Secretary of State David MacDonald from Prince Edward Island; Treasury Board President Sinclair Stevens, House leader and Privy Council President Walter Baker, Minister of State for Federal-Provincial Relations William Jarvis, External Affairs Minister Flora MacDonald and Robert de Cotret from Ontario; Energy Minister Ray Hnatyshyn from Saskatchewan; Postmaster General and Environment Minister John Fraser from British Columbia.

Only two members of this group—Flynn and Crosbie—had ever been part of a Government in power. The rest had served their apprenticeships for power during part of the Conservatives' sixteen years in Opposition. More experience might have been available had the Conservatives been able to attract provincial ministers to Ottawa over the years. The federal party had chosen provincial premiers as leaders—John Bracken of Manitoba, George Drew of Ontario, and Robert Stanfield of Nova Scotia—but only a handful of provincial ministers had successfully made the leap to federal politics. Many prominent Conservatives in provinces where the party was strong preferred to remain in provincial politics, where they could exercise power rather than undergo the frustrations of serving in the Opposition in Ottawa. Some federal Conservatives such as Davie Fulton, Angus MacLean, and Hugh Horner chose to return to provincial politics.

David MacDonald, John Crosbie, and Sinclair Stevens were the most influential members of the inner Cabinet by dint of their astonishing capacity to master the Cabinet documents prepared by departments other than their own, and by their own keen intellects. David MacDonald, saddled with two portfolios—secretary of state and communications—nevertheless intervened sensibly on issues beyond his domains. Crosbie, after a hesitant start in the finance portfolio, became the strongman of the inner Cabinet, occasionally pushing aside objections from other ministers with the assertion that he was the Minister of Finance and, as such, knew better than anyone else what was good for the economy. Stevens was a loner, mistrusted by some of his colleagues, who suspected he was playing fancy games with numbers. But he was appreciated for his tenacity and capacity for hard work.

The presence of Stevens allowed the inner Cabinet to stretch across the political spectrum of the Conservative Party. Stevens, however, was the only representative of the party's right wing; the other members of the inner Cabinet were all moderates or progressives in the terms of reference of the Conservative Party. The Cabinet, therefore, represented but did not faithfully reflect the ideological makeup of the party. Certainly, the Conservative caucus was more right-wing than the inner Cabinet. Conservative backbenchers grew restless when the inner Cabinet moved slowly in reducing expenditures and examining cutbacks in social programs. There was also the feeling that the Cabinet was too technocratic, by which the backbenchers meant that ministers were too enamoured of their civil servants and were insufficiently bloody-minded about shaking up the civil service and replacing Liberal appointees with Conservatives.

The weakest members of the inner Cabinet were Jacques Flynn, Roch LaSalle, and Ray Hnatyshyn. Flynn possessed neither the interest nor the energy to be an effective minister; he was sixty-four years old, and performing the inconsequential duties of Opposition leader in the Senate for twelve years had dulled his appetite for work. LaSalle was handicapped by his weak command of English. Clark ordered simultaneous translation for Cabinet meetings to help LaSalle, but his attention span was still limited. He was deliberately given a portfolio with a light workload so that he could concentrate on the political fortunes of the Conservative Party in Quebec. However, major decisions about candidate selection were still handled by Clark and his Quebec organizer Rodrigue Pageau; Montreal lawyers Jean Bazin and Michel Cogger; Brian Mulroney, president of Iron Ore of Canada Limited, and national-party director Paul Curley. Hnatyshyn was overwhelmed by the energy portfolio. He never got a firm grasp on the issues and lost important battles in Cabinet.

Hnatyshyn's problems stemmed partly from constant infighting between the Prime Minister's office and individual Cabinet ministers or their departments. There were constant struggles between Clark's staff and the inner Cabinet, or some of its members, over energy and economic policies and foreign policy. Most of the disagreements revolved around promises made by the party in Opposition that the Prime Minister's principal advisors— Jim Gillies, William Neville, and Lowell Murray—were intent on keeping once the party was in power. Some of those policies, such as mortgage-interest and property-tax deductibility, the $2-billion tax cut, and moving the Canadian embassy in Israel from Tel Aviv to Jerusalem, had been initiated by Clark's advisors. They strengthened their personal commitment to these policies by insisting that the Government needed to keep its promises or its credibility would be destroyed. Many ministers—who either believed that the policies were in error or were so persuaded by their civil servants—began fighting with Clark's advisors or with Clark himself.

Although the Cabinet is a Government's most visible extension, the Prime Minister's office arguably wields more power in shaping the political fortunes of a Government, especially in an era when the perception of the Prime Minister's "leadership" is the most animating factor in elections. In the Prime Minister's office, reputations can be bled dry by the criticisms of whispered conversations. In the wake of the Liberals' 1979 defeat, no one's reputation suffered more than that of Trudeau's principal secretary, Jim Coutts. He was blamed not only for his own shortcomings but also for some of Trudeau's, which rank-and-file Liberals were too timorous to voice publicly. Similarly, when the Conservative Government collapsed like a snowbank in spring, disgruntled or bewildered Conservatives fingered Clark's principal advisors as those responsible for the Government's defeat.

Any Prime Minister chooses a coterie of advisors who in performing their responsibilities become extensions of himself. They are his eyes and ears, absorbing and distilling information from the civil service, the party, and the country. Quite often, their influence is resented by the party, which feels that its voice is not being heard clearly by the Prime Minister because it has been filtered by his advisors. The party finds it easier, and safer, to criticize the advisors than the Prime Minister, who can punish dissidents in a way his advisors cannot. Nor is the party alone in its complaints. The civil service also views with suspicion the advisors' influence, fearing that the sanctity of factual presentations and careful analyses will be violated by the advisors' profane political calculations. The influence of advisors on a Prime Minister stems from the judiciousness of their counsel and from their loyalty. Loyalty is indispensable; it often overshadows failings undetected by a Prime Minister who is grateful to find, in the uncertain world of politics, associates in whom he can invest absolute trust. Loyalty can be blind, whereas wisdom requires a discerning eye; so advisors are occasionally torn between delivering unpleasant news to a Prime Minister and sugaring the message.

The Prime Minister's office is the nerve centre of government and politics in the country. Its budget grew from $900,800 in 1970 to $2.8 million in 1979. The information flowing into that office each day would overwhelm the most energetic Prime Minister. His advisors act as gatekeepers, deflecting the irrelevant and drawing to his attention only the most germane information. Similarly, his advisors must sift through the avalanche of requests to see the Prime Minister. They must shape events to put the Prime Minister, and therefore the Government, in the most flattering light. They write the Prime Minister's speeches, or at least provide a framework and some phrases that he can develop into a speech. They recommend which invitations the Prime Minister should accept or decline, and they work to extract the last drop of favourable publicity from his performance. Their vision must be bifocal, placing the day's decisions into a broader political context.

Although the partisan world of politics and the administrative concerns of government meet in the Cabinet, the Prime Minister's office can often predetermine the outcome of the encounter. Before entering a Cabinet meeting, the Prime Minister is briefed on the likely flow of debate: which ministers will persist and which will yield, which trade-offs are possible, which solutions desired. Ministers, too, are given probable Cabinet scenarios by their departments, but none of their documents is as thorough as those at the Prime Minister's hand. The Prime Minister can best force trade-offs or, like Lincoln, listen to the "nays" from around the table, vote "yea" himself, and declare that the "yeas" have it—just as Joe Clark did when he overrode objections from the inner Cabinet to his PetroCanada policy.

It is the Prime Minister who must pilot the Government towards re-election; his advisors are the navigators, checking course in mid-route, testing political winds, and warning of storms ahead. A Prime Minister may lose his course, even with excellent advice; without it, his failure is more likely, as Joe Clark learned.

At the top of Clark's staff was William Neville, a former Liberal who became disillusioned with the Trudeau Government in the late 1960s and joined the Conservatives. He had worked for Liberal ministers Edgar Benson, Judy LaMarsh and Paul Hellyer. When he left the Liberals, Neville embraced his new political affiliation with the conviction of a convert, as well as his own fierce competitiveness.

Believing Trudeau preferred to lead by picking fights with those who disagreed with him, Neville cut his ties with the Liberals after Trudeau became their leader in 1968. In the 1972 election, some Conservatives thought he was "some kind of Liberal spy," he said later about their reaction to his work for Conservative M.P. Jim Gillies in Don Valley West. After the election, Neville returned to his consulting business, advising clients about which doors to knock on in Ottawa and what to expect if the doors were opened. He was earning about $100,000 a year from that business, but the work satisfied neither his fascination with politics nor his competitive instincts. In 1974, "in one of the great kamikaze acts of all time," as he later called it, Neville took on Liberal Finance Minister John Turner in the riding of Ottawa-Carleton. He attacked Turner personally throughout the campaign and lost by 10,940 votes—a "defeat that proved my loyalty, even if it did nothing for my intelligence."

A year later, Neville joined Stanfield's office as director of research, a thankless job with a party leader who had just lost his third election and was soon to retire from politics. Neville could have made more money in his consulting business, but politics was his passion. When Stanfield stepped down, Neville made sure the party research staff stayed neutral in the leadership fight.

The morning after the leadership convention, Clark asked Neville to become chief-of-staff. Neville was willing (the job was too enticing to refuse); able (he had spent nearly fifteen years around Parliament Hill); and available (most of Stanfield's staff had cleared out and none of Clark's own campaign organizers knew Ottawa well enough to run the Opposition leader's office).

Neville quickly became the most indispensable member of Clark's staff. A self-described workaholic, Neville took command of every phase of Clark's office. As a former journalist—United Press International bureau chief before he became a Liberal ministerial assistant—Neville designed the Conservatives' media strategy. As a former executive assistant and consultant, Neville interested himself in policy. More than anyone else, Neville pressed on Clark the Conservatives' 1978 promise to offer homeowners partial income-tax deductibility for mortgage interest and property taxes. His stance was a reflection of an interest in housing kindled while working for Liberal Minister Paul Hellyer's task force on housing in 1968. Neville also recruited Clark's personal staff, developing such a personal loyalty to many of them that he waited too long before firing or transferring some of the ineffective recruits. No one within Clark's office rivalled Neville's influence with the leader. Jim Hawkes, a close friend of Clark and a pivotal figure in his leadership campaign organization, worked with Neville for six months after the leadership convention but returned to the University of Calgary when his sabbatical ended. Duncan Edmonds, a long-time Liberal executive assistant and a friend of Clark, replaced Hawkes, but he left within a year, resentful of Neville's influence and questioning Neville's political judgement.

Only Lowell Murray surpassed Neville's influence with Clark, but this was never a source of resentment for Neville; he recognized the long-standing friendship between Clark and Murray. For his part, Murray was pleased to leave the daily strategy of the Opposition leader's office to Neville. Murray wanted to be heard only on important decisions affecting the party's footing for the 1979 campaign. Although Clark listened to Murray for broad strategy, he depended on Neville for practical advice.

Neville rubbed a lot of Conservatives the wrong way, and Clark was under pressure to find a new chief-of-staff after the 1980 election. Neville was especially distrusted by some of the Conservative elite in Toronto—with their pinstripes, private-school ties, and lunches at the Albany Club—who looked at

Neville's Liberal background and florid attire—initials on the cuff, patent-leather or white shoes—and concluded that Clark was poorly advised. Neville's detractors within the Conservative caucus, remembering encounters with his abrupt and occasionally sarcastic personality, concurred.

A quick study, however, did not do justice to Neville. He could be an engaging man, knowledgeable about a wide variety of subjects. He was loyal to his friends, visiting Judy LaMarsh when she was afflicted by cancer and making a special effort to console Cabinet ministers such as Ray Hnatyshyn after they lost battles in Cabinet. He was a bit of a romantic, who quietly provided money to keep *Saturday Night* magazine afloat.

Neville's extreme competitiveness showed itself in every aspect of his life. A rabid fan of the St. Louis Cardinals, he would want his team to bunt for an insurance run when they were leading by nine runs. He carried a paunch the size of a small watermelon and smoked heavily, but he was a jock at heart, never happier than when talking about baseball or hockey. A stationary bicycle sat in his basement and he played an occasional game of tennis—a picture hung in his office showed him swinging off-balance at a tennis ball—but he had little time for exercise. He worked at a killing pace, rising early several mornings a week for French lessons with a private tutor and returning home in the evening with a briefcase full of Cabinet documents or office memoranda. He did everything in Clark's office except run the photocopier. He wrote speeches, directed media strategy, worked with the caucus and the party, listened to interest groups and provincial governments, shaped Clark's itinerary, battled with the civil service, prepared Clark for meetings, sat on committees doling out patronage, and accepted specific assignments, such as drafting conflict-of-interest guidelines for ministers. It was too much, even for a chief-of-staff, and his political judgement suffered. In this vortex of work he did not see the storm clouds building around the Government.

Neville's competitive instinct coloured his political judgement. He had a passion for whipping the Grits, as he liked to call Liberals with a mixture of disgust and admiration. He also knew that many voters perceived Clark as a weak leader; Neville thought that only by demonstrating toughness could that image be reversed. Applying the sports adage that a good offence is the best defence, Neville advised Clark to be unyielding, when discretion would have been wiser counsel. When the Government faced mortal peril on the day of its collapse, Neville foolishly advised a full-scale attack rather than a tactical retreat.

When Joe Clark took office, only Lowell Murray and William Neville had a stronger call on the Prime Minister's attention than did Jim Gillies. Gillies commanded Clark's complete respect and could have remained one of the most influential men in the Conservative Government, but he was at heart and by profession an academic who could not use effectively the power he had helped Clark to win. Gillies' influence had faded long before the Government fell, and he tagged along on the 1980 campaign like a lost puppy, perplexed and sad.

Gillies entered the Commons in 1972 with impressive academic credentials; he was the sort of candidate the Conservatives needed to overcome the suspicion of academics and intellectuals within the party. Gillies had degrees from Western, Brown, and Indiana universities. He had taught at the University of California at Berkeley, served as the first dean of the faculty of administrative studies at York University, and sat on the boards of directors of companies such as General Foods, McGraw Hill-Ryerson, Zenith, and Eddie Match. He was a happy blend of the academic and the businessman. He even dressed like a split personality: he wore expensive clothes but always looked like an unmade bed. He was a charming man, gracious, urbane, and much in demand on the Ottawa social circuit.

Gillies was full of ideas, and that was the problem. He was fascinated by ideas, especially economic ones, and the more arresting they were the better. It seemed that he either had too many ideas bouncing around in his head to reflect carefully enough on any of them, or that he thought through an idea to its logical conclusion without giving sufficient consideration to its political implications. If Gillies persuaded himself that an idea was right, he mistakenly believed others would agree with him. Before the 1974 election, Gillies helped to sell the party on its promise of a wage-and-price freeze followed by controls. Gillies later hesitated when Stanfield committed the party to the policy in the 1974 campaign, but he took the blame within the party, since it was easier for the Conservatives to attack him than Stanfield. Gillies gained a measure of vindication when the Liberals introduced controls in 1975, but the Conservative caucus thought of him as a cross between Savonarola and Harold Stassen.

Still, the Conservatives did not have many M.P.s who could

discourse learnedly on a Phillips curve or the intricacies of monetary policy. Leaning back in his chair, waving a Cuban cigar, Gillies sounded like an economic wizard; but to those who did not share his views, Gillies represented the motto on the button given to him as a joke during the 1980 campaign: "If you can't beat them with brains, baffle them with bullshit."

Gillies demonstrated his political maladroitness in the Conservative leadership race, finishing seventh on the first ballot. His campaign button—"Jim Gillies: United We Win"—was the size and shape of an egg, which was the way most of the delegates figuratively saw his head. He was an academic in politics, a poor platform performer given to windy answers. As the 1979 election drew near, Gillies decided not to seek re-election. If he did not return to York, he would lose his tenure; he had already been given extensions of academic leave for public service. But Joe Clark wanted his special talents in the 1979 campaign.

Gillies had a marvellous knack of responding to a Clark observation or question on economics without ever undermining Clark's shaky self-confidence in the field. Gillies often started his observations with "Gee, you might be right," or "I hadn't thought of it that way," and these genuine expressions of good-will put Clark at ease. Gillies never put down Clark for asking untutored questions about economics; instead, he patiently ran through the problem with Clark like a sensitive classroom teacher who lets the pupil feel that he has done all of the thinking himself.

After the 1979 election, Gillies was asked to remain in Clark's office with the title of policy advisor. He agreed to stay until September 1, then until January 1. He attended Clark's morning staff meetings and when asked by visitors how he was enjoying himself, he cheerfully pointed to Clark's nearby office as a symbol of his influence. He helped to design the inner and outer Cabinet system, worked on a new way of managing expenditures—the so-called "spending envelopes" (see Chapter Eight)—and assumed specific duties for the new Prime Minister.

Slowly, however, his influence and ebullience waned. Gillies was an ideas man, not an administrator. The stream of paper flowing from the bureaucracy irritated him: couldn't the bureaucrats write shorter memos? he complained. He was instrumental in the firing of William Hood as Deputy Minister of Finance and the recruiting of Grant Reuber from the Bank of Montreal to replace Hood. But he could not persuade Clark to consider replacing the governor of the Bank of Canada, Gerald Bouey, whose policy of high interest rates Gillies did not agree with. Nor could he persuade Clark to transfer Ian Stewart, Deputy Minister of Energy. Gillies became involved in energy negotiations with Alberta, vigorously contesting the analyses of the federal energy department and the Ontario government. His interventions irritated other federal officials in the negotiations. They were working full-time on the negotiations, and Gillies was flitting in and out with ideas they considered half-baked and politically unwise. Gillies liked the global approach to problems—lower interest rates, vastly higher oil prices, a massive tax cut—the kind of ideas worth discussing in the classroom or raising in Opposition, but too audacious and politically risky for his colleagues in the Government.

After the 1979 election, the new Prime Minister leaned on Gillies for economic advice, but as time wore on Clark was exposed to new sources of advice from the civil service, some of which he found more compelling than Gillies' analyses. Ministers in economic portfolios resented Gillies' intrusions in their domains. Lacking the administrative savvy necessary to fight bureaucratic battles and increasingly frustrated by his dwindling influence, Gillies began to look forward to leaving Ottawa. He was going to depart in January 1980, but the election intervened and Clark asked him to join his campaign team again.

This time, Clark was more familiar with the economic issues of the campaign. He neither needed nor asked for Gillies' advice as often as in the 1979 campaign. Gillies was along for the ride. Disillusionment soon spread across his deflated countenance, a reflection of his recent, unhappy past and the Conservatives' impending defeat.

Neville and Gillies were Clark's advisors-in-residence; Lowell Murray was the Prime Minister's advisor-in-absentia. The day before the 1979 election, Murray had packed his bags and cleared off his desk. On election day he greeted a visitor to Conservative headquarters in an office stripped of everything but the furniture, a telephone, and his briefcase. That night he slept for five hours and rose early the next morning to go salmon-fishing in New Brunswick, en route to a cottage near Smelt Brook, Cape Breton Island.

Murray remained there for nearly three months while the Conservative Government settled into Ottawa. He was summoned twice from Smelt Brook: to an inner Cabinet meeting in Jasper in late August, and to the Senate in early September. Not only did his Senate appointment force him to leave Smelt Brook, it persuaded him to buy a condominium in Ottawa, a city he disliked, because senators must own at least $4,000 in property in the province they purport to represent. Murray, a Maritimer, was named Senator from Ontario, a quirk in the long and sorry history of paying off victorious national campaign chairmen with Senate sinecures.

Murray's absence and the role he defined for himself upon his return to Ottawa irritated some Cabinet ministers, who thought Murray wanted influence without responsibility. Murray sat on a screening committee for patronage appointments along with Neville and Pigott. He had a standing invitation to attend Clark's morning staff meeting. Beyond these formal responsibilities, Murray preferred to resist entangling commitments. Murray wanted unfettered access to Cabinet ministers, and he complained when ministers' secretaries replied, "Lowell Who?" when he called. Ministers, considering themselves to be shrewd politicians, resented Murray's influence and often disagreed with his advice. Those who lost the PetroCanada battle at Jasper blamed Murray for bending Clark's ear with the foolish advice that the Government had to keep all of its election promises. Murray, however, complained when he heard ministers disavowing party policies or protecting their civil servants. If Murray had been in charge, more civil servants would have been replaced. Murray was a partisan, and proud of it, as he explained in his maiden speech in the Senate:

> The political direction that is given by a Cabinet to the public service has to be informed by some cohesive sense of purpose that animates the ministers as a group. One of the roles and prerogatives of the party is to keep the ministers' feet to the fire, to make sure that the leadership remains faithful to the mandate it sought from the Canadian people.
>
> Governments have gone wrong in the past because politicians did not have the courage of their convictions; because politicians were somehow embarrassed, once they attained high office, by their political origins . . . because politicians thought that they had to become better technocrats than administrators, when they should have been consulting their own best instincts, the motives that brought them into political life in the first place, and when they should have been consulting the traditions of their parties and the philosophical and historical context of their actions.

In Murray's view the party organization and the Government should touch, but not join; they should respect each other's spheres of competence. Murray himself was one of the touch-points, and most of his interventions with ministers related to patronage and party problems.

Having been out of power so long, the Conservatives were anxious not to repeat the mistakes they believed the Liberals had made in enfeebling Liberal Party headquarters and allowing Coutts and Davey to represent the interests of the party to the Government. The Conservatives believed that the overwhelming power of Trudeau's office had rendered the Liberal Party a eunuch, impotent to express its opinions. The Conservatives wanted to put some distance between the party and the Government, to ensure that the party's interests were not perverted by a powerful advisor in the Prime Minister's office.

Without a political nerve-centre in the daily operation of the Government, the Conservatives drifted towards disaster. While Coutts was instructing Goldfarb to take regular samples of public opinion throughout the fall, the Conservatives contented themselves with one national survey in August. Neville was too busy with his many tasks to notice the dangerous drift. Gillies had no political sixth sense, and Murray was an irregular influence on the Government. Ministers were preoccupied with their departments, with Cabinet committees, and with the rest of their workloads. The full Cabinet, supposedly the "political" Cabinet, met less frequently and exercised less power than the inner Cabinet did.

By mid-November, the Prime Minister was overwhelmed with work. His office staff resolved to use the Christmas break to examine an improved allocation of his time. Once Trudeau resigned on November 21, the Government breathed a collective sigh of relief. Clark issued instructions to bring Parliament back in early January for a session packed with new legislation, the preparation of which further burdened his hard-pressed ministers. The Government cruised towards the Christmas recess like a doomed ocean liner, all hands busy with appointed tasks, so confident of safe passage that no one took note of the emerging peril.

One floor below Clark's office in the Langevin Block, across Wellington Street from Parliament, a cheerful, fifty-three-year-old woman sat in her rocking chair surrounded by antique furniture, jars and boxes of cookies, and her own collection of porcelain pigs. She smiled so often and extended such understanding to those with problems that she looked like everyone's favourite aunt.

Jean Pigott was impossible to dislike. When Pigott's defeat

was announced on election night May 22, 1979, Joe Clark's wife, Maureen McTeer, cried. Many Conservative M.P.s were equally saddened. Pigott had not been an effective housing critic after her election to the Commons in a 1976 by-election, but her glowing personality was much appreciated in the Conservative caucus. After her defeat in the 1979 election, Pigott could have had any public service position that was within Clark's power to give, but such an appointment might have blocked her return to electoral politics. So she joined Clark's staff to act as a liaison between the leader's office and the Conservative caucus and interest groups. More importantly, Pigott was Clark's principal advisor on patronage. She had apparent qualifications for the job: popularity within the party, business experience, and Clark's trust. But when the Conservatives were defeated, party members across Canada were angry with Pigott and a perplexed Clark remarked: "One of the things we didn't do well was appointments. . . . It's astonishing to me."

When the Conservatives finally got their hands on the faucets of federal patronage after sixteen years in Opposition, rank-and-file Conservatives wanted the Government to crank open the taps. After all, the Liberals had used patronage shamelessly, spoiling exemplary appointments by handing jobs to party hacks, ineffective M.P.s, burned-out Cabinet ministers, and Liberal bagmen. Finally, the Conservatives had a chance to reward their own faithful; but instead of a torrent of appointments, the Conservative Government produced only a dribble.

A handful of Conservative lawyers were appointed to the bench, and Conservative lawyers and advertising firms replaced their Liberal counterparts. Ralph Stewart, an undistinguished Liberal M.P. who crossed the floor to join the Conservatives two weeks before the 1979 election was called (only to lose the Conservative nomination in his northern Ontario riding), hung around the Prime Minister's office for a few months after the election, until he received his payoff as Canadian counsul in Atlanta. Hugh Horner, a former Conservative M.P. and party leader in Alberta, was named grain transportation co-ordinator. Jean Casselman Wadds, a Conservative M.P. from 1958 to 1968 and national secretary of the Conservative Party from 1971 to 1975, replaced Paul Martin as Canadian High Commissioner to Great Britain. Mr. Justice Julien Chouinard of the Quebec Court of Appeal, Conservative candidate in the 1968 election, was appointed to the Supreme Court of Canada.

Eight Conservatives, including Murray, were appointed to

the Senate (each receiving with the appointment a $28,700 salary and a tax-free expense allowance of $6,200)—Richard Donahoe, a former attorney general of Nova Scotia; Guy Charbonneau, vice-chairman of the P.C. Canada Fund and Quebec Conservative finance chairman; James Balfour, a former Conservative M.P. for Regina East and head of Clark's transition team; William Doody, a Conservative warhorse from the Newfoundland legislature who was defeated by Brian Peckford for the Newfoundland party leadership in March 1979; Nathan Nurgitz, national president of the Conservative Party from 1970 to 1971 and Conservative campaign chairman for Manitoba in the elections of 1972, 1974, and 1979; Cyril Sherwood, former Conservative leader in New Brunswick; and Heath MacQuarrie, a twenty-two-year veteran of the House of Commons from Prince Edward Island. For a party that hoped for more, these appointments represented insufficient fare, but the flap caused by the summoning of MacQuarrie to the Senate offered a hint about why appointments came slowly.

Heath MacQuarrie held a strong claim for the Senate if the Conservatives ever took power. He had been M.P. for Queen's since 1957, defending the seat until his retirement in 1979 with the tenacity of a Scottish soldier protecting the Highland passes. MacQuarrie had wanted a Senate seat while still an M.P., but the Liberals appointed a Conservative M.P. to the Senate only if they thought his seat could be won in the ensuing by-election.

Despite MacQuarrie's excellent claim, tradition demanded that there be Prince Edward Island senators from both Catholic and Protestant communities on the island. Three Prince Edward Island senators were Protestants. When rumours began circulating that MacQuarrie, a Presbyterian, was going to get Prince Edward Island's fourth seat, Catholics on the island mounted a strong lobbying campaign for one of their own: Leo Rossiter, the garrulous Minister of Fisheries and the dean of the provincial legislature, first elected in 1955. Rossiter was an obstreperous man, and Conservative Premier Angus MacLean would not have been sorry to see Rossiter leave the provincial Cabinet. Nor was any love lost between MacLean and MacQuarrie, long-time rivals as M.P.s for supremacy among federal Conservatives in Prince Edward Island. Even the Catholic bishop got behind Rossiter's campaign, contacting Pigott and other Conservatives in Ottawa to plead the case for a Catholic.

Clark, Pigott, and Secretary of State David MacDonald, Prince Edward Island's representative in the Cabinet, were determined to reward MacQuarrie, whose legislative experience the outnumbered Conservatives needed in the Senate. After weeks of considering the problem, the trio hit on a solution. To mollify the bishop and others pressing for a Catholic senator, the Conservatives decided to appoint Dr. Joseph Doiron, a Catholic, as lieutenant-governor. The selection of Doiron, a dentist and MacDonald's riding president, placated some Catholics, but the squabble surrounding MacQuarrie's appointment to the Senate showed the Conservatives how prickly feelings could be where patronage was involved.

So hungry were Conservatives for a taste of patronage that Clark made himself unpopular when he offered appointments to persons not identified with the Conservative Party. The Conservative caucus was extremely upset when Clark, after six weeks of deliberation, appointed John Meisel as chairman of the Canadian Radio-Television and Telecommunications Commission. Meisel, a professor of political science at Queen's University, was regarded as an egghead by some Conservative M.P.s. He knew little about the practical side of the communications business. Most importantly, Meisel had never been a Conservative or publicly supported Conservative causes. Meisel came recommended by Flora MacDonald and David MacDonald and he fit perfectly with Clark's wish to bring talented people into the senior civil service, but this did not cool the passions that Meisel's appointment aroused in the Conservative caucus.

The angriest reaction, however, greeted Clark's appointment of Arthur Tremblay as senator from Quebec. Tremblay had a distinguished career in the Quebec civil service; he was Deputy Minister of Education in the early days of the Quiet Revolution and Deputy Minister of Intergovernmental Affairs from 1971 to 1977, when he retired to teach at Laval University. No one in Canada was more conversant with federal-provincial relations, and few knew Quebec better. For a party scorned by the political and cultural elites of Quebec, the Conservatives pulled off a masterstroke in persuading Tremblay to join their ranks.

That was not the way Tremblay's appointment appeared to the bagmen and militants who had worked so hard to plant the seeds of the Conservative Party in the inhospitable soil of Quebec. Two days before Tremblay's appointment was made public, word of it spread through a reception for Conservative supporters that Clark was attending in Quebec City. Angry that one of their own would not be appointed, the militants buzzed around Clark,

Murray, and national-party director Paul Curley like blackflies in May, extracting their ounces of flesh for the outrage of Tremblay's appointment.

Of special concern to the Conservative rank-and-file were Liberals whom Trudeau had deposited in government jobs. If the Conservative caucus had been granted its wish, most of the Liberals would have been fired shortly after the change of government, but Clark resisted this kind of pressure, except in the case of Bryce Mackasey. Of all Trudeau's patronage appointments, the selection of Mackasey as chairman of Air Canada was the most offensive to the Conservatives. Mackasey, a loquacious and often blubbering politician, had resigned from the Liberal Cabinet to contest the 1976 Quebec provincial election. During and after that election, he ranted so incessantly about the separatist menace that his credibility was eroded everywhere in Quebec, including within the provincial Liberal Party. Ostracized by the party leadership from a position of authority, Mackasey resigned his seat in the National Assembly and began looking for a riding from which to return to federal politics. The Ottawa Centre Liberals, desperate for a presentable candidate, selected Mackasey as a candidate in the October 1978 by-election, in which he finished a disappointing third. Mackasey was by then a burned-out case, a tragic but altogether too familiar example of a man clinging to politics for the lack of anything better to do. Since length of service to the Liberal Party rather than talent was often the depressing criterion for patronage appointments, Mackasey was made chairman of Air Canada, at a salary that the Conservatives claimed was $90,000 a year. His appointment was an affront to the Conservatives and to the whole system of government appointments, and Clark, under intense pressure from his own party, fired him.

The Government's dilatoriness in making appointments, however, related more to the method the Conservatives designed for handling the problem than to the inevitable political controversies surrounding patronage. The Liberals, old pros at the patronage game, left behind a system the Conservatives tried to broaden. The Liberals' system rested on the selection of a "political" minister for each province, who recommended to the Prime Minister's office appointments, which Jim Coutts sifted through.

The Conservatives kept the same system by designating political ministers for each province: David MacDonald for Prince Edward Island, Robert Howie for New Brunswick, Elmer MacKay for Nova Scotia, Roch LaSalle for Quebec, Jake Epp for Manitoba,

Ray Hnatyshyn for Saskatchewan, Don Mazankowski for Alberta, and John Fraser for British Columbia. Ontario was so big that the province was split between Ron Atkey, responsible for Metropolitan Toronto, and William Jarvis for the rest of the province. In Newfoundland, neither John Crosbie nor Fisheries Minister James McGrath could bear seeing the other get the plum job, so both were made political ministers for Newfoundland.

The political ministers were responsible for liaison with provincial parties as well as for recommendation of appointments, a job that could take up a quarter of a minister's time. Most of the political ministers designated a staff member to assist them with these responsibilities, and some established committees of local Conservatives to search out talent and screen applications. For example, Atkey's committee of Toronto Conservatives included William Saunderson, the Ontario campaign chairman; lawyers Jeffery Lyons, Allan Blott, and Gordon Sedgwick; and businessmen Irving Gerstein and Hal Jackman. Prominent Conservative lawyers such as Richard Bell of Ottawa and Eddie Goodman of Toronto were consulted on judicial appointments in Ontario.

The ministers, their staffs, and local committees worked from the "yellow books" prepared in Jean Pigott's office. The Conservatives were surprised when they took power that no summary existed of the hundreds of part- and full-time order-in-council appointments. Pigott ordered that the information be compiled and put in binders with yellow covers, listing every appointed position, the salary or stipend attached to the position, and the expiry date of the incumbent's term of office. The positions in the yellow books were then matched against a computerized talent bank developed by Pigott. Within a month of the election, the Government was deluged with more than 5,000 job applications. To these were added recommendations from M.P.s and party officials.

In theory, the system should have worked as follows. If the yellow books showed that, say, a new director from Newfoundland was needed for the Canadian Saltfish Corporation ($100 per day plus travelling expenses), Pigott could search in her computer and find qualified applicants from Newfoundland. She would then alert the political ministers for Newfoundland. The ministers or their staffs would consult the provincial government, Newfoundland Conservatives, and members of Newfoundland's fishing industry and add recommendations to those culled from Pigott's talent bank. Important appointments were then screened by a committee that included Pigott, Lowell Murray, and William Neville before a recommendation, or a short list, was passed on to Clark.

The system was laudably designed. It was based on the premise that the Liberals had acted too haphazardly and made too many egregious appointments. If the Conservatives had been longer in power, the system would certainly have produced the quantity of appointments desired by the Conservative rank-and-file and, perhaps, higher-quality appointments than those made by the Liberals. But in the early stages, the system was plagued by bottlenecks. It took three months to get the yellow books together, and that retarded the operation of the system.* The avalanche of applications delayed the creation of a talent bank. Those ministers, such as Secretary of State David MacDonald, who had a large number of boards and agencies attached to their departments were too busy with other matters to focus on appointments. The Conservatives had also pledged to consult extensively with provincial governments—a concern seldom shown by the Liberals, since few provincial Liberal parties were in power—and this consultation slowed up the appointments.

Believing they would be in power for at least eighteen months, the Conservatives waited for their system to be fully in place before cranking out the appointments. The day after the Government fell, Clark and Pigott met to consider about 150 appointments, half of which required only Clark's signature to become official. Other prime ministers had made appointments after the issuing of election writs, and Clark was still Prime Minister of Canada. But he told Pigott that his Government had been defeated in the Commons and lacked the moral authority to make any more appointments. It was a noble gesture, but it left plenty of bad feeling in a party that had anticipated loaves and fishes and had received only crumbs.

These men and women of the Conservative Government—Prime Minister, advisors, ministers—operated under a set of assumptions that were fatally in error. Some of the assumptions were articulated by Clark and his ministers; others were taken for granted.

The perception that time was the Government's ally rather than its foe, as events subsequently demonstrated, was the most dramatically erroneous assumption. The Conservatives did not

*Once returned to power, the Liberals refused to make the yellow books public.

believe that the other parties would dare to overturn the Government within at least the first eighteen months, and probably not before twenty-four months had passed. The Conservatives were convinced, without ever discussing the matter in depth, that the Liberals had destroyed themselves by playing politics in the eighteen months preceding the 1979 election. The electorate was tired of politics and wanted a stretch of vigorous governing. That meant that the Conservatives did not have to budge from their campaign commitments; the other parties would have to adapt themselves to the election result. This inflexible position—putting the onus on the Opposition parties to compromise—set the tone for the entire performance of the Clark Government. Clark made the point clearly on the day after the election.

> I think that in the circumstances like this, where we are so very close to a majority Government, it will be in the interests of the other parties in Parliament to support sensible measures that we put forward. My program is clear. We intend to act on that program and the decision as to the response of other parties—the Liberals, the NDP, the Créditistes—will rest with the leaders and the members of those parties. But I am making very clear now my intention to carry the program for which we have a mandate, and I would expect, *looking back at the history of these things*, that the other parties will first of all find it in their interest and secondly to consider it to be fair, to give a new government the opportunity to govern.

The key phrase in Clark's statement was "looking back at the history of these things." Joe Clark clearly had in his mind the experience of John Diefenbaker in the elections of 1957 and 1958. Elected in 1957 with a thinner minority than Clark had won, Diefenbaker dissolved Parliament nine months later and won the biggest landslide in Canadian political history: 208 seats, compared to forty-eight for the Liberals. While Clark never dreamed of winning 208 seats, he did think the election of 1979 was the first of two steps that would give the Conservatives a majority government. He preferred to govern for several years with his minority Government, but believed that if the Opposition parties plunged the country into an election, the Conservatives would complete the knockout that they nearly recorded in the May 1979 election. In a television interview during the campaign, Clark showed that the Diefenbaker precedent was in his mind.

I think there is a very classic lesson in what Mr. Diefenbaker was able to do. He was able to bring in his program,
not make modifications, not make concessions, not be
held up for ransom by minority parties. It was a very
effective and creative time in government. He went on to
call an election that won an overwhelming majority. But
that was in a different time and I think that what the
primary obligation upon whoever is Prime Minister after
the 22nd [of May]—whether majority or minority—is
going to be to restore some sense of stability and certainty and calm. . . . If we had to go through the next two
years [with] the kind of atmosphere that pervaded the
Parliament in the last two years—when you didn't know
from day to day whether an election was going to be
called—nothing would get done.

Joe Clark, however, forgot Diefenbaker's course of action after his
minority win in 1957 to set the stage for his 1958 landslide.
Shortly after his election, Diefenbaker attended the Commonwealth Conference in London, where he was an instant hit with
his vigorous affirmations of faith in the Commonwealth. Upon his
return to Canada, Diefenbaker spent thirty-seven of the next
sixty days travelling around the country, his flair and presence
confirming the excitement that greeted his astonishing victory.
While Diefenbaker paraded across Canada, his Cabinet was busy
in Ottawa making announcements of popular new policies, and
the level of activity quickened appreciably when Parliament
convened. Parliament was inundated with legislation, so that
"when the House adjourned for Christmas, there was a well-
justified feeling in the nation that the Conservative Government
had lived up to its promises."* Five weeks after the House rose for
Christmas, Diefenbaker dissolved Parliament for the 1958 election.

When Joe Clark sought re-election, Parliament had adopted
six bills: three financial measures left over from the Liberal
Government; one bill authorizing postal rate changes; another
changing tariff schedules in trade treaties with New Zealand,
Australia, and South Africa; and a bill widening the eligibility for
spouses' allowances. This was hardly a record on which re-elections
are made.

---

*For further details, see Peter Newman, *Renegade in Power* (McClelland and
Stewart, 1963), pgs. 60-65.

And yet the Conservatives never expected to have to face another election on that record alone. When Trudeau resigned, they reasoned that the Liberals would be preoccupied with their leadership contest. The Government prepared a lengthy list of legislative measures for the post-Christmas period, figuring that once the Liberals chose a new leader they would press for an early election and the Government would need a substantial legislative record for a spring or fall campaign. The list of legislation and proposed policy initiatives included: a meat import law, a telecommunications act, and privacy legislation restricting access to social insurance numbers; amendments to the Indian Act removing sections discriminating against Indian women; "sunset" laws, an expanded youth employment program, and further de-regulation of Canada's air travel industry; federal-provincial conferences on women's issues and a shelter allowance program; and publication of policy papers on fisheries, non-medical use of drugs, and pensions.

The Conservatives did face two inescapable impediments to faster action after they took power. The first was the backlog of bills left over from the Liberal Government. The second was the foreign travel Clark was required to undertake: to Tokyo for the economic summit and to Lusaka for the Commonwealth Conference. Saddled with a poor reputation in foreign affairs after his Jerusalem-embassy promise and his world trip as Opposition leader, Clark spent an inordinate amount of time preparing for these international conferences.

In the months following their election, the Conservatives were forced to confront many of the disciplines of power: shaping policy according to changed circumstances, establishing a healthy working relationship with the civil service, listening to the voices of organized interest groups, learning how to judge today's decisions by the measure of a longer time-frame, moving swiftly to take advantage of an adversary's temporary weakness. The Conservatives were slowly and often painfully learning to master some of these practices but they still had a long way to go when they were defeated.

Clark, Neville, Murray, Gillies, and some ministers believed that the Conservatives had been given a mandate to change the fundamental direction of the country. They convinced themselves that the Liberals had been punished for abandoning principles and governing by expediency. The electorate desired change, and the Conservatives must deliver that change or face defeat. In August, when the Conservatives discovered that the Government had not experienced a honeymoon period, Clark and his advisors concluded that the public was dismayed that the party had not fulfilled its election commitments. A wiser analysis would have concluded that the public was dismayed with some of the promises themselves, not their failure to be implemented.

It was so seductive and comforting, after sixteen years in Opposition, to believe that the electorate had finally embraced the Conservative Party. For men and women who had stood in the Commons day after day, month after month, year after year, warning the nation of the ruinous course charted by the Liberals, the election of 1979 was blissful vindication for all their backbreaking labour. They were like marathon swimmers who, having finally reached the other side of the lake, collapsed in sweet ecstasy, forgetting the chill of the air until just before they were frozen stiff.

The Conservatives shared a naive belief approaching fantasy that the election of 1979 heralded the beginning of a new era in Canadian politics in which conservative causes would be in the ascendancy. In the United States and Great Britain, electorates seemed to be rejecting the solutions of liberalism and social democracy, with their heavy reliance upon state intervention to solve social and economic problems. In Canada, the Conservative Party had toppled Liberal and NDP Governments in Manitoba, Newfoundland, Prince Edward Island, and Nova Scotia. The Conservative Party in Saskatchewan was growing stronger at the expense of the Liberals. The federal Conservatives, therefore, saw their own election as part of a wider political trend, rooted in disillusionment with the state's failure to cure social and economic ills. There was also a conviction that the electorate hungered for something more than the incrementalism of the Liberals. Fundamental changes—"real change" as the Conservatives put it later—were required for the country and desired by the electorate.

In fact, the Conservatives were given a tentative mandate based on the electorate's desire to change the Government, which was not necessarily synonymous with fundamental change in the direction of the country. That mandate grew weaker, as Allan Gregg explained in his post-election memorandum, once the electorate had registered its protest vote against the Liberals. The Conservatives received 36 per cent of the popular vote in the election, but half of it was unreliable; it needed constant reinforcement. To keep the allegiance of the Liberals and New Democrats who had left their natural political homes to support the Conservatives, the Government needed to offer measures attractive to these groups.

The Conservative Party has prospered in the past by reaching out to these groups with imaginative policies in which the state played an indispensable role. This belief in the utility of state intervention in the economy is an honourable part of the Conservative tradition in Canada and the prerequisite for a Conservative Government to sustain itself in power. The building of a transcontinental railway and radio network, the offering of a "vision" of northern Canada opened by government-built roads and public works projects, the creation of provincial hydro-electric companies, the establishment of publicly owned airlines—these, along with a reputation for fiscal prudence and political stability, are part of the Conservative political heritage in Canada. Privatization of PetroCanada, mortgage-interest and property-tax giveaways, cutbacks, and slogans such as "real change," "tough times," and "short-term pain for long-term gain" were all offensive to this Conservative tradition and disastrous politically for the Clark Government.

In the first two months in power, the Government's most visible minister was Sinclair Stevens. His message of slashing spending and selling off crown corporations was enormously satisfying to the Conservative rank-and-file, but it offered nothing to disaffected Liberals and New Democrats whose support was crucial for the Conservative Government's survival. Instead of directing every effort to consolidate its protest vote, the Government seemed determined to drive away the disaffected Liberals and New Democrats. Trapped in a misreading of their mandate and forgetful of all of the traditions of their party, the Conservatives stumbled back into Opposition.

~ 5 ~

Confronting the Mandarins

The Conservative Government and the federal bureaucracy greeted each other like partners on a blind date. Neither knew quite what to expect of the other, and they awaited the meeting with apprehension and excitement, determined at the very least to act correctly. Many of the senior civil servants had never before worked for a Conservative Government. Those who had served under Diefenbaker had done so at an earlier and less influential stage in their careers. On the other side only two M.P.s in Joe Clark's Cabinet had ministerial experience, and both of these men—John Crosbie and Allan Lawrence—had been provincial Cabinet ministers.

Naturally, both Conservative ministers and senior civil servants had formed a mental picture of each other before the Conservatives took office. Having served in Opposition for so long, the Conservatives were suspicious of the civil service. The mandarins' secrecy had frustrated the Conservatives' efforts to get information, and their advice had helped sustain in office the Conservatives' principal political foe. For its part, the civil service could not help but feel apprehensive after hearing rumours of a Conservative "hit list," as well as attacks by Conservative spokesmen on government inefficiency and waste. Clark also arrived in power promising freedom-of-information legislation, open government, and parliamentary reform. All of these causes challenged established procedures of the civil service, but were of absorbing interest to a party long out of power.

At first, relations between the two groups were tense because Clark and his advisors thought the civil service was merely protecting vested interests in policies that the Conservatives were committed to changing. The Conservatives could not distinguish between the motives they ascribed to those who provided the advice and the advice itself. Once the Government was hurt by ignoring the civil service's advice (on the Jerusalem-embassy issue, for example) or understood that a department was providing a better method of implementing Conservative promises than the party devised (as on mortgage deductibility and energy policy), the Government began to trust the civil service, judging its advice on merit rather than by imputation. As the Conservatives approached the election that returned the party to Opposition, they were learning how to co-exist with the civil service—one of the prerequisites of the successful exercise of power.

The civil service the Conservatives inherited had changed almost beyond recognition since the party was last in power in 1963. A compact set of institutions in the late 1950s and early 1960s, the civil service exploded in the late 1960s and 1970s into a sprawling network of departments, central agencies, and crown corporations that seemed to defy rational control. New departments and ministries of state—urban affairs, environment, regional and economic expansion, science and technology, multiculturalism—were created, and traditional departments saw their budgets tripled, then quadrupled and, in some cases, more than quintupled during the Trudeau years. The Indian Affairs Department's budget increased from $256 million in the fiscal year 1968 to 1969 to $1.2 billion in 1978 to 1979; Health and Welfare's budget grew from $1.6 billion to $13 billion in the same period; External Affairs' budget rose from $85 million to $307 million; Canada's foreign aid program grew from $142.5 million to $1 billion. In 1963, when John Diefenbaker fell from power, federal expenditures were $7.6 billion. When Trudeau arrived in 1968, they were $12.2 billion. When Joe Clark took office, federal expenditures had grown to more than $49 billion.

So busy was the civil service in administering new programs and collecting vast amounts of additional information before launching new programs that no one thought much about how efficiently money was being spent. In the heady days of the early 1970s, the Treasury Board seemed more like a sieve than an obstacle to new spending. The Cabinet itself opened wide the floodgates to new spending in the period 1973 to 1975, sweetening social programs and attempting to avoid a recession by a rapid increase in federal spending.

By the waning years of the Trudeau Government, however, the free-spending days were coming to an end, and "restraint" became the new catch-phrase in Ottawa. Many voters questioned the value of all this government expansion when inflation, unemployment, and income disparities remained stubbornly resistant to reduction. There were horror stories about abuses in unemployment insurance, the Local Initiatives Program, government contracts, and a host of other areas; and although these abuses represented but a tiny fraction of total government spending, the publicity soured an increasing number of citizens on government efficiency. In his report for the fiscal year ending March 31, 1976, Auditor General James Macdonell warned that "the Government has lost, or is close to losing, effective control of the public purse." In subsequent reports to Parliament, Macdonell introduced value-for-money auditing practices and charged that taxpayers were not receiving efficient services for their dollars. After a battle with Treasury Board President Robert Andras, Macdonell persuaded the Government to appoint a comptroller general to improve financial management within the federal government. Alarmed by the public outcry against government inefficiency and prodded by Macdonell, the Trudeau Government appointed a Royal Commission on Financial Accountability (the Lambert Commission) in November 1976 to study efficiency, productivity, and financial management in the federal government. In a damning indictment of 586 pages, delivered on the eve of the 1979 general election, the commission stated its "deeply held conviction that the serious malaise pervading the management of government stems fundamentally from a grave weakening, and in some cases an almost total breakdown, in the chain of accountability of government to Parliament and ultimately to the Canadian people." At the same time, the Government learned that overclassification of positions was rife in the civil service. A benchmark audit of 2,000 employees in the National Capital Commission area found that 16 per cent of federal government employees were working in overclassified positions while only 4 per cent were employed in underclassified jobs. Overclassification was worst among personnel officers, who were supposed to oversee the classification system on which were based the pay scales of the federal government.

The civil service was understandably jittery facing this avalanche of criticism from the public, the auditor general, and the royal commission. This unease was aggravated when the Trudeau Government began to restrain increases in spending: promotions were harder to obtain, departmental man-years were frozen or reduced, academic leaves were curtailed or cancelled, and program managers wondered if the axe might soon fall on their sections. In August 1978, Trudeau suddenly announced $2 billion in spending cuts. Trudeau's swift strike, born of his own frustration at the civil service's reluctance to respond to his request for money-saving ideas, shook up the civil service. If the Liberals, the party the civil service knew best, could flash a switchblade, who knew what havoc the Conservatives would wreak with the cleaver they carried into office.

The civil service's last experience with a Conservative Government had not been a happy one. Although only a minority of civil servants had worked for the Diefenbaker Government, stories of his legendary mistrust of the civil service had been recorded in books and passed by word of mouth from one group of civil servants to another. By all accounts, the civil service tried to provide Diefenbaker with professional, well-balanced advice, but the Prime Minister deeply suspected that the advice was tainted by the Liberal affiliations of many senior civil servants. In 1979 some of Diefenbaker's ministers were still kicking around in the Conservative caucus. They had lost some of their influence over the years, but civil servants could not help asking themselves if the Diefenbaker veterans were filling the ears of younger colleagues with twisted tales of twenty years ago.

Many of the Conservative backbenchers who entered politics from small businesses and farms in the 1979 election complained about excessive government regulation, government inefficiency, and "creeping socialism." Their rallying cry was the reduction in the scope of government in the lives of citizens and in the operation of the free market. In their campaigns, the M.P.s had railed against the civil service, blaming it for many of the nation's ills including inflation, declining productivity, slow economic growth, and excessively generous social assistance programs that discouraged individual initiative.

The cast of mind of the new Conservative M.P.s resembled that of experienced Conservative M.P.s, many of whom had been frustrated in their attempts to pry information or help out of the civil service. Although some of the civil service's information could be obtained by Opposition M.P.s, much of it was reserved for the Government, as was all of the policy analysis and advice that flowed from the information. The civil service was secretive by nature in a parliamentary system based on the principles of ministerial responsibility and Cabinet solidarity. It existed to serve the Government and to administer Government programs, not to provide the Opposition with useful ammunition with which to attack the Government. Civil servants could be called before parliamentary committees; but if the Conservatives pestered a civil servant with questions he did not wish to answer, Government M.P.s invariably rushed to the witness's defence, or the witness passed the question to the minister or his parliamentary secretary.

The Official Opposition's job is to make noise, to raise grievances, and air complaints; the civil service prefers to function discreetly. The Official Opposition's responsibility is also to criticize government policy, which civil servants shape and are sworn to uphold. As the Official Opposition, the Conservatives were more likely to converse with critics of Government policies than with the defenders of those policies, such as the civil service. Occasionally, an unmarked brown envelope would put a Conservative M.P. onto the scent of scandal or blunder; but this merely reinforced the civil service's belief that the Conservatives were a troublesome, rambunctious lot more interested in publicity than effective governing.

The Conservatives' suspicion of the civil service was deepened just by glancing across the aisle of the House of Commons. There sat a party that had worked smoothly with the civil service for sixteen years. It was easy for the Conservatives to reason that the friend of their political enemy could not be trusted. The Liberal Party had a history of attracting men to politics who had worked for the civil service: Lester Pearson, Walter Gordon, Jack Pickersgill, Mitchell Sharp, C. M. (Bud) Drury, John Roberts. More than this, Liberal Cabinets under Trudeau were invariably stuffed with men so lacking in public passion that they looked and sounded like colourless civil servants: Tony Abbott, Ron Basford, Jack Davis, Alastair Gillespie, George McIlraith, Martin O'Connell, Robert Stanbury.

Worst of all from the Conservatives' perspective, Trudeau had deposited former Liberal Cabinet ministers and political aides throughout the civil service. Edgar Benson, a former finance minister, was chairman of the Canadian Transport Commission. Bryce Mackasey, who held four portfolios under Trudeau, was flying high as chairman of Air Canada. Pierre Juneau, a former advisor to Trudeau who served briefly as Minister of Communications before his defeat as a Liberal candidate in the Hochelaga by-election of 1975, was Undersecretary of State. Bud Drury held down two jobs: special representative on constitutional development in the Northwest Territories and chairman of the National Capital Commission. Mitchell Sharp, another former finance minister, was commissioner of the Northern Pipeline Agency. Gérard Pelletier, one of Trudeau's closest friends and a former Minister of Communications, was Canadian ambassador to France. Paul Martin, another long-time Liberal minister, was Canadian High Commissioner in London. Lucien Cardin, a Minister of Justice under Pearson, was chairman of the Tax Review Board. Liberal M.P.s who missed the Cabinet or a Senate sinecure were scattered throughout the civil service and the diplomatic corps. In short, if you were a Liberal who wanted to stay on the public payroll, Trudeau found a spot for you somewhere.

Trudeau also promoted friends or civil servants whose style he admired. The most obvious example was Michael Pitfield, a close friend of Trudeau's who was made Clerk of the Privy Council in 1975, replacing Gordon Robertson, one of Ottawa's longest-serving civil servants. Others in Trudeau's charmed circle included Bernard Ostry, Deputy Minister of Communications; his wife Sylvia, chairman of the Economic Council of Canada; de Montigny Marchand, deputy secretary to the Cabinet for operations; Allan Gotlieb, undersecretary of state for external affairs; Ian Stewart, Deputy Minister of Energy and a former economic policy advisor to Trudeau.

The civil service became more politicized under Trudeau than it had ever been before. Trudeau's own strong personality—as well as his determination to ensure that politicians, not civil servants, made policy—led him to strengthen his own office and the Privy Council office, so that they became the most powerful nerve centres of government. The strengthening of these agencies, combined with the appointment of Trudeau's friends and former Liberal politicians, upset the Conservatives, who observed these changes helplessly from the Opposition. It was no wonder, then, that Conservative backbenchers talked about making heads roll when the party took power; nor was it surprising that such talk made the civil service even more skittish.

The mandarins could not have been reassured when they read what Joe Clark said about the civil service as a backbencher, leadership candidate, and leader of the Opposition. Although his sharpest criticisms were reserved for the "excessive power" wielded by the Prime Minister's office and the Privy Council under Michael Pitfield, Clark's complaints reflected more widespread Conservative fears about the civil service. Clark said in a statement on "political structures" issued to delegates at the 1976 Conservative leadership convention:

> The great majority of Canadian public servants are dedicated professionals who will honour their oath to serve whatever Government is elected. Some, however, have spent their lives constructing programs our Government will want to change; others have political backgrounds which will lead them to oppose or obstruct Progressive Conservative reforms.
>
> The late Richard Crossman, a leading minister in the first Wilson Labour Government, once said: "We have a non-partisan public service, but in Britain non-partisan means Tory." After four decades of virtual one-party rule in Canada, we have a similar problem and [we] will have to balance the traditional public service with some excellent people who share our goals of reform.
>
> Ideally, we should have extensive interchanges of senior executives among federal, provincial and municipal governments, business, unions and other institutions to avoid tunnel vision. In any event, federal public servants should spend more time "under fire" from the people their policies affect so they might understand the society they govern.

In the 1979 campaign, the Conservatives portrayed themselves as the friend of taxpayers who were beleaguered by the frustration of dealing with Big Government. Early in the campaign, Clark told an audience in Cranbrook, British Columbia, many of whom had probably never heard of the report, that the Conservatives accepted the recommendations of the Lambert Royal Commission. He pledged to introduce "sunset laws," which would ensure that existing programs would not automatically continue without a periodic review of their usefulness by Parliament. He promised tighter government control over crown corporations, which he delighted in saying had become so numerous that the Liberal Government had lost count of them. But of greatest concern to the civil service was the Conservatives' promise to reduce the size of the civil service by 60,000 people over three years. Conservative spokesmen, especially in Ottawa ridings where the promise smelled like political death, repeatedly assured the civil service that their jobs would be secure because the reduction would come through attrition. But many civil servants who pondered the possibility of Sinclair Stevens becoming President of the Treasury Board or Minister of Finance agreed with John Smart, NDP candidate in Ottawa Centre: "Civil servants who vote for the Conservatives are like chickens who vote for Colonel Sanders."

Two factors, however, offered room for optimism that the Conservatives and the civil service could co-exist profitably and come to trust each other's competence.

The first reflected the professionalism of the civil service. Change, although upsetting to any bureaucracy, can also be stimulating and even exciting. After working with the Liberals for sixteen years, the civil service would be forced by the Conservatives to re-examine old problems, test different solutions, and tackle new priorities. Clearly, this reassessment would be difficult for civil servants who accepted the wisdom of established programs and feared for their own careers. But the change of Government offered many civil servants a chance to demonstrate their professionalism by serving the new Government with efficiency and loyalty. No one better exemplified this sense of professionalism than Michael Pitfield, who, despite his friendship with Trudeau, was passionately committed to the idea of a non-partisan, highly motivated civil service capable of serving whichever political party formed the Government. Pitfield, more than anyone else, ensured that the civil service worked hard to prepare itself for the transition and to give the new Government every conceivable assistance when it took office. Although he wanted to remain Clerk of the Privy Council, he sensed his fate and selflessly moved his probable successor into a key position in the Privy Council hierarchy a month before the election.

The second factor reflected Joe Clark's study of the Diefenbaker Government. In his Master's thesis, Clark had written about "the oppositionist cast of mind of Mr. Diefenbaker," and he was determined not to repeat his predecessor's error of treating the civil service with undisguised suspicion. Clark certainly harboured doubts about the civil service's biases, but he wanted to keep those thoughts to himself and instead to reassure the civil service that his Government wanted and needed its help. If he could allay the mandarins' fears about a Conservative purge of senior officials, he could win the civil service's confidence and invite understanding for the changes he wished to make.

A week after taking office, Clark summoned the deputy ministers to a meeting at which he insisted that his Government did not have a "hit list" in its pocket of civil servants. He said the Government harboured no ill will towards the civil service. Any changes in personnel would be made with compassion and fairness. Clark's speech impressed the deputy ministers by its precision and tone. It struck them as a reasonable position for a new Prime Minister: Clark was not trying to fool them into believing that all of their jobs were secure, but this necessary uncertainty was eased by his promise of considerate treatment.

The meeting was important because Clark's first act as Prime Minister was to sack Michael Pitfield, the highest-ranking civil servant in the land. Pitfield knew from Clark's speeches that his fate was probably sealed if the Conservatives took power, but he retained a glimmer of hope that he could stay if he demonstrated his loyalty during the transition period. Pitfield flew to Jasper, where Clark and his advisors retreated after the election, to brief the new Prime Minister on the transition of power, but the thoroughness of his presentations could not erase his past friendship and loyalty to Trudeau. His own appointment had politicized the Clerk's job, and Pitfield suffered the inevitable consequences when Clark asked for his resignation during a two-hour meeting at Jasper. A week later, Pitfield discharged his last responsibility as Clerk of the Privy Council, swearing in the new Conservative Cabinet like a prisoner cleaning the rifles of his firing squad. The next day, Pitfield broke down in tears when he bade farewell to his colleagues in the Privy Council.

Pitfield, however, rendered Clark an important service a month before the election without Clark's even knowing. He correctly surmised that his replacement might be Marcel Massé, deputy secretary to the Cabinet for federal-provincial relations. As a result, Pitfield quietly shifted Massé to another position— deputy secretary to the Cabinet for operations—where Massé could better familiarize himself with the functioning of the civil service.

Weeks before taking power, Clark's advisors and his transition team began thinking about Pitfield's replacement. The Clerk's job is of critical importance: he is the principal advisor to the Cabinet, the funnel through which passes much of the sensitive information to the Prime Minister, the key liaison between the Cabinet and the civil service. The more Clark and his advisors considered the problem of Pitfield's replacement, the more obvious Marcel

Massé's appointment became. He was a French Canadian, and Clark wanted to demonstrate that his Government was hospitable to French-speaking Quebeckers despite his party's abysmal electoral showing in Quebec. Massé was undeniably bright, with a curriculum vitae loaded with university degrees and practical qualifications, all obtained by the age of thirty-eight. He also came recommended by two important Conservatives: New Brunswick Premier Richard Hatfield and Lowell Murray, the Conservatives' campaign chairman.

Massé's appointment was a spectacular success; it was the best appointment the Clark Government made in seven months in power. In one move, Clark reassured French-speaking civil servants of his good-will, showed the civil service that he valued talent, and gave his Cabinet an outstanding source of advice.

At first glance, Massé did not look like the prototype Clerk. He often dressed carelessly, as if he were stricken with an obscure eye disease each morning when matching tie and suit. At thirty-eight, he was prematurely bald and overweight. He was unfailingly polite, never putting on airs to suit his lofty position. Those who bantered with him would never have suspected that he possessed a steely determination that once sent him hiking in the Himalayas, although he had never before climbed a mountain, and steered him to McGill, although he did not speak English when he applied.

Massé may have looked a trifle dishevelled, but his mind operated like a finely tuned instrument, a reflection of his brilliant academic career, which included a Rhodes Scholarship. He went on to work for four years at the World Bank before accepting a job with the Privy Council in Ottawa. That job did not last long, because Premier Richard Hatfield got wind of his reputation and invited him to become New Brunswick's deputy minister of finance and then secretary to the provincial Cabinet. Lowell Murray was Hatfield's executive assistant and chief political aide, and Murray and Massé ran the daily business of New Brunswick while the erratic premier flitted to New York, Montreal, Morocco, Senegal, and other places far removed from Fredericton. Massé left New Brunswick in August 1977 to return to the Privy Council, but Lowell Murray did not forget the admiration he felt for his friend. When Joe Clark became Prime Minister of Canada, Murray pressed Massé's name on the young Prime Minister.

Massé's approach to problems was like that of an accomplished chess player. He always thought three or four moves ahead, balancing short-term tactics against long-term strategy. He tried to understand completely the other parties to a dispute in order to anticipate their probable responses. In this way he came to appreciate politicians, who are often motivated more by emotion than by fact. Although he was careful to allow Hatfield and Clark to make "political decisions," his advice was tailored to the political factors weighing on their minds. It was rooted in fact but sensitive to the special needs of the politicians he served. In other words, he had learned the golden rule of influence in the civil service.

This method of analysing problems sprang from his intellectual training and his experience in federal-provincial relations, Canada's own exhausting domestic diplomacy. Making progress in federal-provincial relations requires, at the very least, a sophisticated understanding of the motivations of the other ten governments in Canada. This understanding can only come through extensive consultation, as players probe for compromise. Before any federal-provincial meeting, Massé analysed the other actors as carefully as Bismark sized up the Great Powers of Europe. Occasionally frustrated, Massé was never surprised. Massé did not share the belief widely held in the federal civil service that "consultation" meant informing provincial governments of impending federal initiatives. Having worked in New Brunswick, he thought "consultation" required Ottawa to shape its initiatives in concert with the provinces. He had been instrumental in persuading the federal government under Trudeau to convene a federal-provincial conference on the economy at which the two levels of government committed themselves to targets for civil service renumeration and growth. The conference did not produce the degree of federal-provincial co-ordination in economic policy Massé sought, but it was a first step along a road Massé thought was inevitable. In this, he fell out with the finance department, which was inclined to look disdainfully at other federal departments let alone provincial governments, and with mandarins like Gordon Robertson, who saw the federal government shackled like a medieval French king. After several years in Ottawa, Massé became more sceptical of the clamorous self-interest of provincial governments, but his general view blended perfectly with Clark's vague notion of "community of communities."

Massé wielded even more power than Pitfield as Clerk of the Privy Council, because he was serving a Prime Minister who did not know the civil service. But Massé himself was not as intimately familiar with the civil service as either Pitfield or Robertson. As a new boy in the most powerful civil service job, Massé needed to

130 / Discipline of Power

convince the civil service that he was their friend in the councils of the Prime Minister. For his own purposes, therefore, Massé wanted as much stability in the civil service as possible and urged moderation on Clark every time Gillies, Murray, or Conservative backbenchers sought the sacrificial blood of civil servants. But Massé could not bow to civil service pressure to tell Clark that some of his election promises were foolish or unworkable. Massé, who did not know Clark well, could hardly win the Prime Minister's complete confidence if he lined up with the civil service's complaints about some of the promises. His counsel on fulfilling promises was always restrained and subtle.

At Joe Clark's first Cabinet meeting, he instructed his ministers to provide him within six weeks with a report on their deputy ministers, since the appointment of deputy ministers is a prime ministerial prerogative. In early August, he sat down with each of his ministers in turn and discussed their reports, beginning a month-long review that culminated in changing seven deputy ministers, six of whom came from within the civil service.

The new deputy minister recruited from outside the civil service was Grant Reuber, who replaced William Hood at the finance department. Hood's dismissal sent shock waves through the civil service. To an outsider, Hood looked like a dull civil servant: grey suit, striped tie, cautious language, inexperienced in the private sector, an economic theorist who knew about all the numbers except those below the bottom line. Within the civil service, however, Hood was considered a model bureaucrat: dedicated to public service, experienced, loyal. He had spent nine years as assistant and associate deputy minister of finance before becoming deputy minister six weeks before the election campaign that brought the Conservatives to power. Colleagues in the senior bureaucracy had applauded his appointment.

Suddenly the Clark Government confirmed the civil service's worst fears by firing William Hood. If the Conservatives could treat a discreet bureaucrat like Hood this way, what would prevent them from firing civil servants more clearly identified with the previous government? Several weeks of soothing talk from Clark and Massé were needed to calm fears created by Hood's dismissal. And when the next round of changes came, it amounted to little more than a game of musical chairs; those shifted were given senior positions in the bureaucracy.

Hood, unlike the other deputy ministers, was done in by politics and by his own performance. Long before the election, Clark, Gillies, and Neville assumed that the Department of Finance needed a complete overhaul in personnel. Convinced that the Liberals' policies had been ruinous, the Conservatives assumed that the fault lay, at least partially, with those who had been offering economic advice to the Liberals. Gillies and Neville eventually wanted to make changes in personnel reaching two or three ranks down in the department, but the deputy minister's office was a good place to start. Clark himself, who barely knew Hood, had pledged to bring fresh blood into the bureaucracy. Thus, when the Conservatives took office, the noose was already lowered around William Hood's neck, and he unknowingly tightened the cord in his first two presentations to the new Government.

Shortly after the Conservatives took office, Hood delivered to the Cabinet a *tour d'horizon* of the country's economic outlook and the government's financial position. Not only did the Conservatives dislike the sombre economic music, but they were unimpressed with the performance of the piano player. Hood groped for some of his answers and struck some ministers as ill-prepared. Whether or not they were reading their own biases into Hood's performance, many ministers emerged thinking Hood had not been as impressive as Ian Stewart, the Deputy Minister of Energy, who presented a similar briefing on energy.

Shortly thereafter, Hood delivered to Clark a paper on mortgage-interest and property-tax deductibility that politely but firmly told the new Prime Minister that the idea was economically regressive. The paper had been requested by Crosbie, and it helpfully sketched several alternatives to deductibility. The problem was that Clark, Neville, and Gillies were not looking for alternatives; they had just won an election on a platform they believed the country had supported.

Hood's only defender in the Cabinet and the Prime Minister's office was Crosbie. Crosbie had not been instrumental in developing the Conservatives' economic policies in Opposition; he frankly disagreed with most of them. Crosbie had worked with civil servants in five portfolios in the Newfoundland Government, and he believed that strong ministers had nothing to fear from civil servants. Crosbie told Clark that William Hood should stay. But the appointment of deputy ministers is a prime ministerial prerogative; Crosbie registered his objection, shrugged his shoulders, and watched Hood depart.*

While John Crosbie was putting up an indifferent fight to keep his deputy minister, Flora MacDonald was struggling fiercely to get rid of Allan Gotlieb, her undersecretary of state for external affairs. MacDonald's and Gotlieb's personalities met like metal on stone; the more they rubbed against each other, the more heated became their arguments, until every clerk and waitress at external affairs heard about the fiery debates upstairs. MacDonald and Gotlieb were both headstrong, each certain they knew what was best for Canada's foreign policy. MacDonald hired a trusted friend, Hugh Hanson, as her executive assistant, and within a short time he also came to distrust and dislike Gotlieb, whom he considered vain, arrogant, and insufficiently respectful of Mac-Donald's ministerial role. MacDonald and Hanson especially disliked Gotlieb's temper tantrums, thrown when he and Mac-Donald fell out. Gotlieb, MacDonald felt, was undermining her position in the department, and she resented the access he was granted to Clark and his advisors.

MacDonald demanded that Gotlieb be transferred or fired, but Clark would not budge. Clark thought Gotlieb had delivered dependable advice at the economic summit in Tokyo and the Commonwealth Summit in Lusaka. He had already fired two civil servants—Pitfield and Hood—and another firing would cause further uncertainty in the civil service. Nor did Clark agree to a transfer for Gotlieb. MacDonald's pressure simply got his dander up. He was the Prime Minister, with the right to appoint deputy ministers. If he yielded to MacDonald, an independent power within the party, she might feel she could press any demand on Clark. He could not give in right away, but he was planning to transfer Gotlieb eventually.

Other ministers also felt uncomfortable with their deputy ministers, but none developed MacDonald's anger. Transport Minister Don Mazankowski did not work effectively with Deputy Minister Sylvain Cloutier; Indian Affairs Minister Jake Epp was

---

*Hood was offered several international assignments by the Clark Government. Embittered by his treatment, Hood declined the offers and joined the World Bank. Thomas Shoyama, a former Deputy Minister of Finance, was also angry at Hood's dismissal. He resigned as chairman of Atomic Energy of Canada Limited and as a member of the Board of the Export Development Corporation. Shoyama was also upset with the Government's plans for PetroCanada, the EDC, and federal-provincial relations.

uneasy with Arthur Kroeger, and both Cloutier and Kroeger were shifted to new jobs. Sinclair Stevens was granted his wish for a new secretary of the Treasury Board when Jack Manion moved over from the Department of Employment and Immigration to replace Maurice LeClair, who became vice-president of Canadian National.

Some ministers, however, were delighted with their deputies. David MacDonald got on famously with two men closely identified with the Liberal Government—Bernard Ostry, Deputy Minister of Communications, and Pierre Juneau, undersecretary of state. Health and Welfare Minister David Crombie took an instant liking to Bruce Rawson, whom Clark moved to another job, much to Crombie's annoyance.

Whatever the personal relations between Conservative ministers and their senior civil servants, the Government as a whole moved warily in accepting advice from the civil service in its first three months in office. The ministers were all new to their jobs, and Clark warned them against launching initiatives prepared by the civil service before they felt comfortable in their portfolios. Clark instructed several ministers to keep a low profile during the summer in order to master the intricacies of their ministries. The advice was a public-relations error that hurt the Conservatives when autumn arrived and the public had seen little activity. But there were other reasons for delay, best illustrated by the cases of William Jarvis and Ray Hnatyshyn.

William Jarvis was an enormously likeable lawyer from Stratford, Ontario. So homespun were his genial virtues and so solid was his integrity that he could have played himself in a Canadian version of *Mr. Smith Goes to Washington.* He even looked a bit like Jimmy Stewart. In the Commons Jarvis was an effective critic of the solicitor general's department. He made Solicitor General Jean-Jacques Blais' vacuous replies seem all the more unintelligible by the precision and persistence of his questioning. In southwestern Ontario, Jarvis knew just about every Conservative who ever organized a rally or pulled a vote on election day, having learned his politics as a cog in former Ontario Premier John Robarts' electoral machine in London. He was a natural choice to be political minister for Ontario in Clark's Cabinet.

But William Jarvis knew little, if anything, about federal-provincial relations, the portfolio he was given by Clark. Any minister may experience difficulty in assuming a new portfolio, but entering federal-provincial relations without experience is like being lost in Harlem with pocketfuls of cash. Not only did provincial ministers and bureaucrats think that Jarvis was hopelessly naive; his own civil servants did not know what to make of him, nor he of them. Jarvis was so obviously well intentioned that he was impossible to dislike, but he was so evidently uneasy with the intricate diplomacy and numbing complexity of federal-provincial relations that he was immobilized. Part of Jarvis' problem stemmed from the Conservatives' inability in Opposition to articulate a comprehensive approach to federal-provincial relations. The Conservatives took one stab at drafting a paper recommending a provincially appointed Senate, but the Conservatives arrived in power exuding only good-will and promising to "put a fresh face on federalism." The party's two specific promises—disbanding LotoCanada and granting control of offshore resources to coastal provinces—were both handled by ministers other than Jarvis. Similarly, the Prime Minister wanted to make major policy decisions in federal-provincial relations, so Jarvis became a federal emissary flying about the country meeting provincial ministers to convey and receive information.

Jarvis seemed in awe of his civil servants. His bureaucrats worked in the Privy Council, the elite corps within the civil service. They could dazzle an untutored minister with explanations of the constitutional implications of flower gardening, since agriculture was a concurrent jurisdiction between Ottawa and the provinces. Or they could put him to sleep with an analysis of the Established Programs Financing Act, which apportioned money to provincial governments for hospital insurance, Medicare, and post-secondary education according to formulas calculated to the cube root. Such talent did not go unnoticed by Jarvis, who looked at the top of his federal-provincial relations hierarchy and saw Gordon Robertson. The dean of the civil service, he had spent twenty-six years as a deputy minister and was Pitfield's predecessor as Clerk of the Privy Council. As if dazed by the brilliance of his own civil servants, Jarvis kept them in the dark about his own intentions. All summer, his civil servants waited in vain for instructions that never came. The media was kept at bay, too, as Jarvis shunned publicity that might expose his uncertainty.

Gordon Robertson, however, had been around Ottawa long enough to understand that the Conservatives' federal-provincial relations policy was not to his liking. If there was to be a "fresh face on federalism," Gordon Robertson was not the man to apply the make-up; his vision of the country was too centralist for that. He personified the style of administering federal-provincial relations that the Conservatives were going to change. Robertson told Clark in June that he was prepared to retire immediately, but Clark asked him to stay for one year to help the Government make changes in the civil service. Once the first two rounds of changes were made in the civil service, Robertson handed Clark a model letter of resignation:

> . . . The considerations which have led me to this con-clusion have to do with the important decisions of policy that will have to be taken in the near future concerning national unity and the Constitution. I have been person-ally involved in and identified with all the work relating to these problems since I became Clerk of the Privy Council and Secretary to the Cabinet in 1963.
>
> While that background and experience provide a somewhat exceptional knowledge of the problems and of the difficulties inherent in various possible solutions, they have also identified me in a personal way with the former policies and former governments to a degree that could embarrass your efforts to establish your own approach in these areas. . . . I would not want my presence, as the official head of the Federal-Provincial Relations Office with a direct responsibility in these matters, to inhibit in any way your capacity to establish and to carry out whatever new policies you think may be needed to preserve the unity of Canada and to create a better federalism for the future.*

Robertson's resignation removed one source of Jarvis' uneasiness; the destruction of the Tellier group took away another. After the election of the Parti Québécois, the Liberal Government estab-lished a six-man group of civil servants in the Privy Council to monitor developments in Quebec under the direction of Paul Tellier, a charming and intelligent man who had risen meteorically through the civil service. The Tellier group, as it was called, became the bureaucratic spearpoint in the Liberal Government's

---

*Before the Government fell, Clark had settled on Robertson's replacement, Dr. Peter Meekison, Deputy Minister of Intergovernmental Affairs in Alberta. Of course, Trudeau appointed his own man, Michael Kirby, director of the Institute for Research into Public Policy.

aggressive policy of counterattacking the Parti Québécois Government. The Conservatives, without strong representation in Quebec, could not realistically contemplate the same strategy. Moreover, Clark believed that the aggressiveness of the strategy had become counterproductive. Jarvis was uncertain what to do with this high-powered group: it represented a strategy Clark wanted changed; but it was also Jarvis' best source of information on Quebec, a province Jarvis did not know well. Eventually, Clark decided that the group should be disbanded, and Tellier was appointed Deputy Minister of Indian Affairs and Northern Development. The group's disappearance satisfied the Government's political need to demonstrate a new approach to Quebec, but it left Jarvis even more uncertain than before about federal-provincial relations.

If William Jarvis represented a minister co-existing uneasily with civil servants in a policy vacuum, Ray Hnatyshyn symbolized a minister overwhelmed by the complexity of his dossier. Hnatyshyn never wanted to be Minister of Energy; as a lawyer from Saskatoon, he would have preferred the justice portfolio. But geography worked against him. Clark needed a Minister of Energy from a province with credibility in Alberta and the consuming provinces: Saskatchewan produced enough oil to make Alberta think of the province as an ally, but it did not produce enough to make Ontario, Quebec, and Atlantic Canada nervous. Hnatyshyn, like Jarvis, was enormously likeable, and this was thought to be an important virtue for a minister negotiating politically explosive agreements with provinces and industries. Knowing little about energy, Hnatyshyn accepted Clark's advice and dropped out of sight for nearly two months, trying to learn about it. When energy grabbed the headlines during the summer, Hnatyshyn was nowhere to be seen; he was buried in the energy department while his officials answered the Cabinet's call for "remake-the-world" Cabinet papers on energy policy. (See Chapter Seven.)

Hnatyshyn quickly learned that the department's view of energy problems differed from the perception the Conservative Party had developed in Opposition. Most notably, the department vigorously opposed the Conservatives' PetroCanada policy. The department also doubted the practicability of the party's commitment to energy self-sufficiency by 1990. Finally, the department rejected the party's assumption that rapid increases in the domestic supply of oil were possible.

These views reflected the strong influence of Deputy Minister

Ian Stewart and the economic analysis of Edmund Clark, assistant deputy minister. Stewart had been Trudeau's economic-policy advisor and, as such, was considered vulnerable if the Conservatives possessed a "hit list." But Stewart, a quiet man with a quizzical look on his face, won Clark's confidence with exemplary briefings at the Tokyo Economic Summit and with an extensive description of Canada's energy problems for the full Cabinet.

Hnatyshyn, without firm views of his own, wedded himself to those of the department. His recommendations to Cabinet reflected the department's thinking about PetroCanada, oil pricing, and the need to funnel more money from higher prices to federal coffers. This got Hnatyshyn into serious trouble in the Prime Minister's office, where neither Clark, Gillies, nor Neville shared the department's dislike for Conservative policies. Gillies, in particular, thought of himself as an expert in energy policy. He so thoroughly disagreed with the department's analysis that he pressed Clark to replace Stewart with Thomas Kierans, the chairman of the Ontario Economic Council. Clark refused, and Kierans said he would only come to Ottawa to be deputy minister; an offer to become an energy policy advisor to Clark was not sufficiently enticing. Finally, Gillies persuaded Clark that the department needed a new assistant deputy minister based in Calgary to listen to the oil industry, but Hnatyshyn ignored the request.

Hnatyshyn watched this manoeuvreing in the Prime Minister's office with increasing dismay. Gillies was trying to undermine his credibility, of that Hnatyshyn was certain. But Hnatyshyn's confidence was further damaged when he lost his first important Cabinet battles on PetroCanada. Hnatyshyn had allies in Cabinet who wanted to preserve PetroCanada as a crown corporation, but he did not think any of them fought hard enough against Clark, who pushed aside objections and insisted that PetroCanada be restructured. When he lost the PetroCanada fight in Jasper in late August, Hnatyshyn's normal ebullience turned to nervous laughter when forced to defend publicly a policy he believed to be in error.

Hnatyshyn never mastered the complexity of the energy portfolio. He felt and looked uncomfortable when he confronted provincial energy ministers, like Merv Leitch of Alberta, who knew every phase of the energy business. Beholden to his department for ideas, beleaguered by Gillies, and defeated in Cabinet, Hnatyshyn was the unhappiest member of Clark's Cabinet. He fumbled for answers in the Commons, crippling the Government, which needed a convincing salesman for its controversial energy policies.

As Canada's party of the Official Opposition, the Conservatives had beaten their heads against the wall of secrecy that surrounds the activities of the federal government. Conservative M.P.s had repeatedly met refusals from Cabinet ministers and civil servants to release information or to comment on news stories based on documents the Opposition had not seen. After sixteen years in power, the Liberals and the civil service had assumed each other's values and mores; each supported the other's wish to keep confidential any information that might have cast the Government in an unfavourable light. The Liberals promised freedom-of-information legislation for years, but it took a party that arrived in power after an extended spell in Opposition to give freedom of information the priority it deserved. That the Liberals introduced a freedom of information bill after returning to power was partly related to the visibility the Conservatives had given the issue.

The Conservatives repeatedly pressed for freedom-of-information legislation while still in Opposition. Gerald Baldwin, M.P. for Peace River, became the most visible champion of the issue, tabling private members' bills for freedom of information and taking a personal interest in cases of individuals denied access to their files by government fiat. The press rallied to Baldwin's crusade, seeing in freedom of information a new tool it also could use to pry information out of the government. The Canadian Bar Association, the Canadian Civil Liberties Association, and other interest groups took up the cause. All individuals and groups pressing for government action pointed to the United States' freedom-of-information law, adopted after the Watergate scandal.

The general public, however, remained indifferent to the issue, and this indifference allowed the Liberals to respond feebly to the demands for freedom-of-information legislation. The Liberals put through Parliament in 1977 the Canadian Human Rights Act, which gave citizens the right to inspect information placed on their personal files compiled by the federal government. The Liberals changed the structure of Cabinet documents, so that information was contained in the first part of the document and policy recommendations in the second. The Liberals promised to make public the first sections of Cabinet documents, but rarely did so. Secretary of State John Roberts, the Liberal minister responsible for freedom of information, talked piously about his party's commitment to the idea. But all the Liberals ever produced was a self-serving green paper on freedom of information that rejected any third-party review of ministerial decisions to keep information secret. The Liberals, despite many promises, never put a freedom-of-information bill before Parliament in the eleven years that Pierre Trudeau was Prime Minister of Canada before the 1979 election.

The Conservatives, conditioned by their extended spell in Opposition, swept into power resolved to bring freedom-of-information legislation to the federal government. Clark himself pressed the civil service and his ministers to get a freedom-of-information bill ready for the opening of Parliament. He correctly sensed that the longer the Conservatives were in power, co-existing with the civil service, the faster the party's enthusiasm for freedom of information might wane. Opposition to freedom-of-information laws came from the usual places in the civil service— external affairs, defence, the solicitor general's department, and the RCMP. But these departmental objections were met when the Conservatives indicated that the bill would provide exemptions for national security, crime prevention, and international affairs.

The Conservatives hesitated in making decisions in other policy areas, but they plunged ahead with freedom of information and accomplished more in five and a half months than the Liberals had in eleven years. On October 24, 1979, the Government introduced Bill C-15, the freedom-of-information bill that the Liberals had always promised but never delivered. The bill was imperfect: its exemptions for the release of information were still too broad. But it was a reasonable attempt to balance the right of citizens to know what their government was doing and the government's need to act confidentially in matters of national security, crime prevention, diplomacy, and Cabinet decision-making. Most importantly, the bill provided review by a freedom-of-information ombudsman and the federal court of ministerial refusals to make information public. The Conservatives' bill died on the order paper when the Government was defeated, but the party's efforts helped widen the consensus in Canada that freedom of information was an idea whose time had come.

The freedom-of-information bill was the most dramatic illustration of a more open approach to information and a more relaxed style of government that the Conservatives brought to Ottawa. Unaccustomed to power, the Conservatives were not impressed by its trappings. The result was a refreshing change from the false majesty of the Liberals.

The change was the product of small, but revealing, incidents and decisions. On the night of his election win, Clark arrived at the arena in Spruce Grove riding in an enormous car escorted by a cavalcade of policemen on motorcycles. The next morning, he sounded embarrassed by the spectacle: "I was surprised by that big car and I have given instructions to the RCMP that I do not want to travel in cars of that size." Back in Ottawa, he mothballed the $90,000 bullet-proof Cadillac that Trudeau had used for travelling the two miles from 24 Sussex Drive to Parliament. He instructed his ministers to make less frequent use of government JetStars, remembering the misuse of the planes by Liberal ministers like Otto Lang.

Clark was more accessible to the media than Trudeau had been. He did not share Trudeau's profound contempt for the press, so he gave interviews more readily than Trudeau and tried hard to answer questions. He instructed the civil service to help him provide "a more open government for Canada." In a letter to deputy ministers, Clark said, "one of the things we can do is encourage open and responsive behaviour among public servants in their day-to-day dealings with the public, including particularly Members of Parliament and representatives of the news media." He attached to his letter guidelines approved by Cabinet:

1. Communications with the public, including particularly Members of Parliament and news media representatives, are a part of the duties and responsibilities of managers in the public service. A staff function in support of this management role is performed by information officers in most departments and agencies.

2. Public servants should be prepared to discuss frankly information within their areas of responsibility that describes or explains programs and policies that have been announced or implemented by the Government.

3. Public servants should not go beyond this discussion of factual information. It is not appropriate to discuss advice or recommendations tendered to ministers, or to speculate about policy deliberations or future policy decisions.

4. It will be normal in many instances for public servants to be quoted by name and to be interviewed for radio and television as well as by print media.

5. These guidelines cannot and do not authorize the disclosure of information which is specifically prohibited by law. Public employees acting in good faith under these guidelines will not be considered as having violated their oaths of secrecy.

The Conservatives also published a compilation of order-in-council positions and a list of the membership of Cabinet committees, both of which were kept secret by the Liberals. Minister of State for Federal-Provincial Relations William Jarvis, asked by *The Globe and Mail* for a confidential and highly controversial study of federal programs in Quebec, released the study over the objections of his officials. Finance Minister John Crosbie published five-year government-revenue and expenditure projections, which the Liberals had always refused to publish, fearing the projections might someday prove embarrassing.

Pierre Trudeau, in one of his rare unguarded moments, once claimed that Opposition M.P.s were "nobodies" when they left Parliament Hill. The remark bears a kernel of truth. Parliament is where Opposition M.P.s can receive a national exposure denied to them elsewhere. Opposition M.P.s may be big fish in their own constituencies or provinces, but their personalities ripple across the nation's political consciousness only if they make a splash in Parliament. The Government gets a hearing wherever the Prime Minister or his senior ministers travel in Canada or abroad. The Opposition leader is "news" when he travels, but his senior colleagues must fight for attention and his backbenchers are largely ignored outside of their own constituencies. It is in Parliament that Opposition M.P.s can act like town criers, their voices ringing with alarm, drawing the nation's attention to unfolding events. If they are lucky, Opposition M.P.s will find their cries amplified by the media and eventually heeded by the Government. But more often the cries echo against the stone walls of Parliament, reverberating in the Opposition M.P.s' ears and heightening their frustration with their own political impotence. Still, an Opposition party's most important weapon is talk, and Parliament provides the best, and often the only, stage from which the Opposition parties can be heard.

The Official Opposition is often unhappy with its lot in Parliament. Of course, it wants to form the Government, and it invariably feels that the rules and procedures of Parliament inhibit the full exposure of the Government's ineptitude. Government majorities on parliamentary committees blunt amendments or initiatives. Government M.P.s kill private members' bills presented by Opposition M.P.s by talking them to death. The Opposition is often forced to respond with little preparation to statements by ministers. In the Commons, ministers give vague and unsatisfactory answers. They ignore suggestions made by the Opposition. The Government, if it has a majority, wins all the votes. Many aspects of Parliament are designed to assist the Opposition— Question Period, points of order and privilege, an independent Speaker, Opposition Days on which an Opposition party can choose the subject for debate. But inevitably the Opposition overlooks the institutional protections afforded it and concentrates on the restraints placed upon it.

The Opposition's frustration and its dependence on Parliament seem to inspire the desire to reform the institution: the last two Conservative Governments have made parliamentary reform one of their rallying cries. In the 1957 election, the Conservatives under John Diefenbaker—out of power for twenty-two years and fresh from the pipeline debate of 1956—promised the abolition of closure, the appointment of a permanent Speaker, and stronger parliamentary committees. In 1979, Joe Clark also promised stronger committees and the study of a permanent Speaker in his first Speech from the Throne. Unlike Diefenbaker, however, Clark acted on his promise, offering a white paper on parliamentary reform that suggested questioning of ministers about previously held portfolios, smaller committees, and tighter time limits on speeches; twenty days per session for private members' bills; a mandatory Government response within twenty-one days to reports from parliamentary committees; and the right of the leader of the Opposition to choose the estimates of any two departments for scrutiny by committee of the whole of the Commons.

In Parliament the Conservatives also made a public show of putting their theories into practice. They accepted motions from other parties, including one referring the question of high interest rates to a parliamentary committee, where the daily criticism of the Bank of Canada's policy did not help the Government. Clark and Marcel Massé, Clerk of the Privy Council, appeared before a parliamentary committee to explain and defend the estimates of their offices; this gesture contrasted with Trudeau's refusal to appear before committees or to allow his Privy Council Clerk Michael Pitfield to testify before Commons committees.

In the Speech from the Throne, the Conservatives created four special parliamentary committees to study services for the handicapped, the role of voluntary organizations, foreign ownership, and cost overruns in government. Standing committees were asked to conduct reviews of cultural and foreign policy. These initiatives reflected the Conservatives' concern, expressed in Opposition, that M.P.s' talents were underutilized. The initiatives also indicated that the Conservatives did not know what to do in these policy areas; the party thought the subjects were important, but it had not developed comprehensive policies in these areas before coming to power.

Although some of the hidebound members of the civil service opposed these Conservative initiatives, many civil servants recognized the salutary nature of the proposals. Some of the more thoughtful civil servants understood that if these reforms enhanced the legitimacy and credibility of the federal government, they might also sweep away some of the public mistrust of the civil service.

Indeed, the acceptance of the spirit of these reforms by some civil servants was part of an effective partnership that was developing between the Conservative Government and the civil service. It had taken a few months for both sides to understand the motivations of the other, but the senior civil service—with a few exceptions—warmed to the Conservatives' eagerness. Many senior mandarins even came to respect Joe Clark, more for his capacity to learn and his friendliness than for his innate abilities. He treated them fairly, listened to them with the respect they considered their due, and surprised them with his willingness to tackle complicated subjects of policy. They were another group whose expectations he exceeded. After his defeat, Clark met with the deputy ministers for a final time before he turned power back to the Liberals. He wanted to thank them collectively for serving his Government so well. Before he could speak, they gave him a standing ovation.

~ 6 ~

Promises, Promises

Promises are such an integral part of a party's restless search for votes that they are woven through the political life of a nation. So many promises are often made during an election campaign that the most conscientious voter despairs of remembering, let alone analysing, them all. The sceptics say that promises are intended to bribe us with our own money. And often they are right. But there is another motivation for political promises that is neither counterfeit nor contemptible. Promises are the tangible expressions of where a party wants to take the nation. The care with which the promises are crafted and the values they reflect say something about the men and women who seek the nation's trust on election day. The wisest promises, those given the widest likelihood of implementation, are consistent with the noblest traditions of a party, since promises born of expediency rather than conviction will lack defenders even within the party itself.

In making promises, it helps to have scouted the territory. A man may think he can climb a mountain when he views it from afar; only after he begins his ascent does he find his spirit sagging and his equipment ill-designed. Good intentions are an insufficient guarantee of success in mountain-climbing or politics, and if the initial expression of resolve is designed merely to impress one's fellows, then failure is assured and ridicule invited.

Of course, all parties make promises, some more outlandish and foolish than others, and the Liberals have made their share of them. The next ice age will be upon us before the CNR is double-tracked to Vancouver. The saplings and craft shows at Harbourfront are not what the citizens of Toronto were promised in the dying stages of the 1972 campaign. Municipal transit systems across Canada are still waiting for the money that was supposed to flow from Ottawa after the same campaign. But, as the governing party, the Liberals could always divert attention from unkept promises by taking action on other fronts.

An Opposition party, however, is alone with its promises, especially if it has been long-removed from office. The governing party defends its record in an election campaign; the Opposition party winds up justifying its promises, since it has no record to defend. If elected, the Opposition party finds that its promises are a substitute for a record, at least in the early stages of its mandate. They are the yardstick by which the party is judged. If the promises were conceived in haste or were otherwise poorly designed, they can cause a new Government unending grief when it struggles to adjust the promises to the realities of power.

Joe Clark and the Conservative Party arrived in power groaning under the weight of all the promises they had made during the 1979 campaign. Two of the most dramatic were the plans to move the Canadian embassy in Israel from Tel Aviv to Jerusalem and to dismantle PetroCanada as a crown corporation. The embassy promise was whipped together in the heat of the campaign, but the PetroCanada promise had slowly become a political issue before the campaign. Both promises suffered two critical liabilities: they had been given insufficient attention by Clark and his party before the election and they seemed to abuse the public interest. They also defied the wishes of the electorate, many of whom had cast their ballots more to rid themselves of Trudeau than to move the Canadian embassy or to dismantle PetroCanada.

Joe Clark, however, believed that he had a mandate for fundamental change. He thought the country was tired of incremental Liberal rule, the continuous shifting of direction that had marked the Liberals' last two years in office. He held to this belief even when prominent members of his own party implored him to drop the promises, and when the civil service counselled delay or retreat. The mandarins possessed, as it turned out, a sure grasp of the substance and the politics of both issues, but Clark believed the civil service's advice reflected a concern for protecting its own vested interests in PetroCanada and for directing foreign policy, rather than an understanding of what the public wanted. So Clark dismissed the advice of the civil service and insisted on his very first day in office that he would keep both promises.

Ironically, a more confident man might have dropped both promises or delayed their implementation until he could build a constituency for his proposed initiatives. But Clark knew that the public thought of him as a vacillating leader. For him, Jerusalem and PetroCanada became issues cutting to the heart of his own credibility. Only by standing firm could he overcome the image of vacillation; only by ploughing towards a stated goal could he demonstrate an inner strength that the public doubted he possessed.

Of all the errors Joe Clark made as leader of the Conservative Party, none rivalled his promise to move the Canadian embassy in Israel from Tel Aviv to Jerusalem. Through a numbing mixture of unforgivable stupidity and crass politics, Clark stumbled into a promise that was to haunt him through all his days as Prime Minister. Nothing he could say—not even his plaintive plea that he had made a mistake and was man enough to admit it—could repair the political damage when, after the election, the issue moved from one of concern to Canada's Jewish community to one touching many Canadians.

As a middle-ranked power in the world, Canada has limited freedom of movement in foreign affairs. But Canadians feel, and comfort themselves in feeling that their country is widely respected in the world community. If we have not got the political, economic, nor military clout to impress the world, at least we keep our noses clean and our self-esteem intact. We have a reputation—or so we believe—for fairness in dealing with other nations. We are a good neighbour to our allies, a nation offering little offence to our foes; in short, a moderate, sensible influence in the world community.

Clark's blunder shattered all the myths Canadians hold about themselves in the world community. Instead of working with our allies, we were out of step, and more than that, we were being told by the United States and the countries of western Europe to get back into line. We no longer looked like a helpful fixer in the Middle East, where our peacekeeping forces had served honourably in the Gaza Strip and Golan Heights. The Arabs were now angry at Canada. After the election, large Canadian companies like Bell Canada, Westinghouse, and Canadair, along with many smaller Canadian firms, feared for their contracts with Arab countries. Arab newspapers and spokesmen condemned Clark's policy, some threatening retaliatory action. In the age of OPEC's supremacy in fixing the price and supply of oil, talk of retaliation sent shivers through Canadians, whose country had become increasingly reliant on Saudi Arabia and other Arab countries for oil.

Isolated from our allies and chastised by the Arab world, Canada appeared foolish and naive. For a nation that prided itself on shrewd diplomacy and common sense, appearing foolish and naive was too painful to bear. What's more, no group in Canada, apart from some members of the Jewish community and a few of Joe Clark's advisors, could see how moving the embassy helped Canada's own interests or aided the search for peace in the Middle East. Any foreign policy initiative must at least provide some prospect for enhancing a nation's self-interest, but Clark's promise and subsequent actions offered the opposite: fewer jobs because of lost contracts, reprisals against Canadian nationals in Arab countries, a possible threat to oil supplies, and strained relations with Arab nations.

Jerusalem, of course, is more than just a city; it is an important symbol to Jews, Moslems, and Christians. Struggled over for centuries, the city has been a flash point in relations between Israel and its Arab neighbours since the creation of the state of Israel. After the 1949 armistice, the city was left divided between Israel and Jordan, and Israel moved its capital from Tel Aviv to West Jerusalem in 1950. In the 1967 Six-Day War, Israel pushed the Jordanian border back to the Jordan River, about forty kilometres to the east, and integrated East Jerusalem into Israel. Canada never recognized this integration, nor did the United Nations, which adopted a resolution calling for the "withdrawal of Israeli armed forces from territories occupied in the recent conflict." Of course, the Arab states, which claimed Jerusalem a holy city sacred to the Moslem faith, never accepted the integration.

For the Israelis, it became a matter of national pride and a goal of their diplomacy to persuade states recognizing Israel to move their embassies from Tel Aviv to Jerusalem.* It was not surprising, therefore, that Israeli Prime Minister Menachem Begin tried unsuccessfully to enlist Canada's support for an embassy move during a state visit to Canada in November of 1978. During private meetings with Begin, Trudeau refused to change Canada's position, but the Israeli Prime Minister heightened the issue's importance during a subsequent trip to Toronto. There he urged Jewish leaders in both private meetings and public speeches to increase their pressure on the Canadian Government. By the time he left for Israel, the Canadian Zionist Federation National Executive had passed a resolution advocating the embassy move and the Canada-Israel Committee had debated the issue and agreed to debate it

---

*The following countries maintained embassies in Jerusalem: Bolivia, Chile, Columbia, Costa Rica, Dominican Republic, Ecuador, El Salvador, Guatemala, Haiti, Holland, Panama, Uruguay and Venezuela.

again. Begin made an overt pitch for the embassy move in a speech at Beth Tzedec Synagogue. "Ladies and gentlemen, Jerusalem, reunited, indivisible, [is] the eternal capital of the state of Israel, [and] culturally, morally, historically, of all the Jewish people, as long as the Jewish people will live, and the Jewish people will live forever," Begin said. If Canada placed its embassies in the capitals of other countries, why not in Jerusalem? Begin asked.

This question left the Jewish community buzzing after Begin's departure. The embassy move, never the highest priority for Jewish organizations lobbying Ottawa, suddenly assumed a new urgency, especially with a federal election looming and many Toronto ridings likely to change hands.

Six weeks after Begin's departure, in January 1979, Joe Clark embarked on a world tour to Japan, India, and the Middle East. Preparing for the trip, Clark was warned by U.S. officials that the Israelis would probably raise the embassy move with him. The external affairs department offered the same warning and underlined many reasons why Canada should not consent to the Israeli request. Douglas Roche, M.P. for Edmonton South and a party critic on external affairs, gave similar advice, based on a world trip, including a visit to the Middle East that he had undertaken at Clark's request.

For the Middle East portion of his trip, Clark was joined by Maureen McTeer, two Conservative candidates in the upcoming election, and two personal friends from Toronto's Jewish community: Irving Gerstein, president of Peoples' Jewellers, and Jeffery Lyons, a likeable Toronto lawyer who had been one of Clark's supporters for the Conservative Leadership.* Both Gerstein and Lyons urged Clark to commit the Conservative Party to moving the embassy, although they thought the announcement should be made in Canada rather than in Israel.

The two Conservative candidates with Clark were Rob Parker, a television personality who had won Eglinton-Lawrence riding—which was about 35 per cent Jewish—in an October 1978 by-election; and Ron Atkey, an M.P. for St. Paul's from 1972 to 1974 who had already been nominated to run in the same riding in the 1979 election. Parker had spent ten days in Israel before Clark's arrival, discussing a wide range of issues with Israeli officials including

---

*After Clark became Prime Minister, Lyons was put in charge of dispensing some legal patronage in Toronto, although he wisely resisted efforts by Clark and other Conservatives to persuade him to run in the losing election of 1980.

moving the embassy, a policy Parker urged Clark to consider. Atkey, whose Toronto riding was about 25 per cent Jewish, had prepared for Clark a report on the embassy question, which was read by the Opposition leader before his arrival in Israel.

Atkey's report recommended moving the embassy, but in two other ways the report was highly cautionary. First, it said the embassy move was not the most important priority issue in the Jewish community. "Of all the Jewish-Israeli issues directly relevant to Canada and the next election, I would rank this third, next to the Egypt-Israel peace negotiations and the economic boycott," Atkey said in his report.

Then Atkey warned that moving the embassy while peace negotiations were in progress "might be interpreted by the Egyptians as an unnecessary 'taking of sides.'" Atkey said it would be "unwise for Canada to make any commitment regarding transference of the embassy until after the conclusion of the peace talks and the signing of the treaty."

Clark's most important meeting in Israel was with Begin, who received the Conservative leader knowing that he might soon be Prime Minister of Canada. Begin promptly delivered to Clark the same pitch he had given to Trudeau: move the embassy to Jerusalem as a sign of solidarity with Israel. Clark's aides later reported that Begin had hinted he might further encourage Canadian Jews to increase pressure on the Canadian government if action was not forthcoming from Canada.

After their thirty-minute meeting, Clark and Begin met reporters at the heavily guarded entrance to Begin's office, where Clark was predictably asked about the embassy move. He replied, as Atkey had suggested, that the proposed move was ill advised while Egypt and Israel were involved in the so-called Camp David negotiations, part of which touched the future status of West Bank Palestinians and Jerusalem. Until the peace negotiations were completed, Clark said any move of the Canadian embassy would be premature and possibly upsetting to the peace negotiations themselves. Clark had been briefed on the problems of moving the embassy by Ted Lee, Canadian ambassador to Israel, and Clark's remarks at the time showed he appreciated the dangers implied in the course of action urged by his friends and candidates. Several days later, Clark repeated the same statements at a breakfast press conference in Amman, Jordan, the last stop on his world tour.

It had not been a very successful world tour for Clark, but at least he had shown sufficient understanding of the embassy problem to avoid committing his party to the move. Upon his return, members of the Jewish community continued to press the issue, but it appeared they would be unsuccessful with both major parties, because Clark had spoken against the move and Trudeau had already spurned Begin's request.

There the matter rested until the election campaign, when the crassest of political considerations overwhelmed Joe Clark. From the outset of the 1979 campaign, all parties knew that the outcome would be determined largely in southern Ontario, especially in Metropolitan Toronto and the surrounding suburbs. Unless the Conservatives could make substantial gains in and around Toronto, they could certainly not form a majority Government and might not even win the election. Both Atkey and Parker were in political dogfights. Atkey had won St. Paul's in 1972, but lost the riding to Secretary of State John Roberts in 1974, and the two men were locked in a rematch in 1979. Parker's Eglinton-Lawrence constituency had been changed by redistribution; a heavily Liberal section of Italian-Canadians had been added to the west end of the riding. To save both Atkey and Parker, the Conservatives started casting about for an issue of specific appeal to these constituencies.

Clark was scheduled to meet the Canada-Israel Committee on April 25, about a month before voting day. As the meeting approached, it became clear that the committee would expect Clark to make a statement on the embassy question; in fact, the agenda proposed by the committee listed the embassy move as the first item of business. In preparation for the meeting, Clark asked Lowell Murray to phone prominent Jewish Conservatives to ask them about the embassy move. Most, including Eddie Goodman, the prominent lawyer and Conservative bagman in Toronto, counselled caution in the middle of an election campaign. Even Rob Parker said he did not need a promise to move the embassy to win his riding.

Four days before Clark's meeting with the Canada-Israel Committee, the Conservative policy committee met in Ottawa to discuss the embassy move. The three most powerful members of the committee were chairman Bill Nobleman, a businessman from Toronto, William Neville, and Murray. Nobleman favoured the embassy move, although he worried about ensuing security problems for Canadian embassies in other countries. He also wondered about the political gains to be won by releasing the policy during a campaign when it might be attacked by Trudeau.

Neville and Murray, however, were convinced that the policy was correct in substance and that its release would aid Parker, Atkey, and other Conservative candidates in ridings with substantial Jewish populations in Ontario. Murray had favoured moving the embassy since his visit to the Middle East in the early 1970s, after which he wrote a speech for his boss, New Brunswick Premier Richard Hatfield, endorsing the idea. Murray always pointed out that the Democratic Party had included moving the U.S. embassy in Israel from Tel Aviv to Jerusalem in its 1976 platform, although Jimmy Carter quickly forgot about the idea after winning the presidency. The policy committee recommended the Conservative Party support the embassy move, although Clark was not given a recommendation about when or how to announce the policy. This recommendation had no particular status. It had not been approved by a party convention, nor had it been discussed by the Conservative caucus. But the recommendation had political allure for Clark, who thought he was close to a majority Government and needed every seat he could get.

The night before his meeting with the Canada-Israel Committee, Clark discussed the embassy move with his close advisors without committing himself to announcing the policy. The Conservative Party research office had prepared a report pointing out many of the negative consequences for Canada if the embassy were moved. Clark was given the views of those Conservative Jews who argued against the policy, although he also knew of the support of Jewish Conservatives such as Jeffery Lyons, who had written Clark a "Dear Joe" letter in favour of the move after Clark's world tour. Clark went to bed apparently undecided about what to do, although his aides got the feeling he would probably resist making any positive announcement. Just in case, however, Atkey drafted a press release with Neville's help, explaining why the Conservatives favoured moving the embassy.

Clark's meeting with the Canada-Israel Committee was scheduled for 2 p.m. At an early morning press conference, Clark said nothing about the embassy move. Atkey had asked for a session with Clark before the meeting with the Canada-Israel Committee, and he joined Clark in his suite about an hour prior to the meeting with the committee. From there, Clark phoned Murray in Ottawa. Murray repeated to Clark the objections he had received from Jewish Conservatives; but Clark already knew Murray's personal views on the issue and his political judgement that an announcement might be important to Parker, Atkey and others. Clark put down the phone and decided that, after all, the Conservatives would announce their support for moving the embassy from Tel Aviv to Jerusalem. Clark's staff immediately began rounding up copies of Atkey's press release and distributed them to the press before Clark's meeting. The tactical ploy was meant to show sceptical reporters that Clark had made the decision without pressure from the Canada-Israel Committee, but it was a transparent effort that did not fool anyone about the real motives behind the announcement. Clark emerged from his meeting with the Canada-Israel Committee to say that the embassy move was now appropriate because the Camp David negotiations had been successfully completed in March.

> Thankfully, those difficult negotiations have now borne fruit. Both Egypt and Israel, assisted by President Carter, have signed the peace agreement. The result has been dramatically affirmed within both countries. This historic peace event opens the way for Canada to take positive initiatives in the Middle East.
> One such initiative would be the recognition of Jerusalem as the capital of Israel, with free access to the holy places provided to all faiths. As a symbol of the recognition, my Government would be prepared to move the Canadian embassy from Tel Aviv to the western part of Jerusalem, which has been part of Israel since the creation of the country in 1948.

In fact, only the first phase of the negotiations between Egypt and Israel had been completed; the second phase, on the status of West Bank Palestinians and Jerusalem, remained. Further, Clark was wilfully ignoring the symbolic importance of Jerusalem in the broader context of Middle East affairs, a context he had ostensibly gone to the Middle East to learn more about. Nevertheless, Clark then added two other assertions:

> This is not to be construed as a taking of sides in Arab-Israeli negotiations respecting the West Bank, the Palestinians or the broader terms of a comprehensive peace agreement between all countries in the Middle East. Rather, this foreign policy initiative is only a recognition of the political, administrative and legal realities of Jerusalem in 1979.

Arguing that moving the embassy, a policy strongly supported by Israel and opposed by Arab states, did not constitute "a taking of sides" was a complete misreading of Middle East politics. Similarly, his promise did not recognize the "realities" of Jerusalem; it ignored them, as Clark was to learn in the months ahead.

Finally, Clark accepted the basis of the Israeli position:

> Jerusalem . . . is and always has been the capital of the Jewish people and the Jewish spirit. "Next year in Jerusalem" is a Jewish prayer which we intend to make a Canadian reality.

Atkey was visibly delighted with Clark's announcement. Elsewhere within the Conservative Party there was widespread consternation. David Crombie took public issue with the promise. John Crosbie, campaigning in Newfoundland, thought the announcement just about the silliest decision he could imagine. Flora MacDonald held her tongue in public, but muttered to her friends about the stupidity of it all. Trudeau, of course, pounced on the promise as further evidence that Clark knew nothing about foreign policy.

No one can quantify the effect of the promise on the election. Atkey won St. Paul's, Parker lost Eglinton-Lawrence, and the Conservatives took Willowdale, Don Valley West, and Don Valley East; the Liberals held York Centre. Thus, in the ridings with a sizeable Jewish population, the Conservatives won four and the Liberals two. But Conservative campaign organizers said later that the embassy promise was, at best, a marginal factor in the six ridings. (In 1980, the Liberals won five of six, losing only Don Valley West.)

During the campaign the promise was attacked from many quarters: on the editorial pages of many newspapers, by academics specializing in international affairs, and by businessmen. When Clark took office, many hoped he would jettison his promise, or at least delay its implementation. Certainly, that was the advice given Clark by the external affairs department, which produced a briefing paper pointing out all the reasons why the embassy move was inappropriate. That was also the position taken by Flora MacDonald when she met Clark to discuss her appointment as Secretary of State for External Affairs. At the very least, MacDonald urged Clark to postpone any action on the promise, to bury it as Jimmy Carter had done with his party's promise in 1976.

Clark, however, had just survived an election campaign in which he had been saddled with the image of flip-flopping on major policy questions. He had already changed his mind once on moving the embassy; he was not about to change direction again. His personal credibility had become more important than the substance of the issue. He also was annoyed by the rumblings of discontent, which were being reported in the press. He was anxious to show the civil service, in particular the external affairs department, that a new Government was now in charge.

Sitting at his post-election retreat in Cape Breton, Lowell Murray felt the same way. On June 5, the day after the Cabinet was sworn in, Murray called Clark. Murray could not get through to the Prime Minister, so he dictated a note to Clark advising him to bring the civil service into line, especially on the embassy move. Murray did not recommend that Clark deliver a public lecture, but, later in the day, that is what Clark proceeded to do. His performance astonished reporters attending his first press conference as Prime Minister. In response to a question about keeping his embassy promise Clark replied:

> We certainly intend to do that. Miss MacDonald will be indicating to officials in external affairs that we will be expecting from them recommendations fairly directly as to how it can be accomplished and what other policies will be followed that will be necessary to make that goal realizable.
>
> I say that simply to indicate that the position she and other ministers will be taking in relation to matters that have been part of party policy in the election campaign will be to indicate that those questions are now beyond discussion as to their appropriateness and that what we will be seeking from the public service will be indications as to how we accomplish what we have undertaken to do.

Flora MacDonald learned about Clark's lecture when she circulated through a reception with her civil servants at the external affairs department, where officers were buzzing about the putdown they had just received. MacDonald, who thought Clark would ignore the promise for awhile, was shocked. Instead of spending the next few days settling into her department, she was bombarded with requests for interviews from the media, with representations against the Prime Minister's bold declaration from Arab ambassadors and Canadian businessmen, and with negative reactions from party supporters across the country. Her job from that point on was to minimize the disruption in her own department and the political damage to the party caused by Clark's public ineptitude.

For the next two weeks, the public clamour grew steadily against Clark's decision. Businessmen warned of lost contracts. Newspaper stories reported that Canadians were being harassed in Saudi Arabia. The Arab Monetary Fund, in a move more symbolic than anything else, withdrew its capital from Canadian banks. The Islamic Conference, representing forty-two Arab states, told Canada that moving the embassy would have an "adverse effect on Canada's relations."

After a week of hearing the cacophony of protesting voices, MacDonald left Canada for a meeting of the Organization for Economic Co-operation and Development. She left as much to get away from the embassy controversy as to learn something at the OECD. By the time she left, Clark, in an interview with American television journalist Barbara Walters, had reaffirmed his intention to proceed with the embassy move.

Several days after returning from the OECD meeting, Mac-Donald drew Clark aside at a luncheon that the Prime Minister was giving for Prime Minister Kriangsak Chamanan of Thailand. Why not appoint a special envoy to study the Jerusalem question, to take the heat at least temporarily off the Government? she asked Clark. Did she have anyone in mind? Clark replied. Mac-Donald asked for some time to think about a possible candidate and agreed to get back to Clark with a recommendation. Her choice turned out to be Robert Stanfield, the former leader of the Conservative Party, who was in Halifax when contacted by Clark. Upon hearing of the request, Stanfield asked for time to consider his answer. The next day Stanfield called back while Clark and MacDonald were attending a Cabinet meeting. Neville left the Cabinet room to take the call and returned nodding to both Clark and MacDonald. Stanfield had come once again to the aid of his party.

The next day, Clark and MacDonald met first with a delegation of Arab ambassadors and later with the Israeli ambassador to Canada. Shortly thereafter, Clark told reporters waiting outside 24 Sussex Drive that Stanfield had agreed to undertake a study of the embassy move in the context of a general review of Canada's relations with the countries of the Middle East.

"I want to see the implementation of our policy on Jerusalem in a way that will be compatible with the efforts to achieve a comprehensive peace settlement," Clark said, still holding to the link between the embassy move and the peace negotiations.

In fact, in appointing Stanfield, Clark assumed that his predecessor as party leader would find an honourable way of extricating him from a messy political situation of his own making. Within a week of taking office, Clark had become convinced that he had to back down, and he needed both to prepare his party and the public for the coming *volte-face* and to find the least politically damaging way out of his promise. Having announced the Stanfield mission, Clark departed for the Tokyo Economic Summit. On the way back, he began alerting the public to his coming policy change. "It was a mistake of tone from which, I am convinced, we can recover to the good of the country," Clark told Richard Gwyn of *The Toronto Star* in a reply to a question about his post-election declaration on the embassy move. "The permanent damage was to me in the nature of a scar that will always be there, although not too large."

Stanfield began his work immediately, collecting an impressive library of articles and books on the Middle East and, with customary thoroughness, immersing himself in briefings with academics and external affairs department officials. MacDonald had asked to receive a report from Stanfield in 1980; but Stanfield soon discovered, while touring Arab countries, that progress could not be made in reviewing Canada's policy with Arab countries—part of the broad task he had been given by the Government—until the embassy promise was revoked. As he made his way through the capitals of the Middle East, jokes circulated throughout Canada about poor "Stanfield of Arabia" and his rescue mission for the inexperienced Joe Clark. After he returned to Canada early in the week of October 24, Stanfield drafted a three-page letter summarizing his recommendations about the embassy move. He delivered it to Clark on Friday, October 29. To no one's surprise, Stanfield told Clark that the embassy move was a mistake. Without even acknowledging the possible arguments in favour of moving the embassy, Stanfield outlined the overwhelming case against the idea. He wrote:

> Expectations arose with the conclusion of the Camp David accords and the Peace Treaty between Egypt and Israel that there would be rapid movement towards a comprehensive peace settlement in the area which would include as one key element the question of Jerusalem. These expectations have not been met. . . .
> To use effectively whatever influence we may have in the area to encourage moderation and compromise we must retain credibility with both sides as a fair-minded interlocutor. We could not do this if we were to move our embassy to Jerusalem. . . . It is my view . . . that the question of the relocation of the embassy must await the resolution of Jerusalem's status as part of a just and lasting comprehensive settlement.

Even if he had so desired, there was nothing Clark could do but accept the inevitable; his reaction was that of a student receiving a failing grade on a term paper for which he had done insufficient work. Once again Clark would have to change his position, and the tactical question became how to break the news in order to minimize the negative political consequences. Since the Government could not fudge its reversal, Clark and his staff decided to make public Stanfield's report on the following Monday. They also agreed that nothing could be gained by tortured explanations. It would be preferable, although painful, for Clark to say simply that he had made a mistake, hoping such a reply would elicit sympathy for its honesty. (Coincidentally, Trudeau had been quoted that same week in *The Toronto Star* as worrying about the rise of Zionism in the world. Although Trudeau's office subsequently denied the story, the Conservatives felt the reaction in the Jewish community against the report of Trudeau's remarks might offset the anticipated negative fallout from what Clark would say.)

On Monday, Neville and other members of Clark's staff spent the day phoning Jewish leaders to warn them about what was coming. The news was then broken to Atkey and to the inner Cabinet, where there was little sympathy for Atkey, whose political skin had never been deemed of sufficient value to justify the high price the Government had paid to protect it. Finally, Clark told the House of Commons in a 194-word statement:

> As a result of extensive consultations, Mr. Stanfield has concluded that a change in the location of the Canadian Embassy in Israel could be seen as pre-judging negotiations among parties in the Middle East and might, in fact, work against progress to a just and lasting peace settlement.
>
> The purpose of this Government is to encourage that peace. Consequently, the Government accepts the recommendation that no action be taken on the location of the Canadian Embassy until the status of Jerusalem is clarified within a comprehensive agreement between Israel and its Arab neighbors.

Thus the curtain rang down on Joe Clark's worst performance as Prime Minister. Try as he might, the memory of his Jerusalem promise never fully faded from the Canadian political consciousness. The Jerusalem promise shackled Clark with a reputation for political opportunism and poor judgement.

Clark's promise was made in haste during the hurly-burly of an election campaign, and as such was given less serious consideration than it needed. But the promise fit snugly into the Conservatives' political strategy for that election. It broadened the party's narrow base with a specific appeal to an individual group of voters. Just as mortgage-interest and property-tax deductibility was a promise to attract upper-middle-class Canadians living in suburbia, so the Jerusalem-embassy promise was a blatant pitch to a selected ethnic group.

The Conservative Party has always struggled to attract ethnic voters, many of whom think of the party as a WASP-dominated group oriented towards big business. John Diefenbaker helped to change the party's image, especially among the Ukrainians and other central and east European groups in western Canada. But among Canada's other ethnic minorities—French Canadians, Catholics from southern European countries, and Jews—the Conservatives have had little luck in building political support. Among Jews, the Conservatives are generally not as well regarded as the Liberals are. Jewish feelings towards the Conservative Party sank in the fall of 1978 when Clark refused to repudiate allegedly anti-Semitic statements made by Roger Delorme, a Conservative candidate in a by-election in Terrebonne riding. The Jerusalem-embassy promise was seen by Clark as the surest way of expunging the memory of the Delorme affair and building bridges to an influential ethnic group.

Unfortunately for Clark, the embassy promise etched more deeply in the public consciousness his image as a political leader who changed his position exclusively for political gain. If the facts of the Middle East situation had changed between Clark's world tour in January and his election promise four months later, then he could have defended his election promise. All that had changed, however, was the signing of the first phase agreements under the Camp David accords. Further and more difficult negotiations remained between Egypt and Israel, and nothing at all had changed between Israel and its other Arab neighbours. Clark knew the arguments against the embassy move. He had repeated some of them on his world tour, so neither he nor his ministers could argue convincingly that Stanfield's report had provided new information to justify the Government's final change of heart. Further, Jerusalem showed up Clark's inexperience in foreign affairs, and once that impression took hold he never seemed credible when talking about the subject, although he tried to make foreign policy an issue in the 1980 campaign.

Finally, the Jerusalem promise called into question Clark's judgement and left the public wondering about his conception of the public interest. Since few could see how moving the embassy would enhance any of Canada's own interests or its self-appointed role in the world community, the promise was seen for what it really was: a naked bribe for votes. A political leader is always engaged in the search for public support, but there comes a point at which his entreaties become so blatant that the public is repelled. Once that point is reached, the public starts, understandably, to ask itself how willingly the political leader in question will sell off other parts of the public interest for a handful of votes. When that suspicion arises, the political leader loses any trust vested in him by the voters. Such was the political legacy of the Jerusalem-embassy fiasco for Joe Clark.

Nothing so clearly illustrated the divisions within the Conservative Party as the question of what to do with PetroCanada, the crown energy corporation. The party's initial position that a crown corporation in the energy field was unnecessary reflected the views of those within the party who deeply distrusted state intervention in the economy. They happened to occupy the key shadow Cabinet positions shaping the party's energy policy, but once the party came to power a wider range of views within the party was brought to bear on PetroCanada. Representatives of another strain of Conservative thinking supportive of state undertakings to expand Canadian ownership of industry made their objections known to their hard-line, free-enterprise colleagues.

PetroCanada stuck in the party's craw like a bone in a dog's throat. The more the Conservatives struggled with the problem of how to fulfil their election promise, the worse the pain became. Once in power, the Conservatives were burdened with a promise to dismantle PetroCanada as a crown corporation, and they thrashed about searching for an escape-hatch from a dilemma of their own making. Eventually it was Joe Clark, against the advice of his inner Cabinet, who insisted on fulfilling the party's election promise because he feared that failure to act would be construed as another sign of his own weak leadership. He blinded himself to the mood of the public, which strongly supported the retention of PetroCanada as a crown corporation. As a result, the public credited Clark not with fidelity to principle, but with making a mistake.

The Conservatives' problem with PetroCanada started in 1975, the year before Clark became leader of the Conservative

Party. Returned with a majority in the 1974 election, the Liberals introduced a bill the following year creating the crown corporation to give the federal government a toehold in the exploration and research end of the oil and natural gas industries in Canada. With an initial capital investment of $500 million, PetroCanada was hardly a threat to the giant multinational oil companies, whose vertically integrated operations stretched across Canada and around the world.

The Conservatives were still regrouping after their 1974 election defeat, when the electorate repudiated the party's proposal for a ninety-day wage and price freeze followed by controls. Having seen their proposed state intervention in the economy rejected by the voters, the Conservatives retreated to hard-line, free-enterprise positions, fostered in the case of the party's response to PetroCanada by the close links between members of the Conservative caucus and the oil industry.

In its fledgling stages, PetroCanada was greeted with suspicion and hostility by the industry. Many oil-company executives scorned government intervention in the marketplace. Others complained about what they said were preferential rules created by Ottawa for PetroCanada. The federal government was dependent on the industry for its information about supplies; now Ottawa would have a "window" on the industry. By the time the Conservatives took office in 1979, many of the industry's views had changed; PetroCanada had become a source of federal money for joint ventures. But when the crown corporation was first established, the industry made its views known to important members of the Conservative Party.

Jim Gillies and Harvie Andre, M.P. for Calgary Centre, were two prominent Conservatives who agreed with the industry's complaints. Both Gillies and Andre were convinced that the industry had done an acceptable job in finding new oil and gas. Whatever impediments the industry faced were those imposed by the federal government. What the industry did not need was a government-backed competitor nosing about in the business of finding oil and gas.

Joe Clark did not have a closer personal friend in the Conservative caucus than Harvie Andre, one of only three M.P.s who supported Clark's bid for the Conservative leadership. Andre had hesitated before endorsing Clark, hoping that Alberta Premier Peter Lougheed might contest the leadership. When Lougheed declined, Andre threw his own support to Clark, serving as convention chairman for the Clark campaign.* Andre was the party's official spokesman in the PetroCanada debate when the bill was first introduced by the Liberals. Clark, then a backbencher, took his lead on PetroCanada from Andre and from Gillies, the party's energy critic.

"The basic objection one has to take to Bill C-8 [the bill creating PetroCanada] is that it is a fraud. It does not do what it purports to do," Clark told the Commons during debate on the legislation. "It is clearly going to change, without any cause, the relationship between the private and the public sector in the country; it is going to change the climate which exists in the petroleum-exploration industry, and it is going to change this relationship for the worse."

Clark then added a non-sequitur, noting that PetroCanada's $500-million investment was half what the Liberal Government had spent on consultant fees in 1974. Then he arrived at the nub of his argument:

> If the Government sees something moving in the country, it wants to get into the act, not as a mediator, not as a regulator or in the traditional way that the federal government and governments as a whole have operated, but as a controller. It wants power. It is prepared to extend its influence and its activities by intruding upon the jurisdiction of the provinces, by moving into the private sector whatever the consequences. It is preoccupied with extending its own power and influence whatever the cost. That is the real reason why we have this piece of legislation before us tonight.

Clark concluded that PetroCanada would wind up becoming a "$500-million white elephant," a view he never changed, even as Prime Minister, despite considerable evidence to the contrary.

Clark delivered his PetroCanada speech in April 1975, the same month in which he made his first political soundings about running for the Conservative leadership. Months later, when he was a candidate for the leadership, he raised the PetroCanada

---

*Andre was assured of a place in Clark's Cabinet until investigations were launched into the business activities of a development company of which Andre had been a director. Both Clark and Andre regretfully agreed that Andre's Cabinet post would have to await the outcome of the investigations. Still, Andre wept in his office the day Clark's Cabinet was sworn into office.

162/ Discipline of Power

issue again, advocating sale of the corporation to the public via a share offering. The suggestion was not a central part of Clark's leadership bid; but it did reflect the admiration Clark had always shown for the Alberta Government's distribution of shares to the public of Alberta Gas Trunk Line, a move that had proven hugely successful and politically popular. The suggestion also fit the party's ideological preference for free enterprise, although it ignored another honourable tradition of the Conservative Party: using public corporations to enhance and protect distinctly Canadian values and interests.

Clark made PetroCanada an issue as leader of the Opposition. In the two years preceding the 1979 campaign, Clark and his party tried to paint the Liberals as reckless spenders. They made much of the number of crown corporations that had been established under the Liberals, using the point as part of a larger illustration of Big-Government-Gone-Wild. Bloated bureaucracy, excessive regulation, insensitive political leadership; no Conservative spokesman could open his mouth without touching these arguments. PetroCanada became entwined in the Conservatives' broader criticisms of the Liberal record. But it was Clark who put Petro-Canada front and centre in the party's critique. He used it repeatedly when asked just how the Conservatives would reduce the size of government and lighten the heavy hand of bureaucracy.

The Liberals, sensing the public mood, had begun in the meantime talking half-heartedly about "privatizing" crown corporations. Predictably, the Conservatives picked up the expression and repeated it so often in relation to PetroCanada that "privatization" became almost synonymous with PetroCanada. Anxious, as Opposition leaders frequently are, to provide a ready-made answer to every question, Clark dragged PetroCanada into so many of his speeches that it took on an incandescent political life of its own. Instead of being presented as one of several crown corporations the Conservatives might dismantle, PetroCanada became *the* crown corporation the public associated with the Conservatives' program. But PetroCanada was, after all, an energy corporation. Focusing attention on PetroCanada inevitably placed the party's plans for the corporation in the context of national energy policy, not in the context of Big Government, where the Conservatives wanted the debate.

Having created an issue, the Conservatives found themselves with only half a policy—the proposition to end PetroCanada's life as a crown corporation. As the 1979 election drew near, the other half of the policy question remained unanswered: what did the Conservatives propose to do with PetroCanada? This dilemma was the source of the trouble. Some Conservatives actually liked PetroCanada, and when asked what a Conservative Government might do, they fumbled for a politically safe reply, saying perhaps only part of the corporation would be sold. Others, like Flora MacDonald and David MacDonald, held their peace rather than embarrass the party by disavowing publicly its stand. John Crosbie, appointed the party's energy critic after entering the Commons in an October 1976 by-election, returned from a trip to the west a supporter of PetroCanada. The free-enterprise hawks, their appetites whetted by all the satisfying rhetoric about taming Big Government, cried loudly about what a carrion PetroCanada was about to become.

Clark stepped into this perfectly splendid and politically dangerous confusion with a compromise to paper over the cracks, at least until the party was safely in power. Once elected, he said, the Conservatives would appoint trustees to recommend how best to distribute the shares of PetroCanada to the public. Unfortunately, this compromise raised more questions than it answered, both for the party and the public. Its vagueness neither expunged the previous confusion nor suggested that the party had a clear notion of what it wanted to do. It left much room for the dissidents without offering sufficient solace to the free-enterprisers. The compromise held open so many options that Clark spent the entire election campaign of 1979 trying to explain his clarification. The promise, however, became the basis for a task force on Petro-Canada, set up by the Conservatives in power.

There was understandable curiosity about Clark's determination to keep his PetroCanada promise when he became Prime Minister. Having made the dismantling of the crown corporation such an issue in Opposition, Clark was predictably asked about the timetable for fulfilling his promise at his first press conference as Prime Minister. He replied that the Government "would start this summer with the nomination of trustees who would begin the process of evaluating the assets of PetroCanada."

By mid-August of 1979, scarcely two months after taking office, the Conservative Government knew its imprecise Petro-Canada policy had become a severe political liability. Polls indicated that the public was giving wide support to the crown corporation. An attack on PetroCanada, Canada's largest domestically owned energy company, looked like a defence of the multinational oil companies, with whom politicians nest at their peril. Canadians are not ideologues for or against free enterprise. They are accustomed to a mixed economy, hoping for, if not always receiving, efficiency from either privately or publicly owned corporations. Much as the Conservatives deplored PetroCanada's corporate record, the corporation seemed to be engaged in sensible activities, such as drilling in frontier areas, negotiating state-to-state energy deals, and generally expanding Canadian ownership in a field dominated by the multinationals. A July Gallup Poll confirmed the public sentiment: 48 per cent said they opposed selling shares of PetroCanada to the private sector, 22 per cent supported the idea, and 30 per cent had no opinion. A *Calgary Herald* poll taken in mid-August showed that even in Canada's oil capital residents overwhelmingly (81 per cent) favoured retaining PetroCanada, although 80 per cent of the respondents favoured selling shares of the crown corporation to the private sector.

Even the private oil and gas companies had swung around and now supported PetroCanada. They still did not like PetroCanada's preferential treatment, and oil-company executives felt their counterparts at PetroCanada passed secrets on to Ottawa; but PetroCanada was a vehicle for the financing of joint ventures, a spigot tapped into the federal money tree.* By mid-summer of 1979, PetroCanada was locked into major exploration and development projects with private companies all across Canada. Petro-Canada invested $80 million in the Arctic Islands Exploration Group with Imperial, Gulf, and Panarctic. PetroCanada had a 40-per-cent interest in a large acreage off Sable Island in the Atlantic Ocean, and a stake in a Chevron-Standard project off the coast of Labrador. The Eastcan Group of France had entered into a deal with PetroCanada whereby the crown corporation was drilling off the coast of Newfoundland. Gulf, Saskoil (the Saskatchewan Government's oil company), and PetroCanada were embarked on development of heavy oil near the Alberta-Saskatchewan border. And PetroCanada was involved with the private sector in the Syncrude project, in further tar-sands projects in northern Alberta, and in exploration for natural gas in the high Arctic. In short, PetroCanada was busy, prosperous (showing a profit of $13.7-million in 1978), and popular with the public and the industry.

---

*The Canadian Chamber of Commerce is the country's most inveterate booster of the private sector, yet H. L. Wyatt, elected the chamber's president in September 1979, said about PetroCanada: "It's there. It's serving a purpose and my own feeling is that it should be left alone."

What's more, the Canadian public was becoming increasingly worried about energy. Throughout the summer of 1979 stories poured across the border reporting line-ups for gasoline in the United States. Newspaper stories speculated about the possibility of heating-oil shortages in Canada during the winter. The energy department reported that the heating-oil-supply situation was "tight but managable, but an unusually cold winter or a refinery breakdown could create a shortage." The Organization of Petroleum Exporting Countries (OPEC) had again raised the price of oil to consuming countries and Canada's dependence on imported oil was growing. A sense of energy insecurity was everywhere in the air, and the possibility of dismantling PetroCanada as a crown corporation merely added another element of uncertainty for an already troubled public.

The message that Allan Gregg, the Conservatives' polling expert, delivered in a November memorandum to members of the party's program committee was based on his August polling. His message cut to the heart of the Conservatives' self-imposed dilemma on PetroCanada, warning them how untenable the party's position was.

> The reason that this particular issue area is going to present a problem for us is not because the people of Canada are either for or against institutional changes to PetroCanada as a crown corporation. Rather, the public is increasingly aware that the future is, at best, uncertain.
>
> More particularly, the entire energy issue and energy-related issues tend to bring this belief into focus for the average individual. Our action, therefore, is being presented through the opposition and the media as fueling the uncertainties of the future.
>
> In other words, in the face of an *impending* "energy crisis" and excessive profits by multinational companies, we are seen to be dismantling the only *Canadian* entity standing between the people and the problem. We must therefore, when explaining these changes to PetroCanada, present something more than a knee-jerk commitment to free enterprise.

Finally, conflicting public statements were deepening confusion about the Government's intentions. Shortly after the election, Clark reaffirmed PetroCanada's demise as a crown corporation. He told an American television interviewer that he still intended to take PetroCanada out of government control. In mid-July, the Government created further confusion when PetroCanada was ordered to stop integrating into its structure an American company PetroCanada had acquired, Pacific Petroleums Limited. The order, contained in a letter from Energy Minister Hnatyshyn to the crown corporation, also warned PetroCanada not to make any other corporate changes until the Government's review was completed.

By mid-August, however, Hnatyshyn announced that circumstances had changed dramatically since the Conservatives had taken power. In a front-page story in *The Globe and Mail*, Hnatyshyn said that PetroCanada would not be split up and sold to the private sector, although minor PetroCanada holdings might be offered for sale. Hnatyshyn also said PetroCanada would continue to negotiate state-to-state oil deals with other countries, an activity Clark had argued during the campaign could easily be handled by other federal agencies like the National Energy Board. With Hnatyshyn's statement, the Conservatives had changed direction completely since their days in Opposition: they had gone from arguing that PetroCanada was unnecessary (1975), to allowing that PetroCanada was necessary but better off entirely in private hands (1978), to conceding that PetroCanada would be only partially sold off (1979), to deciding that PetroCanada would remain largely intact.

Hnatyshyn was struggling for a handle on the energy portfolio. He had been persuaded of the need to keep PetroCanada by his department early in his tenure as energy minister. At the beginning of August, his department prepared several long documents for the Cabinet on energy-pricing and PetroCanada. Hnatyshyn signed both, supporting the department's argument that PetroCanada should be kept largely intact. The documents, sensitive to the Conservatives' political dilemma, suggested that some minor assets of PetroCanada could be sold to the private sector, some special privileges accorded PetroCanada rescinded, and tighter Cabinet control imposed on PetroCanada's budget. In a confidential submission to his Cabinet colleagues on August 13, Hnatyshyn said:

> It is my view, however, that a direct agent of federal Government energy policy is likely necessary if we are to achieve our goals. The instruments available to the Government (taxes and regulations) are either not available, or have already been used to their limit. Retention of PetroCanada in a modified form is important.

Predictably enough, Clark and his advisors were annoyed at the department and at Hnatyshyn for having proposed a policy to

Cabinet so at odds with the Conservatives' public position on PetroCanada. From that point on, Hnatyshyn's political stock started sinking within the Prime Minister's office. Gillies, who wanted Ian Stewart replaced as Deputy Minister of Energy, saw the Cabinet documents as confirmation that the department could not be trusted. Gillies thought that Hnatyshyn was simply parroting the department's views. Neville believed the department was being stubborn, if not a trifle mischievous, in presenting a Petro-Canada policy so out of whack with what the Conservatives wanted. Clark, who believed that the share-offering might prove to be an enormous political success, was also unhappy with the department's advice. But Hnatyshyn pressed ahead, winding up where a minister should never find himself: aligned with his department against a determined Prime Minister.

A Prime Minister is more than the first among equals in Cabinet; he sets the general tone for the style and policies of the Government. He cannot possibly attend to all of the problems confronting his Government, nor is he vitally interested in all of them. But there are usually a handful of policies that a Prime Minister believes require his ongoing attention, because he views them as essential either for the country or for his own political credibility. In these instances, ministers are directed to carry out *his* instructions, and when they balk or cast doubt upon the wisdom of the Prime Minister's course of action, they can wind up being ostracized or stripped of the confidence of the man to whom they are beholden for their jobs. Bucking Clark's determination to dismantle PetroCanada simply weakened Hnatyshyn's position in the inner Cabinet, whatever the merits of his arguments.

With Cabinet ministers inadvertently sowing confusion, it became clear to Clark and his advisors that the Government had to find a fixed position. Apart from the energy department's submission to Cabinet on PetroCanada in early August, the ministers had been dealing with other matters. Clark himself had not assigned PetroCanada a high priority; he had been preoccupied with forming his Government and with preparing for and attending the Tokyo Economic Summit in late June, as well as the Commonwealth Conference in Zambia in August. Clark therefore decided that PetroCanada should be placed on the agenda of the inner Cabinet's late-August meeting at the mountain resort at Jasper. There the Government finally settled on its PetroCanada strategy, following a stormy inner Cabinet session that pitted Clark and his political advisors against most of the inner Cabinet. Arriving at Jasper, many members of the inner Cabinet thought

that the sharpest debate would come on the new system of expenditure management. (See Chapter Eight.) Instead, the debate raged
over PetroCanada, which for Joe Clark became a symbol of his
Government's credibility.

Clark had asked Lowell Murray to leave his Cape Breton
retreat in order to give a political report to the inner Cabinet based
on a major national polling survey Allan Gregg had conducted in
August. On the first morning, Murray delivered to the inner
Cabinet some bad news, and then a political lecture. Gregg's polling
showed that the Government was being severely wounded by the
public's impression that the Government was not keeping its
promises. The Jerusalem-embassy affair, Crosbie's first press conference at which he made light of the party's campaign promises,
and waffling on PetroCanada were undermining the party's credibility. When asked which party was most likely to break its
promises, 42 per cent of the respondents to Gregg's poll said the
Conservatives—not the Liberals, whom the Conservatives had
portrayed throughout the 1979 campaign as never having kept
their promises. Murray said that the party had been elected by
voters who expected the Conservatives to make changes in the
way the country was governed, and breaking promises eroded the
electorate's faith that changes were on the way.

The image of a Government that broke its promises was
related to the sombre political overview Murray then delivered.
Instead of basking in the political warmth of a post-election honeymoon, the Conservative Government had slipped marginally in
public esteem since taking office. The mere fact of having been
elected had deprived the Conservatives of their protest vote.
During the May election, Gregg's polling had shown that a
majority of both Liberals and New Democrats considered the Conservatives as their second favourite party. Now, the party enjoyed
less second-choice support than either of the other parties did.
Murray told them bluntly that the Government's political position
was untenable unless ministers began implementing the platform
on which the party had been elected. That meant, among other
things, getting rid of PetroCanada as a crown corporation, just as
Joe Clark had promised. In Murray's analysis, the key to political
survival lay in keeping faith with those who expected the Conservative Government to fulfil its election promises.

At one point during a long afternoon Cabinet session at
Jasper, Clark, his face flushed, said in exasperation that all he
wanted was to be able to say in one year that something called
PetroCanada no longer existed as a crown corporation. To his

surprise, Clark found himself with few allies in the inner Cabinet. Only de Cotret and Stevens came close to sharing Clark's analysis of the PetroCanada problem. Everyone else was opposed. Hnatyshyn was the most persistent defender of PetroCanada. Baker, LaSalle, Jarvis, and Fraser were worried about the political fallout from tampering with PetroCanada. Crosbie, David MacDonald, and Flora MacDonald thought PetroCanada had become a security blanket for Canadians worried about energy; it made no political sense to tamper with it.

The Cabinet understood, however, that the party was publicly identified with the dismantling of PetroCanada. Even those ministers who thought dismantling the crown corporation might be a political mistake knew that the party's broader credibility was at stake, as Murray had argued. The debate therefore centred on how much of PetroCanada to offer to the private sector, and on what terms of reference to give the PetroCanada task force, which the Government had promised to establish even before the election campaign. Most of the Cabinet wanted the terms of reference written so that the task force would examine only a few of Petro-Canada's assets. Clark and his advisors wanted looser terms of reference, giving the task force a broad mandate to turn most of the crown corporation into a private company.

Without resolving the issue, the Cabinet broke for dinner, and Stewart returned to his cabin to draft the proposed terms of reference. As he was working on his porch, Flora MacDonald strolled by, and Stewart beckoned her to join him. The two discussed the terms of reference, commiserating with each other about Clark's decision.

Later that evening, Stewart and Hnatyshyn presented the proposed terms of reference to a meeting in Clark's cabin where the proposals immediately set off a resumption of the intense Cabinet debate. Neville, Gillies, Murray, and Clark all thought that Stewart's proposed terms of reference were designed to leave PetroCanada intact. Neville and Stewart, friends who occasionally played tennis together, found themselves in a heated and prolonged argument. While the debate raged, Flora MacDonald returned from dinner and joined in the fray on the side of Stewart and Hnatyshyn, who felt crushed by the weight of Clark's opinion and complained privately about having been undermined by Gillies. Finally, Clark called a halt to the discussion, saying he would work on the terms of reference. Eventually, they were drafted by Neville and Murray, but not before Flora MacDonald had one last try at changing the course of events. Increasingly upset by Clark's intransigence, she went to Murray's cabin, where she argued fruitlessly with him for nearly an hour.

It was no use. Clark and his advisors were convinced that more than PetroCanada was at stake. Policy was being made on the basis of how to minimize the Government's political losses, and Clark was convinced that more harm would be done by breaking another promise than by courting public displeasure by tampering with PetroCanada. Faced with a determined Prime Minister, supported by his closest political aides, there was nothing the Cabinet dissidents could do. Clark's terms of reference were dutifully approved. It fell to Hnatyshyn to release them to the public, along with the names of the five members of the task force.

Several days after the Jasper meeting, Hnatyshyn walked into the television hot room in the basement of the House of Commons to unveil the terms of reference. He looked distinctly uncomfortable, shifting nervously and sweating profusely, as he dodged reporters' questions about just what the Government wanted to do with PetroCanada.

The Government chose one of its own to lead the task force: Donald McDougall, a former president of Labatt's and a prominent Conservative fundraiser in Ontario who ran unsuccessfully for the Conservatives in London West in the 1980 election. He and three other task-force members were charged with "advising as to the procedures for transferring PetroCanada to private ownership, which of the existing assets of PetroCanada might most beneficially be returned to the private sector, as well as means of broadening Canadian participation and ownership in the petroleum industry." The task force was specifically told that the Government still wanted to be involved in three areas of activity: negotiating state-to-state crude oil contracts, encouraging exploration in frontier areas, and promoting tar-sands and heavy-oils research and development.

Six weeks later the task force, having received consulting help from several Toronto financial houses, produced its report. The task force recommended creating a new government agency to handle the three functions that the Government wanted to retain. The remaining activities of PetroCanada would be taken over by a newly created private company, shares of which would be given to every Canadian citizen. The government had already invested $1 billion in PetroCanada and had guaranteed an additional $1.5 billion in debt. The task force proposed that this debt be assumed by the government. The new private company, to be called Petro-Canada Exploration Limited, would retain all of PetroCanada's holdings from previous takeovers of Atlantic Richfield and Pacific Petroleums. The new company would also have a 10-per-cent interest in the Polar Gas Project (PetroCanada's remaining 15 per cent would be retained by the new government agency), and 15 per cent of Panarctic Oils Limited, the wholly owned government agency.

By appointing the task force, the Government had at least quieted public debate on PetroCanada's future; but the publication of the task force report rekindled the fires of discontent. The Government had come to expect considerable public criticism of its PetroCanada policy, but when the criticism came from within the Conservative Party itself then the Government could scarcely contain the damage.

On October 16, the day after publication of the task force report, Ontario Premier William Davis delivered a lengthy address on energy policy in the Ontario legislature, during which he managed to kick the props out from under the federal government's entire energy policy, including plans for PetroCanada. Davis said:

> Our Government believes the present national responsibilities of PetroCanada should be retained and that the federal Government should retain ownership of Petro-Canada as a national publicly owned petroleum institution. We have advanced this position on several occasions with the federal government, and I sense that on this matter we are reflecting the unanimous concern of the legislature.
>
> I do not believe a new federal government absolutely must retain "every bit" of this company or should not even review its structures of relationship to Parliament. . . . Nevertheless, I do not feel the federal government and our mixed economy have anything to fear from a financially viable PetroCanada operating as a crown corporation to enhance energy security for all Canadians.

Davis was protecting his own political position in Ontario by staying on the popular side of the PetroCanada issue and keeping a safe distance from the Clark Government's energy policies. The Davis Government never understood Clark's misgivings about crown corporations; in Ontario, crown corporations such as Ontario Hydro had always been the pillars of the province's resource policies. Davis' message was designed primarily for political consumption in Ontario, but it went unheeded in Ottawa. Federal Conservatives understood Davis' political requirements in Ontario but wondered why he persisted in his attacks on federal energy policies. After all, the Cabinet had taken its decision on Petro-Canada at Jasper in late August and the task force had finally produced its report. Davis' message came too late to change Ottawa's course, but it helped to undermine further the federal Conservatives' political position in Ontario.

The task force, instead of providing the Government with a ready-made policy for PetroCanada, produced a report unpalatable to a Cabinet committed to fiscal responsibility. By mid-October, Finance Minister Crosbie was well along in the initial stages of preparing his budget designed to attack the deficit, the fastest growing component of which was interest on the public debt. Telling Crosbie and his colleagues to absorb PetroCanada's debt was like asking Hannibal to call off his march on Rome. Since the task force report was unacceptable, Clark asked Hnatyshyn and Minister of State for International Trade Michael Wilson, a former vice-president of Dominion Securities, to head a special Cabinet committee to study the task force report and give Clark a PetroCanada policy once and for all.

The Cabinet committee went to work several weeks after the opening of Parliament. Sensing the Government's vulnerability on the issue, the Liberals and New Democrats zeroed in on Petro-Canada. The NDP attacks were especially effective, since Broadbent made PetroCanada and rising interest rates the focal points of his party's performance in Question Period. Even before Parliament opened, Broadbent had undertaken a cross-country speaking tour designed to warn the public against the Government's Petro-Canada's policies. He received extensive media coverage everywhere he went, defining the issue for the public with the help of buttons that read, "Sell Clark, Save PetroCanada."

In the Commons, Clark and Hnatyshyn struggled to fend off Opposition attacks, their job made more difficult by the Government's lack of a clear policy. Clark defended the emerging direction of Government policy by arguing that a change in the structure of PetroCanada would enhance Canadian participation in energy development. The point was seized upon by the Opposition parties, who wondered how Clark could increase Canadian participation in PetroCanada when the crown corporation was already 100-percent owned by Canadians through the federal government.

When the Government fell, it had undergone two months of intensive parliamentary criticism for its confusion on PetroCanada, with the result that the Conservatives found themselves in the campaign without a clear policy, but facing a public already alarmed about what they thought the Government wanted to do. An election campaign is usually a poor time to explain policy to the voters, many of whom form their impressions of parties, policies, and leaders before the campaign. Nevertheless, Clark was being hit so hard by the Opposition parties on PetroCanada that he was forced to respond with a definitive statement. He had received the report of his special Cabinet committee, and he chose a board of trade meeting in Vancouver at which to unveil his final Petro-Canada decision in the first week of the campaign:

First, PetroCanada will remain intact as a company but it will become a publicly traded commercial corporation. Its mandate will be broadened so that it can become not merely an oil company, but a major energy resource corporation able to expand, as its directors decide, into all aspects of the energy sector.

Second, in recognition of the $1 billion in tax revenues already invested in PetroCanada equity and to let all Canadians have an opportunity to participate personally in owning the company, every adult Canadian will be given the chance to acquire free of charge five shares of PetroCanada.

Third, individual Canadians and Canadian institutions will be offered the right to purchase additional equity in the company, subject to a limit of three per cent of the outstanding shares by any single private shareholder. Only Canadians will be eligible to receive, buy or hold shares.

Fourth, the Government will continue to hold about one-third of the company's shares. This will allow us to oversee and ensure PetroCanada's transition to a commercial corporation.

Fifth, all Canadian children alive on the date of the share issue also will be given the chance on their eighteenth birthday to acquire five free shares in PetroCanada.

Sixth, the current assets of PetroCanada will remain intact. Any changes in assets—be they the disposition of existing holdings or the acquisition of new ones—will be the responsibility of the company's board of directors.

Seventh, the Government will be free to enter into

contract with PetroCanada to take on any public assignment, as the Government can do with any private corporation. The legislation will specify that the Government
may contract with PetroCanada in regard to state-to-state
oil trading, for frontier exploration not justified by
commercial considerations and for special research and
development projects. It would be our intention to utilize
those provisions within the law.

From an initial position taken in Opposition that PetroCanada was
unnecessary, Clark had moved to embrace the idea of a privately
managed PetroCanada whose largest single shareholder would be
the federal government. After arguing that PetroCanada was not
needed for state-to-state energy deals, Clark was now saying the
government might sign contracts with PetroCanada to enter
state-to-state deals on its behalf. If Clark thought his speech
would demonstrate a boldness of vision, he needed only to glance
at the next day's headlines to convince himself of the contrary:
"Conservative Turnaround Seen Over Policy for PetroCanada"
(*The Globe and Mail*); "Now Clark Says He'd Keep Control of
PetroCan" (*The Toronto Star*); "Clark's Miracle: A New, Unchanged
PetroCan" (*The Toronto Star*); "Behold PetroCan, The Latest
Model" (*Victoria Daily Colonist*); "Third Thoughts on PetroCan" (*St.
John's Evening Telegraph*); "Clark Retreats Slightly" (*Windsor Star*);
"PetroCanada Est Sauvée" (*Le Devoir*). For months, the nation's
press had chronicled Clark's "flip-flops" on policy; now, they drove
home the point a final time on PetroCanada.

To be fair to Clark, if the Government had stayed longer in
power, his PetroCanada policy might have become a political
trump card for his Government. He occasionally thought of how
his policy might aid national unity by giving Quebeckers direct
shares in wealth being generated elsewhere in Canada. If shares
had been distributed successfully to Canadians and the value of
those shares had risen over time, Clark might have found a con-
crete demonstration of the model of citizens' capitalism he always
admired.

But the early election caught the Conservatives without a
policy, after months of confusion. As a result, PetroCanada
saddled Clark and his Government with an image of incompetence
for having waited so long to formulate a policy, as well as an image
of arrogance—even stupidity—for having so obviously flouted the
wishes of voters.

~ 7 ~

The Limits of Loyalty

Next to the thorny question of Quebec's status in Canada—which Joe Clark suggested he could solve by putting a "fresh face on federalism"—nothing touched off more rancorous federal-provincial debates during the 1970s than energy policy, especially the pricing and taxation of oil and natural gas.

Into the expensive and complicated field of energy pricing came Joe Clark, confident that with enough good-will and perseverance, and with appeals for co-operation to his Conservative friends in the provincial capitals, he could reach a speedy agreement on a new energy policy. He discovered that with such friends, a man does not require enemies.

Clark's oft-repeated phrase "community of communities" resonated with harmony and brotherhood. It was pleasing to the ear, soothing to the mind, and even inspirational for the soul. As long as no one asked what the phrase meant, or how it should be applied, it stood the test of political rhetoric by offering no offence and inviting a wide range of interpretations. Although Clark used the phrase to laud the cultural diversity of Canada, he also applied it to the political realm of federal-provincial relations. It seemed to mean, in his vague definition, that the federal government had grown too powerful at the expense of provincial governments.

Clark pointed to LotoCanada, the federal ministry of state for urban affairs, and to Ottawa's refusal to cede complete jurisdiction for offshore resources to the provinces as examples of the federal government trampling on provincial territory. He never offered countervailing examples of provinces nosing about in federal domains such as monetary policy, international tariff negotiations, and fisheries policy.

Federal-provincial relations are difficult for the untutored observer or participant to understand. Much of what goes on is hidden from public view; the relative strengths of the two levels of government change periodically through agreements of numbing complexity, which are understood by only a handful of bureaucrats. For example, the Established Programs Financing agreement of 1976 was the single most important development in federal-provincial relations in the 1970s; it changed the financing of post-secondary education, health and hospital insurance, and extended medical care, all of which cost the federal government alone about $7 billion in 1980. But the agreement was negotiated largely by bureaucrats and ministers at closed conferences, and the formulas for apportioning the staggering sums were so complicated that they defeated politicians who sought a rational debate on the issue. The EPF bill passed through Parliament with only a cursory debate.

The EPF was part of a long-term decentralization of power in Canada, a shift that was accompanied, ironically, by increasing provincial complaints about the growing power of the central government. Although the EPF program gave the provinces more tax points and greater flexibility in spending the revenues generated by the tax points, the premiers clamoured that Ottawa was frustrating their economic aspirations. At the beginning of the 1970s, Ottawa's revenues represented 18.1 per cent of gross national product, compared with 16.2 per cent for provincial revenues. By the end of the decade, Ottawa's portion had fallen to about 16 per cent, while the provinces' had risen to about 20 per cent. While higher revenues from oil and natural gas swelled provincial treasuries, Ottawa was burdened with oil import compensation payments to subsidize the price of oil to eastern-Canadian consumers. The same burgeoning revenues for oil- and gas-producing provinces widened the gap between wealthy and poor provinces, driving up the cost of federal equalization payments by about 50 per cent from 1977 to 1980.

The 1970s saw an exponential increase in provincial complaints about the federal system and demands for more money and constitutional power. Before 1970, Quebec was alone in pressing for sweeping new powers. In the 1970's the resource-rich western provinces, then several of the Atlantic provinces, notably Newfoundland and Nova Scotia, picked up Quebec's lead. Even Ontario, which had preferred to play a conciliating role at federal-provincial conferences, began to defend its own interests, as the other regions did. While the provinces demanded more power, they used what considerable powers they already possessed under the constitution to erect new barriers to interprovincial mobility of goods, services, and labour. They imposed preferential purchasing and hiring policies, passed laws restricting the sale of land to non-residents, and acted as "province-firsters" in dealings with Ottawa and neighbouring provinces.

The federal Liberals, in power for all but the last seven months of the 1970s, made a convenient target for provincial governments and parties of different political stripes. At the beginning of the decade, the Liberals were in power in six provinces; by the end of the decade, the party had been wiped out of every provincial government. The principal beneficiary of the Liberals' decline was the Conservative Party. It knocked the Liberals out of office in all four Atlantic provinces, toppled the NDP in Manitoba and the Social Credit Party in Alberta. When Joe Clark took office there were six Conservative premiers in Canada, and a seventh, John Buchanan of Nova Scotia, came to power four months after Clark.

In the 1979 election campaign, Joe Clark told the country that the election of a Conservative Government in Ottawa would reduce tensions between the federal and provincial governments. After all, the election of Clark's Conservatives would give the party control of seven of the eleven federal and provincial governments in Canada. Trudeau warned that Clark would be nothing more than a "headwaiter" for the Conservative premiers, but Clark replied that "the Canadian federation is a community of communities, and the whole is strong when the local communities are strong." By yielding jurisdiction in selected areas, by increasing the intensity of consultation with provincial governments, and by counting on reciprocal co-operation from Conservative provincial governments, Clark promised to end the bickering that characterized relations between the federal government and the provinces. "We have the capacity, uniquely, to draw together the premiers of six of the provinces—premiers of our party—and to find common cause with other premiers who want to make the kind of changes that will make the system work. We can establish the trust that Mr. Trudeau has wasted," Clark promised.

His promise was put to the test when he entered negotiations with Alberta for a new oil pricing agreement. Under the constitution, the provinces own and manage resources within their territories. The federal government has jurisdiction over interprovincial and international trade. Both governments are equipped with authority to tax revenues and profits from resources. Throughout the 1970s, the governments used their respective powers in ways that provoked confrontations and stirred tensions. After the world oil crisis of 1973, the federal government and the producing provinces entered into a series of agreements to regulate the price of domestic oil and natural gas. The agreements were designed to eliminate the differential between domestic and international prices by the early 1980s through a series of increases in domestic prices. From 1974 to 1979, the price of domestic crude oil in Toronto increased by 18 per cent a year, and the gap between domestic and imported oil prices narrowed from 79 per cent in 1974 to 25 per cent at the end of 1978. Soon afterwards, the Organization of Petroleum Exporting Countries (OPEC) launched another series of massive price increases. As a result of these increases, the domestic price began falling behind the leapfrogging world price.

Negotiations over energy pricing between Ottawa and the producing provinces had always been attended by mutual suspicion. The governments of consuming provinces, especially Ontario, did not play a direct role in the negotiations; their best ally was public opinion in their own provinces. The producing provinces usually figured that Ottawa was cocking a more attentive ear to consuming provinces' demands for the lowest possible price increases than it was to their own demands for rapid price escalations.

Five weeks after becoming Prime Minister of Canada, Joe Clark received a memorandum from Ian Stewart, Deputy Minister of Energy, advising him that the country's energy problems were so serious that "perhaps only an heroic approach in a defined and urgent time frame has a reasonable chance of success." Clark and Stewart had just returned to Canada from the Tokyo Economic Summit, where the leaders of the seven leading industrial nations had been preoccupied with energy, especially the Western world's growing reliance on oil imported from OPEC. Impressed by the urgency of the energy problem for Canada and the Western world, Clark set out to develop a new energy policy for Canada.

Nothing had adequately prepared either Joe Clark or his party for the task at hand. In Opposition, the Conservatives drafted an unrealistic energy policy based on a number of misconceptions and a refusal to confront the key question in any sensible energy policy: the price of oil and natural gas. Once in power, the Opposition party found its illusions shattered by the civil service, which produced a series of policy recommendations for which the

(CP Photo)

Jim Coutts

(Ted Grant)

Senator Lowell Murray

Pierre Trudeau on the night of the Conservative Government's defeat in the House of Commons

(CP Photo/Fred Chartrand)

Jim Coutts and Pierre Trudeau aboard the Liberal plane in the 1979 campaign

Senator Keith Davey

Martin Goldfarb, the Liberals' polling expert

Allan Gregg, the Conservatives' polling expert

(Photo Features Ltd.)

Robin Sears, NDP federal secretary

John Crosbie

(CP Photo/Dave Buston)

(CP Photo/Fred Chartrand)

Joe Clark, with wife Maureen McTeer in background

William Neville, Clark's chief-of-staff

(CP Photo/Roger Arar)

Joe Clark

NDP leader Ed Broadbent   Jim Gillies, Clark's economic policy advisor

The Conservatives' brain trust with Clark at the Prime Minister's morning
staff meeting. Left to right: André Payette, Ian Green, Nancy Jamieson,
Donald Doyle, Jock Osler, Lowell Murray

Pierre Trudeau: the approaching victory put joy into his campaign

Conservatives were unprepared. Similarly, the Conservatives had convinced themselves, more by constant repetition than by cogent analysis, that energy and other federal-provincial problems could be solved if the new Government in Ottawa spread sufficient good-will around the country. Never having known power before, the Conservatives under Clark were surprised and then disillusioned when their foray into the energy domain proved more difficult than they had ever anticipated in Opposition.

To Joe Clark's credit, he made the "heroic" effort Stewart recommended to forge a new energy policy. He nearly succeeded, but he failed because his Government collapsed just when it finally appeared that a pricing agreement might be signed with Alberta Premier Peter Lougheed. It had taken months of excruciating bargaining with Lougheed even to approach an agreement, and the story of those months is, in part, Joe Clark's slow disillusionment with the Alberta premier and the shaking of the young Prime Minister's conviction that the Conservative premiers of Canada really wished him to succeed. He was naive on entering the negotiations; nothing in Opposition had prepared him for the intractability of provincial governments. He believed that by showing good-will and making early concessions he could consummate a speedy energy agreement that would fulfil his election promise to end the warring between Ottawa and the provinces. An early agreement would show a sceptical public that he possessed the vision and toughness to be Prime Minister. Instead, he discovered that the premiers cared at least as much about their own provinces as about the national interest, and cared much more about their own political necks than about helping Joe Clark.

As the negotiations dragged on with Alberta, Clark found his political position undermined in Ontario by the public perception that he was capitulating to Alberta. That perception was strengthened enormously by Ontario Premier William Davis, who launched a systematic campaign to discredit Clark's energy policy in order to protect the Ontario Conservative Party's standing in Ontario. Rather than preparing Ontario for the inevitability of higher oil and natural-gas prices, Davis told his province that any increase in oil prices would prove disastrous for its comfortable way of life. With every speech he delivered, Davis hammered another nail in Clark's political coffin.

Struggling with Lougheed and undermined by Davis, Clark was also forced to reconcile divisions within the federal government over energy policy. PetroCanada illustrated one issue on which the Government was divided; the energy policy negotiations revealed others, especially between the Department of Energy, Mines and Resources and some of Clark's own political advisors.

Most damaging of all was the Clark Government's failure to explain its emerging energy policy to the people. Clark knew from a wide variety of sources that the public would resist higher energy prices. Canadians simply did not believe that there was an energy problem, let alone an "energy crisis," in their country. They were paying the lowest prices for gasoline and heating oil in the Western world. The real price of gasoline had not risen since 1961. Canadians believed the country possessed an inexhaustible supply of natural resources, including oil, that would see the nation through the future. Yet all the talk about an energy crisis created public concern that the comfortable blanket of energy security at low prices might soon be ripped away. Uncertainty breeds suspicion, and across the country Canadians searched for appropriate villains. Albertans found their *bête noire* in William Davis and the prosperity he represented in Ontario. Ontario looked enviously at Alberta's burgeoning Heritage Fund and listened angrily to Lougheed's insistent demands for more money; but there was no direct outlet for Ontario's frustration with Peter Lougheed. There was an outlet, however, when Joe Clark faced the voters of Ontario on February 18, 1980.

Joe Clark's Cabinet received a full briefing on Canada's energy predicament from Ian Stewart and other energy department officials in the Government's first week in office. Although the energy field is fiendishly complicated, the essence of Stewart's message was quite straightforward: Canada had an oil problem that was getting worse. Canada possessed a surplus of other energy forms—natural gas, electricity and nuclear power—but oil imports were increasing rapidly and Canada's own supplies of conventional crude oil were running down. The importing of ever-larger amounts of foreign oil was increasing the federal deficit, since Ottawa was subsidizing the price of imported oil in eastern Canada to maintain a one-price system across Canada. That price—$12.75 per barrel when Clark took office—was about half the world price. The twice-yearly increases of $1 per barrel in the domestic price—increases negotiated between the Trudeau Government and the producing provinces—were so small that the gap between the Canadian and world prices was widening.

Little could be done quickly to increase Canada's own oil

supplies. There were enormous quantities of oil lying in Alberta's tar sands, in heavy oil deposits in western Canada, and in prospects for commercial production in the Beaufort Sea and off the Atlantic Coast, but these would take years to develop. For Canada to reduce its dependence on imported oil—the supply of which could be threatened at any time by political events far beyond Canada's control—Canadians would have to curb their appetite for oil. Policies were needed that would reduce demand, preferably by sharp domestic price increases that would induce conservation and encourage Canadians to switch to cheaper and more abundant energy sources like natural gas. Even then, achieving energy self-sufficiency by 1990—the Conservatives' election promise—would be difficult.

This was a disconcerting overview for a group of men and women who had proposed in Opposition very different solutions to the energy problem. For about eighteen months before the 1979 election, the Conservatives had been hardening their commitment to energy (meaning oil) self-sufficiency. In August 1978, the Conservative caucus' energy committee published a policy paper recommending that Canada be "self-sufficient in energy possibly as early as 1990." By March 1979, that recommendation had been toughened to read: "A Progressive Conservative Government will institute policies which will assure that Canada is self-sufficient in energy by 1990." In his first statement of the election campaign, Clark said: "We know this country can be self-sufficient in energy by 1990, and we are determined that eastern Canadians no longer should have to rely on uncertain foreign sources to heat their homes and put gas in their cars."

The Conservatives in Opposition believed that increasing domestic supplies, not reducing demand, provided the key to self-sufficiency. The party's position papers exuded confidence that the private sector could unlock the riches of the tar sands and the offshore frontier to make Canada self-sufficient. The papers did mention reducing demand, not by raising prices sharply, but by a series of voluntary conservation measures. The Conservatives had been stung by the price issue in 1973, the year of the first substantial OPEC price increases. The Ontario and Alberta wings of the Conservative caucus had not been able to agree on the appropriate speed for oil-price increases in Canada. The party was embarrassed by its failure to reach a consensus in 1973, so rather than expose itself to another internecine debate, the Conservatives took the easy way out and ignored the price question altogether during the 1979 campaign. Once in office, however, the Conservatives quickly learned that their promise of self-sufficiency could only be achieved by dramatic price increases. Such increases meant following a treacherous political course that would take enormous political skill to negotiate, given the vested interests of Alberta and Ontario. Indeed, the promise of self-sufficiency, laudable as an objective, was never given sufficient study by the Conservative caucus, whose principal spokesmen on the issue were Jim Gillies and Harvie Andre. Andre, in particular, was much influenced by the analysis of the private oil companies in his home city. Their basic credo was: give us enough money and incentives and we'll find all the oil there is. Acceptance of that credo, however, risked ignoring a range of other energy issues: the distribution of revenues among governments, the impact on consumers, the healthy state of oil-company profits. But Andre and Gillies had their way; energy self-sufficiency became a Conservative slogan before and during the 1979 election—a rallying cry that obliterated the need for careful questioning of what the goal implied.

Shortly after the Cabinet's initial energy briefing, Flora MacDonald and John Crosbie left for Paris for a meeting of the Organization for Economic Co-operation and Development. There they discovered to their astonishment that everyone was talking about oil. They had expected a general overview of the international economy; instead they found the member countries preoccupied with the precariousness of the international oil situation, especially in the wake of the revolution in Iran, one of the most important oil-producing countries in the world.

Upon their return, MacDonald, Crosbie, and Clark began preparing themselves for the Tokyo Economic Summit where, once again, the international oil situation would dominate the agenda. The Tokyo summit coincided with a price-fixing meeting of OPEC, and the western European summit partners were determined to push the United States, a profligate energy-user, into setting strict limits on its consumption. The western Europeans reasoned that they could not convince OPEC to moderate price increases unless the consuming nations, especially the United States, were serious about reducing their demand for oil.

Clark was nervous when he arrived in Tokyo—more nervous than he had ever been in public life, one of his aides said later. His own world trip as Opposition leader in January had shaken his confidence in his ability to master foreign policy. He left behind in Ottawa the Jerusalem-embassy affair, having announced the Stanfield mission on the eve of his departure for Tokyo. In short, his credentials in foreign affairs were poor, and he wanted desperately to succeed at the summit.

As so often happens, Canada found itself trying to suggest compromises to the Europeans and the Americans. Canada had nothing to brag about—we had the highest per-capita energy consumption in the Western world—but the Europeans were primarily upset with the consumption record of the United States. The Americans, in turn, were peeved that the Europeans had arrived at the summit proclaiming the need for all the summit partners to freeze oil imports until 1985. This was a somewhat disingenuous position for the Europeans; their oil-import targets looked impressive because British North Sea oil, not available to western Europe, was nevertheless included in their calculations.

Although Clark entered his first meeting with the other six Western leaders feeling extremely nervous, he had been well briefed. After the first round of discussions his nervousness began to disappear. He remarked to an aide that sitting with the mighty of the Western world was not so different from political meetings he had attended in Canada. The leaders argued, squabbled and postured just like any group of politicians back home. Feeling progressively more confident, Clark intervened regularly in the discussions, impressing some of the participants with his grasp of facts and his ability to make his points in both English and French. Behind the scenes, Clark, MacDonald, and Stewart worked to find accommodations between the western Europeans and the Americans. When the conference ended with a communique acceptable to all the participants, Clark was delighted with his own performance. He was also pleased with the advice he had received from Marcel Massé, Ian Stewart, and Undersecretary of State for External Affairs Allan Gotlieb. This satisfaction later helped to persuade Clark to keep Stewart and Gotlieb in their jobs, despite pressures from within his Cabinet and his inner circle of advisors to transfer both men to new positions.

At a summit designed for participants to commit themselves to reduce consumption, Canada had to offer a target for itself. First, Clark agreed to hold Canada's 1980 imports at 1979 levels, a forlorn hope given increasing consumption in Canada. Second, he pledged that Canada would reduce its yearly increases in oil consumption from about 3.5 per cent to one per cent by 1985. Given declining conventional crude-oil production in Canada, that would mean importing 600,000 barrels of oil per day, instead of 650,000 per day.

Before he left for home, Clark said Canada would meet its

commitments by pushing conservation, accelerating domestic supply, and negotiating new and higher domestic prices with Canada's producing provinces.

"It is clear that prices in Canada are now seriously out of line with those in the United States and even further out of line with those prevailing in the rest of the world," Clark said.

Clark did not mention moving the Canadian price to world levels, but the final communique said:

> We agree on the importance of keeping domestic oil prices at world market prices or raising them to this level as soon as possible. We will seek to minimize and finally eliminate administrative action that might put upward pressure on oil prices that result from domestic under-pricing of oil and to avoid new subsidies which would have the same effect.

On his return to Canada, Clark and Energy Minister Ray Hna-tyshyn asked Ian Stewart to outline how the Government might meet its international obligations. More generally, they wanted advice on developing an energy strategy and on fulfilling their election promise to make Canada self-sufficient in energy by 1990.

Stewart's reply, a memorandum dated July 12, began by underlining energy's importance in economic policy and added prophetically: "It is also clear . . . that a strong public sense of the Government's control of energy issues will have a great deal to do with the Government's political fortunes." To reach self-suffi-ciency by 1990, the Government needed to move quickly to increase domestic supply, although new energy projects would take many years to develop. But more crucial was "the degree to which the Government will employ the pricing of oil as a central pillar in its policy structure." After laying out a timetable of work for the months ahead, Stewart ended with a shrewd assessment of the need to sell any energy policy to a sceptical public:

> The success of a dramatic adventure of this kind would clearly depend on the most careful attention to the process of preparing the public, the various publics and the provinces. . . . One is also, of course, seeking to con-vince Canadians that there is opportunity in all of this and not just blood, sweat and tears.
>
> The task in the time-frame proposed here is perhaps too heroic. One can only note that Mr. Carter's difficulties lie less in the quality of his ideas than in the deep lack of

public acceptance. To public acceptance difficulties one adds in Canada the perhaps deeper difficulty of seeking federal-provincial and inter-provincial consensus. Perhaps only an heroic approach in a defined and urgent time frame has a reasonable chance of success.

In mid-July, the Clark Government began in earnest to tackle the energy problem. If Clark could get an agreement on oil pricing with Alberta that offered ways of cushioning the impact for consuming provinces, Clark believed that he could show the country that the Conservatives were capable of solving important national problems. A successful energy policy would demonstrate that federalism could be made to work effectively if the federal government improved the climate of relations with the provinces. In Opposition, the Conservatives had decried Liberal energy policies and tactics; here was a splendid chance to show that the new Conservative Government was possessed of a sure sense of direction. Action would further show that the Conservatives were fulfilling an election promise. The issue was crucial, cutting to the heart of economic policy and federal-provincial relations. The stakes were high and the risk of failure was great. The Conservative premiers would want the new Conservative Government in Ottawa to succeed—or so Joe Clark reasoned.

Federal officials began drafting comprehensive energy policy papers in July. These were discussed with the provinces and forwarded to the Cabinet, under Hnatyshyn's signature, on August 13, several weeks before the late-August meeting of the inner Cabinet at Jasper. They were remarkable documents that provoked a sharp debate within the federal government and contained the seeds of subsequent disputes with Alberta and Ontario.

The first Cabinet document, entitled "Background to Energy Policy Choices," laid out the basic facts of Canada's energy (read oil) predicament:

1. Canada had become a net importer of oil since 1976. The nation's deficit in oil would grow rapidly in the 1980s unless substantial new supplies were discovered or domestic prices increased rapidly.

2. Even with "dramatic increases in the price of oil and substantial restraint on the price of natural gas, oil imports would still be 430,000 barrels per day in 1985 and 315,000 barrels per day in 1990."

3. As a result, "oil self-sufficiency by 1990 is unlikely, but with pricing policies emphasizing substitution by gas, movement of oil prices to the world level and an ambitious non-conventional and heavy oils program, imports of oil might be reduced to about 170,000 barrels per day."

4. The department was sceptical about large new domestic supplies of oil in the 1980s, even if prices moved up quickly. Reducing the increase in the demand for oil was a more effective policy for self-sufficiency than waiting for dramatic oil discoveries.

5. High energy prices hit low-income groups the hardest. Government fiscal measures would be needed to offset the impact of higher prices.

6. An excessively generous tax system had allowed some petroleum companies to pay little, if any, tax. The system also favoured large, integrated multinational companies at the expense of smaller companies, many of which were Canadian.

7. The oil-producing provinces were reaping an unexpected bonanza from the existing tax and royalty system. Even if domestic prices continued to rise by only $1 per barrel every six months, Alberta's Heritage Fund would swell from $5 billion to $25 billion by 1985. Any acceleration in the schedule of oil-price increases would make the fund obscenely fat.

8. The oil and gas industry possessed sufficient funds to finance future exploration projects.

This forty-eight-page document contradicted many of the assumptions the Conservatives held about energy in Opposition. The department was saying that energy self-sufficiency by 1990 was "unlikely," a discreet bureaucratic phrase meaning "almost impossible." The Conservatives' emphasis on new supplies was wrong; the department said new discoveries were improbable. The oil and gas companies, friends of Harvie Andre and other Conservative M.P.s, were overflowing with money. Finally, the department warned the Cabinet that any energy policy must give Ottawa a larger percentage of additional revenues from higher prices than the federal government had been receiving.

Needless to say, the document annoyed those close to Clark, such as Jim Gillies and William Neville, whose solution to the energy predicament was not reflected in the department's analysis. But no sooner did they finish reading the background document when their eyes fell on an accompanying twenty-eight-page Cabinet document, also signed by Hnatyshyn and written in an exhortatory style.

"The Government is at a fork in the road. . . . Self-sufficiency requires much higher oil prices, and the sooner the better," Hnatyshyn's document stated. Then, in a sentence that captured the political task that the Clark Government never mastered, the document warned: "The Canadian consumer and his provincial government will have to be persuaded that there is a basic link between the two [self-sufficiency and higher oil prices]; that something is being gained in exchange for higher prices."

In a classic example of the Opposition-party mentality at work, Hnatyshyn's document argued that only fundamental changes could put things right.

> The need is evident and the time propitious for this Government to demonstrate by its energy policies that it is different from the one that preceded it. . . . The repeated promise of technical fixes, big projects and generous subsidies that characterized the former Government may have lulled Canadians into believing that they alone in the world were to escape relatively un-scathed from the OPEC trauma. The truth needs to be brought home to them. . . . If we do nothing, as time passes and tensions mount, it will be this Government and not the old which will be held responsible, for we will have foregone the opportunity to change.

The document then recommended moving the domestic price to world levels in the next three years. Such a move "would strike hard at consumers and enrich producers beyond any reasonable or acceptable expectations." This meant that the federal government needed revenues to offset some of the negative economic conse-quences for consumers of higher energy prices and to minimize economic dislocation in oil-consuming provinces. In order to finance these measures Ottawa would need to take a healthy slice of any additional price rise above the $2-per-barrel yearly increase already in place. The document warned the Cabinet that:

> We should have, however, no illusions about the dangers of the path I suggest. Unless skilfully sold, consumers will react violently to such draconian price rises. A major con-frontation with Alberta is not unlikely. Indeed, it is hard to believe we could possibly reach a solution involving the changes I propose without some conflict with Alberta, and perhaps more importantly, without Alberta believing that we were prepared to take them on in a major con-frontation if they refused to compromise.

If the Cabinet rejected higher oil prices and preferred to maintain the existing $2-per-barrel yearly increases until the agreement with Alberta expired on July 1, 1980, then the document proposed "an immediate, large increase in the excise tax on gasoline—in the order of 30 to 50 cents per gallon." The seed of a politically poisonous weed had been planted.

Now, for the crux of the proposal outlined in the Cabinet documents. Ottawa would agree to raise the price of oil by $18 per barrel over the next three years, an acceleration of $12 per barrel from the existing schedule of price increases. But, in return, Ottawa wanted all of the industry's additional revenues and some of the producing provinces' to "offset the economic impact of higher energy prices, conserve energy and finance new energy projects" through the creation of an Energy Self-Sufficiency Fund and a Canada Resource Corporation. The new corporation—part public, part private—would invest in energy projects. This was the essential trade-off: Alberta would get substantially higher prices if Ottawa could be assured of enough money to mitigate the economic impact of higher prices in the rest of the country. The subsequent tortured history of the Clark Government's energy negotiations turned on that trade-off.

Jim Gillies, Clark's policy advisor, did not like what he saw in those Cabinet documents. Gillies had been instrumental in developing what passed for a Conservative energy policy when the party was in Opposition. That policy set self-sufficiency as a goal by 1990, but it relied on vastly increasing the supply of Canadian oil. Gillies especially disliked the department's combination of two questions: higher oil prices and the distribution of revenues resulting from the higher prices. He thought the department should concentrate on developing policies to increase the supply of oil and let the finance department worry about the macroeconomic impact of higher prices. In Gillies view, there was nothing to fear from Alberta's enormous Heritage Fund: "when our regions prosper, the whole country prospers," he used to say. Clutching for some of Alberta's revenues was a sure way of provoking a confrontation that would injure federal-provincial relations. Gillies reasoned as follows: get the price increase first, to speed up new projects and increase supply; recoup some money for energy projects elsewhere in Canada, again to increase supply or to induce substitution by natural gas; offer some help to those hit hardest by higher prices, but don't mix a new division of revenues into the pricing negotiations; put the revenue question over until later, perhaps until the creation of a royal commission into federal-provincial fiscal relations.

A week after the documents arrived at the inner Cabinet, Gillies called together in Toronto a group of oil executives and energy experts, including Thomas Kierans, chairman of the Ontario Economic Council. Clark had asked Gillies to arrange the meeting, and Ian Stewart was invited so that the department would benefit from this outside advice. Gillies' August 24 memorandum to the inner Cabinet summarized the results of the meeting and the difference between his approach and that of the department. The memo was written in point form, outlining Gillies' argument that the recycling of revenues from higher oil prices should be left until later.

> Take problems as they develop and clearly begin analysis of fiscal implication in context of entire fiscal framework of the nation—not in context of energy policy alone.
> The group more or less (but without consensus) . . . saw the problem of recycling and wealth distribution changes inherent in higher prices *but* urged that this be examined in broader context than energy and not let the problem delay energy progress.
> Increase in price clearly means more wealth for provinces that have resources, but also more prosperity for the nation in general.

This fundamental difference between Gillies and the energy department plagued the federal government's efforts to arrive at an agreed-upon negotiating strategy with Alberta. Valuable time and effort were spent within the federal government in arriving at a consensus. Personal relations were strained when Gillies began pressing Clark to replace Stewart as Deputy Minister of Energy. Gillies wanted Thomas Kierans for the job, but Clark would not sack Stewart, who had won Clark's trust at the Tokyo summit. Gillies' presence also embittered relations with Ontario, whose officials felt that he had an inordinate influence on Clark. And, of course, Clark himself was constantly torn between the advice of his principal economic policy advisor and his own Minister and Department of Energy.

During the summer, the provincial governments learned of the emerging federal policy when federal officials circulated their thoughts to test provincial reaction. As the federal policy took shape, Ontario Premier William Davis started to feel distinctly uncomfortable. The Ontario Conservatives were in a minority position at Queen's Park, where the Opposition parties were making noises about fighting hard against oil-price increases. Like their federal counterparts, the Ontario Conservatives assumed that a federal election lay some distance away; but a provincial election could come soon, if not in the fall then probably in the spring of 1980. Davis had worked hard for Clark in the 1979 federal campaign; if the Ontario Conservatives were to face the voters first, Davis certainly did not relish being tied politically to a federal Government hell-bent on raising oil prices to world levels.

By mid-summer, some of Davis' political aides and Cabinet ministers began to believe that the coalition of voters that had brought the federal Conservatives so much success in Ontario, especially in the politically volatile suburbs of Toronto, was breaking down. Similarly, the Ontario Conservatives, who seldom undertook any initiative without commissioning public-opinion polls, had polls of their own showing opposition in Ontario to higher energy prices. In September, they communicated to Ottawa the results of a province-wide poll, taken by the federal Conservatives' polling expert, Allan Gregg. He had left Ottawa after the 1979 federal election to join a public-opinion research firm in Toronto. Gregg's polling confirmed that higher prices meant political trouble for the offending Government in Ontario. Hugh Segal, Davis' chief political aide, took the message to Ottawa, where the warning did not receive the notice it warranted. The federal Conservatives simply did not believe that an early federal election was possible. None of Clark's Cabinet ministers from Ontario worried about the political fallout from higher prices. In fact, Flora MacDonald, the most influential minister from Ontario in Clark's Cabinet, had become a convert to higher energy prices following her attendance at international economic meetings. Minister of Finance John Crosbie agreed with her. The federal Conservatives said they understood Davis' own political requirements, but their policy was in the best interests of Canada.

Gillies, of course, believed that the Ontario Conservatives were poor economists. The Ontario Conservatives went one better; they thought Gillies was a dangerous economist, preoccupied with supply to the exclusion of concern for the impact of higher prices on inflation and growth. After all, the federal Cabinet's own energy background paper predicted that inflation would rise by 0.6 per cent and unemployment by 0.2 per cent for every $1-per-barrel price rise in oil. A $6-per-barrel price increase would bring disastrous economic consequences for the Ontario economy. Moreover, Gillies had been the major proponent of wage-and-price controls before the 1974 election, and that spoke volumes about his political acumen to Davis' aides at Queen's Park, several of whom had worked in Robert Stanfield's office before the 1974 election.

The Ontario Conservatives had maintained themselves in power since 1943, governing like experienced tracking dogs, nose down following the scent of public opinion. Joe Clark's coalition in Ontario was crumbling: the disaffected Liberals and New Democrats who voted against their party in the 1979 election had returned to their accustomed political homes. Clark came from western Canada. His commitment to higher oil prices was political suicide in Ontario. William Davis had helped to elect Joe Clark, and the Prime Minister of Canada was becoming a political liability. The Ontario Conservatives needed to put distance between themselves and Joe Clark.

The Ontario Conservatives warned their federal cousins to expect a public parting of the ways, and the breach opened when Davis released a policy paper on energy prices on the eve of the annual premiers' conference at Pointe Au Pic, Quebec, in late August. The policy paper irritated the premiers, who resented the attention lavished on it by the media. But the paper was really intended to influence the inner Cabinet—meeting after the premiers' conference at Jasper—and public opinion in Ontario. The energy negotiations were between the federal government and Alberta; the Ontario Government's best hope for leverage lay in galvanizing public opinion in the province against the emerging federal energy policy.

The Ontario policy paper opposed any "immediate" price increase beyond the $1-per-barrel increase already scheduled for January 1, 1980, under the existing agreement between Ottawa and the producing provinces. Ontario officials said privately that there was no need for a comprehensive, three-year agreement when the existing agreement expired on July 1, 1980. At the very least, Ontario wanted to forestall an initial whopping increase that could hurt the province's economy.

That position, of course, was unacceptable to Alberta, whose oil was dramatically undervalued in relation to world prices. It was also unacceptable to Ottawa, where the new Government wanted a comprehensive agreement to show it could successfully manage federal-provincial relations. Ontario's piecemeal approach would also have required negotiations stretching over the next few years, a depressing prospect to both Ottawa and Alberta.

Even if the province could not say so publicly for political

192 / Discipline of Power

reasons, Ontario understood that higher oil prices were inevitable. The economic facts demanded them, and the producing provinces would not support a renewal of the existing agreement with its $2-per-barrel yearly increases. Ontario was seeking a change in the flow of revenues resulting from higher prices. The province wanted the federal government to take a bigger slice of those revenues and recycle them through the Canadian economy in order to offset the impact of higher prices. Ontario also insisted that the producing provinces relinquish some of their revenues to help mitigate the economic consequences of higher prices in the consuming provinces. If the producing provinces balked, then Ontario urged Ottawa to consider using its draconian constitutional power to alter unilaterally the revenue flows.

"It should be well understood by the federal Government that it is charged with the responsibility and has the legitimate constitutional authority to avert an intolerable economic and social danger. If necessary, the federal Government must use its influence and constitutional authority to direct oil and natural gas revenue flows in accordance with agreed national objectives," said the Ontario Government in its policy paper.

This threat of using the "declaratory" power in the constitution, coupled with Ontario's resistance to immediate price increases, enraged Alberta Premier Peter Lougheed. He and Davis met in Montreal before the premiers' conference and the discussion ended in a stalemate. Lougheed had hoped that the Clark Government had convinced Ontario to be quiescent in the upcoming negotiations. Ontario's policy paper killed that possibility. Ontario had four times as many voters as Alberta; if Ottawa bent to any political pressure it would be Ontario's, and Alberta would have to fight as hard as ever against the combination of the federal government and Ontario voters. At the premiers' conference, Lougheed angrily denounced Ontario's policy paper, claiming that it represented the economic status quo that Albertans were determined to change. The energy negotiations had not yet started, and already Alberta and Ontario were locked into fixed positions, with the federal government caught in the middle and Joe Clark still hoping that by imparting good will he could produce an early and acceptable settlement.

In this climate of controversy, the inner Cabinet met in Jasper in late August to consider the Cabinet papers prepared by the energy department. With surprising ease, given the enormous political stakes, the inner Cabinet came to a decision about an initial offer to Alberta, which was communicated to the province in the following week by federal officials. Clark himself met Lougheed in Calgary on the way back from Jasper to brief him on the thrust of the federal position.

By conceding an enormous price increase, Ottawa hoped that its proposals might find favour in Alberta. Ottawa proposed that the domestic price rise by $6 per barrel for three years, pushing the domestic price from $13.75 per barrel to $31.75 per barrel by 1983.* Similarly, Clark made it clear that his Government would never threaten Alberta's cherished jurisdiction over natural resources. With those two concessions, Clark hoped Alberta would accept Ottawa's national responsibility to mitigate adverse economic consequences in the consuming provinces. To achieve that goal, Ottawa proposed taking half the additional revenues from higher prices. The producing provinces, principally Alberta, would get the remaining 50 per cent, but some of that money would be contributed to a Stabilization Fund to offset negative macroeconomic consequences. The producing provinces would also put up money on an equity basis to a National Energy Bank to finance energy projects across Canada to enhance self-sufficiency. To make natural gas an attractive substitute for oil, Ottawa wanted new natural gas to be priced at 65 per cent of the value of the energy equivalent in oil, although gas already under contract would continue to be pegged to 85 per cent of the price of oil.

Lougheed was again furious. He refused to make any equity contribution to a National Energy Bank or a Stabilization Fund. It was for Alberta, which owned the natural resources, to determine what to do with the provincial revenues from those resources. He rejected the dark picture of economic recession painted by Ontario and apparently accepted by the federal government. The consuming provinces had been living on cheap oil ever since the OPEC crisis of 1973. Alberta's conventional crude oil was being sold at half the world price. What more did Ontario want, and what more did Ottawa expect Alberta to give? Lougheed demanded. Alberta's conventional crude oil was running out; it would be seriously depleted by the early 1990s. Alberta needed its Heritage Fund to guard against that day, and not one penny was going to be diverted from that Heritage Fund to an Energy Bank or a Stabilization Fund controlled by the federal government.

The fact that Joe Clark was a Conservative scarcely moved

---

*The price had risen automatically from $12.75 per barrel to $13.75 per barrel on July 1, 1979.

Peter Lougheed. Clark had once worked for Lougheed, and the Alberta premier considered Clark to be his intellectual inferior. He simply did not have much respect for the Prime Minister of Canada, whom he felt was poorly briefed and not quite up to the job. In such circumstances, Lougheed felt it inevitable that Clark and his ineffective Energy Minister Ray Hnatyshyn would yield to the advice of federal bureaucrats in the energy and finance departments. Men like Ian Stewart were just the sort of federal officials Lougheed had in mind when he railed against Ottawa bureaucrats who desired only to gather more power unto the federal government. He had no use for them and he had a profound suspicion of their every motive, having battled with them for eight years since becoming premier of Alberta. The feeling was mutual, but held more deeply on the Alberta side, reflecting the defensive mentality in the political and bureaucratic circles around Lougheed. Lougheed knew more about energy than Joe Clark did; his ministers were better informed than Clark's team, so Lougheed reasoned that the federal civil servants were Clark's best and only weapon. And how he distrusted those civil servants.

Alberta refused to budge: there would not be a grant to the Energy Bank or the Stabilization Fund. The longer Ottawa persisted in pushing the recycling problem, the more insistent Alberta became. The answer was no, a thousand times no, and with that answer disappeared all hope for an early and amicable deal.

Still, the essential trade-off remained: higher prices required offsetting policies initiated by the federal government. If Alberta refused to help Ottawa fulfil its national obligation to manage the economy and cushion the impact of higher energy costs for low-income consumers, then the price increase must be smaller. With that in mind, the federal government developed a variation on its original offer. Instead of a $6-per-barrel yearly increase, Ottawa suggested a $4-per-barrel increase, provided that the Canadian price did not rise above 90 per cent of the U.S. benchmark price, the so-called "Chicago" price. The natural gas offer remained the same: an 85 per cent differential for gas under contract; a 65 per cent differential for new gas. The federal government would consider dropping its Stabilization Fund and its request that Alberta contribute equity to the Energy Bank. But Ottawa still wanted the Energy Bank, so it asked Alberta to loan money to the bank at concessionary rates of interest. Ottawa preferred interest-free loans, but the federal fallback position was loans at half the prime rate. Ottawa also suggested that it would use its own taxing powers to discourage consumption, either by increasing the 7-cents-per-gallon excise tax on gasoline or by raising the federal manufacturing sales tax.

Again, Alberta balked. The $4-per-barrel price increase was insufficient. The 65 per cent incentive pricing for natural gas was too great; 75 per cent was more like it. Any loans to the Energy Bank would be at prime rates minus brokerage fees; there would not be any loans at concessionary rates. Any money loaned by Alberta would have to be guaranteed by the federal government.

Through September and early October, federal and Alberta officials and ministers talked about the elements of a deal. On the federal side, there was still hope that Alberta would appreciate the federal concessions, but the Albertans insisted that the federal government still did not recognize the sacrifices Alberta had already made by selling its oil for less than world prices. The failure to make progress persuaded Clark to cancel a speaking tour he had planned for September to promote conservation and explain the need for higher prices. Two meetings of federal and provincial officials went badly in early September, when the Albertans continued to insist that Ottawa drop its Stabilization Fund and its insistence that Alberta put up equity money for the Energy Bank. Meetings among ministers went scarcely better. The Albertans continued to think that Hnatyshyn barely knew what he was talking about and simply mouthed the words prepared for him by his civil servants. Only marginal progress had been made when Clark, Hnatyshyn, Crosbie, and Gillies met Lougheed and several Alberta ministers in Montreal on Thanksgiving Day.

The meeting was a disaster. Lougheed was at his cantankerous worst, giving the Prime Minister and his ministers a lecture on everything that Alberta was doing for Canada. With scarcely an exchange of pleasantries, Lougheed laid down the Alberta position, more or less on a take-it-or-leave-it basis. Lougheed said Alberta would commit the necessary resources to build two more tar sands plants in Alberta. He was willing to change the tax structure on existing tar-sands plants to give Ottawa more revenue and to change the tax structure on existing wells for crude oil, to encourage more secondary and tertiary extraction. Alberta would invest its own money in energy projects across Canada. It would loan $2 billion over five years to an Energy Bank, but the loans would be at near-commercial, not concessionary, rates. The domestic oil price increase must be $4 per barrel in the first year and at least $4.50

per barrel thereafter, moving to 90 per cent of the Chicago price, although a *force majeure* clause would protect consumers if OPEC prices skyrocketed. Lougheed did agree that Ottawa should heavily tax the oil companies unless the companies reinvested their profits in new energy-related projects, but the nature of the tax was left unresolved. It was later to cause major problems.

After listening to Lougheed's lecture and proposals, Clark and his team retired to a nearby room to consider their response. Gillies, whose view of the energy situation closely paralleled Alberta's throughout the negotiations, thought Clark should accept Lougheed's proposal as the outline for a deal. Clark, Hnatyshyn, and Crosbie hesitated. There were far too many details left open to accept Lougheed's outline. Federal officials had not yet abandoned all hope that Lougheed might change his mind on the Stabilization Fund or on equity contributions to the Energy Bank. Neither Clark nor Hnatyshyn felt capable of agreeing to a deal of this magnitude on short notice. Crosbie deeply distrusted Lougheed. He used to call the Alberta Premier "Ayatollah" or "The Emperor Bokassa II," a reference to the psychotic dictator of the Central African Empire. Clark and his ministers returned to their meeting with Lougheed and announced that they would take his offer back to Ottawa and think about it. At that, Lougheed, with scarcely a parting word, gathered up his papers and stomped out of the meeting.

By this point in the negotiations, Joe Clark was beginning to wonder about Peter Lougheed. The Alberta premier had not been impressed by Clark's declaration of good intentions; or if he had been impressed, he had not said so publicly or privately. Instead, Lougheed was bargaining like Clemenceau at Versailles, of whom the historian Alfred Cobban wrote, "he tried to make obstinacy do the work of finesse." The practical concessions Lougheed was offering did not seem to amount to much: the infrastructure for the two tar-sands plants would have to be built eventually; the tax changes were also in Alberta's interest; the list of projects receiving Alberta's own money remained vague and the near-commercial interest rates for loans to the Energy Bank were hardly the stuff of which compromise was made. In private conversations with his officials, ministers, and caucus, Lougheed was disparaging about the federal Conservatives, and word of these remarks reached Ottawa directly or through the Alberta M.P.s in Clark's own caucus. In October and November, stories about the negotiations appeared in publications such as *The Globe and Mail* and *Maclean's* based on leaks from federal sources—all of which annoyed Lougheed, who considered them deliberate and malicious, a sign of the incompetence of Clark's Cabinet ministers or the bias of the federal civil service. He kept informing his own caucus of developments in the negotiations as he saw them; caucus members would then either contact their federal-caucus counterparts or the petroleum industry, which would in turn complain to the federal government. By November, Lougheed was talking about splitting the provincial from the federal Conservative Party, a sure sign that Lougheed was pulling together the wagons for a fight with the federal government.

Clark continued to put the best public light he could on the negotiations. Indeed, once Ottawa accepted the formula for price increases of $4 per barrel in 1980 and $4.50 for three years thereafter and agreed that Alberta could provide loans at near-commercial rates, it appeared that an agreement was at hand. But each time Clark permitted himself a whiff of optimism, Lougheed entered the discussions with new demands. When asked about the state of negotiations, Clark, desperately wanting a deal, kept saying the two sides were very close. Each time he gave that answer without an agreement being signed shortly thereafter, he undermined his own position in Ontario, where it appeared that Clark was giving in to Alberta.

That image of weakness was deepened when William Davis began delivering a series of speeches denouncing higher energy prices and warning Ontario that higher prices would bring slower growth, more inflation, and higher unemployment. Ontario had witnessed apprehensively the growth of the new west, as businesses shifted headquarters from Toronto to Calgary and Edmonton. So rich had Alberta become that the federal equalization formula, based on twenty-nine revenue sources including oil and gas revenues, actually made Ontario eligible for equalization payments. Regulations were drafted in Ottawa, with Ontario's consent, preventing payments to the province, since the idea of Ontario receiving equalization would have been incomprehensible and politically inexplicable to Quebec and Atlantic Canada. But Ontario was watching some of its accustomed power and wealth slip westward, and its citizens were worried when their premier warned of even tougher times ahead. In speeches across Ontario, Davis questioned the need for Canada to move towards the world price, which was the commitment Canada had given in signing the communique at the Tokyo summit. He rejected the linchpin of federal energy policy: that stiff price increases would reduce consumption and so move Canada towards self-sufficiency. As Davis told the legislature on October 16 during a debate on energy policy:

> There is no honest consensus that significant oil price increases, by themselves, lead effectively to reduced consumption. The only thing we do know is that a massive increase in the price of oil can stall economic activity and slash employment growth. I will oppose this course so long as I am charged to serve this province. Ontario is not a "have-not" province, but it is not about to be bled white either.

The image of Ontario being "bled white" by Alberta, aided by Joe Clark's federal government, was considerably overdrawn, but it served Davis' political purpose to portray himself as the only defender of Ontario's economic interests. The more he defined himself as the last line of defence, the more the federal Conservatives appeared to be on the other side of the line, helping the aggressive Lougheed bleed Ontario white.

Davis' speechmaking was only partly understood by Clark and his political advisors. Davis aides such as Hugh Segal and Les Horswill, both of whom had worked for the federal party under Stanfield, and prominent Ontario Conservatives such as lawyer and fundraiser Eddie Goodman kept telling federal Conservatives that Davis' speeches were designed only to protect the Conservative Government's precarious minority position in the Ontario legislature. Publicly, Davis had no alternative but to oppose price increases; otherwise he was too vulnerable to attacks from the provincial Liberals and New Democrats. He kept dropping hints his Government understood that prices had to increase. And privately, Clark's political advisors thought that Ontario had reconciled itself to stiff price increases and was only holding out for the best possible package of policies to offset the impact of the increases. The federal Conservatives thought they had found this package. The Canadian price would be pegged to 85 per cent of the Chicago price, giving Ontario industries a permanent 15 per cent cost advantage in energy over their American competitors. The budget would contain measures to help those hit hardest by price increases. The federal Conservatives promised not to increase the price of oil in the first six months of 1980, a concession to Davis, who worried about higher heating-oil costs during the winter. Tying new gas to only 65 per cent of the price of oil would encourage Ontario homeowners and industries to switch to the cheaper resource, thus lessening the province's dependence on oil from Alberta or anywhere else. Although Alberta had refused to provide equity to an Energy Bank, at least there was going to be a bank. Finally, Ottawa was insisting on a royal commission to investigate federal-provincial fiscal relations, at which time Ontario could present its case that higher oil and gas prices were distorting the nation's economy and impeding the federal government's capacity to manage the national economy. As a final gesture of goodwill, Clark agreed to hold a first ministers' meeting on energy November 12 to give Bill Davis a national platform from which to make a public presentation against higher prices and for more extensive recycling of revenues from higher prices. As it turned out for the federal Conservatives, this was the political equivalent of self-immolation. Davis' message was rejected by the other nine premiers, several of whom dreamed that their provinces might strike it rich in oil or natural gas, and by the federal government; but it was heard clearly by the voters of Ontario, who remembered it when they voted on February 18, 1980, to defeat Joe Clark. Davis told the conference and a national television audience:

> No appreciation on our part of the desire of the federal government to share its intentions on national energy policy can constrain our intense frustration and alarm about what appears to be a seemingly unrelenting commitment to chase an artificial, erratic and soaring world price—a price set by interests and circumstances foreign to Canada and our economic realities.

Worse blows were yet to fall on the federal government before Davis finished his remarks.

> I must also say, in frankness, that the oil-pricing proposal which is being negotiated between [Clark's] Government and the province of Alberta appears, from what we now know, to be an excessive and imprudent response to the claims of the producing provinces and the petroleum industry.

Davis argued that the contemplated increases in the price of oil and natural gas, coupled with a rumoured 30-cent increase in the excise tax on gasoline, would "risk a national recession." These policies would represent the equivalent in 1980 of a $5.4-billion tax increase, costing every household in Canada about $700.

Without equally massive income assistance to consumers, which does not seem to be under any serious considera- tion, such a decision would, in our opinion, constitute an unprecedented raid on the consumer, not a meaningful attack on our energy problems.

Davis had arrived in Ottawa thinking that the federal and Alberta governments might soon sign an energy-pricing agreement; his strong speech was considered by Clark and his aides to be Ontario's last hurrah before an agreement was signed. But Peter Lougheed had not finished bargaining. He and the federal government had reached an impasse over how Ottawa would get its revenues from higher oil prices. The two governments had agreed that the exist- ing formula for dividing revenues from a $2-per-barrel increase would remain the same: roughly 45 per cent for the producing provinces, 45 per cent for the petroleum industry and 10 per cent for the federal government. Anything above $2 per barrel would be split between the producing provinces and the federal govern- ment. To get its share, Ottawa proposed a wellhead tax, imposed directly on companies for every barrel they produced. Revenues from the tax, called an energy self-sufficiency tax, would be used to finance an Energy Bank and to finance offsetting macroeco- nomic policies. To Peter Lougheed, the proposed wellhead tax amounted to a royalty, which he said only the provincial govern- ment could levy on the resources it owned. The wellhead tax was an invasion of the federal government into provincial jurisdiction and, as such, was unacceptable. The day after the first ministers' meeting Lougheed told the legislature:

I have made it very clear to the Prime Minister on a number of occasions that federal tax measures cannot be designed as a means of skimming off resource revenues which belong to the people of Alberta. . . .
We have made it abundantly clear to the federal government that we would not in principle find acceptable a federal royalty upon Alberta's oil. This is an entirely different matter from federal tax measures on the profits of petroleum producers.

The next day, on November 14, Lougheed and Clark met in Sas- katoon, where Lougheed repeated his opposition to any federal wellhead tax, leaving the negotiations again at a standstill. There were other problems, too. Lougheed was still unhappy with Ottawa's offer of a $4-per-barrel increase in 1980 and $4.50 for the next three years. That offer provided for a review in 1981 to see if the gap between the Canadian and Chicago price had narrowed; if not, the increases could be greater. Lougheed insisted on a formula that provided a basic $4 per barrel plus a percentage of the difference between the Canadian and Chicago price. He conceded that the Canadian price should be 85 per cent of the Chicago price (he had been holding out for 90 per cent), but he wanted to close the gap by allowing increases of up to $6 per year if the Chicago price rose rapidly. That seemed to Ottawa a sneaky proposal designed to secure $6 per barrel price increases, which Ottawa had originally offered and then withdrawn when Alberta would not help Ottawa offset the economic impact of higher prices. It appeared Lougheed was still holding to his original bargaining position, but dressing it in a new disguise. Lougheed still was not happy with the 65 per cent differential pricing for natural gas, but he said he would not insist on that point. In return, however, he wanted Clark to commit himself to exporting more gas to the United States, a commitment Clark gave publicly. The Prime Minister said he approved in principle more gas exports, provided the National Energy Board found that Canada had gas surplus to meet its needs. When the NEB report later concluded that there was surplus gas, Clark authorized greater exports to the U.S.

In mid-November Clark and Lougheed exchanged letters, outlining the positions of the two governments. Most interesting was the difference in tone: Clark's letter was low-key, almost conciliatory; Lougheed's was pointed and almost accusatory in several passages. In his letter dated November 26, Lougheed said:

> Before commenting on your proposals and outlining Alberta's position, I feel it necessary to make a general observation. In your letter, you refer to "the major considerations which have shaped our attitude toward" the outstanding energy questions. In examining your position, I find considerable symmetry between your position and the one advanced by the Government of Ontario.

Lougheed then quoted from the Ontario policy paper's threat to urge Ottawa to use its declaratory power against Alberta's resources, adding:

> It would appear that you have accepted this policy position of the Government of Ontario. As you know, the Government of Alberta wholly rejected the Government of Ontario's proposals during the Premiers' conference

last August. You appear to have ignored completely Alberta's conclusions at that conference.

Later in his letter, Lougheed returned to the same point, referring to a comment in Clark's letter explaining that the federal government had finally set a budget date and sought an energy agreement before then:

> I am deeply disturbed by the final comments in your letter. I agree that it would be desirable to conclude, as early as possible, an agreement on these matters, but I find it impossible to accept the veiled threat that unilateral federal action would be necessary if the matter is not concluded in time for the budget presentation on December 11, 1979. Given your commitment to improved federal-provincial relations, I find such warnings surprising. Any unilateral action on the part of the Government of Canada serves only to undermine provincial ownership of resources.

As if he had not repeatedly done so, Lougheed explained "the massive contribution Alberta is prepared to make in an effort to reach an overall 'energy package' agreement aimed at achieving energy self-sufficiency." This effort included new tar-sands plants, incentive taxing for companies in energy production, loans (at commercial rates guaranteed by the federal government) to the Energy Bank, and billions of dollars in foregone revenues by virtue of the domestic price having remained so far below world levels.

Instead of an early and amicable energy settlement, Clark found himself heading into winter without an agreement, wounded politically by Davis' attacks and making only laborious private progress with Lougheed, who Clark now figured was determined to hurt the federal Conservative Government. Each week in the House of Commons, Opposition M.P.s demanded to know the state of play in the energy negotiations. Enough information had already been published, especially about the anticipated price increases, to allow the Liberals and New Democrats free rein to whip up public sentiment against the increases. Clark and Hnatyshyn, a weak parliamentary performer, struggled to defend a policy not yet in place. They tried manfully to argue that the coming price increases were the country's best guarantee of self-sufficiency. But the link between price and supply had not been accepted by the public, as Allan Gregg pointed out in a memorandum to the Conservative program committee in early November:

The same set of belief structures that cause us problems on the PetroCanada issue come together in a different way to create even larger problems for the Government in terms of its energy proposal.

We should recognize first and foremostly that, regardless of the complexity of the proposal, the average individual will focus on the price side and not really comprehend any of the other implications of the policy. The feeling among the electorates is that things are getting worse, and in the face of massive profits in the oil industry, their inclination is to suggest that the prospects of energy shortages are a "hoax" or a problem to be relegated to the future. This makes excessive price increases at the pump extremely difficult to justify from a public policy perspective.

Therefore, we must once again emphasize how this will push us further towards energy self-sufficiency both in terms of having to rely less on foreign supplies and more on domestic supplies. Equally, we must be more than aware that this particular aspect of our policy proposal is going to give the Government of Ontario a very difficult time, given the political ground they have already staked out.

To counter the opposition's and public's reaction to price increases, our proposals should be presented and communicated in such a way as to engender the sense of moral duty—that is, Canadians now are being asked to make the short-term sacrifice in order to guarantee the long-term prosperity of Canada in future generations. In short, this proposal should not be put forward as a belt-tightening measure. Rather, it should be viewed as a stepping stone towards future prosperity.

Clark's previously cancelled series of major speeches on energy policy, which would have emphasized the need for conservation, might have built some public support for the Conservatives' proposals. That they were not given lessened the possibility of public acceptance. Clark had also been warned by Ian Stewart's first memo that failure to reach an early agreement would be politically costly. As the weeks dragged on, the price of failure mounted.

The Conservative budget, which the Government thought would be the clearest indication that it was prepared to govern in a way dramatically different from the Liberals' cautious style, was pushed back, opening yet another avenue of attack for the Opposition parties. The Government, which entered the energy negotiations believing early success would bring enormous political rewards, found itself in a public-relations quagmire by early December. It was attacked from all sides and trying to fight its way to political safety with arguments based on a hypothetical agreement.

Similarly, the Government was unsuccessfully imploring Canadians to fix their sights on the distant goal of self-sufficiency, instead of on their gasoline tanks and furnaces. When Gregg conducted his national survey for the federal party in August, he learned how difficult the Government's political task would be. His survey asked respondents how closely attuned Joe Clark was to their aspirations on a range of issues. Gregg found Clark furthest removed from public aspirations on energy.

On Tuesday, December 11, the day of the Government's fateful budget, Joe Clark spoke to Peter Lougheed by telephone. A committee of officials led by Mickey Cohen, Deputy Minister of Industry, Trade and Commerce and a taxation expert, had proposed a new formula for the energy self-sufficiency tax that seemed acceptable in principle to Lougheed. But four other points remained to be clarified, Lougheed said. Maybe an agreement could be signed the following week, maybe not, Lougheed concluded. They would see at the first ministers' conference on the economy the following week.

That conference was never held. Joe Clark's Government fell two days after the budget. Its energy components were the political poison in John Crosbie's fiscal recipe for Canada. Joe Clark laboured hard and fruitlessly in the 1980 campaign to sell Canadians his energy vision for the 1990s, but his credibility in Ontario had been too severely eroded before the campaign began for him to be successful. Perhaps if his Government had lasted another year or two, he might have brought more public support to his side. As it was, he entered the campaign with nothing tangible to show for all his efforts and good-will.

Clark learned a lesson that a more experienced Prime Minister would have understood. In federal-provincial relations, premiers are colour-blind when the vital interests of their provinces are at stake; in fact, it is often easier politically for them to have a federal government of a different political stripe to blame at provincial-election time. Mitchell Hepburn, former premier of Ontario, and Prime Minister Mackenzie King were both Liberals and yet they fought tempestuous battles with each other. Jean Lesage and

Robert Bourassa were Liberal premiers of Quebec, but that never prevented them from attacking the federal government when the Liberals ruled in Ottawa.

If one believed that Canada could continue to enjoy the Western world's lowest energy prices without penalty, then Joe Clark was a political fool for having proposed sharply higher energy prices. Certainly, he never put his case for higher prices until the 1980 election campaign, when it was far too late. But if one believed with most economists that Canada's energy prices were a cuckoo-land fantasy, then Clark's stand was politically courageous. If he had secured an early agreement, his political position would have been more defensible, even in Ontario. For that failure, Clark could blame Peter Lougheed and draw small solace from the cruel irony of Lougheed's position. Lougheed had helped to undermine Joe Clark, from whom he had already won more than he could easily extract from Liberal Prime Minister Pierre Trudeau. The one-eyed sheik still ruled the oil-rich kingdom of the blind.

~ 8 ~

The New Economic Catechism

> I'm not an economic genius. I'm just a lawyer from St.
> John's, Newfoundland, with a reasonable amount of
> intelligence, who's already been Minister of Finance once,
> barely survived it, does not expect to survive it this time,
> and am trying to do my best.
>   —Finance Minister John Crosbie

Some of his Cabinet colleagues called John Carnell Crosbie a cynic, which is the Conservative definition of a Liberal. By this, his colleagues meant that Crosbie was disrespectful of the promises the Conservative Party had made in Opposition. Crosbie certainly thought that many of the Conservatives' election promises were foolish. He muttered privately about Clark's promise to move the Canadian embassy in Israel from Tel Aviv to Jerusalem. He disagreed with the party's commitment to dismantle PetroCanada as a crown corporation. In the economic field, he disliked mortgage-interest and property-tax deductibility, the $2-billion tax cut, and the exemption of common shares of publicly traded Canadian corporations from capital gains tax. Instead, he selected only those aspects of the Conservatives' economic platform that he considered essential—a reduction in the federal deficit and energy self-sufficiency—and fashioned a new Conservative dogma, neatly summarized in the phrase "short-term pain for long-term gain" that did not resemble in tone or substance the Conservatives' 1979 campaign themes of economic optimism and rising expectations.

A finance minister is usually the strongest member of the federal Cabinet next to the Prime Minister, and seldom has this been more evident than in the case of John Crosbie. Newfoundlanders seem to require salt, blarney, and steel in their political leaders, so it took awhile for other English-speaking Canadians, accustomed to more anodyne political performers, to appreciate the mixture. After a hesitant start in his portfolio, Crosbie's political stock soared when Canadians heard more of his New-foundland twang and spicy comments. They might not have liked his message, but it was hard not to be entertained by a minister who called Trudeau's Cabinet "Disco Daddy and the Has-beens"; told an audience at the Canadian Tax Foundation, "You won't believe this, but there's a move afoot to move our interest rates to Jerusalem"; called himself "Canada's first ethnic Prime Minister"; and sported mukluks instead of the traditional new pair of shoes worn by a finance minister on budget night. Shortly after his election to the Commons as M.P. for St. John's West in a 1976 by-election, he criticized those opposed to the seal hunt, especially French actress Brigitte Bardot, who "did a lot of twitching over here—twitching in ways you wouldn't believe; then again, you might." In jesting retaliation, he moved in the Commons to ban the importation of French wine "because [the French] brutalize the grapes when they pound them with their feet." He delivered his cascade of one-liners with the twang of the Newfoundland outports, thicker in public than in private, that turned "barrels" into "burr'ls," "tough times" into "toof toimes," "Conservatives" into "Consarrvatives," and "budgets" into "boogets." "With a Polish Pope and a Newfie finance minister, you mainlanders had better watch your jokes," he told a Toronto audience.

The day after Crosbie's appointment, Newfoundland Liberal leader Don Jamieson, who campaigned with Crosbie against the Dominion of Newfoundland joining Confederation in 1949, said of Crosbie: "He has by his very nature an opposition kind of mentality. I'm not at all certain he's fully equipped to do what one has to do as Minister of Finance when every word you utter in the House of Commons is likely to have a bearing on the stock market and prices and goodness knows what else." Crosbie turned out to be a popular finance minister with the business community and with his parliamentary colleagues, but in the early months of the Conservative Government, his Cabinet colleagues and Joe Clark's advisors wondered about Crosbie's loyalty to the Conservative team. While Clark and other ministers kept insisting that the Conservatives would keep all their election promises, Crosbie was trying to persuade his colleagues to scuttle some of them and to prepare the public for their abandonment. Crosbie was not an Opposition party politician who suddenly found himself in Gov-ernment; he had served for five years in the Newfoundland

Cabinet. He was not plagued with the naïveté of some of his colleagues; he did not believe that governments were judged on their faithfulness to promises. He knew that they won or lost support based on their ability to adjust policies to changing circumstances—which is another reason why he was called a cynic. At a July press conference, he amazed reporters with his flippant comments about some of his party's promises, especially concerning tax cuts and the "stimulative deficit."

> I don't know what's going to be in the budget yet, because it depends on our analysis of where Canada is when we bring down the budget. And conditions have changed somewhat since stimulative deficits were talked about. We already have a budget which I hope is stimulative, but it's a large deficit now.
>
> There are areas of the Canadian economy where stimulation still is necessary. Some of those are regional sectors and there might be stimulative deficiting in relation to those areas if we can do it. We have got some room for manoeuvre, as you know, and if we can't make large leaps forward or backward, you know, we do have some room. So it's possible that we may do some stimulative deficiting in that respect. But then there are other areas where if we can do it we will restrain expenditures. Whatever deficit you've got, some deficits are more stimulative than others, and ours are going to be more stimulative than the previous ones if we can do it. That's our stimulative deficit policy. We don't think the deficit is going to disappear. I mean we're going to have a deficit for a long time to come yet. So, I mean we're going to take a different approach to it, and whatever the Prime Minister says will certainly have a lot of influence on me.

This message and its slightly sarcastic tone did not sit well in the Prime Minister's office. There Clark's advisors were also hearing privately from Crosbie about the foolishness of another of Clark's campaign promises—mortgage-interest and property-tax deductibility. Crosbie appeared eager to overturn the electoral canons of the Conservative Party, but there was little Clark could do, for John Crosbie was a most determined man.

Born into one of Newfoundland's wealthiest families, Crosbie received blue-chip academic training: the political science medal for his bachelor's degree at Queen's University, university medal at Dalhousie law school, the Viscount Bennett fellowship from the Canadian Bar Association as the top Canadian law student in his graduating year, graduate from the Institute for Advanced Legal Studies at the London School of Economics. His wealth and academic brilliance made Crosbie an independent thinker in the disciplined world of party politics. He joined the Newfoundland Liberal Cabinet of Premier Joey Smallwood in 1966, but two years later their bulky egos collided. The two men fell out over Smallwood's plans to advance an unsecured $5-million loan to New York promoter John Shaheen for a $30-million oil refinery and chemical complex at Come-by-Chance. He resigned from Smallwood's Cabinet to sit as an Independent Liberal, received instruction in public speaking from a friend who taught a Dale Carnegie course, and challenged Smallwood for the leadership of the Newfoundland Liberal Party. Rebuffed, he joined the provincial Conservative Party before its triumph over Smallwood in the 1971 election. Before his entry into the House of Commons, Crosbie had held six portfolios in the Newfoundland Cabinet, including the finance portfolio.

For all his public bluster, Crosbie was a shy, hard-working man whom his bureaucrats felt was an ideal finance minister. He could sell the department's thinking, protect it from assaults by other departments, and understand detailed fiscal and monetary policies. His Liberal predecessor, Jean Chrétien, refused to read the department's lengthy briefing notes, but Crosbie devoured them like a paper shredder. Once Grant Reuber was appointed Deputy Minister of Finance—with a letter from Clark asserting that Reuber and Crosbie would not be overruled by other departments in establishing the Government's economic policy—the two men set about restoring the finance department to its former pre-eminence in Ottawa. Their efforts did wonders for morale within the department, where bureaucrats had seen their power eroded by the influence of the Privy Council office and the Prime Minister's office under a succession of Liberal finance ministers and deputy ministers of finance. Little did the finance bureaucrats know that Reuber also had a mandate to clean house in the upper echelons of the department, work that had just begun when the Conservative Government was defeated.

Crosbie was not about to be second-guessed by anyone. He took his time coming to a conclusion, but once he had made up his mind he brushed aside further objections. When he was drafting his budget, he became exasperated at interventions by other Cabinet ministers and went directly to Clark, demanding that the Prime Minister end the Cabinet bickering and stand behind his finance minister. Although Crosbie did not threaten to resign, he phrased his demands so assertively that Clark's advisors thought Crosbie might consider resignation if he did not get his way.

Crosbie had gone to Clark with a similar demand early in his term as finance minister when Treasury Board president Sinclair Stevens was preparing to hold a press conference on government expenditure projections. Stevens' appointment as finance minister had been blocked by opposition from the Toronto financial community, which considered him an unreliable wheeler-dealer because of his days as president of the ill-fated Bank of Western Canada. Nevertheless, he grasped his ministerial responsibilities more rapidly than any of his colleagues. In the first two months of the Clark Government, Stevens' name was all over the newspapers. His missionary zeal to cut government spending propelled him to announce a freeze in civil service hiring, privatization of crown corporations, and cancellation of a Liberal plan to move parts of government departments in Ottawa-Hull to other Canadian cities (mostly in Liberal ridings). His colleagues were still learning about the operation of their departments while Stevens plunged ahead; he slowed down only when he smashed against the imposing self-assurance of John Crosbie and the territorial imperative of the finance department. Stevens' proposed press conference was designed to provide a platform from which he could expound on the financial mess the Liberals had bequeathed to the nation, including the soaring public debt and the federal government's weakened fiscal position. Fiscal policy, however, is the jealously guarded prerogative of the finance department, and a minister as powerful as John Crosbie could not countenance another minister trespassing on his department's domain. Acquiescence in Stevens' design would have weakened the department's traditional role, from which a finance minister derives his power.

On July 17, three days before Stevens' proposed press conference, Crosbie wrote Clark demanding that Stevens be prevented from undercutting the finance department's traditional role. The next day, he wrote Stevens a stern letter outlining his objections to Stevens' plans. Stevens was headed off when Clark supported Crosbie. The briefing paper on federal expenditures was released at the press conference under the names of both Stevens and Crosbie, although it was Stevens who rose from his seat, pointer in hand, to lecture Canadians through the media that "We must arrest this trend towards more and more debt. You, in effect, are mortgaging the future by piling up this debt."

The scrap between Crosbie and Stevens over the appropriate jurisdiction of the finance department and the Treasury Board was part of a larger disagreement between the two men about the way to tackle the federal deficit. For Stevens, the answer lay in dramatic reductions in government spending, the pursuit of which earned him the nickname "Slasher"; for Crosbie, the deficit could only be reduced by whopping increases in revenues. But at least both men agreed that the deficit was a spur to inflation and a drag on the nation's resources.

An early attack on the deficit seemed to the Conservatives to be both sensible economics and good politics. It is a rule of thumb that a Government should make unpopular decisions early in its term of office so that more appealing measures can be introduced closer to the next election. The Conservatives reasoned that they had at least two, and perhaps three, years in office. An immediate attack on the deficit might free up fiscal room in 1981 or 1982, when the Conservatives thought they would next face the electorate. The Conservatives also understood that economic issues, especially inflation, were the most salient electoral issues. The Conservatives wanted to enter the next election showing that they had lowered the rate of inflation, and that meant, to the Conservatives' way of thinking, a reduction of the deficit. "We feel, and we believe the Canadian people feel, that the deficit has to be brought under control. It is one of the major causes of inflation in the country," Crosbie told *The Financial Post* in one of his first interviews as finance minister.

"Moving towards a balanced budget" was also part of Joe Clark's campaign pledge to restore sound management to Ottawa, a promise he made in Guelph on May 1, 1979.

> Inflation in this country has been caused by a government in Ottawa that consistently spent more money than it raised, and consistently printed new money to cover that kind of overspending. Inflation will be cured in Canada only when a government in Ottawa is prepared to reduce its deficits, only when a government in Ottawa is prepared to stop using the printing presses of the Bank of Canada to cover its own waste.

When Clark charged that the Trudeau years had been a "decade of deficits," he was offering an accurate picture of the nation's recent fiscal history. In the calendar year 1969, the federal government's budgetary deficit was $576 million; in 1979, it was $12.1 billion. Put another way, the federal deficit for 1979 was almost as great as

federal expenditures in 1969 ($12.4 billion). The budgetary deficit
had risen by about 130 per cent from 1976 to 1979, and businessmen, independent economists, and research institutes pointed to
the burgeoning deficit as a major contributing factor to Canada's
sluggish economic performance and high inflation.

The last half of the 1970s saw a dramatic worsening in the
federal government's fiscal position. Throughout the decade,
federal revenues grew by 11.6 per cent a year, while expenditures
increased by 14.6 per cent a year. From 1974 to 1979, the federal
deficit grew steadily larger. Slow economic growth towards the
end of the decade played a part in reducing the federal government's new revenues and increasing its expenditures on social
programs such as unemployment insurance. The finance department reported that the federal government's own tax-cutting
initiatives had deprived the treasury of $14 billion in revenue since
1972. The largest revenue loss—$6 billion—followed the indexing
of personal income taxes in 1973. The elimination of sales tax on
clothing and footwear, the reduction in the sales tax for building
materials, a 3-per-cent reduction in the federal sales tax, an
increase in personal employment expense deduction, and a range
of other fiscal measures also lowered the increase in federal
revenues.

John Crosbie examined the government's fiscal position and
decided that the deficit could only be reduced by raising new
revenues. For political reasons, he could not scrap mortgage-
interest and property-tax deductibility. But he drew the line at
three other promises: the $2-billion tax cut, exemption of shares
of publicly traded Canadian corporations from capital gains tax,
and $125 million for research-and-development credits. The tax-
cutting promises developed in Opposition by Gillies and de Cotret
were based on economic reasoning that Crosbie did not accept.
Both de Cotret and Gillies, economists trained in the United
States, were much influenced by conservative economic thinking
in that country. They had been impressed by the academic work of
Arthur Laffer and like-minded economists, and by the political
arguments of Republicans, like Treasury Secretary William Simon
and Alan Greenspan, chairman of the U.S. Council of Economic
Advisors, in the Nixon and Ford administrations. They held that
massive tax cuts, coupled preferably with severe expenditure
restraints, would stimulate the economy and quickly produce
revenues from stronger economic growth to offset the government's initial revenue loss from the tax cuts. Crosbie, however,

did not believe that the deficit could be reduced quickly by stimulating the economy through tax cuts. Such stimulation would
encourage Canadians to continue to live beyond their means,
would spur inflation, and would deepen, not reduce, the federal
deficit.

Crosbie also explained his lack of fidelity to the party's
promise to cut taxes by pleading that circumstances had changed
since the party took power. In fact, the indicators by which the
health of the economy is measured began changing before the
Conservatives won the election. When the party set forth its
strategy for stimulating the economy in 1978, growth was sluggish
and unemployment was high. Many independent economists
called for some kind of stimulus because gross national product in
1978 grew by only 10 per cent (or by about 1 per cent adjusted for
inflation) and unemployment stood at 8.4 per cent. Two months
after the Conservatives took power in May 1979, it appeared that
growth for the calendar year would be more than 13 per cent (or 4
per cent adjusted for inflation). Unemployment had fallen to 7.1
per cent by July 1979. Meanwhile, inflation, which had been 8 per
cent in 1977 and 8.9 per cent in 1978, crept ahead to 9.1 per cent in
the first quarter of 1979 and to 9.3 per cent in the second quarter
of the year. These changes suggested that the economy was entering a period of steady growth. The critical economic problem
seemed to be a resurgence of inflation, which stimulative measures
might simply accelerate. Stimulative economic policies developed
by the Conservatives in Opposition, perhaps defensible at the
time, were no longer appropriate under a different set of economic
circumstances. Having jettisoned the party's tax-cutting promises,
Crosbie then turned to confront Sinclair Stevens' consuming
passion for slashing federal expenditures.

Those who seek to slash federal spending soon find themselves
chipping at an iceberg. Only a tiny percentage of federal spending
can be touched in a given fiscal year because most of the federal
government's budget is locked into public debt charges, remunera-
tion for federal employees, and transfer payments to provincial
governments and individuals.

Transfer payments to provincial governments, for example,
are tied to binding federal-provincial agreements, the largest of
which is the Established Programs Financing plan. In 1978, the
Liberal Government tried to lower EPF payments to the provinces
during Trudeau's $2-billion expenditure reduction program, but
the provinces balked, pointing to a clause in the five-year agree-

ment that prevented a reduction in federal payments without provincial consent. The EPF agreement, as well as equalization payments, transfers for welfare programs, and a host of smaller federal-provincial programs accounted for more than $11.7 billion in federal spending in 1979, or about 20 per cent of the federal budget.

Transfers to individuals for such programs as unemployment insurance, family allowances, and old-age pensions ate up another $14.7 billion, or about 28 per cent of the federal budget. The unemployment-insurance program, despite amendments effective in 1979 that provided for a longer period of work before qualification for benefits and a reduced rate of benefits, still cost the federal treasury about $2.3 billion in 1979, compared with $880 million in 1972, the year after the Liberals widened eligibility and increased payments under the Unemployment Insurance Act. Family allowances cost another $1.7 billion in 1979, a more than three-fold increase since the beginning of the decade. The costliest social program of all was old-age security: $6.3 billion in the fiscal year 1979 to 1980.

Stevens was prepared, and in some cases eager, to reduce the cost of these programs immediately. But Crosbie, supported by the rest of the inner Cabinet, believed Stevens' obsessions would entail economic hardship for the disadvantaged as well as political catastrophe for the Government. Condemning unemployment-insurance abuses, for example, might have been good politics in southern Ontario; but not so in Atlantic Canada, where unemployment ran three or four points above the national average. In Newfoundland, politicians complained about excessive federal spending at their peril, since unemployment exceeded 15 per cent, per capita income was two-thirds of the national average, and one-third of provincial revenues came from federal equalization payments.

The battle between Stevens and Crosbie intensified during the summer. Stevens was prepared to support increased taxes to reduce the deficit, but his support was offered only after he had lost an inner Cabinet struggle to keep the increase in federal expenditures to half of what Crosbie proposed in his budget.

Stevens lost his case at the inner Cabinet's late-August meeting at Jasper. All summer, he had been pressing his colleagues to restrain expenditures and to cut back their new spending plans. In preparation for the Jasper meeting, where the inner Cabinet was to make preliminary decisions about expenditure levels for the next four fiscal years, Stevens instructed Treasury Board officials to prepare a document outlining how billions of dollars could be lopped off federal expenditures. He proposed to keep the increase in federal spending to 5 per cent, instead of Crosbie's target of a 9-per-cent increase. In a letter to his colleagues dated August 24, Stevens said "significant reductions in expenditures for existing programs" and resistance to "new programs" would create more wealth in Canada. He predicted that by holding spending increases to 5 per cent—about half the level of inflation—the Conservatives could produce a balanced budget by 1985. He also sketched out alternative scenarios for spending increases of 6 and 7 per cent. For those ministers who complained that Stevens' ideas were too abstract, he displayed a Treasury Board document that outlined daring alternatives for reducing expenditures. Options included a means test for pensioners; ending the indexing of personal income taxes; making the unemployment insurance plan self-financing; replacing family allowances by tax deductions; privatizing Via Rail; substituting compensatory rates for the Crow's Nest Pass freight agreements; limiting equalization payments to 8 per cent a year; and chopping incentives for companies locating in slow-growth regions. These were draconian political options, too drastic for the other members of the inner Cabinet, who believed that a government could not be re-elected by altering such politically sensitive programs as wilfully as Stevens suggested. Crosbie, armed with a critical analysis of the Treasury Board's options from his finance department officials, said Stevens' target of 5-per-cent growth in spending would slow growth in the economy and lock the federal government into an excessively rigid fiscal position. Instead, the inner Cabinet opted for spending increases of 9 per cent.

The inner Cabinet also resisted Stevens' efforts to end the $179-million Canada Works program, established in October 1976 as a five-year job-creation program. Stevens considered the program a waste of money, inefficiently administered, and ineffectual in creating jobs, but Crosbie and Secretary of State David MacDonald from Prince Edward Island, representing provinces of high unemployment, stayed Stevens' attack for the fiscal year 1979 to 1980. The Government did promise to eliminate Canada Works in the next fiscal year and to replace the program with a new employment strategy.

Instead of a frontal assault on spending, therefore, the inner Cabinet set in motion a series of reviews of social programs. A group of Conservative M.P.s, under the direction of Paul McCrossan from York-Scarborough, launched a review of the unemployment insurance program. Health and Welfare Minister David Crombie began considering new methods of directing family allowances to those most in need of government help. And the Government invited the provinces to join a federal-provincial study of fiscal relations between the two levels of government.

But the Government's most significant initiative was the introduction of a new Cabinet system for reviewing expenditures. The Privy Council office had begun developing the new system after the Royal Commission on Financial Management (Lambert Commission) chastised the federal government for its inadequate controls on public spending. The Conservatives fleshed out the new system and made it the cornerstone of their efforts to control government spending. The new system made such compelling good sense that the Liberals adopted it when they returned to power.

The system revolved around nine "spending envelopes." Each envelope included related policy areas of the federal government. The inner Cabinet allocated money for each of the envelopes, and it was then up to the committees of Cabinet charged with administering the envelopes to decide how the money should be apportioned among the departmental budgets included in each envelope. Any minister seeking additional funds for a new or enriched program was forced to find money in his envelope, either by persuading other ministers to restrain the spending of their departments or pruning programs within his own department. Ministers could not circumvent the system by proposing tax incentives rather than additional expenditures, because the system also measured "tax expenditures," or revenues foregone by federal tax incentives.

The Conservatives' system offered two improvements on the system it replaced. Previously, a minister seeking additional money fought directly with the Treasury Board, without concerning himself with the impact of his demands on other departments or on the government's overall fiscal position. The political dynamics of spending decisions were usually bi-polar: the president of the Treasury Board against each of his colleagues in turn. There was no ongoing incentive for ministers to attack each other's spending designs, and ministers often rallied support for their spending schemes by promising to support additional spending by other ministers. The new system imposed restraint on every minister, instead of making restraint the preoccupation of only the president of the Treasury Board.

The new system also forced ministers to think ahead, since each "spending envelope" was given expenditure ceilings for the next four fiscal years. If the minister's cost projections were wrong, the budget of the entire envelope could be affected. The system did contain, however, a measure of flexibility. The envelopes and the five-year projections were to be reviewed periodically by the inner Cabinet and adjusted according to economic (and political) circumstances.

These structural changes needed time to slow down increases in federal spending; so did the reviews of social programs and the study of federal-provincial fiscal relations. All were overdue, but they could only provide solutions for the long haul. Having fixed a reduction in the federal deficit as the prime target of the Government's fiscal policy and having rebuffed Stevens' draconian designs for expenditure reductions, Crosbie was left with no alternative but to raise new revenues. The tax increases proposed in his budget were more substantial than they might otherwise have been because of another of the party's campaign promises—mortgage-interest and property-tax deductibility—that would have reduced federal revenues at the same time the Government was trying to move towards a balanced budget.

These tax deductions had been intermittently debated in the Conservative Party since Robert Stanfield's period as party leader. Stanfield had always rejected the scheme, arguing that it was too expensive and socially regressive. But Joe Clark, yielding to the arguments of advisors such as Jim Gillies and William Neville, saw the deductibility scheme as a political magnet for homeowners, especially in the suburban ridings the Conservatives needed to capture from the Liberals. Clark and his advisors also suspected that the Liberals were contemplating a similar policy, so they wanted to make the deductibility scheme Conservative policy before the Liberals embraced the idea. During the October 1978 campaign for fifteen by-elections, Clark unveiled the grandiose Conservative promise: deductibility of up to $5,000 for mortgage interest and $1,000 for property tax, to be phased in over four years. The Conservatives estimated, wrongly, as it turned out, that the scheme would cost $400 million in lost revenue in the first year and $1.6 billion in the fourth year.

John Crosbie did not like the campaign promise. How could the Government attack the burgeoning deficit when it was proposing to cut its own revenues? he muttered privately. Like Stanfield, he felt the scheme was socially regressive: it would help homeowners, who tended to be better off than renters. Shortly after assuming the finance portfolio, he asked the finance department to prepare a paper examining the Conservatives' campaign promise. The department, increasingly preoccupied with the size of the federal deficit, eagerly seized the opportunity to explain why the program was fiscally unsound. In a July 6 memorandum to Crosbie, which the finance minister forwarded to Clark, Deputy Minister of Finance William Hood tore apart the Conservatives' campaign promise. His memorandum read, in part:

The major goals of the measure would seem to be to reduce the cost of home ownership, to promote the construction industry, and to provide tax reductions for middle and upper-income Canadians. Before considering detailed policy options and the issues involved in implementing the proposal, it can be noted that a straightforward mortgage interest and property tax deduction measure has been criticized on several grounds. . . .

1. The measure stimulates the demand for existing and new houses; that is its basic thrust. As such it tends to put upward pressure on house prices and mortgage interest rates. . . . In the extreme it is possible for all of the tax savings to be capitalized into higher house prices and interest costs, which would defeat the purpose of the measure and make it harder for lower-income, new home-buyers to purchase their first home.

2. As a technique for helping new home-buyers and encouraging new home construction, the use of a mortgage interest deduction is not efficient. This is because over 80 per cent of the tax savings (i.e. government revenue loss) would go to existing home-buyers, and less than 20 per cent would go specifically to new home-buyers.

3. The measure does not benefit renters. . . . The current system is, in fact, biased in favour of homeowners in that imputed income and the capital gains on investments made in one's home are tax free, while income and capital gains on other forms of investments are generally taxable.

4. A long-standing principle of Canadian income taxation has been that expenditures of a personal nature are not deductible. Every year, the government receives many requests for tax relief for particular expenses. Deductibility of such personal expenses results in ine-

quities between taxpayers with different spending patterns. A mortgage interest deduction would breach this principle and could heighten pressure for deductibility of other personal expenditures in future.

5. The measure provides the largest benefits to those with highest incomes. This is because higher-income families can afford more expensive homes with bigger mortgages and also due to the fact that the value of a tax deduction is larger the higher the marginal tax rate applicable to the taxpayer.

6. The benefits of the measure would vary significantly from province to province due to regional variations in the incidence of home ownership and the percentage of homeowners with mortgages. The incidence of home ownership is the lowest in Quebec (50 per cent of families) and the highest in the Atlantic provinces (70 per cent of families). However, a very large percentage of families in the Atlantic provinces own their homes without any mortgage debt outstanding, and would thus not benefit from the measure unless they began to engage in refinancing. . . .

7. Under any scheme of this nature, there is an understandable incentive for individuals to refinance their home in order to purchase other consumer durables such as boats, automobiles, vacation homes and the like. . . .

8. The medium-term outlook suggests that housing requirements will be falling. It thus may not be appropriate to over-stimulate housing demand in the face of other emerging investment requirements such as in the field of energy.

Neither Clark nor his advisors appreciated being told by the finance department that their economic reasoning was puerile. The Conservative Party had made mortgage-interest and property-tax deductibility its most glittering election promise, and the party simply could not renege on so important a commitment. But the finance department provided still another argument against deductibility that even Joe Clark could not ignore. The department pointed out that provincial income taxes were based on federal income taxes, and any reduction in federal income taxes would cost provincial treasuries millions of dollars. This elementary observation had eluded Clark when he was asked about the impact on provincial revenues shortly after unveiling the promise in the by-election campaign. To a question about the provincial impact, Clark replied incoherently:

> Well, what I'm saying is that we would—the calculus that we issue, coming to a $1.6 billion total cost figure over four years of operation, is based upon federal tax. That would be the cost to the federal treasury. We would only be rebating to the provinces, to use your term, something that we—an effect upon taxation that would—an effect upon their—I'm trying to put this clearly. The rebating to the provinces would be a sum in excess to the cost to the federal treasury and we would be rebating to the provinces something that would not have come to the federal government in the first place without this program. It would also not be a new—the cost would be an administrative share, an administrative cost but a very insignificant one.

This gobbledegook from Clark did not impress the Ontario Government, which estimated its revenue loss at $300 million. Clark's "very insignificant" administrative cost turned out to be $1 billion, as he was informed in a July 17 memorandum sent to Crosbie by the finance department and passed on to Clark. "The paper will illustrate that to proceed by way of a deduction could result in a total budgetary cost of $1 billion in addition to the cost of the measure itself," the memorandum began, before analysing in detail the impact of mortgage-interest and property-tax deductibility on provincial revenues. Clark simply could not proceed with a deductibility plan likely to cost vastly more than he had originally estimated.

For his part, Crosbie recognized that the Government's credibility was inextricably linked to providing significant tax relief to homeowners. Although opposed to mortgage-interest and property-tax deductibility, he recognized grudgingly that the Conservatives had reaped a political benefit from the promise in the by-elections of 1978 and the federal election of 1979. Clark and Crosbie, therefore, settled on a compromise first put forward by the finance department. Instead of a tax *deduction*, the Government offered a tax *credit* of up to $1,250 for mortgage interest and $250 for property taxes, with a maximum credit in the first year of $375. The credit program would cost the treasury as much as the deductibility scheme, minus the impact on provincial revenues. That meant the Government would still forego about $1.5-billion in revenues while trying simultaneously to reduce the deficit.

The credit plan avoided the obvious political conflict in Clark's original deductibility scheme, but it still left the Government in a fiscal dilemma partly of its own making. Not only was the credit regressive, it would leave the federal government with an additional tax loss that deepened the federal deficit and made more imperative the stiff tax increases in Crosbie's budget that proved so unpopular in the election.

Seven weeks after taking office, the Conservatives were hit with an economic issue—high interest rates—that savaged their political credibility. The party had denounced high interest rates in Opposition but soon found itself defending them in power, at considerable political cost. The soaring rates even robbed the mortgage-interest and property-tax credit scheme of some of its lustre, because escalating mortgage rates erased the anticipated benefits of the tax credit.

The Bank of Canada's bank rate—the level at which the central bank makes infrequent loans to the chartered banks—is largely symbolic. When the rate moves at the behest of the governor of the bank, it is a signal to the chartered banks to raise or lower their commercial rates in tandem with the bank rate. Throughout 1978, the Bank of Canada had pushed up the bank rate in order to stifle inflationary pressures in Canada, to attract foreign capital into Canada, and to sustain the level of the Canadian dollar. At the beginning of 1978, the bank rate stood at 7.5 per cent; by December, it had risen to 10.75 per cent. In early January 1979, the bank rate increased to 11.25 per cent, where it remained for six and a half months. But on July 25, the bank rate jumped to 11.75 per cent. It was the first of three increases within three months that left the bank rate at 14 per cent in late October. Each increase represented an historic high. With each one, the chartered banks, trust companies, and other lending institutions followed suit, until small businessmen, farmers, homeowners, and others reliant upon credit were paying interest rates of up to 18 per cent. Such interest rates were unbearably painful for many Canadians, and no amount of explaining by Gerald Bouey, governor of the Bank of Canada, or John Crosbie could ease their discomfort.

The Bank of Canada's high-interest-rate policy put the Conservatives in a political vise that grew tighter with each increase. In Opposition, the Conservatives had castigated the Liberals for permitting interest rates to rise by 3.75 per cent in the eleven months preceding January 1979. On the twenty-second of that month, Jim Gillies, M.P. for Don Valley West, asked Finance Minister Jean Chrétien:

> Given the fact that our unemployment rate is over 8 per cent, our inflation rate is over 8 per cent, and now very reputable forecasters say that real growth in the economy will be less than 3 per cent, will the Government change its high-interest-rate policy, which everyone says is taking us into a serious recession, reverse itself and move to a low-interest-rate policy?

Gillies returned to the attack on high interest rates in a debate three weeks later (although Crosbie steered away from criticizing the bank's policy, calling it only a "symptom" of a wider malaise):

> Presumably, [the Government] does not care about high interest rates, high consumer borrowing costs, high mortgage costs or high costs for starting businesses. Every economist in this country and, indeed, the governor of the Bank of Canada, have said that a high-interest-rate policy, given the domestic economic situation in the nation today, is wrong. The last thing Canada needs right now is a high-interest-rate policy.

With Gillies at his side, Clark also promised lower interest rates during a 1979 campaign speech in Guelph:

> We also intend as a national government to move this nation towards lower interest rates. Mr. Trudeau has pushed interest rates in Canada to the highest level in the history of this country. That in itself is inflationary. It's a cost of production to industry, and that is often passed on so that it becomes another pressure on the consumer, another pressure on people who are seeking legitimately in many cases higher wages so that they can keep up with the high cost of living. We're going to move this country towards lower interest rates as part of our movement to get inflation under control in Canada.

Although no one likes high interest rates, except perhaps the chartered banks, the negative reaction is often strongest among small businessmen and farmers who depend upon credit for capital costs and inventory financing. High interest rates have always been an anathema in western Canada, whose history has been chequered with political movements challenging corporate power in central Canada, as well as restrictive monetary policy that made credit prohibitively expensive or simply unavailable. The Conservative backbenches were stocked with small businessmen and farmers, and the party's national strength was rooted in western Canada. When the M.P.s returned to their constituencies, all they seemed to hear were complaints about high interest rates. It was scarcely surprising, therefore, that Conservative M.P.s grumbled and complained privately.

Party discipline, however, imposed a public silence on most of them. Alvin Hamilton, M.P. for Qu'Appelle-Moose Mountain, could not be stilled. Hamilton had always been one of the most independently minded men in the Conservative Party, his exuberance for new ideas infecting his every speech. He was an elder statesman on the Prairies, where farmers remembered how effectively he had sold their wheat as Diefenbaker's Minister of Agriculture. He delighted in playing the role of iconoclast. He knew that at the age of sixty-seven, he was too old to aspire realistically to the Cabinet. He could not be held hostage to ambition by Clark or anyone else within the Conservative Party. Hamilton took up the cry against high interest rates, giving interviews condemning the policy. The Liberals and New Democrats were delighted—here was a crack in the Conservative ranks—and some Conservative M.P.s were privately pleased that a senior colleague was questioning the bank's policy despite the additional ammunition Hamilton's remarks provided the Conservatives' political opponents.

Hamilton's criticism was an irritant rather than a threat to John Crosbie, who had never shared the breezy optimism of Gillies and Clark that the country's economic problems could be resolved with several new, dramatic policies. Although Crosbie fulminated against the Liberal Government, his speeches revealed a man convinced that the Canadian economy needed strict fiscal and monetary discipline to dampen inflation, reverse a worsening current account deficit, and restore investor confidence. As a politician, he did not like high interest rates, but as finance minister, he considered them a necessary evil. "Certainly, I'm reluctant as finance minister because our interest rates are already very high, but under the circumstances I felt I had no choice," Crosbie explained after the first interest rate increase in July. Crosbie shared Bouey's analysis that high interest rates were needed to restrain inflation in Canada and to support the Canadian dollar by keeping Canadian interest rates slightly above those in the United States. As a result, when the U.S. Federal Reserve Board pushed up its lending rate, the Bank of Canada followed suit within a matter of hours or days. Each time, Crosbie explained that Canada had no choice but to match leapfrogging U.S. rates. His explanations echoed those of his Liberal predecessor Jean Chrétien, who said in January 1979: "The monetary policy is established by the governor of the Bank of Canada. When he raised interest rates, he stated his reasons for doing so in a press release, and I approved his decisions. . . . Canada is a new country which imports capital from foreign countries . . . so we must have competitive interest rates."

Even if Crosbie had disagreed with Bouey's analysis, politicians have been reluctant to spark a confrontation with the governor of the Bank of Canada since the messy removal of Governor James Coyne by the Diefenbaker Government in the summer of 1961. The Bank of Canada Act makes clear that the Government is ultimately responsible for the nation's monetary policy, but the governor handles the bank's day-by-day decisions and also traditionally makes important policy decisions. In the case of a severe conflict with the Government, the governor would have little choice but to resign. Ever since the Coyne imbroglio, Governments have feared the political fallout from a confrontation with the governor, whose position ostensibly protects the nation's currency from the sway of partisan politics. In Bouey's case, the nation's financial community stood solidly behind the Bank of Canada's policy. Several prominent economists such as writer Arthur Donner and Douglas Peters, vice-president of the Toronto-Dominion Bank, questioned the need for high interest rates. But along Bay and St. James streets, there was quiet approval for Bouey's policy. Financial experts warned that Bouey's removal would shake investor confidence in the stability of the Canadian dollar.

The Government's acceptance of the Bank of Canada's high-interest-rate policy was especially troublesome for Clark's policy advisor, Jim Gillies, who had led his party's denunciation of high interest rates in Opposition. Gillies griped about the governor's refusal to understand that high interest rates encouraged, not dampened, inflation, and that interest-rate differentials between Canada and the United States were less influential in determining investment flows than the relative health of the two economies. But Gillies did not press Clark as hard to replace Bouey as he had done to fire William Hood as Deputy Minister of Finance. Crosbie, after all, was solidly behind Bouey, and Clark was not prepared to take on both his finance minister and the financial community by offering Bouey's head to Gillies and to restless members of the Conservative caucus. To ease fears in the financial community that the Conservatives might change the direction of monetary policy, the Conservatives reappointed Bouey for another seven-year term before his existing term expired in February 1980.

Bouey's reappointment confirmed the Government's continued acceptance of the Bank of Canada's policy. Canadian interest rates remained in tandem with American rates, and although this made compelling economic sense, it did not placate those pressing the Conservatives to fulfil their election promises. NDP leader Ed Broadbent lumped the Conservatives and Liberals together as the pageboys for high finance. The Liberals managed to forget their previous defence of Bouey's policies, arguing disingenuously but effectively that they would never have pursued the same policy had rates continued to rise.

Under the circumstances, the Conservatives were following an economically defensible policy, but whatever the economic wisdom of their policy, they had promised something else in Opposition so that their policy seem a betrayal of principle. Inevitably, their own political credibility suffered. If the Conservatives had remained longer in office, the party might have profited politically when interest rates plummeted in the spring of 1980. Instead, the Liberals accepted the credit for the falling rates, leaving the Conservatives to reflect again on the blindness of their leaders, who threw the party into electoral battle with pennants, bugles, and damp powder.

Having rejected both stimulative fiscal measures and drastic expenditure cuts, the Conservatives settled on raising new revenues as the only way of attacking the deficit. The search for new revenues in turn led the Conservatives to include in the budget an additional 18-cents-per-gallon excise tax on transportation fuels, which became the most damaging issue for the party in the 1980 campaign—apart from the perception of Joe Clark's leadership. The excise tax provided an easy target for the Opposition parties, who hammered the tax so vigorously that the Government was never able to make clear its case for the tax. The idea of the excise tax arose from within the civil service, where it sparked a fierce debate among bureaucrats. But it also provoked a row within the inner Cabinet that exposed the lack of consensus on economic policy within the Conservative Party.

The Liberals first imposed a 10-cents-per-gallon excise tax on gasoline in their budget of June 1975. At the time, the federal government faced declining revenues from a levy on oil exported to the United States and from growing payments for its oil-import compensation program, which subsidized the price of imported oil in the five eastern-most provinces. The Liberals subsequently reduced the excise tax on gasoline to 7 cents per gallon, but the tax was still raising badly needed revenue for a federal government whose budget was plunging each year more deeply into the red. In 1975, when the excise tax was first imposed, Canada was a net exporter of oil, although the nation's exports had fallen sharply after 1973. By 1976, Canada was importing more oil than it exported, and the situation worsened relentlessly through 1979, when the federal government was paying $628 million in oil-import compensation payments and staring at the prospect of spending $1.5 billion in 1980 for the same program.*

The idea of raising the excise tax originated within the energy department. In documents prepared for the inner Cabinet in August, the department urged the Government to increase dramatically the price of oil and natural gas to reduce consumption. The department recommended a yearly price increase in oil of $6 per barrel, but if this level of increase could not be negotiated with the producing provinces the department suggested an excise tax "in the order of 30 to 50 cents per gallon" on gasoline in order to shock consumers into curbing their appetites for transportation fuels. The department was convinced that sharply higher prices would reduce consumption. The real price of gasoline had not risen since 1961, and that had encouraged Canadians to gobble up gasoline at what the department called "alarming" rates. In the first nine months of 1979, while gasoline consumption rose in Canada by 4 per cent, it fell by 4 per cent in the United States, where consumers adjusted their consumption habits to the government-directed movement of oil prices to world levels.

The energy department's general view had been accepted by the Liberal Government. In its 1976 *Energy Strategy Report*, the Liberal Government agreed "to move domestic oil prices towards international levels" without necessarily reaching the world price. At the first ministers' conference of April 1975 Prime Minister Trudeau accepted the link between higher prices and reduced demand: "We cannot go on year after year being extravagant in

---

*Subsequent world oil price increases pushed the projected oil-import compensation payments to more than $3 billion in 1980.

our use of oil far beyond what almost every country in the world consumes—mainly because it is being sold cheaply in Canada, a lot cheaper than elsewhere and a lot cheaper than our future supplies will cost."

When the Conservatives discovered in their energy negotiations with Alberta that the federal government would not receive adequate revenues from the proposed $6-per-barrel oil-price increases, Ottawa dropped the yearly increases to $4 and $4.50 per barrel. But this lower increase would produce a smaller impact on demand and generate less revenue for the federal government. So the excise tax, first discussed as a fallback position, acquired a life of its own. An additional excise tax of 30 cents per gallon, piled atop price increases arising from the crude oil pricing negotiations with Alberta, would force a significant reduction in consumer demand and provide the federal treasury with about $3.5 billion.

The finance department looked covetously at the excise tax proposal. The $3.5 billion was just what the department needed to attack the federal deficit. Once the finance department began eyeing the excise tax, two debates started in the federal government: one between the energy and finance departments; the other among Cabinet ministers favouring or resisting the excise tax. The two debates proceeded simultaneously until the finance department won the revenue battle; then the ministers were left with a clear field for their donnybrook.

The debate between the energy and finance departments turned on a straightforward question: how to use the revenue from the excise tax? The energy department, supported by Privy Council Clerk Marcel Massé, wanted the money for energy-related projects. The department argued that the nation could only become self-sufficient by 1990 if the federal government invested in energy projects across Canada. The tax could be made acceptable to consumers only if Canadians saw the government pumping revenues from the excise tax into projects to enhance self-sufficiency. The tax must be made to look like an insurance program into which consumers made payments now for future security of supply.

The finance department's sights were fixed elsewhere. Having ruled out draconian expenditure reductions and assumed a costly mortgage-interest and property-tax relief plan, the department was starved for additional revenues to reduce the Government's deficit. The excise tax was a swift method of raising revenues, and even if the money was used for deficit reduction, the tax would still satisfy the energy department's goal of shocking consumers into reduced demand. Crosbie saw to it that the debate was resolved in the finance department's favour. He argued strenuously that reducing the deficit was the Government's highest priority, noting that the energy department had secured an Energy Bank from the negotiations with Alberta for energy-related projects. Clark, against the advice of Marcel Massé and Energy Minister Ray Hnatyshyn, supported his finance minister, and the debate ended.

But there were still those in the Cabinet opposed to the excise tax, the most vocal of whom was Sinclair Stevens. Stevens mistrusted bureaucratic thinking, and the excise tax confirmed his suspicion that civil servants assumed they knew what was best for citizens. He dismissed the energy department's argument that sharply higher prices necessarily reduced consumption. People would pay the higher prices and continue to drive as much as before, he countered. Bureaucrats might think that people would drive less frequently, but they did not understand human nature, conditioned by the car-oriented society of North America.

Stevens, however, was most alarmed by the potentially negative political reaction to the excise tax. Stevens did not oppose tax increases; in fact, he wrote to Crosbie in November suggesting a variety of revenue-generating measures, such as a surtax on personal and corporate income tax, an excess profits tax, or an increase in federal sales tax. But Stevens, supported by House leader Walter Baker, considered the excise tax dangerously visible; motorists would notice the tax every time they filled up their gasoline tanks. Perhaps the tax could be increased by two or three cents, he suggested. At worst, the existing 7-cents-per-gallon excise tax could be doubled, so that at least the Conservatives could argue that they had not imposed a higher tax than the Liberals. But anything greater than 7 cents per gallon was political suicide.

The inner Cabinet was split: Crosbie insisting that the excise tax of 30 cents would provide revenue for the government and a shock for consumers; Stevens and Baker warning that the excise tax would bring political trouble. The other ministers were torn between two emotions—a belief in the economic reasoning behind the tax and a nervousness about its political implications. Gradually, the inner Cabinet inched towards a compromise: the excise tax dropped from 30 cents to 25 cents, and finally to 18 cents; roughly halfway between Crosbie's original proposal and Stevens' maximum increase of 7 cents.

Settling on an 18-cents-per-gallon increase, however, did not resolve another dispute. The Liberals had exempted all commercial fuels from their original excise tax. Motorists using gasoline were paying the tax, but farmers, fishermen, and other users of diesel fuel were exempted. The finance department's original proposal to the inner Cabinet would have ended this exemption so that farmers and fishermen, for example, would have felt an even sharper jolt than other consumers from the proposed increase in the excise tax. Crosbie argued that no group should be exempt from the fight to reduce the deficit and move Canada towards self-sufficiency. But this was too politically risky for some ministers, who battled either for an exemption from the tax for these groups or for another form of relief. Again, the Cabinet reached a compromise position: farmers, fishermen, and municipal transit systems would receive a 10-cents-per-gallon refund for the additional 18-cents-per-gallon excise tax.

Crosbie had not won a total victory, but he was still satisfied with what emerged from the inner Cabinet. The 18-cents-per-gallon excise tax would produce about $2 billion in revenues for the federal government. Any public anger directed towards the Government would wane before the next election, which Crosbie assumed still lay some distance away. By then, the voters would be thinking of other issues, and perhaps the Conservatives could show progress in reducing the deficit and inflation.

Unfortunately for Crosbie and his party, the link between the excise tax and self-sufficiency was never accepted by the voters. If the revenues from the tax had been funnelled into energy projects, perhaps the tax could have been sold as an insurance program. But the Conservatives would still have experienced great difficulty in persuading Canadians that the excise tax was indispensable for self-sufficiency, because the Government was asking Canadians to bear sacrifices in the absence of a sense of crisis. Although news of disconcerting political developments in oil-producing countries appeared periodically on their television screens, Canadians had always been able to secure adequate supplies of oil and to pay the lowest energy prices in the Western world. Self-sufficiency was a distant goal, but the excise tax was an immediate burden. It represented "short-term pain" that Canadians were unwilling to forbear for the "long-term gain" of self-sufficiency, the lack of which had not yet been brought home to consumers in the form of interrupted supplies or world prices. Nor did the Conservatives' energy tax credit of $80 per adult and $30 per child in a family with income of less than $21,380 ease the "short-term pain," because it was to be phased in over two years, whereas the excise tax was imposed immediately.

As it was, the excise tax looked like a revenue grab by a federal government determined to lower its deficit, a cause for which a majority of Canadians would not willingly pay higher prices nor cast their votes.

John Crosbie's budget—"a budget that faces the facts," as he called it—grew from his profound conviction that Canadians had been living beyond their means. "The only way we can come out of this crisis in Canada is by asking the Canadian people to tighten their belts," Crosbie said on the eve of the 1979 election. His analysis was undoubtedly sound; the proof lay in the nation's staggering current-account deficit, the budgetary deficit, a devalued currency, and a growing dependence on foreign oil. But for all his humour and proselytizing, he could not persuade Canadians either that he was correct or that his solutions were equitable.

Whether from upbringing or conviction, it is often those born to wealth who lecture their fellow citizens on the need to lower their expectations. John Crosbie was the scion of one of the Water Street merchant families of St. John's. Their children are sent to Bishop Field College high school to begin their training to replace their parents as the economic elite of Newfoundland. He was a "thousandaire" with enough money to be comfortable "unless we can't beat inflation," Crosbie said with rare understatement. Most of his fellow citizens, however, could only dream of the wealth of John Crosbie's family; asking them to lower their expectations—to accept "short-term pain for long-term gain"—smacked of the smugness of the affluent.

As a minority party, the Conservatives must always reach far beyond their core supporters to attract citizens whose usual voting preferences lie elsewhere. The budget, at least the way it was presented by the Conservatives and depicted by the Opposition parties, seemed more onerous for low- and moderate-income Canadians than for upper-middle-class and wealthy citizens. The affluent could better protect themselves from higher energy prices and also could benefit disproportionately from mortgage-interest and property-tax credits which, although not contained in the budget, were in the final stage of parliamentary debate when the Government was defeated. The energy tax credit, a sensible plan to cushion less-affluent taxpayers from the shock of higher energy prices, was never adequately explained by the party. There was no time to do so before the election, and the excise tax was much easier for the electorate to seize upon during the campaign than was a tax credit phased in over two years. In the poor and working-class regions of Canada, voters reacted strongly against the budget, and the Conservatives lost seats and popular support in Atlantic Canada, the industrial ridings of Ontario, and on the Prairies, where the excise tax was especially unpopular with farmers.

It was a budget for a majority Government. Six weeks before the budget was introduced, Government House leader Walter Baker had remarked at an inner Cabinet meeting that the budget had an "extremely slim" chance of parliamentary approval. But Baker's comment was uttered before Pierre Trudeau resigned as Liberal leader. His impending departure led the Conservatives to believe that the budget, despite its contentious clauses, would sail through the Commons while the Liberals were engrossed in their leadership review.

Even a minority Government might have survived in Parliament or won an election on such a budget if it enjoyed a healthy margin of public support. But to present such a budget while trailing by nineteen points in public opinion was politically foolhardy. The budget courageously addressed economic issues left unattended by the Liberals, but courage without prudence can amount to recklessness. The Conservative Government careened blindly from its budget towards an electoral defeat that only divine intervention or a memorable Liberal blunder could prevent.

PART THREE: CAMPAIGN

~ 9 ~

First Stirrings

On the day after their defeat in the House of Commons, the Conservatives contemplated the election campaign in an upbeat frame of mind. They had convinced themselves, despite considerable adverse evidence, that the election was theirs for the winning. The campaign was not to be a fight for survival; it would produce a majority Conservative Government.

The speed with which the Conservatives plunged into the election fight fueled the party's optimism. The Conservatives' campaign organization was mobilized within forty-eight hours of the Government's defeat, while the Liberals were still wondering who would lead their party. Once Trudeau agreed to return, the Conservatives' hopes soared further, since they could not believe that Canadians were ready to embrace the man whom they had spurned seven months before. William Neville, Clark's combative chief-of-staff, summed up the optimism as he wandered through the back of Clark's campaign plane on the second day of Clark's national tour telling journalists: "This is my tenth election and I've never been so up. I really want to kill them this time."

The Gallup Poll of November had shown the Conservatives nineteen points behind the Liberals. As a general rule, the Liberals or Conservatives can hope for a movement of only four or five points in the polls during a campaign. But the Conservatives, blinded by optimism, rationalized the Gallup Poll results. The Conservatives had argued for many years that the Gallup Poll systematically underestimated their strength in Canada's rural regions. That accounted for about three points in the Gallup Poll, they reasoned. They also believed that the Gallup Poll exaggerated the gap between the two parties by incorrectly measuring the Liberals' enormous lead in Quebec. In dozens of Quebec ridings, the Liberals "waste" thousands of votes by piling up huge majorities, which inflate the party's standing in the national popular vote. Observers usually knock four or five points off the Liberals' lead in the Gallup Poll and other national surveys to take account of this "Quebec factor." But the Conservatives conceded such a massive lead to the Liberals in Quebec that they chopped about eight points off the gap separating the Liberals and Conservatives. Combining the Quebec factor with their own conviction that the Gallup Poll underestimated Conservative strength in rural regions allowed those organizing the Conservative campaign to cut the effective Liberal lead in the Gallup Poll from nineteen to about eight points. The return of Trudeau and the anticipated negative reaction against the Opposition parties for precipitating the election more than compensated for the remaining eight points.

The Conservatives also took heart from their splendid election organization. Those running the Conservatives' 1979 campaign made several tactical errors that might have cost the Conservatives a majority Government: the decision to coast through the final week of the campaign; Clark's ill-considered responses to questions about the RCMP; Quebec's right to self-determination and the cost of the party's election promises. But the organization of the campaign had been magnificent. Clark's own tour was superbly organized. The party's polling and media campaigns reinforced each other, driving home the messages that "Trudeau" and "change" were irreconcilable, and identifying the Conservatives with the voters' underlying mood of optimism. The Conservatives were overwhelmed with volunteers in constituencies outside Quebec. The party's election-day organization in English-speaking provinces pulled out a large percentage of committed and probable Conservative voters. There was no reason to doubt that the party could count on the same efficiency in the 1980 campaign.

The Conservatives' organization began to purr even before the election was called. On the day of the Government's defeat, Paul Curley, the party's national director, alerted the party's provincial campaign chairmen that they might be summoned to Ottawa on short notice for a strategy meeting. When the Government fell that night, Curley immediately summoned his provincial chairmen to Ottawa for an all-day meeting at Conservative headquarters on Saturday, December 15. On the same morning, the

Liberal Party's national executive gathered at the Chateau Laurier Hotel to consider Trudeau's return as party leader. Whereas a visitor that Saturday morning to Conservative headquarters found typewriters humming and frenzied activity, the doors were locked and the lights were out at Liberal headquarters two blocks away in downtown Ottawa.

On the night of the Government's defeat, Clark, Neville, Lowell Murray, Nancy Jamieson, and Curley dined in Clark's offices on Parliament Hill. They spent about half of their two-hour dinner meeting discussing the broad themes of the Conservatives' campaign. At that meeting, Curley reported that Air Canada had already agreed to provide a charter aircraft within seventy-two hours. The party's finances were in excellent condition and the organization was on standby alert, he said.

In the 1979 election, the Conservatives as an Opposition party were allowed the luxury of basing their campaign on the Liberals' record, although the Conservatives also outlined an array of promises that later tripped them up. In 1980, the Conservatives could not avoid their own record of seven months in office. Unfortunately for the Conservatives, their premature defeat cut short initiatives either recently launched or in the final planning stages. Tactically, therefore, the Conservatives' campaign would have to centre more on future action than on past accomplishments, an often untenable position for a Government seeking re-election.

The party's most disconcerting problem, apart from the image of Clark's leadership, was the public perception that the party had looked unsteady and at times incompetent, especially in wrestling with its election promises. The Conservatives were wounded as much by their failure to act decisively on their promises as by some of the foolish promises themselves. On the day after the Government's defeat, Clark met with Lowell Murray, Neville, Jamieson, assistant chief-of-staff Donald Doyle, director of communications André Payette, and press secretary Jock Osler to prepare himself for the first press conference of the campaign. Such a meeting was standard procedure for Clark before any of his press conferences as Prime Minister. Anticipating a question about broken promises, those attending the meeting agreed that Clark should confront the accusation directly. Clark was therefore well prepared when the expected question was asked at the press conference: "How are you going to respond to that double questioning of both your competence and your credibility?" Clark replied, using the answer developed at the earlier meeting:

> I am going to respond by pointing out that in the election
> campaign [of 1979] we promised to bring government
> spending under control. We started to do that. We
> promised to bring down deficits and we have already
> accomplished that. We promised to introduce freedom of
> information. It is before the House of Commons. We
> promised to introduce other parliamentary reforms.
> They have been spelled out in the House of Commons.
> We promised to get grain moving in western Canada. The
> Minister of Transport has been moving on that. We
> promised to put in place a national grain transport coor-
> dinator. That grain transport coordinator is in place. We
> promised help to small business. That help was outlined
> in the budget. We promised a spouse's allowance, and
> that has been passed. We promised help to the veterans of
> the country. That was another piece of legislation which
> the Liberals and the New Democratic Party stopped being
> passed by Parliament. I could go on for a couple of hours,
> but it is a short press conference.

Another minute would have sufficed to list the promises fulfilled,
but Clark had at least made a start at cauterizing the wound. This
kind of answer, however defiantly delivered, could not adequately
compensate for the harm the Government had already done to
itself by the Jerusalem-embassy promise, the confusion over
PetroCanada, energy policy, and the budget. Caught in an election
with its liabilities showing and its assets stillborn, the Conservatives began thinking about how to arouse the electorate's sympathy,
since they could not win its affection.

Blaming the other parties for precipitating the election was
the most obvious tactic. Although the Conservatives had impru-
dently discarded their options for avoiding defeat in the Commons,
the Conservatives believed they could pin the blame for the election on the Opposition parties. On the day after the Government's
defeat, the Conservatives published a list of bills "killed by the
Opposition." Listening to the Conservatives' rhetoric, one might
have concluded that the Liberals and NDP had committed a more
heinous offence than simply voting a lack of confidence in the
Government. On the night of his defeat, Clark said:

> The Opposition parties have decided to disrupt the
> nation's business. That was not our choice; we wanted to
> get on with governing the country. . . . Unfortunately,

> from the first day, Opposition parties showed no interest
> in making Parliament work. Instead, they have system-
> atically obstructed its business. Now, they have brought
> it to a complete halt.

Blaming the other parties for the election could only work for the
first two weeks of the campaign; after that, the electorate would
stop assigning blame and begin considering which party should
form the Government. It was an argument only for the short
term. It certainly would leave unmoved the mass of undecided
voters who only turn their attention to the campaign in the final
three weeks.

Assigning blame for the election reinforced the argument at
the core of the Conservatives' strategy: the Government had not
been given a fair chance to govern. There was something plaintive
about the Conservatives' contention that the Government had
been struck down in the flower of its youth, when the Prime
Minister and those around him were hardened political partisans.
But they believed that the voters' desire for "fundamental change,"
as Clark put it on the night of his Government's defeat, was so
compelling and their distaste for Trudeau so deep that hearts would
flutter when the Conservatives depicted themselves as virtuous
innocents cut down by unscrupulous Liberals and New Democrats.
Clark even took to using an analogy between a child and his
Government, saying babies need nine months from conception to
birth, whereas his Government had been given only seven months.

Finally, the Conservatives had to make strategic decisions
about the budget. After the campaign, Liberals like Martin Goldfarb, the party's polling expert, wondered why the Conservatives
stood by their budget and provided the Liberals with a stationary
target to attack. Goldfarb thought the Conservatives should have
dropped the budget, explaining that it had been defeated in the
Commons and would therefore be revised even if the Conservatives were re-elected. But the Conservatives had run their 1979
campaign partly on the Liberals' record of broken promises. The
Government had just endured seven months of criticism for
breaking promises or fudging their implementation. John Crosbie
was proud of his budget; he was the most popular Conservative
minister on the eve of the election. There would be no retreat,
despite the Government's defeat on the budget in the House. "If
you come back with [a] majority or even if you come back with a
minority, would you put forth the same budget?" Clark was asked

at his press conference the day after his Government's defeat. "Yes," he replied, and the issue that toppled the Government in the Commons became the centrepiece of the election campaign. It was part of the Conservatives' broader attempt to portray themselves as the party of principle, in contrast to the opportunistic Liberals and "socialists," as Clark took to calling the NDP, hoping the pejorative term would frighten potential NDP supporters in Ontario and western Canada. The Conservative Government may have vacillated in office, but no one would be able to accuse Clark of that in the campaign. Clark, who told Canadians in the 1979 campaign to raise their expectations, became the man for "tough decisions." The same fear of appearing weak that motivated Clark in power dictated his strategy in the campaign. In January, Crosbie went to Clark and suggested phasing in the excise tax in three 6-cent increases; Clark would have none of it.

The Conservatives spent eighteen months plotting their strategy for the 1979 campaign, but decisions for the 1980 campaign were made on the fly. There was not time for elaborate research; instinct and wide strokes of luck would have to lead those organizing the Conservative campaign to make wise strategic decisions. Nor were there any polls from Allan Gregg to guide the Conservative strategists in those first days after the Government's defeat. There was only the November Gallup Poll, which the Conservatives had satisfied themselves was irrelevant before the campaign began. Decisions taken immediately after the fall of the Government could not be tempered by consultation with either the oracle of the polls or the wisdom of party members across the country.

As in 1979, Lowell Murray and William Neville shaped the broad design of the Conservative campaign. Although Murray had ceded the title of campaign director to Paul Curley, an Albertan who had been Murray's director of operations in the 1979 campaign, Murray was the strategist of last resort for the Conservatives' media campaign and the thematic development of Clark's speeches. Curley was responsible for working with provincial chairmen who co-ordinated the Conservatives' constituency campaigns. Neville travelled with Clark throughout the campaign, writing speeches, reviewing daily plans with Conservative advance men, and ensuring that the Clark tour ran with the same efficiency as it had in 1979. The political judgements of Murray and Neville may have been unsettled by the cares of power, but the two men were like hounds on the chase in an election campaign. It was a testament to their acumen as organizers and tacticians that the Conservatives fought so skilfully against insurmountable odds in the 1980 campaign. Solace is the vinegary wine of losers, but they still merited a bittersweet toast for their campaign efforts.

With the Liberals in deceptive disarray after the fall of the Government, the Conservatives began their campaign as quickly as possible to steal a march on the Liberals. On the Monday following the Government's defeat, while Trudeau pondered his future in Ottawa, Clark kicked off his campaign in Montreal, where he introduced the party's leading Quebec candidates. He might just have well taken their coffin sizes, as things turned out, but illusions spring eternal in the Conservative Party in Quebec. "They're all hoping that this is like 1958," bubbled Richard Holden, a Conservative lawyer in Montreal who lost by 36,700 votes in Dollard riding in the 1979 election but prudently decided to skip the 1980 campaign. The initial planning for the showpiece rally had begun an hour after the Government's defeat, when Clark chatted briefly in his office with Industry, Trade and Commerce Minister Robert de Cotret. During their conversation, de Cotret agreed to give up his Senate seat and run in Quebec, where Clark needed the strongest possible team of candidates to impress Quebeckers and, as importantly, to show Canadians elsewhere that the party might make gains in that province. De Cotret and Murray began studying possible Quebec ridings for the Ontario native to contest. At a weekend meeting with Clark, de Cotret finally decided to run in the riding of Berthier-Maskinongé in the Mauricie region of Quebec, north of the St. Lawrence River between Montreal and Trois-Rivières. De Cotret, Clark, and Murray had also looked at the ridings of Chicoutimi, Trois-Rivières, and Saint Hyacinthe, but they chose Berthier-Maskinongé because the Liberal candidate, Antonio Yanakis, faced court charges for perjury in connection with a previous legal investigation. The Conservatives had lost Berthier-Maskinongé by 6,800 votes in the 1979 campaign. That was a Liberal landslide all right, but from the Conservatives' perspective Berthier-Maskinongé had been a near thing: the party lost Chicoutimi by nearly 9,000 votes, Saint Hyacinthe by 11,200 and Trois-Rivières by 14,500. Joliette, the riding of popular Conservative M.P. Roch LaSalle, bordered on Berthier-Maskinongé; perhaps LaSalle's popularity, combined with plenty of federal *bonbons* for the good citizens of Berthier-Maskinongé, might get de Cotret into the Commons. Once de Cotret's riding was selected, the other ridings for "name"

240/ Discipline of Power

Conservatives fell into place: president of the Quebec Conservative Party Marcel Danis for Saint Hyacinthe; former Union Nationale Cabinet minister Marcel Masse in Labelle; Clark's director of communications André Payette in Ste. Marie.

The first week of Clark's campaign was the first phase of a phony war. Elections usually catch the attention of a majority of the voters only in the last month of the campaign. Parties organize their campaigns on the premise that the undecided voters do not start "tuning in," to use the inelegant but appropriate expression of the television age in politics, until several weeks before voting day. The first week of any campaign, therefore, is not directed at the undecided voters; it is for the committed party workers whose enthusiasm needs kindling for the arduous labours of a two-month campaign. Thus Clark sallied forth from Ottawa before Christmas with three limited objectives in mind: to capitalize on whatever annoyance he could find with the calling of an election; to rally the Conservative faithful; and to shore up several weak spots in the party platform. All week, he railed against the Liberals and New Democrats for "plunging the country into an unnecessary election," listing the accomplishments of his Government and the initiatives cut short by the election. In Kitchener, on the second day of his campaign, he summarized his accusation with standard campaign hyperbole:

> When we formed the Government last June, we knew that we had a nation to heal, a Parliament to respect, and an economy that we had to rebuild. We had begun that work as a new national government. Yet the Liberals and the socialists did not want that work to continue. With a referendum coming in the province of Quebec, with energy and economic challenges that we simply cannot avoid as a nation, with an international situation that needs Canada's mediation, the Opposition parties plunged this country into an unnecessary, expensive election.

The next night in his own riding of Yellowhead, Clark spoke about his aborted plans for a royal commission into fiscal relations between Ottawa and the provinces.

> We must face the fact that the federal government is not as able as it should be to manage the national economy, to help overcome regional disparities, and to conduct major national policies. There has grown up a serious fiscal imbalance, not only among the provinces but between the provincial and federal levels of government.

It was a surprising speech for someone who viewed Canada as a "community of communities," because he was admitting that the fiscal powers of the central government had become dangerously weakened. If the Liberals had not decided to avoid national unity and federal-provincial relations in their campaign, they could have pounced on Clark's speech as another "flip-flop." As it was, Clark's accurate analysis of the fiscal imbalances of federalism simply indicated how his thinking about federalism had shifted since his days as Opposition leader.

From Alberta, Clark moved on to Vancouver, where he hoped at last to set straight his PetroCanada policy for his party and the country. Ever since the report of the Government's task force on PetroCanada, a Cabinet committee under Minister of State for International Trade Michael Wilson had been trying to figure out what to do with the crown corporation. The task force's report was unacceptable; the Government could not assume an additional $2 billion in debt when Sinclair Stevens and John Crosbie were screaming that the interest on the public debt was bleeding the federal budget. Instead, the Wilson committee hit upon a less costly scheme which Clark announced in a speech to the Vancouver Board of Trade. The Government would give away 50 per cent of the shares of PetroCanada and sell 20 per cent, keeping 30 per cent for itself. That would make the federal government the largest shareholder in the new company. Every Canadian above the age of eighteen would receive five free shares of the new company. Each share would be worth $100, and no institution or individual could own more than 3 per cent of the outstanding shares. It was a politically attractive scheme, but it came too late to erase the image of confusion and uncertainty that the Government had already established for itself on PetroCanada.

An election campaign is a poor time to announce a major shift or clarification in policy. Those who organize political campaigns know that if a policy is unclear to the public before a campaign, it will be too late to explain the policy during a campaign. Extensive explanations during a campaign create the impression of confusion; they dilute the focus a party tries to put on issues and leadership. Only a minority of the electorate changes its voting intention during a campaign. These "switchers" and undecided voters usually make up their minds on the basis of "leadership" and the parties' general images, rather than on promises or policies. Nevertheless, the Conservatives' confused PetroCanada policy had become such an open sore that Clark felt he had to act early in the campaign to minimize the possibility of further political damage during the campaign.

On the final day of his first week of campaigning, Clark was in superb form as he outlined his party's energy policy to the Winnipeg Society of Financial Analysts. During the entire first week of the 1980 campaign, he delivered his speeches with more assurance than at any time in the 1979 campaign. The Winnipeg speech was his first extensive effort to make the link between higher prices and self-sufficiency for Canada.

> We are relying more and more as a nation on energy supplies over which we have no control, and energy supplies on which we simply cannot depend. The evidence of that ... is on our television screens every night. Today the problem is in Iran. Tomorrow it could well be in another country on whom we now depend to fuel our cars or heat our homes or run our industries. Ladies and gentlemen, I do not intend to let the energy security of Canada depend on OPEC or the Ayatollah.

"OPEC or the Ayatollah"—the businessmen liked the phrase, responding with prolonged applause. Clark had finally found a striking way of putting his case for higher prices. But, again, it was too late. He was fighting a deeply held belief in Canada that the energy problems of the world did not touch this blessed land of abundant resources. He had delayed taking his case for higher prices to the people during the fall, waiting for the conclusion of energy negotiations with Alberta Premier Peter Lougheed. As a result, he was left to argue a compelling but politically unpalatable case in the hopeless forum of an election campaign against two other parties that promised cheaper energy than the Conservatives.

Still, it was a good week. Trudeau had barely begun campaigning. Clark had delivered six speeches, laying out the basic themes of his campaign. If Clark had not reached the mass of the electorate preoccupied with Christmas rather than politics, he had at least addressed the Conservative faithful, bucking up their spirits with his own enthusiasm. On the flight back to Ottawa Friday night, his staff decked out the plane in Christmas decorations, broke open the champagne and distributed gifts to the passengers. Standing at the front of the cabin, his tie loosened and wearing a yellow cardigan, Clark joined the accompanying journalists who sang songs of political satire they had composed to the music of

Christmas carols: "The Twelve Days of Depression," "Deck Me Follies" and "We Three Turkeys."

Alas, while the revelry continued in the sky, the first results were pouring in from the Conservatives' polls. As soon as the election writs had been issued, Allan Gregg had launched the party's first polling survey since August 1979. By the end of the first week of the campaign, Gregg had assembled his data. On Sunday night he joined Murray, Neville, and Curley for a meeting with Clark at 24 Sussex Drive. There, the five men studied the disaster foretold by Gregg's polling.

The Conservatives were in deep trouble everywhere in Canada except Alberta. Across the country, the party trailed the Liberals by twenty-one points; they were even further behind than Gallup had indicated in November. In Ontario, where the Conservatives had fashioned their 1979 victory, they trailed the Liberals by twenty-one points; west of Yonge Street in Metropolitan Toronto, the Conservatives were thirty-five points behind. In western Canada, except in Alberta, the Conservatives were trailing the NDP, and the Liberals were showing surprising strength in British Columbia and Manitoba. The Conservatives had finished the 1979 campaign four points behind the Liberals; in seven months, the party had dropped seventeen points. Most of the decline came in the two months preceding the election. Parties try to enter a campaign on the upswing, hoping that momentum can be built upon during the campaign. The Conservatives were not only without momentum, they were sliding backwards when the campaign began.

The raw numbers measuring voting intentions did not tell the whole gloomy story. By more than a two-to-one margin, voters disapproved of the Clark Government's performance in office. The electorate still wanted "change" in the management of the country, but the largest number of voters did not support the Conservatives' proposed changes, especially on the energy issue, where few voters accepted the link between higher prices and energy self-sufficiency. The 18-cents-per-gallon excise tax on gasoline was unpopular in every region.

The worst news of all was yet to come. The Conservatives were delighted when Trudeau re-entered the fray, believing that the electorate could not countenance his return to power. But Gregg's polling data showed that antipathy to Trudeau had largely subsided; it was as if the electorate had blocked from their minds his eleven years in power. Asked which man was better equipped to handle national problems, 60 per cent said Trudeau, 20 per cent Clark. Despite everything the Conservatives had said about Trudeau running a one-man show in Ottawa, Trudeau was thought to have a more capable team of candidates than Clark. Trudeau was an asset for the Liberals, not a liability, as the Conservatives had believed.

No one could be optimistic after studying Gregg's poll, but a campaign infected by pessimism turns on itself, magnifying errors, inducing recriminations, and sapping energy. Clark took the news stoically while the others began searching for thin rays of hope. The Liberals' lead in Quebec was so overwhelming that perhaps the Quebec factor would count for as many as ten points. The winter weather would keep down the voter turn-out, and the Conservatives' election machine could turn out more of the party's solid supporters than the Liberals could produce of theirs. But the more the five men sitting in 24 Sussex Drive studied the data, the closer they came to the inescapable conclusion that the key to the election was Trudeau. If the Conservatives could remind the voters of their previous feelings towards Trudeau, perhaps the election might yet be saved. It was their only hope.

Those organizing the Liberals' campaign, notably Jim Coutts and Keith Davey, understood the Conservatives' thinking. It was, after all, the Conservatives' only strategy, given the Government's sorry standing in public opinion—a condition Coutts and Davey had recognized before it dawned on the Conservatives themselves. Coutts and Davey had helped to persuade Trudeau to return to politics, but for his return to be triumphant, Trudeau would have to conduct a different style of campaign from the one he had waged in 1979.

There had been a touch of heroism in that campaign. Defeat seemed inevitable from the outset; the accumulated grievances of eleven years in power had soured the electorate on the Liberals. And yet Trudeau had railed against his fading power. He had campaigned with the burden of his estranged wife's prattling memoirs splashed across the pages of the nation's newspapers. Perhaps as a result, he had lashed out at the unemployed, at farmers, and at those who did not share his urgency to revitalize Confederation. He had spoken eloquently of the need for a strong central government, warning Canadians against Clark's "community of communities." He had occasionally discarded his advisors' speeches and their counsel, and wound up the campaign discussing the constitution. He had campaigned with vigour and passion and, at the very end, with dignity. In the final week of the campaign, Trudeau was speaking as much for the historical record as for votes.

Of course, most of Trudeau's campaign in 1979 was carefully planned. Burdened with an unpopular record and abandoned by some of his strongest ministers, Trudeau gambled everything on drawing a comparison between himself and Clark. If he could make the electorate forget their grievances by concentrating instead on his forceful personality, perhaps the anticipated result could be reversed. He stood behind a solitary microphone, hands hooked in his belt, his ice-blue eyes piercing through the television cameras into the living rooms of the nation, inviting Canadians to contrast his strength with Clark's weakness. "A Leader Must Be A Leader," boomed the Liberal advertisements as Trudeau punctured the air with his hands, rousing another crowd by vehement speechmaking. In the televised debate among the party leaders, Trudeau bloodied Clark's nose without flooring the challenger. Trudeau could not prevent a Liberal defeat, but he helped to deprive Clark of a Conservative majority and to sow seeds of doubt about Clark that bloomed when the young Prime Minister took office.

Trudeau all but disappeared from public view after the Conservatives' victory. Following Coutts' advice and his own desire for a respite from politics, Trudeau travelled with his children and with friends, reappearing occasionally at regional caucus meetings of Liberal M.P.s. The low profile undoubtedly dissipated some of the antipathy towards him, and it also made good tactical sense. There is usually little that an Opposition party can do to undermine a newly elected Government in its honeymoon period. Similarly, Canadians' interest in politics slackens during the summer. Convenience and smart tactics, then, suggested that Trudeau should yield the limelight to Clark, who gradually frittered away his election mandate in the first months in office. While the Liberals regrouped after their election defeat, the NDP acted like the Official Opposition, leading the attack against high interest rates and the dismantling of PetroCanada as a crown corporation. By doing next to nothing for four months after the election, the Liberals inadvertently benefited from these NDP attacks, because disillusioned Conservative supporters were more likely to swing to the Liberals than the NDP.

Without even trying, the Liberals found themselves nineteen points ahead of the Conservatives by early winter. That was an abnormally large lead that could not be sustained indefinitely, because the Liberals' and Conservatives' "core" votes were only about ten points apart. But the Liberals did have a larger base of support in the country than the Conservatives, so unless the Liberals ran afoul of many of their own supporters, they were better placed to win an election than the Conservatives were. If the Liberals did not make a major mistake in the 1980 campaign, if they kept reminding voters of the weaknesses of the Clark Government, the Liberals could not fail to win the election.

From this analysis flowed the most important decisions made at two meetings of the party's strategy committee. In past campaigns, the Liberals had dispensed with or ignored the advice of strategy committees, leaving decisions in the hands of Trudeau and a few close advisors. But the defeat of 1979 gave rise to demands within the party that the 1980 campaign be differently organized. The national executive of the party, provincial chairmen, and rank-and-file Liberals insisted that the party organization be consulted on strategic and policy decisions during the campaign. So a strategy committee was established for the 1980 campaign with Trudeau as chairman, and with caucus president Jacques Guilbault and party president Alasdair Graham as vice-chairmen. The other ten members included three former ministers—Jean Chrétien, Marc Lalonde, and Allan MacEachen—and Senator Keith Davey, Newfoundland Liberal leader Don Jamieson, and five Liberals from across the country: Gordon Gibson from British Columbia, Jean Gagnon from Quebec, Ted Malone from Saskatchewan, and Irma Melville and Kathy Robinson from Ontario.

The committee met twice at the beginning of the campaign and made six strategic decisions that shaped the Liberal campaign. First, the entire Liberal campaign would be focused on the Clark Government. Second, the party would announce only four or five policies during the campaign, enough to satisfy party members that the Liberals cared about policy but not enough to divert attention from the performance of the Clark Government. Third, Trudeau would speak from written texts. The gunslinger style of the 1979 campaign was discarded for fear that it might awaken latent resentment against the leader and invite the media to concentrate on Trudeau's style rather than on his attacks against the Conservatives. Fourth, the Liberals would use a team approach, surrounding Trudeau with former ministers, M.P.s, and candidates to reassure voters who worried that in voting Liberal they would be getting only Trudeau. Fifth, there would be a televised debate among the leaders only on Trudeau's terms: either a series of rotating debates among party spokesmen, or an extensive one-on-one debate against Clark. If those terms could not be negotiated, and the committee suspected they could not, then Trudeau would not enter a debate. Sixth, the campaign would be built around providing a news item each day for the 6 p.m. newscasts. It would be a leisurely campaign—no more than three events per day and often only one per day—to prevent Trudeau from tiring and to offer the media only one daily package of criticism of the Conservative Government. In short, nothing was to divert the campaign from its focus on Clark's Conservatives. Neither the Liberal campaign nor Trudeau must become issues in the campaign.

Coutts drafted a five-page summary of the committee's conclusions, and Davey further distilled the Liberals' strategy into a three-page "private and confidential" memorandum sent to all Liberal candidates on January 11, the end of Trudeau's first full week of campaigning:

1980—Election Strategy
If the election were today, Canadians would elect a Liberal government—with gains of seats in the Atlantic, Quebec, Ontario, B.C. and possibly the Prairies. Therefore, our campaign must be designed to: (1) reinforce the feelings that turned Canadians against the Clark government (2) keep public attention directed toward issues that are based on those feelings.

The large number of Canadians who turned against Clark and the Tories, and toward us, did so in July, September, October and early November. They did so before Mr. Trudeau's resignation and before the budget. They were *never* confident in Mr. Clark, but were willing to "wait and see" what he could do. He quickly failed them and as the fall progressed, their "wait and see" attitude changed to dislike and eventually embarrassment and anger.

Jerusalem was an important early sign that *he didn't know what he was doing.* At first the Jerusalem decision seemed naive and silly but when the Arab countries reacted it proved harmful to Canada. There was no honeymoon for the Clark government, and a foolish mistake in the early days of uncertainty immediately cost them support.

Two other issues undermined Canadians' confidence

in the Clark government, pre-budget. *First,* the failure to decide on energy policy worried Canadians. This failure was highlighted by their flip-flops over what to do with Petro Canada and Mr. Clark's inability to set the oil price without a major row with Davis and Lougheed. The outcome of that public feud cost Clark a great deal of support in Ontario as Davis turned against Clark and as Clark bungled his way to a decision that clearly favored Alberta. *Second,* interest rates climbed to an all-time high. The new interest rates frightened small businessmen and home-owners who know that at some point they would be facing 5-6% increases in mortgage payments. The introduction of the Tory, "watered-down" mortgage plan (another broken promise), was in stark contrast to the new worry of higher interest rates.

To many, the list of broken promises was irritating but not conclusive evidence of a bad government. Many do not believe any government keeps their election promises. What changed the attitude of Canadians was generally worsening economic conditions (inflation, unemployment, high interest) and a government that didn't know what it was doing in facing the problems. The broken promises added a lack of credibility to ineptitude.

The *Clark budget* finally arrived with its three political weaknesses. It is a further double-cross on promises, it is badly timed for the economy and it is grossly unfair. Canadians deeply resent the 18 cent Clark gas tax, the inflationary effects of the budget and the fact that it advocates and plans for higher unemployment. To partisan Tories and the business community, it is touted as the strong medicine that was required for the times. We should be quite careful to make our three points about it and link those points firmly to the mistakes, the failures, and the waste of the Tory government's first seven months.

We must point out that the Tories had ample time— more than eight months in power to bring forward their own programs and policies for solving the economic problems of the country. They had a fair chance. The fact is that they delayed calling Parliament for five months— the longest such delay in Canadian history. They had more than a fair chance.

The final point of 1979 history to note is where we were, and where the NDP was while all of this was happening during the summer and fall. By and large, except for the dramatic events of Mr. Trudeau's resignation, we were not a factor. Our troops were getting organized in the House of Commons and succeeded only in early December in hitting hard on the six months anniversary attack. It would be wrong to say we were attracting voters through our actions. The NDP never stopped campaigning. What it appears they did was accentuate the energy—Petro Canada issue—further loosen Tory votes that have come more to us than to themselves.

The conclusion is that the Tories through perceived mismanagement were defeating themselves, the NDP were advertising Tory failures and Liberals who remained relatively low profile were the major beneficiaries. It was hard to look power-hungry when we were in the early stages of re-building in the fall and leaderless in the early winter. The party's decision to ask Mr. Trudeau to lead seemed more popular than unpopular and the blame for the election falls more to the government than the opposition with a surprising 60% being so unhappy with the Tories that they preferred an election to more Clark Government.

Canadians are in the mood to defeat another government that they feel has let them down. In doing so they will elect our party. *Our major element of strategy* should be to reinforce the determination of the people to defeat the *Clark Government*. Therefore our major campaign plan should be to attack the *Clark Government* and remind Canadians what it is they dislike about it. Mr. Clark has ventured forth with new promises but voters do not seem to believe that he means these or could carry them out.

People do not like Tories, and they like Joe Clark even less. We must constantly link these Tory programs and policies to Mr. Clark—who we should *never demean or attack in a personal way*. We should be the last ones to tell Clark jokes. We should use every means at our disposal to focus on Mr. Clark's ongoing inability to deal with either Peter Lougheed or William Davis. We have lots of ammunition in statements by both of these (and other) Premiers.

The NDP has also made gains over six months. For many they are the champion of ordinary Canadians.

The NDP will likely collaborate with the Tories in various attempts to change the public mood. They must continue to soften the Tory vote and have more of it go to themselves, thus they will likely join in on an anti-Trudeau theme which they will combine with, "A plague on both their houses."

Mr. Broadbent seems caught between socialist dogma and a move to the right to attract middle-class Canadians. He is showing that the two cannot be reconciled. He is simply a spoiler because Liberals would introduce many of his non-socialist ideas.

The Liberal campaign structure is open. Caucus and party input have been an integral part of the process. The Liberal Party platform is a case in point. It will be announced by the leader and other leading Liberals. Our platform will clearly point to new directions and will show that these new directions will not create massive new spending. We are determined to solve the energy crisis, to protect ordinary Canadians from inflation (especially those with low-middle income) to create jobs for young Canadians and move toward more Canadian control of the economy. If our platform "directives" are progressive, tough, fair and nationalistic, they will attract favorable media attention. They will also cut off NDP gains.

Another theme of the Liberal campaign is teamwork. The spotlight will be less on the leader and more on the team. The leader's tour will be less extensive, sharper, and much friendlier. Mr. Trudeau will always be accompanied on his tour by several prominent Liberals from in and out of Parliament, and from in and out of the region being visited.

Our support continues to be strongest with the ethnic Canadians, young people and ordinary Canadians. Every aspect of our campaign should be targeted in ways which lead to these strengths.

It will be imperative for all of us—the leader, candidates and every last party worker to say the same thing, in the same way, at the same time. This is how we maximize impact. Timing will be an essential ingredient of our campaign. Please follow Mr. Trudeau's lead.

Work and win!

"Work to win" could have served appropriately as the personal motto for Senator Keith Davey, the mastermind who designed with Jim Coutts what Davey later described as a "brilliantly cynical" campaign. The Liberal Party had insisted on a "strategy committee," but once again it was Davey and Coutts who made the critical decisions to capitalize on the Conservatives' blunders and restore the Liberals to power.

Part carnival huckster, part idealist, Keith Davey had been the happy warrior of Canadian politics for nearly twenty years. His relationship with politics was that of a middle-aged man madly in love with a beautiful woman twenty years his junior; he kept muttering about breaking off the relationship until he recognized that separation from the object of his passion would be too painful to bear. Some men derive their satisfaction from only certain aspects of politics, but Davey revelled in everything that politics demands of its participants. He would no more have complained about the long hours than voted Conservative. He could not have been happy unless he arrived at his office to find a stack of message slips from callers across the country. He was an irrepressible story-teller, swapping tales and gossip with anyone.

Keith Davey was a man of powerful enthusiasms that had usually been applied to selling someone else's goods. As a teenager, he discovered that he was a poor athlete, so he took to arranging publicity for his high school's teams. At the University of Toronto's Victoria College in the late 1940s, he was always the booster. The president of the student union in his final year and a tireless organizer of pep rallies, he dreamt up ingenious publicity schemes. He once hired a plane to drop leaflets over the campus, only to find that they thumped in bundles to the ground rather than fluttering individually through the air. He lasted one year in law school, failing his first-year examinations. Then it was back to promoting. After a brief stint peddling space for a suburban Toronto newspaper, he was hired as the sales manager for Foster Hewitt's station CKFH in Toronto.

Davey was born to Liberalism. His father began working in the pressroom of *The Toronto Star* in 1917 when Joe Atkinson was the publisher. In those days, the newspaper was a stentorian supporter of the Liberal Party. Davey's father worshipped Atkinson, consulting the publisher about the proper education for his son Keith and adopting the publisher's politics as his own. It was natural, therefore, for Davey to gravitate towards the Liberal Club at the University of Toronto, which included contemporaries who would later sit as Liberals in the House of Commons, such as Paul Hellyer, Judy LaMarsh, and Phil Givens.

In the late 1950s, Davey began marrying his salesmanship to his politics. The Liberal Party in Ontario had grown complacent and crusty on the eve of the Diefenbaker maelstrom. After the Liberal defeats of 1957 and 1958, Davey and a small group of friends decided that the Ontario wing of the party needed rejuvenation. They successfully plotted and executed a takeover of the organizational machinery of the party in the province. The motto of the group, which called itself "Cell 13," was "Work or Resign," and within a year of the takeover party membership in Toronto alone had more than tripled.

Davey's work did not go unnoticed in Ottawa, where Liberal leader Lester Pearson was casting about for a new national director to prepare the party for the next general election. He asked Davey to take the job, and Davey moved to Ottawa in 1961, beginning a six-year relationship with Pearson that was marked by warm friendship and indifferent political success.

Davey's enthusiasms often extended to those for whom he worked. He idolized Pearson, just as he came to lionize Trudeau, but he could never secure a majority Government for Pearson. In the 1963 election, with Diefenbaker tottering, the Liberals presented the fading Conservative leader with two openings that breathed life into his campaign. Neither was Davey's idea, but he expedited them in the heat of the campaign. The first was a "truth squad," a group of well-known Liberals who sat at a table at the front of Diefenbaker's rallies, ostensibly to point out all of the errors in the Prime Minister's speeches. Diefenbaker pounced on the "truth squad" like a starving jackal, making it the focal point of his campaign even after the embarrassed Liberals pulled the squad off Diefenbaker's trail. "I never made any record of his witticisms at my expense—I hope no one ever did—but I still bear the scars," Judy LaMarsh said later of her hours sitting helplessly at Diefenbaker's rallies. Then, the Liberals unveiled a colouring book of political satire so tasteless that it was quickly withdrawn—but not before Diefenbaker tore it apart. The Liberals won the 1963 election in spite of the campaign they ran against the discredited Diefenbaker.

The next year, Davey and Liberal campaign chairman Senator Dan Lang descended on Waterloo South for a by-election. They pushed aside the local organization, hand-picked the Liberal candidate, and watched the party slide from second place in the 1963 election to third in the by-election. In 1965, Davey and Walter Gordon counselled Pearson to call a quick election to win a majority Government. Pearson heeded their advice, but gained only two seats and remained in a minority position.

For these services, Davey was rewarded with the sinecure prime ministers usually bestow upon their campaign chairmen or national organizers: a seat in the Senate. At thirty-nine, Davey was one of the youngest men ever appointed to that somnolent institution. A lesser man—and there are many of them in the Senate—might have counted his paycheques and sunk into oblivion, or parlayed his station into membership on the boards of directors of private companies. But Davey was too restless for that. Ever the salesman, he reckoned that what the Senate needed was a public-relations campaign. He conducted personal polls to discover what Canadians thought about the Senate, knocking on doors for several months on Saturdays asking people about the institution.

Davey's zeal to reform the Senate was sidetracked in 1967, the year after his appointment, when the club owners of the Canadian Football League asked him to become the league's commissioner. Davey served on a trial basis for six months, but his ambitious plans for the league—including the drafting of a "Football Fan's Bill of Rights"—were more than the owners had bargained for. Davey gave them an ultimatum: accept his terms for the commissioner's job or part company. The owners chose the latter option. They claimed Davey had been fired; he insisted that he had resigned.

Davey had been at the centre of Liberal campaigns in 1962, 1963, and 1965, so it was disconcerting to be ignored by Trudeau in the 1968 campaign. Trudeau had his own admirers, who organized the 1968 campaign and then took up residence with the new Prime Minister after the election. Isolated from the centre of political power, Davey threw himself into an old enthusiasm: investigating the role of the press. Having grown up in a family where *The Toronto Star* put bread on the table, Davey had always been fascinated by the press. As a boy, he cut out mastheads from the world's newspapers and put them on the walls of his room. All his adult life he read three or four newspapers a day and at least a dozen magazines a month. He was a consumer of news, but also its maker. In his early political campaigns, he came to appreciate the importance of the press in creating a saleable image for a candidate, a point repeatedly illustrated in Theodore White's *The Making of the President, 1960*, a book that excited Davey's imagination.

With the Senate's consent, Davey organized a special committee under his leadership to investigate the mass media in Canada. It turned out to be the most thorough study of the press in recent Canadian history, and it paved the way for legislation that encouraged the flourishing of the Canadian magazine industry. The report's other recommendations on the concentration of media ownership and the establishment of a press council were ignored, but the report still stood as an excellent analysis of the press and as a testament to Davey's interest in the fourth estate.

The 1972 campaign was agony for Davey. Consigned again to the sidelines, he watched Trudeau float across Canada giving philosophical discourses on man, government, and society, using the vapid slogan "The Land is Strong." It was certainly a novel kind of campaign, and it fizzled. The Liberals came within two seats of losing power.

Stung by his near-defeat, Trudeau sought explanations for the dissipation of the enthusiasm that had surrounded his 1968 victory. The answer from the Liberal Party organization was clear: he had run a hopeless campaign. He had surrounded himself with intellectuals who ran the government like a post-graduate course in public policy. What Trudeau needed was a dose of partisanship; he had to become more "political." Trudeau had never had a kind word to say about the Liberal Party until he joined it; after that, the party was something to be tolerated rather than nurtured. He had won the 1968 election without much help from the party, or so he thought. But the rebuff of 1972 changed his thinking; the party apparently counted for more than he had believed. He needed stronger links to the party and more partisan advice.

Re-enter Keith Davey, salesman. With customary enthusiasm, Davey scooped up Trudeau's offer to direct the next Liberal campaign. After engineering their own defeat in the minority Parliament, the Liberals won a majority Government in the 1974 election under Davey's guidance. It was a tactically astute campaign; the focus stayed on Conservative leader Robert Stanfield's promise of a wage-and-price freeze followed by controls. Trudeau replaced philosophy with sharply partisan attacks—"Zap, you're frozen"—and Davey made sure that Trudeau was kept as far removed as possible from the press in case a Trudeau answer might hand the Conservatives an issue. The members of the media were there to be manipulated, fed a steady diet of complicated (and soon abandoned) policy announcements just before deadlines. "To Keith, the man who makes the sun shine, with a thousand thanks," Trudeau scribbled on a cartoon he sent Davey after the campaign. The friendship between the aloof, austere, shy Prime Minister and the backslapping salesman was cemented by victory.

Under the tutelage of Davey and Coutts, Trudeau became a relentlessly partisan Prime Minister, doling out patronage so shamelessly that even a few Liberals blanched. Conservatives were appointed to the Senate to open up seats the Liberals thought they could win. More attention was paid to extracting political mileage from each of Trudeau's appearances. Policies were abandoned and new ones embraced if they aided the Liberals' political fortunes.

Davey advised Trudeau on the formation of his Cabinets, on patronage, on political strategy, but he exercised only a minimal influence on policy. Davey described himself as a small-l liberal, out of conviction as well as for tactical reasons: the Liberal Party usually does best from a position slightly to the left of centre on the political spectrum. If asked, Davey would have pressed for measures to promote Canadian nationalism and social reform. But the reform would have been gentle, since Davey was satisfied with the socio-economic status quo in Canada: he had benefited from it as much as anyone, rising from the home of a pressman to the Canadian Senate. Sitting in his wide pinstriped suit at a table in the Canadian Grill at the Chateau Laurier Hotel, where he often dined, he did not seem to have the fires of reform burning in his well-fed belly.

Davey had always been deceptively well organized. Seeing him slumped in a chair, surrounded by files strewn about his hotel room floor, a casual observer might have thought that his mind was flying in a dozen directions at once. But every night before he went to bed, he made a list of phone calls to make and letters to write the next day to his network of contacts across the country. That network, built over twenty years in politics, was loyal to the Liberal Party and to Davey. He always had a talent for spotting budding political organizers and integrating them into his network. For example, Davey immediately recognized the capability of Kathy Robinson, a young Toronto lawyer, and brought her into the inner circles of the federal party organization. Robinson, who had agreed to manage Donald Macdonald's short-lived leadership campaign, was given responsibility for organization of half the ridings in Ontario in the 1979 campaign and became vice-chairman of the Ontario campaign in 1980. She was also a member of the strategy committee for the 1980 campaign, although the Ontario campaign chairman Norman MacLeod was not appointed to the committee.

Successful organization demands an astute plan of action and recruitment of skilled people to execute the plan. Although the Liberals looked disorganized on the eve of the campaign, Davey's network of experienced and professional organizers was ready to start working as soon as they received the word from Davey. The night of the Clark Government's defeat, Davey returned to his Senate office to begin contacting his network across the country and to sketch a rough outline of the party's strategy for the campaign. Davey had learned from his unsuccessful campaigns in the 1960s that campaigns must not be sidetracked from a single-minded execution of the strategic plan outlined before the campaign. Thus, when the strategy committee hammered out the plan for the 1980 campaign, it was Davey's job to see to its execution across the country. He became bitter at British Columbia Liberals who campaigned on local rather than national issues, a tactical error that Davey believed cost the Liberals several seats in British Columbia.

It was one thing, however, to devise an elaborate plan and quite another to implement it by telephone from Ottawa. Someone had to travel with the leader, keeping him on track as he moved across the country and dealing ruthlessly if necessary with the media, local organizers, and members of the leader's staff who might want to vary the plan. Keith Davey had asked Jim Coutts to travel with Trudeau in the 1974 campaign. After the meandering campaign of 1972, Davey insisted in the 1974 campaign that Trudeau and the party stick to the strategy devised before the campaign. No more philosophy. No more "dialogues with Canadians." No more vacuous slogans such as "The Land is Strong." Just punchy and relentless attacks on Stanfield. The success of that venture launched Davey and Coutts on a seven-year partnership that was eclipsed in intensity and success by only one other in federal politics: the one between Jim Coutts and Pierre Trudeau.

Jim Coutts was born too late and in the wrong country. He should have grown up in the United States and joined one of the political machines that used to run the large cities of that country: Tammany in New York, Pendergast in Kansas City, or Thompson, Kelly-Nash, and later Daley in Chicago. He would have been so at ease dispensing patronage, inquiring after every wardheeler's son and daughter, hanging around the taverns swapping stories with cronies, arranging new sidewalks for neighbourhoods that supported his bosses, and keeping the machine apprised of every quiver of political activity in his ward. He would have been so deferential to his superiors and so charming to his underlings that no one would have suspected his ruthless determination to hold power.

As it was, the Liberal Party was his machine, Pierre Trudeau his boss, and the whole of Canada his ward after he became Trudeau's principal secretary in 1975. Sitting in the principal secretary's office, Coutts had more ready and continuous contact with Trudeau than anyone in Canada. He screened information for the Prime Minister, briefed Trudeau for meetings, acted as a link between Trudeau and the party, advised Trudeau on Cabinet and patronage appointments, and cast his partisan eye over every event and policy that affected the Prime Minister or his Government. He personified the confluence of government, administration, and politics, differing from his predecessors as principal secretary in the weight he assigned to political considerations in governing the country. Coutts was wedded only to the fickle bride of power; he had no political convictions other than keeping the Liberal Party in power. He was prepared to alter any policy or contrive any situation that would enhance the romance between Trudeau and the Canadian electorate. He was a master of expediency; for him, politics was a shell game in which each move, more dazzling than the last, left the electorate dizzy from the excitement of a hundred headlines.

Coutts was always scheming. The Anti-Inflation Board's popularity was plummeting from inaction on price increases: pay the board a visit and watch the CBC begin its national newscast with a story about the board's decision to roll back beer prices in Quebec. The public was alarmed at the enormous growth in government expenditures: encourage Trudeau to announce a $2-billion reduction in government expenditures. The public wanted a return to capital punishment: suggest floating the idea of a referendum on the subject. The public was upset about high mortgage costs: examine mortgage-interest and property-tax deductibility. The Liberals were unpopular in western Canada: recruit Jack Horner from the Conservatives and ignore his earlier opposition to bilingualism, a canon of the Liberal Party. The Conservatives were planning an announcement in the afternoon: organize a government briefing on another subject in the morning. The media had sniffed out a potentially embarrassing story: stonewall or dissemble.

When he first joined Trudeau's staff, Coutts was a Liberal Party man. The two men worked together for the first time in the 1974 campaign, and they got on famously. Trudeau admired Coutts' political savvy and his ability to synthesize information into cogent analyses and recommendations. Coutts was supposed to represent the Liberal Party's new-found influence on Trudeau, but gradually he became Trudeau's man in the Liberal Party, warning his boss of dissidence and shaping the party's policies to suit the political convenience of the leader.

Coutts idolized Trudeau. He bought a painting of the Prime Minister from a neighbour and hung it on the wall of his home in Toronto. He stood at the edge of Trudeau's rallies, giggling like a small child, his face turning red with glee, when the audience laughed at a joke or applauded a line that Coutts had either written himself or vetted before it was uttered by Trudeau. In the 1979 campaign, when he knew that Trudeau was beaten, a tear rolled down his cheek at a rally in Charlottetown as he listened to Trudeau shake the iron bars of fate. More than anyone else, Coutts prepared Trudeau's return to politics in 1980.

Such uncommon loyalty did not go unrewarded. When Trudeau met his caucus after deciding to return to lead his party in the 1980 election, he announced that he had heard grumblings about Coutts' excessive influence. That was too bad, Trudeau said defiantly, because "Coutts stays." And so he did, travelling with Trudeau throughout the 1980 campaign, counselling Trudeau on the execution of the strategy drafted before the campaign. Coutts knew he would soon be again at the centre of power, and his joy at the prospect loosened the self-imposed shackles of his considerable charm. He wandered amiably up the aisle of the campaign plane or chatted with reporters at late-night poker games, bantering so effortlessly that some reporters found it a pleasure to be misled by him. The press could not get to see Trudeau until the dying stages of the campaign, but they could always talk to Coutts, for what little that was worth in terms of hard information. Or they could listen to the tales he told, drawn from a lifetime in politics.

Coutts grew up in the Alberta town of Nanton (population 1,100), about sixty miles south of Calgary. A town of that size could not contain the energy of young Coutts, who occasionally ran the projector at the local theatre, swept floors and set type at the *Nanton News*, indulged in amateur theatre, and was captivated by politics. He read Hansard while his classmates looked at less imposing, and boring, material. To be a Liberal in Alberta in the 1950s was to be anti-establishment; the Social Credit Party had been governing without interruption since 1935. Coutts, a bit of a hell-raiser, fell into Liberal politics, working at the age of fourteen in the 1952 provincial campaign and finding a summer job organizing the local Liberal candidate's campaign in the federal election of 1953.

At the University of Alberta, Coutts was the leading Liberal on campus; prime minister one year and leader of the opposition the next in the university's mock parliament, trading places after the election with a fellow-Albertan named Joe Clark, about whom Coutts was reported to have remarked: "In this game you have to be a bit of a sonofabitch. Joe doesn't quite have it."* He received his law degree from the University of Alberta, although he was subsequently required to article for an additional three months because politics consumed so much of his time during the apprenticeship. In the 1962 federal election, the Liberals lost all seventeen seats in Alberta, including the one Jim Coutts contested. By then, his profession was law but his passion was politics. He moved to Ottawa to join Prime Minister Lester Pearson's staff as appointments secretary, two years after Davey became the party's national director. Until his departure for an MBA degree at Harvard in 1966, he was a popular fellow around Ottawa, much in demand for his side-splitting mimicry of Pearson, Paul Martin, John Diefenbaker, and other political luminaries. He delighted those older than himself with his capacity for hard work, his puckish sense of humour, and his storytelling. After Harvard, he worked in Cleveland and Toronto for the large American consulting firm, McKinsey and Company. But he felt constrained by the enormity of the McKinsey empire, so he left the company to found the Canada Consulting Group with five other MBA graduates, and the company soon became one of the most sought-after consulting firms in English Canada.

Consultants are the high-priced firemen of the business world. They must apply managerial and organizational skills to solve problems companies cannot master themselves. Their work revolves around systems, information flows, restructuring of hierarchies, and marketing. To be successful, the consulting firm must be disciplined, tactful, and ruthless in pinpointing weaknesses, especially in personnel. Coutts brought the skills of a consultant to his job as Trudeau's principal secretary. His mind moved easily from one problem to another. He organized information efficiently for the Prime Minister, weeding out irrelevant material and presenting carefully considered options that reflected an understanding of partisan considerations that Trudeau did not possess. None of Coutts' predecessors as principal secretary—

*David Humphreys, *Joe Clark: A Portrait* (Ottawa: Deneau and Greenberg, 1978), p. 31.

Marc Lalonde, Martin O'Connell, and Jack Austin—functioned as Trudeau's chief political advisor. They offered political advice, but so did many others outside the Prime Minister's office. Coutts, however, put political considerations at the centre of the PMO, enduring the wrath of civil servants who distrusted him for his ruthlessness in tearing apart their proposals that did not suit his strategic game plans.

A year after Coutts joined Trudeau's staff, the Liberal Government slumped in public-opinion polls, but in mid-1976 the Liberals had three years remaining in their mandate. Clark, the newly elected Conservative leader, was still enjoying his political honeymoon, and no one in the Liberal Party worried about the lead the Conservatives held in public opinion. The election of the Parti Québécois on November 15, 1976, changed the fortunes of the major parties. Three months after the PQ victory, the Liberals shot ahead of the Conservatives in the polls, widening their lead to more than twenty points in mid-1977. Coutts smelled the scent of a massive majority if an election were called. He and Davey, knowing that Liberal polls confirmed public surveys showing the Liberals with a huge lead in public esteem, counselled Trudeau to call an election in the fall of 1977. Trudeau demurred, arguing that a compelling reason did not exist for going to the people. The opportunity for a smashing re-election vanished with that decision. From that point until the election of the Conservative Government in May 1979, the Liberals suffered an irreversible decline in public support, and there was nothing that Coutts could do to arrest the slide.

Not that he was idle. He turned every page in the handbook of political survival, but nowhere could he find the cure for the Liberal malaise. The $2-billion expenditure reductions announced in a nationally televised speech by Trudeau in August 1978 might have served as the springboard for an election—that was one reason for the announcement—if subsequent events had not rendered the expenditure reduction program such a public-relations fiasco. Ministers were not consulted; Jean Chrétien, the Minister of Finance, was forced to give a press conference to provide details he did not have about a program he knew little about. A month passed before the Government released details of the spending cuts, by which time the shock value of the program had worn off and the whole exercise looked like another cynical ploy for votes.

Working with Davey, Coutts tried to paste a new face on the

Government. Feeble ministers such as Joe Guay and Stanley Haidasz were dispatched to the Senate. John Evans, the former president of the University of Toronto whom the Liberals had showcased on the task force on Canadian Unity, became the party's star candidate in Rosedale. Other fresh candidates were found: Toronto alderman Arthur Eggleton, Scarborough mayor Paul Cosgrove, former *Chatelaine* editor Doris Anderson. All were defeated in October 1978 by-elections. A shuffle in November brought three new ministers into the Cabinet. Nothing worked; in fact, the policy and personnel shifts made matters worse. They merely confirmed the electorate's suspicion that it was watching the last performance of an aging vaudeville player, legs weary, spirit broken, croaking stale songs of yesteryear. When Trudeau promised "A Decade of Development" in calling the 1979 election, the last doubt that the Liberals were tired vanished. They could no longer even dream up catchy slogans.

The 1980 campaign was a form of personal vindication for Coutts, who had been savaged by his critics after the Liberals fell from power. His astute reading of the country's political mood, his persistence, and his loyalty to Trudeau had brought his idol back from retirement into a campaign that Liberals could only lose by making an egregious error. As long as the electorate's attention was directed at Joe Clark and the performance of his Government, the Liberals had a free ticket to power. When Clark sped away from Ottawa to begin his campaign four days after his Government fell, Coutts and Davey were delighted. The more attention Clark received, the better for the Liberals. Nothing should be done by the Liberals to draw excessive attention to themselves. It was a cold-blooded—and winning—strategy, designed by the two shrewdest tacticians in Canadian politics.

~ 10 ~

The Right Question

The frantic activity of an election campaign is directed towards one objective: persuading as many voters as possible to enter the polling booths with the "right" question in their minds. Since each party poses a different right question, a campaign becomes a struggle among parties to make the election revolve around their question, and the answer they suggest to that question. In the 1979 campaign, the Conservatives took power by persuading 36 per cent of the electorate to ask: "Do we want four more years with Trudeau like the last eleven?" Nine months later, the Liberals recaptured power when the largest number of voters asked themselves: "Do we want any more of Joe Clark?"

Both of these questions were defined to suggest negative answers, but such was the style and substance of the Conservatives' and Liberals' campaigns of 1979 and 1980. Indeed, only twice since 1957 has the electorate responded to a positive vision of the country put forward by one of the major parties: in 1958 with John Diefenbaker, and in 1968 with Pierre Trudeau. Put crudely, the other campaigns since 1957 have turned on the electorate's distaste or fatigue with Diefenbaker, Stanfield, Trudeau, and Clark, or its dislike for policies such as wage-and-price controls and higher energy prices.

Campaigns, despite the ubiquitous publicity devoted to them, are seldom decisive in determining who wins or loses on voting day. Party images have usually taken shape before the campaign as the electorate observes the parties wrestling with the nation's problems. It is difficult, if not impossible, in a two-month campaign to recast images that were shaped before the campaign. That is why, as a general rule, parties can hope to gain only marginal ground in a campaign. But campaigns can influence election results when the major parties are evenly matched on the eve of the campaign, or they can tip the balance if one party is on the brink of a majority Government, as the Conservatives were at the outset of the 1979 campaign.

To define the right question with the broadest appeal, the parties piece together from their private polling a sophisticated picture of the electorate as a whole and in its component parts: men and women; English, French, and ethnic groups; urban and rural; young and old; province by province. It is insufficient to know that a given number of voters intend to support one party or another. The parties must know why. What is bothering or motivating voters? How entrenched are these perceptions? Can these perceptions be changed? If so, on what basis? If leadership is the most salient factor, what is it about the party leaders that inspires or erodes trust? The key to any campaign strategy is this initial snapshot of the electorate. It is the single most important factor shaping a party's campaign. Once a party makes its strategic decisions, it must unflinchingly and relentlessly implement those decisions in the campaign. Even with the most severe self-discipline, a party may fail because the electorate is more receptive to the message—that is, the right question—of another party. But without that discipline, a campaign is more likely to fail.

This discipline requires the four basic elements of a campaign—the leader's tour, the local candidates' campaigns, advertising, and a media strategy—to be mutually reinforcing. The most visible element is the leader's tour, since it attracts the attention of the national media. The leader's tour sets the tone and substance for his party's campaign, and local candidates amplify his message at the constituency level. The local candidates are members of the leader's team, subscribing to his views on national issues, reinforcing his definition of the party's right question. Nothing is more disastrous for a party in a campaign than having individual candidates disavow either the leader or his policies, since squabbles detract not only from the authority of the leader but also from the party's disciplined effort to drive home a given message in the campaign. Divisions divert attention, and it is hard enough to compete with the other parties in a campaign without having to quash dissidence in a party's own ranks.

The leader's tour must also be supplemented by an advertising campaign that amplifies the party's basic message. If the message is not appealing to a large majority of the electorate, the most subtle advertising cannot change the voters' minds. But the parties spend millions of dollars and hundreds of hours crafting the commercials with which voters are assaulted during the campaign, applying the same techniques used in promoting dog food and toothpaste to selling political parties.

A party can control the activities of local candidates and plan its own advertising, but it has no direct control over the media, which are the electorate's eyes and ears for the campaign. Since few voters ever see either the national leader or local candidates in the flesh, the media provide voters with the information and images that affect their voting decisions. It is not surprising, therefore, that the parties try so hard to nudge the media towards the kind of coverage that will reinforce the party's definition of the right question. Sometimes, this effort takes the form of outright manipulation; more often, it is subtly calculated to play to the media's weaknesses, especially those of television since its influence pervades the campaign strategy of every party.

Skill, cunning, and discipline are required to run a successful campaign, to make the component parts mutually reinforcing. In the 1980 campaign, depressing as the substance of the campaign may have been, both major parties ran tactically superior campaigns: the Liberals protecting their huge lead, and the Conservatives recovering more ground than most observers thought possible at the beginning of the campaign.

Prudent political parties, their goal the safe haven of an election victory, study private polls like sailors consulting a compass. Maligned and misinterpreted, polls exert an enormous and often decisive influence on parties' decisions in power or in Opposition. The Conservative Government fell partly because those engineering the Liberals' strategy had their own polls, which showed that the public was ready to kick Joe Clark out of office. It is intriguing to speculate about what the Conservatives might have done if they had possessed their own polls showing the same probability, instead of relying on their unguided political instincts. When the Conservatives did receive a poll of their own in August 1979 from Allan Gregg, the party's polling expert, the results persuaded them to reaffirm several of their election promises, notably the dismantling of PetroCanada as a crown corporation and the introduction of a form of mortgage-interest and property-tax relief.

The Liberal Government seldom took a major initiative without first consulting polls provided to the party by Martin Goldfarb, a polling whiz whose services were retained by Keith Davey after Trudeau asked him to run the Liberals' 1974 campaign. Goldfarb, a sprightly, cocky man, surveyed the attitudes of Canadians from the top floor of a half-empty office building in north Toronto. Most of Goldfarb's work was done for private companies, but his political connections with the federal Liberals and the ministries of the Ontario Government gave him notoriety and a reputation for being accurate and influential. He parlayed these attributes into a successful firm with a staff of forty, producing more than one thousand polls a year for a variety of clients. Goldfarb, like any good marketing executive, provided his clients with more than a reading of consumer or voter preferences; he offered comprehensive analyses of the motivations behind those preferences. He was a cheerful proponent of his trade, believing polls to be an indispensable tool for running a government or pumping a product. Promoting politicians was like selling tomatoes, he used to say without a trace of self-doubt.

Keith Davey and Jim Coutts were especially appreciative of polling information, using the profile of public attitudes to shape recommendations about government policy. The Liberal Government's program of expenditure cuts in 1978, for example, flowed from polling results showing the Liberals in electoral difficulty. The repeated postponement of the 1979 election simply reflected Goldfarb's information that the Liberals would lose an election, just as Coutts' and Davey's advice to call an election in the fall of 1977 was based on Goldfarb's findings that the Liberals would win a smashing re-election. So wedded were the Liberals to polling information that they even conducted polls on public reaction to Joe Clark's wife, Maureen McTeer, discovering that her use of her maiden name was unpopular with many women, a fact the Liberals tucked away in case the Conservatives ever made an issue of the collapse of Trudeau's marriage.

The results of Goldfarb's polling taken before the defeat of the Conservative Government were confirmed by a fresh batch of polls shortly after the election was called. The new polls pointed to four factors that guided the Liberals' strategy in the campaign. First, the Liberals were so far ahead of the Conservatives that only a major blunder by the Liberals could deprive the party of victory. Second, the Liberals' lead was built around antipathy to Clark. Goldfarb's poll showed that the public perceived Clark to be

266 / Discipline of Power

honest but lacking in other leadership attributes such as strength of character, decisiveness, and intelligence. Clark was felt to be a weak Prime Minister, changing his mind on issues and unable to control his Cabinet. Third, the Conservatives' budget, especially the excise tax and higher energy prices, was unpopular. Fourth, the election slightly rekindled some of the animosity towards Trudeau, but the level of animosity was decisively lower than in the 1979 campaign.

These four factors persuaded the Liberals to run a tightly controlled, antiseptic campaign. A high-voltage campaign such as the party ran in 1979 might have stirred up more of the latent animosity towards Trudeau and reminded voters of the reasons for their rejection of him seven months before. At all costs, there-fore, the Liberals wanted to direct the electorate's attention towards Clark and the Conservatives' budget; if the focus of the campaign became Trudeau, voters might ask themselves again the Conservatives' right question from the spring campaign: "Do we want four more years with Trudeau like the last eleven?" Fortu-nately for the Liberals, the Conservatives' seven months in power had clouded the electorate's memory of Trudeau's record; the Conservatives' right question would be more difficult to ask in the 1980 campaign. But if the Liberals made startling policy announce-ments, the party might provide the Conservatives with ammuni-tion for their campaign and make the Liberals' promises, rather than the Conservatives' record, the focal point of the entire campaign.

The Liberal Party's national executive, the elected representa-tives of the party's rank-and-file supporters, had insisted on constructing a platform for the 1980 campaign, having complained at the time of Trudeau's return about the sharp shift to the right in the priorities of the Liberal Government in 1978 and early 1979. To satisfy this demand, Trudeau consented to the creation of a "platform committee" of Liberal M.P.s and party officials from across the country. The existence of such a committee cobbling together policies in the heat of a campaign only gave depressing testimony to the intellectual exhaustion of the Liberals. Having grown weary in power and having barely launched themselves on a period of intellectual rejuvenation in Opposition, the Liberals scrabbled about searching for something from previous policy conventions that might suffice for the campaign.

The platform committee held two rounds of meetings in the week after the election was called, with the understanding that

Allan MacEachen, the committee chairman, would report the policy recommendations to Trudeau, who could then use whatever parts of the platform he saw fit in the campaign. Coutts and Davey neither needed nor wanted this platform committee, except as a public-relations exercise to convince the party that its views were to be taken seriously. They intended to focus the Liberals' campaign on the Conservative Government, but at least they were given the freedom to use only those parts of the platform that served the party's electoral purposes. As a result, the policies unveiled during the campaign were those that undercut the Conservatives' budget or gave the Liberals a more progressive image that Davey, in particular, believed was important in attracting marginally committed NDP voters in Ontario. The party's energy policy, which promised a "blended" or "Made-in-Canada" price for oil and 50-per-cent Canadian ownership of the petroleum industry by 1990, was deliberately vague. This bland policy, coupled with a promise not to impose the 18-cents-per-gallon excise tax on gasoline, meant that the Liberals were reinforcing the electorate's unhappiness with Conservative energy policies by suggesting that the Liberal policy would achieve the same objectives without causing as much financial pain.

The Liberals also promised greater Canadian control of the economy, a "progressive" policy that Trudeau made public in the final week of the campaign. Again, the policy was vague, promising an expanded role for the Foreign Investment Review Agency, a greater percentage of purchasing in Canada by the federal government, and further measures to encourage more research and development in Canada. The party's other promises were equally bland.

As the Liberal campaign unfolded, Goldfarb, Coutts, and Davey kept a daily watch on the Liberals' lead. Years ago, when polling techniques were less sophisticated, parties conducted national or regional polls that took four or five days to compile. The polls were spaced at seven- to ten-day intervals during the campaign. Parties did not have access to daily polling information. They were forced to await a fresh batch of polls before deciding on changes of strategy. But modern campaign polling revolves around daily sampling of public opinion, or "tracking." Each day during the campaign, Goldfarb asked 300 persons about every aspect of the campaign. This enabled him to detect immediately any shifts in public opinion, but for greater statistical certainty, he kept a "rolling track" of the responses for the last three, seven, and ten

days. By comparing the movement of public opinion within these
time frames, he could detect the strength of any movement and
pinpoint when the move started. Goldfarb's information was
relayed daily to Davey in Ottawa and to Coutts, who was travelling with Trudeau. If the rolling track had shown an erosion of
Liberal support, the party would undoubtedly have changed its
strategy during the campaign. But the lines of Goldfarb's tracking
graphs showed no narrowing of the gap between the Liberals and
Conservatives in the first month of the campaign.

In mid-campaign, the tracking graphs began to show a small
decline in Liberal support, which Goldfarb suspected reflected the
critical press coverage of the tightly controlled Liberal campaign.
Then two events sent the Liberals' support temporarily tumbling.
The first was the news that the Canadian embassy in Tehran had
successfully smuggled six U.S. diplomats out of Iran; the second
was the beginning of the Conservatives' anti-Trudeau commercials. The Liberals watched nervously when some of their supporters began calling themselves undecided voters in Goldfarb's
polls, the first step in what could have been a substantial shift to
the Conservatives. For about a week, the Liberals' popular vote
totals fell in Goldfarb's rolling track, but the Conservatives' totals
did not increase. It was as if a portion of the electorate had decided
to think again about Clark after the Iranian drama and the Conservatives' commercials. After a week, however, the rolling track
showed the undecided vote falling and the Liberal vote rising,
which Goldfarb believed meant that the voters who had temporarily left the Liberals for a second look at Clark still did not like
what they saw. Once the rolling track revealed a shift back to the
Liberals, Goldfarb, Coutts, Davey, and Jerry Grafstein, the Liberal
lawyer in charge of the party's television advertising, dispensed
with any thoughts of changing the tactics of the Liberal campaign.
Some rank-and-file Liberals objected to the Liberals' negative
advertisements about Clark, but as long as Goldfarb's polls
showed the Liberals retaining their lead against the Conservatives,
the quartet refused to change the party's advertising campaign.
Only in the last four days of the campaign did Goldfarb's rolling
track show the Liberals in decline, but the drop came too late to
endanger the Liberal victory. By then, Goldfarb's polls had done
their work: encouraging key Liberals to defeat the Conservative
Government, shaping the party's strategy for the campaign, and
reinforcing the Liberals' determination to stick with that strategy
throughout the campaign.

The Conservatives placed as much faith in private polls during the campaign as the Liberals did. The Conservatives' polling was conducted by Allan Gregg, who had left the party's employ after the campaign to create a market-research firm in Toronto. Like Goldfarb, he tracked public opinion every day in British Columbia and Ontario, asking a sample of 200 voters thirty questions in a ten-minute interview. The results were tabulated each night and arrived on Gregg's desk the next day at noon. The Conservatives' tracking uncovered different shifts in public opinion during the final month of the campaign from those reflected in Goldfarb's data. Both parties' results showed the Liberals holding an enormous lead until the third week in January. Then Liberal polls indicated some voters were leaving the Liberals to join the ranks of the undecided voters, where they remained for about a week before returning to the Liberals. Gregg's tracking, however, showed the Liberals in slow but steady decline during the last two and a half weeks of the campaign, as the Conservative advertisements rekindled some antipathy to Trudeau. The movement came too late, but it still encouraged the Conservatives to believe that with a superb election-day organization they might win a minority Government. Just before the end of the campaign, Gregg offered the Conservatives three possible scenarios. The "best" scenario showed: Conservatives 142, Liberals 109, NDP 25, Créditistes 5. The "likely" scenario, the one Gregg thought would approximate the final result, showed: Liberals 129, Conservatives 116, NDP 33, Créditistes 3. The "worst-case" scenario showed a Liberal majority government: Liberals 142, Conservatives 99, NDP 39, Créditistes 1. As the election turned out, the returns most closely resembled the worst-case scenario: Liberals 146, Conservatives 103, NDP 32.*

The momentum the Conservatives believed they had generated was also reflected in some of the riding surveys that the party conducted throughout the campaign. Some of these were based on Gregg's data and others on "in-house" surveys by Conservative headquarters in Ottawa. The results were summarized by Ian McKinnon, a Ph.D. candidate in political science from Yale whose father, Allan, served as Clark's defence minister. McKinnon's reports were reviewed by Lowell Murray and Paul Curley, the Conservatives' campaign director, and then discussed with the

---

*The election in Frontenac riding was delayed because of the death of the Créditiste candidate. The Liberals subsequently won the riding, pushing their total to 147 seats.

Conservative candidate in the constituency. Only ridings the party desperately needed to win to form the Government were surveyed. The surveys were used both by the local organization in mapping canvassing and election-day strategy, and by those apportioning the Conservatives' advertising across the country and organizing Clark's itinerary. McKinnon's report on the riding of Ottawa Centre, where Conservative Jean Pigott ran against Liberal incumbent John Evans and New Democrat John Smart, illustrates the detail of all the surveys:*

PROGRESSIVE CONSERVATIVE PARTY OF CANADA
PARTI PROGRESSISTE-CONSERVATEUR DU CANADA

CONFIDENTIAL

MEMORANDUM

TO: Paul Curley   January 22, 1980.
             Lowell Murray

FROM: Ian McKinnon

SUBJECT: Ottawa Centre Polling

This poll was conducted by Decima Research about January 10th. The results are virtually unchanged from the results of the 1979 election—that is, the Liberals hold an insignificant lead over the PCs. Again the NDP, with 20% of the vote, are a significant presence although no threat to win the riding. The size of the "undecideds" is fairly small for this stage of a campaign, although this may result from the proximity to the last election. The Liberal and PC vote is quite hard and about equally so; the NDP vote, on the other hand, is soft. The PCs have the largest core of very firmly committed voters as they have a large number of supporters who refuse to consider any alternative party.

In examining second choice, the Liberals have a very

---

*The Conservatives lost Ottawa Centre. The party also conducted similar surveys in Scarborough West, Selkirk-Interlake, Saint-Hyacinthe, Parkdale, London West, Berthier-Maskinongé, Etobicoke North, Beaches, both ridings in Thunder Bay, Gaspé, Humboldt-Lake Centre, Mississauga North, Willowdale and Kitchener. In the case of Kitchener, the first poll, conducted on January 6, showed the Liberals leading by 47.6 per cent to 29 per cent. With a few days remaining in the campaign, the Conservatives checked again and found that the gap had narrowed to three points. The Conservatives lost Kitchener by two points in the popular vote.

substantial advantage in all areas but the number of
intransigent supporters. Were PC or NDP support to
break, either would go Liberal by a margin of 3:1; Liberal
support would break to the NDP by the same 3:1 ratio. If
we look only at the softer voters the situation remains
about the same: the Liberals enjoy a very substantial
edge.

Turning to voting history, those who think of themselves as Liberals and claim always to have voted Liberal,
once again greatly exceed the analogous core of PC supporters. Also following the normal pattern though, the
PCs are more successful at holding their core vote and are
quite good at attracting those with a "mixed" voting pattern. One of the things which seems particularly to
alienate normally Liberal voters is Trudeau, therefore his
continued leadership should be emphasized.

Candidates:
Jean Pigott is extremely well known—better than even
the incumbent, John Evans—and very very well liked.
Evans is moderately well known for an incumbent, and
people's impressions of him are fairly neutral. Smart, the
NDP candidate, is not well known for someone who contested the last election; in addition, he is not liked at all.
Pigott has a high profile and approval throughout the
riding and, with the normal variations, across the different demographic groups, interestingly, particularly by
those who are less affluent. She is admired even by partisans of other parties. The only area in which she is less
strong is the area north of the Queensway. John Evans'
only real personal strength is among the more affluent
voters, otherwise he is a neutral, fairly well known
member. Unfortunately, Smart is quite a weak candidate;
were he stronger he would probably attract voters from
the Liberals.

The campaign should emphasize Pigott strongly,
however Evans and Trudeau are the opposition, not the
NDP. Any strong attack on the NDP or any "an NDP vote
is a wasted vote" push will probably help the Liberals.

Leaders and Issues:
Although the respondents are very pessimistic about the
course of events over the past five years and their rating
of the economy today, they are less unfavourable about
the course of events since last May than are most of the
ridings surveyed. In addition, almost as many people

272 / *Discipline of Power*

think that things will get better if the PCs stay in power
as think things will get worse. This indicates that here,
more than in other areas surveyed, an appeal based on
our working to improve the future—of a job just begun,
etc., will find a receptive audience. Inflation continues to
be the dominant issue, followed by unemployment and
energy well back. As usual the concern over inflation is
higher for the more affluent, while the fear of unemployment rises in the lower income group.

Trudeau is preferred to Clark by almost a 3:2 ratio, a
reversal of the usual Ontario pattern before the last election. Clark's appeal is limited almost exclusively to people
who intend to vote PC (although that group includes
significant numbers of people who have in the past
supported other parties). Clark is particularly unpopular
with voters under 35 and among the wealthier voters.
There is a sharp area of difference too, with Clark being
mildly preferred to Trudeau in those areas south of the
Queensway, mirrored by very strong preference for
Trudeau in the north.

Demographics:
As with attitudes to the leaders, the PCs are not doing
well with those under 35, while the NDP's strength is in
that same group. PC strength is with the older, WASP,
and middle income voter. The Liberal strength is most
evident among non WASPs where they hold a commanding lead. Interestingly, Pigott's appeal runs across ethnic
lines (as does Evans' general lack of appeal); if possible,
her appeal should be most strongly personal in "ethnic"
areas. The PCs are doing better among residents of single
detached houses; this should be reinforced by emphasizing the mortgage plan there particularly as those residents
are more likely to make the PCs their second choice. The
only demographic variable affecting vote hardness are
age and type of residence: younger voters and apartment
dwellers are softer than are other voters.

Regions:
Ottawa Centre was divided into four areas: area 1
(census tracts 002, 003, 020, 034p) in the south and west;
area 2 (C.T.s 035, 041-043, 047) west of Bronson and
mainly north of the Queensway; area 3 (C.T.s 037-040,
048, 049) east of Bronson and north of the Queensway;
area 4 (C.T.s 016-019, 036) south of the Queensway and
largely east of Bronson.

Area 1: This is predominantly suburbia—younger, well educated, fairly mobile. It includes some areas that are very new developments, with only a small area built before 1945. The francophone population is just under 10%. As in the 1979 election, it is the NDP's weakest area. Jean Pigott is remarkably well liked and Clark is preferred to Trudeau; the PCs lead the Liberals by a wide margin. The vote is somewhat soft so this lead must be protected by heavy canvassing. This is of absolutely critical importance in the new development in the Hunt Club area. Typically for such an affluent area, the prime concern is inflation, energy (supply, price, Petrocan, etc.) is second, with unemployment trailing far behind—the anti-inflationary thrust of Crosbie's budget should be stressed. As well, the canvassers should stress the mortgage plan, particularly in the Hunt Club development.

Area 2: This is a poor, older, relatively non-WASP, reasonably stable area with few single family dwellings—about 70% of the dwellings are rented. Almost 20% of the population has French as a mother tongue, and 25% have a language other than French or English. While inflation still leads as the major issue, unemployment is a solid second concern and should be addressed. While trailing Trudeau, Clark is not disliked too much. Trudeau is clearly admired so attacks on him are likely to be counter-productive. Pigott is well known and liked, Evans is liked but only moderately well known, while Smart is better known and liked here than elsewhere in the riding (although even then he is less well liked or known than the other two). The PCs are now doing slightly better than their rather poor 27% showing in this area last time, moreover the vote is fairly soft and the PCs are doing reasonably well on second choice. Overall, there is significant room to improve in what has until now been a pretty solidly Liberal area.

Area 3: This is a predominantly wealthy, highly mobile (85% of the residences are apartments) area with a substantial francophone minority (15%). Like any core city area, there are great contrasts in relatively small distances. Unemployment just trails inflation as the main issue of concern with energy far behind. The area has pretty heavily been Liberal, reflected in both the large "always voted Liberal" group and in their large votes in the last elections. In this election the Liberals still enjoy a very substantial lead—this being the only area in which they have increased their support since the last election. Once again Jean Pigott is very well known and liked— better than either other candidate. Clark, however, is thoroughly unpopular, trailing even Ed Broadbent as the leader most trusted to lead the country. The vote in this area is hard. While this may seem paradoxical given the volatile voting history of the area, this mobile population is the type most likely to focus almost entirely on the national campaign. In this area drops should be made and canvassing to identify the PC vote and get it out must be done, however the candidate's time should not be spent here except before meetings and specific audiences.

Area 4: This affluent, very stable, dominantly WASP area is one of PC strength. Moreover, the vote is hard. Typically for such an affluent area, inflation is the dominant issue with "good government" (a combination of leadership, good management, the election) a significant minor issue. Pigott is by far the most popular and best known candidate. Clark is marginally preferred to Trudeau. In this area Pigott should be emphasized, however because of the hard vote and very small number of undecided voters, her time should not be spent here. Intense efforts to get out the vote should be made, however this should not be too difficult as this area should produce large numbers of workers.

The most important areas are 1 then 2; in area 3 the vote needs to be identified; in area 4 a high turn-out should be the objective.

Gregg's initial polls, available at the end of Clark's first week of campaigning, led the Conservatives to three strategic decisions. First, the waning of the antipathy to Trudeau forced the Conservatives to raise his profile in the campaign. Second, the election was resented mostly by committed Conservatives, so few additional votes could be won by blaming the election on the Opposition parties. Third, there was still the desire for change that the Conservatives had identified before the 1979 election, but there was also a corresponding feeling that the Conservatives had not fulfilled the hopes entrusted to them in the May 1979 election. From this grew the party's slogan, "Real Change Deserves a Fair Chance."

Political parties expend enormous effort to hit upon the slogan for their campaigns. They carefully research public opinion, often trying out words and phrases on sample voters. The slogan must not only be memorable, it must also lead voters to the right question that the parties want to pose in the campaign. In 1979, an advertising copywriter in Toronto who worked occasionally for the Conservatives suggested the slogan that the party grabbed for its campaign, "Give the Future a Chance." The slogan was upbeat, future-oriented, and indirectly critical of the recent past, all of which fit the Conservatives' attempt to identify themselves with the underlying optimism that their polls detected in the country.

"Real Change Deserves a Fair Chance" tried to address the public impression that the Conservatives had not fulfilled their election commitments. The slogan appealed for sympathy, and as such, sounded whimpering rather than confident. "Real Change," however, reminded some voters of what they did not like about the Conservatives. The Liberals and New Democrat voters who supported the Conservatives in the May 1979 election were voting for a change of Government, not for a fundamental change in the direction of the country, as the Conservatives believed. They certainly did not vote for the dismantling of PetroCanada as a crown corporation, higher energy prices, and the "short-term pain for long-term gain" of John Crosbie's budget. Such voters never wanted to give these real changes a fair chance. Moreover, change, especially fundamental or real change, is deeply unsettling to many people, who prefer marginal adjustments that do not upset established patterns of behaviour. Nor is the Conservative Party, by its very name and tradition, the vehicle voters would normally choose if they wanted major changes. The Conservative Party should stand for order, stability, and organic change, especially for the older segments of the population from which the Conservatives draw more support than do either the Liberals or the New Democrats.

That the Conservative Government had never sufficiently explained the rationale for many of its real changes became clear in the first two weeks of the campaign when Gregg tested voters' reactions to several key issues on which the Conservatives had staked their electoral life. Gregg discovered wide support for Canada becoming self-sufficient in energy, but found no appreciation for the link between higher prices and self-sufficiency. The excise tax, which voters could not see leading to self-sufficiency, was unpopular everywhere in Canada, especially in suburban areas and farming communities. Although an election campaign is a poor occasion in which to explain policies, Clark's policies were so little understood that the Conservatives were forced to spend time during the campaign explaining their positions rather than selling them. Through this effort, the Conservative polls showed the party gaining slowly in public esteem, but the movement came too late to recover all of the ground lost before the campaign began.

Before launching a new product or seeking to expand the market share for an existing product, a company explores the psychology and living habits of those who must be induced to buy the product. Then it advertises the product, meticulously tailoring every word, every intonation, every piece of film to appeal to the dreams and needs of prospective consumers. Of course, the most sophisticated research and advertising cannot guarantee success for faulty or unwanted products, such as the Edsel or Joe Clark, but many a consumer has succumbed to the seduction, hucksterism, and dishonesty of advertising.

A political party, like a company, puts the best possible face on its wares in an election campaign, spending millions of dollars and hundreds of hours designing and presenting the parade of commercials that appear in the last month of a Canadian election campaign. In the 1979 campaign, the Conservatives, Liberals, and NDP spent about $5.3 million on television and radio advertising; in 1980 the three parties increased their spending to about $6.3 million.*

Political advertising on the electronic media has been controversial since the time it was first tried by the Conservatives in the 1935 campaign. In that election, the Conservatives purchased radio time—or "spots"—featuring interviews with a fictional man-on-the-street, Mr. Sage, who, needless to say, could find nothing positive to say about either the Liberal Party or its leader, Mackenzie King. King, a man of considerable personal vanity, won the election and shortly thereafter set about muzzling Mr. Sage. In 1936, Parliament adopted a law entrusting regulation of radio advertising in campaigns to the Canadian Broadcasting Corporation and prohibiting "dramatic" political advertisements such as the Conservatives' Mr. Sage commercials.

By the elections of the 1960s, the parties were pouring an increasing percentage of their advertising budgets into television and radio. In the 1965 election, the parties for the first time spent

---

*This figure was based on estimates provided by the three parties, since spending records had not yet been compiled.

more money ($1,211,973) on the electronic media than on news-paper advertising ($1,191,759). In the 1979 election, the Liberals and New Democrats were spending three dollars on television and radio for every dollar spent on print advertising, and the Con-servatives' ratio was about six to one. Put another way, the Conservatives spent about 63 per cent of their total election expenses on television and radio advertising, compared with 47 per cent for the Liberals and 40 per cent for the NDP, an indication of the crucial role the parties believed television and radio adver-tising played in campaigns.

The importance of television and radio advertising was recog-nized in 1974 amendments to the Canada Elections Act, which limited parties' election spending and provided a partial public subsidy for their campaign expenses. Under the amendments, each broadcasting outlet and network was required to offer six and a half hours of prime time for purchase by the parties during the final twenty-nine days of the campaign. The public treasury then reimbursed the parties for half of their television and radio expenses. The public subsidies offered the greatest boon to the NDP, which did not have ready access to contributions from corporations and wealthy taxpayers that sustained the Conserva-tives and Liberals. But even these parties were grateful for the spending limits and public subsidies, which removed part of the malodorous legacy surrounding relations between the major parties and the corporate sector that stretched back to Sir John A. Macdonald, who begged the Canadian Pacific Railway for funds.

Public subsidies, however, did not change the degree of mani-pulation involved in the parties' advertising campaigns. Instead, the cost of television advertising grew so rapidly after 1974 that parties could not afford to use all of the time broadcasters were required to make available (at the lowest prime-time commercial rates), so parties redoubled their efforts to make each precious second of propaganda count by developing ever more sophisticated appeals to voters. The parties tapped some of Canada's leading advertising executives, who applied their expertise in the subtle arts of salesmanship to the preparation of political commercials. It would have been reassuring to know that the electorate considered the political advertising as so much intellectual garbage, but the evidence on the point was mixed. Some studies in the United States showed that more voters got their information about party positions from advertising than from any other source. These voters apparently considered political advertising to be a direct message from the political parties, unfiltered by the media. A Carleton University school of journalism poll taken after the 1980 election in Canada found that only 10 per cent of respondents admitted that advertising had influenced their vote.

In the 1980 campaign, the first wave of Conservative and Liberal commercials appeared during the popular Super Bowl broadcast and immediately set off a public outcry against "negative" advertisements. Even candidates publicly criticized their party's advertisements for only tearing down the credibility of the leader of the other party. But those who designed the commercials believed that the commercials were indispensable for supplementing the generally negative campaigns that Trudeau and Clark were running against each other. As such, the commercials were merely symptoms of the Liberals' intellectual exhaustion and the Conservatives' pitiful desperation.

The Liberal advertisements were designed by a group of men who first came together before the 1974 election under the direction of Toronto lawyer Jerry Grafstein, who had investments in broadcasting. The group included leading advertising executives from Toronto: Terry O'Malley, president of Vickers and Benson; Ron Bremner, vice-president of Vickers; Hugh Dowd of MacLaren Advertising Ltd.; Hank Karpus, president of Ronalds-Reynolds, and Peter Bonner of Richmond Advertising. They created a company called Red Leaf Communications Limited, the sole purpose of which was to organize the Liberal Party's election campaign advertising. Red Leaf was disbanded after each campaign and incorporated again after the issuance of writs for the next campaign. The creation of Red Leaf enabled the Liberals to bring together talented image-makers from various advertising agencies and to avoid paying the usual 15-per-cent fee to an advertising agency.

The Liberals' campaign strategy was straightforward: keep the electorate's attention on Joe Clark and invite the voters to ask themselves: "Do we want any more of him?" The difficult problem was how to attack Clark without evoking sympathy for him or making the Liberal commercials so negative that they provoked a backlash from angry viewers. The technique that Grafstein and his colleagues devised pitted Joe Clark against himself. Goldfarb's polls had revealed that voters perceived Clark as vacillating and weak, flip-flopping on issues and lacking the attributes of a Prime Minister. Therefore, if Clark's own words and positions were thrown back at him, the Liberals would avoid appearing like accusors and Joe Clark's credibility would be hurt by his own words and those of other Conservatives whom the Liberals put in their commercials.

The Liberals prepared about forty commercials for the campaign, but they used only thirteen after the first series of commercials proved so successful in reinforcing the electorate's doubts about Clark. The most effective was called "The Magician." It showed two white-gloved hands doing card tricks, turning over or fumbling cards on which were written words mentioning Conservative policy changes. The script read:

> For almost a year, you've seen the amazing Joe Clark Conservative trick show. Turn a $2-billion tax cut promise into a $3-billion tax burden on working Canadians. Turn a promise to lower interest rates into the highest interest rates in history. Turn PetroCanada into . . . well, Joe Clark hasn't got that one perfected yet. Turn the Canadian embassy in Israel into, into . . . Don't be fooled again. This is the time to vote Liberal.

The use of a magician triggered three uncomplimentary impressions of Joe Clark and his Government: first, that Clark was a shifty politician devoid of principle; second, that the Conservatives had flip-flopped on policy; third, that the electorate, having been tricked in 1979, could get even in the 1980 campaign.

Grafstein nevertheless pulled the commercial off the air for several days after the U.S. hostages were spirited out of Iran by the Canadian embassy staff. He worried that the commercial might induce viewers to think favourably about the Conservatives because the words *Canadian embassy* were spoken near the end of the script. Although the commercials referred to the Canadian embassy in Israel, Grafstein feared the words might bring to mind the Canadian diplomatic coup in Iran. Grafstein showed "The Magician" to a sample group of voters and discovered that they did not make the connection between the commercial and the heroism of Canada's diplomats in Iran. With that, the commercial was reinserted in the Liberal line-up. But Grafstein's decision to pull "The Magician" illustrated how carefully the Liberals monitored the impact of their commercials. Questions about the Liberal (and Conservative) commercials were included in Goldfarb's daily tracking, and the responses confirmed that the commercials were successfully reinforcing the anti-Clark message of the Liberal campaign, especially with marginally committed Liberals.

Another Liberal commercial played upon Joe Clark's flip-flopping and the Conservatives' confusion over PetroCanada, which the Liberals knew from their polling had soured voters on the Conservatives.

> Earlier this year, PetroCanada was doing quite well. Then along stumbled Joe Clark, who decided it must be changed. First, he said dismantle PetroCan. Then, privatize it. Next, he offered a study. Now, with thinking just as confusing as before, he says Ottawa should keep part, give part away. There's only one thing wrong with Petro-Can—Joe Clark. Nobody voted for the kind of government the Joe Clark Conservatives have given Canada. This is the time to vote Liberal.

This script was accompanied by snapshots of Clark that changed with each sentence describing another Conservative policy shift on PetroCanada. The pictures of Clark and the repeated use of his name—"Joe Clark Conservatives"—put the spotlight on the man the Liberals wanted to highlight in their campaign. The sentence "Nobody voted for the kind of government the Joe Clark Conservatives have given Canada" was a direct appeal to Liberals who voted for the Conservatives in 1979 not to make the same mistake again.

The Magician and PetroCanada commercials used Joe Clark's own positions and policy statements against him to reinforce the impression of Clark as confused and indecisive. The use of Ontario Premier William Davis was also calculated to underline Clark's weakness: the Prime Minister could not even rally support within his own party. Davis' appearance in Liberal commercials was also supposed to send a signal to disgruntled Conservatives that other Conservatives shared their qualms about Clark's policies, and therefore about Clark himself.

> It was the Joe Clark Conservative budget that caused this election. Here's how one prominent Ontarian felt about it: "This will extract a toll of higher inflation and fewer new jobs. One cannot justify the large increase in the excise tax on transportation fuels. This will place a severe hardship on many people." That prominent Ontarian: Conservative Premier William Davis. If the Joe Clark Conservatives let him down, think what they're doing to you. On February 18, vote Liberal.

The Liberals also ran several commercials showing Trudeau at gasoline pumps and construction sights ostensibly engaged in discussions with concerned citizens about energy prices and economic growth. These commercials were supposed to show a softer, people-oriented side of Trudeau, whose adversaries maintained he was out of touch with ordinary Canadians. The Liberal candidates appearing with Trudeau in these commercials were there to scatter the limelight from Trudeau.

But these positive commercials were used less frequently than the ones attacking Clark. Although some Liberals were squeamish about the party's negative commercials, the Liberals running the campaign insisted on showing them throughout the campaign. Strategy dictated that the Liberals were not inviting the electorate to ask questions about the Liberal Party, only about Joe Clark.

The Conservatives who designed their party's 1980 television commercials were seasoned professionals at negative advertising; they had used the same approach in the federal election campaigns of 1972, 1974, and 1979. In those elections, the Conservatives were in Opposition, so the negative commercials were justified as extensions of the party's ongoing attacks against the Liberal Government. In 1980, the Conservatives entered the campaign as a Government with a record to defend, and that made some Conservatives unhappy about using the advertising techniques of an Opposition party.

Three people formed the nucleus of the Conservatives' advertising team: Lowell Murray; Peter Swain, president of Media Buying Services; and Nancy McLean, a freelance advertising consultant in Toronto. Like the Liberals, the Conservatives also used the services of advertising executives from Toronto firms, but Murray, Swain, and McLean were the key Conservatives. Murray was the voice of final authority in the trio, Swain the advisor on purchasing advertising time, and McLean the creative director. Murray had been working in the back rooms of the Conservative Party for twenty years. Swain and McLean first worked for the Conservatives in the Ontario provincial election of 1971, and their services were later used in provincial elections in Newfoundland, New Brunswick, and Nova Scotia, and, of course, in federal elections. None of them had ever entered a federal election with the party so far behind. A spread of twenty points in the popular vote would translate into a Liberal landslide of at least 175 seats and perhaps as many as 200. When Allan Gregg's initial polling results were compiled, it was clear that the Conservatives had suffered massive defections of those who had supported the party in May 1979. The election could only be salvaged if those voters returned to the Conservatives; the party's campaign had to reforge the alliance of solid Conservative supporters and Liberals previously disaffected with Trudeau. The trio reckoned that the coals of disillusionment with Trudeau had to be fanned into the same protest-vote flame that put the Conservatives in power in the spring. The Conservative commercials, therefore, were aimed at two target groups: the Conservatives' own supporters who needed reassurance and the marginally committed voters who supported the Conservatives in 1979 and were inclined to vote Liberal (or NDP) in 1980. The latter group, the one the Conservatives desperately needed, represented what those skilled in the subtle arts of political persuasion call the "core point." Each day the Conservatives scrutinized their tracking data to observe the impact of their commercials on this core point.

The Conservative commercials, distasteful as they appeared to many voters, did seem to have the desired impact on the core point. The Conservatives recovered ground in the final three weeks of the campaign, partly because their television commercials helped to raise Trudeau's profile in the campaign. How could it have been otherwise when viewers were shown a slow-motion film of Trudeau speaking in the House of Commons, tie slightly undone, looking more like a hoodlum than a former Prime Minister? The script for this commercial read:

> Last May, Canadians rejected the Trudeau Liberals and voted for a change, because eleven years of Trudeau Government had brought high inflation, rising unemployment, a growing deficit, confrontation, a shrinking dollar and a growing dependence on foreign energy supplies. Well, there's no new leader, no new team and no reason to believe a Trudeau Government would be better this time. Real Change Deserves a Fair Chance.

It was the most offensive commercial of the campaign because the slow-motion film of Trudeau was a cheap trick that offended rather than startled viewers. As a result, McLean and Murray scrapped the commercial after several days.

Another equally negative, but less offensive, commercial ran throughout the campaign. Trudeau was again the focus of the commercial, his face surrounded by those of prominent Liberals who had left his Cabinet or preferred not to run again after losing in 1979. The Conservatives were stretching a point to include former Regional and Economic Expansion Minister Marcel Lessard in the same league with John Turner and to suggest that House of Commons Speaker James Jerome was a member of the Liberal team. As their names were read out, the faces of former colleagues disappeared from the screen, leaving only Trudeau's face at the end of the commercial. The script read:

> In this campaign, you're being told that if you vote Liberal, you're not voting for Trudeau, you're voting for the Liberal team. Well, John Turner won't run for the Trudeau Liberals. Donald Macdonald won't run. Alastair Gillespie won't run. Nor will Robert Andras. Barney Danson won't run. Iona Campagnolo won't run, neither will Marcel Lessard or James Jerome. Let's face it, if you vote Trudeau, you're getting Trudeau and nothing else. Real Change Deserves a Fair Chance.

Just as the Liberals kept referring to the "Joe Clark Conservatives" to make Clark the focal point in their commercials, so the Conservatives called the Liberal Party the "Trudeau Liberals" and made more frequent use of Trudeau's name than that of the Liberal Party.

The concentration on Trudeau was part of the Conservatives' desperate attempt to compel the electorate to recall his record in office. Gregg's polls revealed that a majority of the voters had put that record out of their minds. To further jog the electorate's memory, the Conservatives ran several commercials that picked up the visual effects from the party's 1979 commercials—a symbolic reminder that the issues had not changed since the spring election. In the 1979 campaign, the Conservatives showed a hockey goalie with the word *Canada* emblazoned in red across his white sweater. In the 1980 campaign, the goalie appeared again at the beginning of a Conservative commercial. The ad then presented a young skater, representing the Conservative Party, carrying the puck until he was slammed to the ice and banged against the boards by two burly defencemen, representing the Liberals and the NDP.

Bashing Trudeau and reminding voters of his record were inadequate responses to the Conservatives' own standing in public opinion. Having allowed themselves to be thrust into a campaign with their principal policies rejected or misunderstood, the Conservatives were forced to explain their policies. For the first month of the campaign, that task appeared hopeless; Gregg's polling data showed that the majority of voters were not listening to the Conservatives' explanations. But the brave action of the Canadian embassy staff in Tehran gave the Conservatives a wider—although still sceptical—audience among marginally committed or undecided voters. As a result, the Conservatives phased out most of their anti-Trudeau commercials and replaced them with commercials explaining Conservative policies. John Crosbie and Clark appeared in separate commercials defending the party's "honest" budget that tried to move Canada towards self-sufficiency in energy. In the final two weeks of the campaign, the Conservatives were running only positive commercials, whereas the Liberals mixed both anti-Clark and positive commercials.

Achieving the proper mix of commercials is essential in a campaign, because the major television-viewing markets are saturated with political advertising. Repetition is required to make an impression on the viewing audience, but excessive repetition either inures viewers to the commercials or leaves them bored. The intensity of political advertising on television during the twenty-nine-day period provided for under the Elections Act means that an average viewer in a major market might see about twenty-five commercials from each of the major parties. That's about three times as many as the same viewer would see in a saturation advertising blitz by a private company, whose commercials would be aired at greater intervals. This level of intensity requires the parties to prepare more commercials than would a private company contemplating saturation advertising.

In figuring out the best mix of commercials for a given market, the parties draw upon a grid of factors before the campaign, including a demographic profile of the target audience, viewing habits, availability of media outlets, and the number of key ridings in the market area. The decision about how much advertising time to purchase in each market is made exceptionally difficult by the Elections Act, which requires the parties to deliver their request for prime-time advertising purchases to the television stations and networks five days after the issuing of the writs. Only skilled professionals in the business of purchasing time could manage such a mind-boggling task for all the major media centres in the country. No wonder, then, that the Liberals needed the expertise of Red Leaf and the Conservatives of Media Buying Services, whose name indicates the company's full-time business, for sorting out the priorities for purchasing time and then negotiating subsequent arrangements with the broadcasters. Inevitably, the parties want to change their purchasing priorities in mid-campaign as voting intentions shift in key market areas. Both the Conservatives and Liberals poured additional money into purchasing extra time in key markets in the final week of the campaign— yet another reflection of the critical importance both parties attached to television advertising.

It is impossible to pinpoint when the importance of television first dawned on Canadian politicians, but it probably emerged in a rudimentary way in the campaigns of the late 1950s when Diefenbaker's magnetism electrified the country. The 1960 presidential campaign of John F. Kennedy in the United States, and the subsequent books and articles analysing his campaign, further alerted those organizing Canadian campaigns to the use a candidate could make of television. But it was not until Trudeau burst into national prominence, first in his leadership campaign and then in the election of 1968, that Canadian political campaigns surrendered themselves to the needs of television. Trudeau, by himself and in contrast to Stanfield, was an instant television star; his body language, arresting face, studied nonchalance and agile phraseology provided television with an endlessly fascinating combination of features. Trudeau, and the kinetic reaction he generated across Canada, created scenes of action and excitement that television craved. Trudeau was restless, vibrant, and charismatic; whereas Stanfield was thoughtful, plodding, and predictable—a fatal combination for television, which prefers confrontation to dialogue, passion to reason, change to continuity, and which presents personalities and images more adeptly than issues and ideas.

So powerful had the influence of television become by the campaigns of 1979 and 1980 that its needs permeated every aspect of the parties' strategies. Leaders flew frantically across the country to appear each day in two, and often three, major media centres. They stood beside grocery stores, copper mines, shipyards, or slaughter houses just to provide pleasing backdrops for the television cameras. They made sure that their major news event—or "Gainsburgers" as the press dubbed the NDP handouts— took place early enough in the day to hit the 6 p.m. newscast. They dropped issues or raised others because of television's coverage of what they were saying. They were animated or restrained according to the preferences of campaign organizers for their leader's image that evening on television newscasts. The campaigns represented the apotheosis of telepolitics in Canada, and sceptical observers could only mix their anger with tears and laughter while watching Trudeau, Clark, and Broadbent pursue the ephemeral bliss of the perfect thirty-second clip.

But who could blame the politicians? Evidence in Canada and the United States pointed to the inescapable conclusion that television far outstripped radio, newspapers, and personal contact between candidate and voter as the most influential source of information for the majority of the electorate. The Carleton University school of journalism asked a sample of 1,099 voters after the 1980 campaign: "Do you think you get most information from television, radio, or newspapers?" Fifty-five per cent said television, 27 per cent said newspapers, and 10 per cent said radio. A comprehensive study of political attitudes based on data from the 1974 campaign concluded:

> Television has the broadest appeal, cutting across all educational levels and socio-economic groups. . . . The importance attached to television by the public and the broad appeal it has to all sectors of the population make it the ideal medium from the point of view of political parties and politicians trying to get their messages across to the voters.*

Nor could the parties be blamed for capitulating to television when the medium offered the best vehicle for reaching that portion of the electorate most eagerly courted by every party: the uncommitted or marginally interested voters. Those who rely on newspapers for most of their information about the campaign, and politics generally, are more likely to be committed supporters of a party than those dependent on television. A newspaper story reaches a greater percentage of committed voters than a comparable television report. The uncommitted voter, in contrast to a partisan, is less likely to have a keen interest in things political. Impressions and images are more influential than issues for the uncommitted voter, and television—which conveys images more adeptly than it does ideas, and impressions more easily than facts—is therefore the medium most likely to provide the information upon which the uncommitted voter makes up his mind.

Television news producers try with varying degrees of commitment to cover the issues in a campaign. The more conscientious

---

*Harold Clark, Jane Jenson, Lawrence LeDuc, Jon Pammett, *Political Choice in Canada*, abridged edition (Toronto: McGraw-Hill Ryerson, 1980), p. 192.

news programs organize teams of reporters to analyse selected issues during the campaign. Some of their reports offer concise explanations of the parties' positions, spiced with a dash of background material about the issue itself. The CBC, for example, provided some exemplary coverage of issues in both the 1979 and 1980 campaigns. This kind of coverage, however, was the exception to the normal practice, whereby television newscasts concentrate on the leaders' tour for the bulk of their campaign coverage. Invariably it is the catchy remark or the offbeat event that quickens the pulse of television reporters, who are captive to their producers' demands for arresting film. To cater to that insatiable appetite for colour, political leaders ride in buggies, sleighs, or boats; walk through mines, mills, and factories, or wait until the cameramen are off the plane and ready to capture yet another airport arrival scene before themselves disembarking. Why else do the leaders' press aides inquire solicitously of television reporters, "How did you like the visuals on that one?" These visuals have nothing to do with the leaders' fitness for office or their platforms, but they have everything to do with obtaining exposure for the leaders on evening television newscasts; many a saddened television reporter has wondered what became of his day's labours when they did not appear on the screen at night, only to be informed by his producer that his visuals were too dull. No wonder the parties scrutinize television coverage so carefully when the entire purpose of a day of campaigning might be lost because a producer or line-up editor decided that the visuals were boring. As a result, political aides rush from dinner, interrupt meetings, or stop socializing at 11 p.m. of each campaign day to watch the newscasts, and their curses are fierce if the coverage is critical or skimpy.

The parties especially fear the "kickers" or "tags" that television journalists are allowed and often encouraged to affix to the end of their daily reports. These "kickers" are five- to ten-second pieces of personal opinion or analysis. A string of uncomplimentary "kickers," such as Trudeau received in 1979, can scuttle days of effective campaigning by repeatedly leaving the viewers with a negative impression of the campaign. Most television news reports of the campaign are predictable: a shot of the leader entering the hall shaking hands with exuberant supporters (the entrance having been planned that way for television); a brief excerpt (usually fifteen to twenty seconds) from the leader's speech; a description of where the leader is travelling; and a concluding comment, often a "kicker." The most attentive viewer must struggle to discover what the party leader actually said that day because of the sparse attention paid to his remarks in the report. The summation, in the form of a "kicker," fills the vacuum left by the rest of the report.

Television reporters, in fairness, are captives of the medium for which they work and of the constraints placed upon them by producers. There is no inherent reason why daily campaign coverage must be so superficial; but as long as the networks shape newscasts out of arresting film of often questionable relevance, the parties will be only too happy to provide endless fodder for the television cameras. Alternatively, the parties can starve the television reporters (and the rest of the press for that matter), as the Liberals did in the first five weeks of the 1980 campaign. Trudeau's theatrics of the 1979 campaign vanished. Instead, he delivered the same speech at every stop. It was dull, and that was what the Liberals wanted. Without any colour, the media was left either to report only Trudeau's daily attacks on the Conservatives, or to minimize the coverage of his activities, which suited the Liberals' purpose of preventing Trudeau from becoming the centre of attention in the campaign. Inevitably, the media became frustrated with the Liberal campaign, describing it as "cynical" and "manipulative," but Coutts and Davey reasoned that all the media whining in the world would not impress voters, whose suspicion of politicians is exceeded only by their mistrust of the media.

The Liberals also understood the fate that befalls a leader's basic campaign speech that is delivered at every stop. The speech contains the same phrases, jokes, and rhetorical flourishes which, as the days roll on, are repeated so incessantly that reporters can startle (and annoy) nearby members of the leader's audience by reciting the lines before they are spoken by the leader. After reporting the basic campaign speech a dozen times, journalists accompanying the leader become bored with the speech; they hunger for new fare, for the spice of the offhand remark or the freshly written paragraph. Normally, campaign organizers see to it that each day the basic campaign speech, which the live audience has not heard before, contains new material that will catch the media's attention and generate coverage on that evening's newscasts. But the Liberals, understanding the media's propensity to become bored with the basic speech, deliberately refused to offer the media any offhand comments or new material. The media had two choices: report the basic speech, which kept the focus of the

Liberal campaign on Clark; or play down the coverage of the Liberals, which kept the focus of the entire campaign away from Trudeau.

The Liberals isolated Trudeau from the media in the early stages of the campaign, because daily encounters with journalists would have diffused the basic message of the Liberal campaign by producing news reports of Trudeau's comments on a variety of subjects. On the fourth night of the campaign, in Moncton, the media were told that Trudeau would be coming down from his room to a dinner given by local Liberals for the press and Liberal aides. Television reporters alerted their camera crews and the journalists began to consider what questions they might ask the Liberal leader. But when his press secretary, Patrick Gossage, saw what the media had in mind, he informed them that Trudeau would not answer any questions or even come to dinner if they bothered him with questions and filming.

For the first five weeks of the campaign, the Trudeau campaign plane was therefore full of disgruntled reporters, and it fell to the gregarious Gossage and his assistant, Suzanne Perry, to minimize the media's unhappiness with a combination of bonhomie, drink, and other pleasures. But so remote did Trudeau remain from the media that twenty-nine journalists signed a petition in the fifth week of the campaign asking Trudeau to hold a press conference. *Fiat media conferenciam*, Trudeau scribbled on the petition,"Let the press conference be held." It took place several days later. By that point in the campaign the Liberals had sufficiently reinforced the negative impression of Clark and were thus prepared to allow a bit of spontaneity to creep into their campaign. The press conference, Trudeau's only one of the campaign, turned out to be a dud, for which the members of the media had only themselves to blame, since their vague, windy questions invited answers in kind.

Holding the media at bay also meant refusing to debate the other party leaders on television. The Liberals offered many spurious reasons during the campaign for their refusal to accept the networks' proposal to repeat the debate of the 1979 campaign, which had been seen by seven million viewers and admired by broadcasting networks from other countries. The Liberals proposed a series of rotating debates among the leaders and party critics, a sound idea that the Liberals knew would prove unacceptable to the networks, who feared a series of debates would be boring and deprive them of too much commercial advertising revenue. Put simply, Trudeau, Coutts, Goldfarb, and Grafstein did not want a debate, and all their protestations about trying to devise a new format for the debate amounted to a smokescreen behind which to retreat. Davey, fearing the criticism such a decision would arouse, counselled participation, but he was overruled by Coutts and Trudeau. In 1979 the Liberals trailed in the campaign and needed the debate to give Trudeau a chance to rough up Clark. "I think we suckered them in a bit on that one," Davey chuckled after the 1979 campaign, referring to the Conservatives' acceptance of the debate. In 1980, the Liberals were far ahead, and they were not about to be suckered themselves. They did not want a debate, and the project collapsed.

The Conservatives naturally screamed foul play when the Liberals scuttled the debate, but in 1979 the Conservatives themselves had wondered about the wisdom of pitting the inexperienced and awkward Clark against so polished a performer as Trudeau. Eventually, the Conservatives accepted the debate, believing that the price of ducking was higher than the price of losing the debate. Indeed, the Conservatives' treatment of the media in 1979 was a less regimented forerunner of the Liberals' strategy in the 1980 campaign. In the first week of the 1979 campaign, Clark made himself available to reporters who squeezed around him in what was appropriately called a "scrum." These encounters did not go well for Clark, who made several ill-considered replies that received prominent coverage. By the second week of the campaign, the scrums became less frequent. At one scrum in that week, Clark answered three questions, two in English and one in French, before dashing for the campaign bus, explaining that he had a pressing engagement even though his next public appearance was four hours later. Throughout the campaign, he was brittle and nervous in all of his dealings with the press, which explained why he kept away from reporters as much as possible.

All was different in the 1980 campaign. The Conservatives, behind in popularity, pressed for a debate. Clark, more confident of himself and his answers after having served seven months as Prime Minister, held weekly press conferences and willingly gave interviews. Tactically, of course, the Conservatives were trying to contrast their "open" campaign with the Liberals' tightly controlled campaign, and the tactic helped generate more sympathy for Clark from the media in the last month of the campaign than he had received since becoming leader of the Conservative Party.

Clark's accessibility, however, was not producing the amount of television coverage that the Conservatives needed in the first month of the campaign. The networks had decided before the campaign that they would not automatically provide full nightly reports on the party leaders' campaigns; instead they often rolled snippets of film of each leader into brief, and often unintelligible, summaries of the day's campaigning. Since January also provided several major international news stories, including the aftermath of the Soviet Union's invasion of Afghanistan, the Canadian election campaign reports often came in the middle or near the end of the newscasts. This was of inadvertent assistance to the Liberals and their low-key campaign. But the lack of television coverage frustrated the Conservatives' attempts to raise the profile of the campaign, to throw Trudeau's record at the electorate, and to explain their Government's policies. Without television to carry his message, Clark might just as well have been talking to himself as to auditoriums full of supporters.

The early indifference of the networks forced the Conservatives to recast their media strategy. They continued to try to provide a lively item for the 6 and 11 p.m. newscasts, but they also put Clark on every available hot-line and local television show willing to entertain him as a guest. Even if Clark were shut out on the evening newscasts, at least he received local media exposure in one major media centre each day.

The NDP, which as the third party in Canadian politics had to fight harder for coverage than the other two parties, shared the Conservatives' frustration. Peter O'Malley, Ed Broadbent's press secretary, became so incensed at the lack of coverage that he demanded that Robin Sears, the NDP federal secretary, write an angry letter of complaint to the CBC. Sears declined. But he found himself in a heated exchange with the producers of *The National* several weeks later, when he wandered into the CBC newsroom in Toronto after taping a program in another studio. The CBC, knowing the sensitivity of the parties to television coverage, kept a computerized account of how many seconds of coverage each party was receiving throughout the campaign.

Studies of voting behaviour all point to the same conclusion: party leadership is the most salient motivating factor affecting the success of a political party. A leader is of crucial electoral importance since he personifies the party and acts as the national spokesman for its ideals and principles. On him, should power be won, will rest the hopes of the nation and the responsibilities of high office. So it is natural that his performance is the yardstick by which most voters measure their appreciation of his party.

But the surrender of political campaigns, and of politics generally, to television has heightened the leader's importance in determining a party's electoral success. Television has provided a new link between leader and voter that neither newspapers nor radio ever offered. Because television, as its programming has been organized, is befuddled by the coverage of issues and ideas, it concentrates on personalities who represent issues and ideas. Quite often, the candidates' personalities and physical characteristics become more important than the ideas they express or the points of view they represent. They are judged as performers, and are accordingly reported on television as impassioned or restrained, tired or alert, amusing or dry, fiery or dull. As a result, much of television's coverage of a campaign revolves around how the leader is "doing"—how effectively he is performing—rather than around what he is saying. In this, all the media, including newspapers and radio, stand accused, but the evidence is most obvious and damning in the case of television.

Trudeau, whatever his other virtues and liabilities, has been the premier Canadian performer in the age of telepolitics. Stanfield and Clark, by contrast and of themselves, were handicapped by television's relentless concentration on speaking style and personal characteristics. While it would be wrong to blame television for the Conservatives' leaders' demise, the medium certainly contributed to the image problem that both men could not escape in their careers. Neither possessed the combination of attractive physical characteristics, expressive body language, a nimble tongue, and powerful but abeyant emotions that are required for effective presentation on television. It was no solace for them to know that Mackenzie King would probably have failed as a politician in the age of telepolitics.

While television accentuates the performing abilities of party leaders, it also carries them into the consciousness of the voters in a way that newspapers and radio could never hope to emulate. In a lifetime in politics, a political leader meets only a tiny fragment of the population, but through television, millions of voters can vicariously believe that they know him. On this link a leader's success depends. A campaign gives the viewers a steady dose of the leader, and his image is the thread that binds the campaign together. He is the spokesman for the party's right question which, shaped by polls and supplemented by advertising, is put each day by the leader and conveyed by television to the voters on whom his fate depends.

~ 11 ~

The Third Party

The aircraft sweeps in a gentle arc above the stark beauty of the Newfoundland coast. Finally, it turns to face the wind and Stephenville, a town suspended between the greys of rock and water like something from a David Blackwood print. The plane touches down just as the sun disappears into the sea, and the light lingers only a few minutes. On the road to Corner Brook, darkness closes in, and chatter and smoke fill the bus.

It is the third week of the 1980 election campaign, and NDP Leader Ed Broadbent is bringing his campaign to Newfoundland, where the party's fortunes have soared in recent years: from 4 per cent of the popular vote in the 1974 election to 31 per cent in the 1979 election. In Corner Brook, a three-man band playing "When The Saints Go Marching In," "John Brown's Body," and other imported American songs, is warming up 150 people clustered in the tiny Paperworkers Hall. It is early in the eight-week campaign, but the size of the crowd is still disappointing. The turn-out is an uncertain portent of what would be the NDP's most shocking setback in all of Canada on election night.

Illusions are the perverted dreams of politics, but they are essential to any leader striving to create the impression of momentum. A leader must fire the enthusiasm of his troops with tales of coming triumphs, especially in a party where defeat is better known than victory. The NDP is plagued by the perception that it cannot win a federal election. Hardcore NDP supporters are the most doggedly faithful workers in Canadian politics, but wavering voters must ask themselves if a vote for the NDP will be "wasted" on a third party without influence in Ottawa. The NDP's best hope for influence in Ottawa lies in winning a handful of additional seats in order to hold the balance of power in a minority Parliament. But the NDP cannot campaign overtly for a minority Government, because such a strategy would imply the party's recognition of its third-party status. Instead, it uses slogans such as "More New Democrats," and campaigns as if this were the first giant step towards the fast-approaching day when the party will be in power. So Broadbent opens his speech in Corner Brook with a little white lie:

> I want you to know that I have come to Newfoundland after having been in Vancouver in the far west, in the Prairies, and in my own home province of Ontario, and in all the meetings the attendance was at least twice what it was last May in every region, including Newfoundland. I want you to know that we are going to make major gains right across the country.

Broadbent is crisp tonight, and he has been well briefed. In most of his speeches, he calls Finance Minister John Crosbie a "millionaire in mukluks," but tonight he inserts a word that makes all the difference in western Newfoundland, where folks resent the city-slickers from St. John's. "John Crosbie, the millionaire townie in mukluks," Broadbent says, and the crowd roars at the cross-island dig.

While Broadbent delivers his standard campaign speech, Fonse Faour stands to one side of the platform. Corner Brook, a pulp and paper town nestled among the hills at the end of Deer Lake, was once a Conservative town when Jack Marshall was the popular Conservative M.P. for the surrounding riding. But, through a Liberal miscalculation, the riding switched to the NDP. The Liberals, sensing that they could win the riding if Marshall departed, appointed him to the Senate in 1978. In the ensuing by-election, however, the NDP found Faour, a young lawyer whose family owned a jewellery store in Corner Brook. Campaigning with the support of the increasingly powerful Food, Fishermen and Allied Workers Union and the Paperworkers Union, Faour brought the NDP from nowhere to victory. He also helped himself by campaigning strenuously against abortion in a heavily Catholic riding. At twenty-nine, Faour arrived in Ottawa with a striking name and the political distinction of being the first New Democrat ever elected in Newfoundland. He was re-elected in the 1979 campaign, and he is considered unassailable in 1980.

But Faour fell victim to fatal circumstances that often confront the NDP.* When enough voters want to defeat one of the major parties, they look for the best political means of achieving that end. Unless the NDP is a major party, as it is in western Canada, the alternative to the Conservatives becomes the Liberals, and vice versa. The NDP in Newfoundland had insufficient time after the 1979 election to parlay its 31 per cent of the popular vote into an improved organization by attracting new recruits wanting to identify with a party on the rise. A few months after the federal campaign, the NDP bombed in a provincial election. Its inadequate organization was worn out entering the 1980 federal campaign. Impressive candidates from 1979 in St. John's and Labrador decided not to run, and the party's entire campaign in Newfoundland reeked of defeatism. The protest vote of 1979 had found another focus: Joe Clark and his budget, with its 18-cents-per-gallon excise tax on diesel fuel for fishermen's boats and higher taxes for residents of Canada's poorest province. Newfoundlanders chose the Liberals as the alternative to the Conservatives, taking five of the province's seven seats.

Nothing in Canadian politics can rival the irreverence of political meetings in Cape Breton, Broadbent's next stop. The region is so dependent on government and has suffered so many broken promises that all politicians are considered untrustworthy, except by the faithful of each party. The bitter weather, the forbidding terrain, and the heartbreaking failures of the mills and mines have produced a prickly independence that the descendants of the Highland Scots bring to their political gatherings. Anger simmers at the hand fate dealt Cape Breton, but the hope for political change is tempered by the desperate desire to preserve what little prosperity exists.

Bob Muir, a Conservative, held Sydney for twenty-two years before the Liberals, in another slice of patronage, appointed him to the Senate shortly before the 1979 election. Muir was tremendously popular in Sydney, and the Liberals knew that as long as he was there, Sydney would probably remain Conservative. They

---

*At the beginning of the campaign, it seemed inconceivable that Faour might lose, so desperate were the Liberals to find a candidate. Brian Tobin, Newfoundland Liberal leader Don Jamieson's executive assistant, was sent into the riding to search for a candidate. Tobin completed his search and reported that a suitable candidate could not be found, to which Jamieson replied: "All right then, you run." Tobin won.

were right: as soon as Muir departed, the Liberals captured the riding, despite the presence of Muir's secretary as the Conservative candidate.

Sydney is one of the two or three most frustrating ridings in Canada for the NDP. Its isolation from Halifax and Ottawa, its unionized workforce and its rebellious nature should make Sydney an NDP fixture. But the party can manage only a second- or third-place finish in federal elections, because in a town split sharply along class lines, the NDP cannot attract enough middle-class votes to win.

At least the NDP had Andy Hogan next door in Cape Breton-East Richmond, a riding that gathers up all the hard-luck mining towns south of Sydney. Hogan was a Catholic priest, another of the local boys who attended St. Francis Xavier University, where he developed a social conscience. A terrier of a man who liked his drink and liked it neat, Hogan was as much a symbol as a politician for the NDP faithful of the island. He gave the NDP its long-sought bridgehead in the Maritimes in the 1974 election, so he represented to New Democrats what hard work and passion could do in politics. As a priest, he stood in a long line of religious men and women who brought a sense of moral outrage and messianic zeal to the secular world of the NDP. To hear him speak was to remember that politics will always find room for oratory from the heart. Hogan was a throwback to an earlier age in politics, before television took the soul from the game by imposing on its participants the need to bridle their passions before the camera's exaggerating eye.

The night after his disappointing rally in Corner Brook, more than 450 people jam the Steelworkers Hall in Sydney to hear Broadbent, but it is Andy Hogan who wins their hearts. Even before he begins, some shout, "Give 'em hell, Andy," "Tell it all, Andy," and later the hall is punctuated with "That's right," "Keep 'er going, Andy," "Right on." He is supposed to speak for five minutes, and he said when he began that he would speak for only ten. But no one believes it, and no one wants to. He could have gone on all night without hearing a murmur of impatience. He is one of them, the local boy who had taken their hurts and their dreams to Ottawa. No matter that his speech lurches uncontrollably, he touches all the nerve ends of their discontent. He is pure theatre, the hero in the morality play whom everyone adores.

After twenty-three minutes Hogan says he must stop. "No, no," "Keep 'er going, Andy," come the cries. But Hogan's speech must end, because further delay might mean less coverage for the man the media have come all this way to hear. The perspiration running off his forehead, Hogan takes his seat, yielding his place at the microphone to the NDP provincial leader Jeremy Akerman, an angular and articulate man from nearby Glace Bay. And Akerman now commences a ritual left over from the days when the NDP was so poor it scrounged to pay its national staff. His appeal is serious, his delivery gentle.

> Every election we keep telling you that campaigning is expensive, more expensive than it used to be. And we always give you a long list of things, of how much it costs to buy an ad in the Cape Breton Post or thirty seconds on CJCB. The fact of the matter is that while there's a rebate that is available to political parties, which we intend to collect, we still need additional money. We do not seek to embarrass anybody. There's no compulsion. But if any of you have a contribution you'd like to make, we'd like to receive it to defray the costs of the campaign. There are going to be some people moving amongst you with buckets.

"Why not barrels?" someone shouts and the crowd erupts in laughter. Akerman just grins that distant smile of his while the buckets go round like offeratory plates, passed by hand throughout the hall, accumulating $650 for the NDP.

Finally, it is Broadbent's turn. Whether from fatigue or poor scripting, he is less impressive than he was the previous night in Corner Brook. His speech is disjointed, as though he had made a mental checklist of all the NDP verities he must touch in twenty minutes: PetroCanada, an industrial strategy, the sins of the Liberals and Conservatives, and a word about local unemployment. The audience, however, does not know Broadbent is off his form; for them, this is the first and perhaps the only time in the campaign that they will see him in the flesh. He receives warm applause at the end of his remarks, but Hogan stole the show.

Alas, one evening does not a campaign make. Whispering about Father Hogan's fondness for drink spread corrosively through the towns of Cape Breton-East Richmond. In the end he was blown away as Faour was by the anger against the Conservative Government—of which the Liberals, not the NDP, were the beneficiaries across Atlantic Canada. Hogan's 5,000-vote plurality in 1979 became a 464-vote defeat in 1980, and the Commons lost his high-pitched voice of hurt.

The following day Broadbent appears at the Halifax Board of Trade, whose membership is overwhelmingly opposed to the NDP. But the crowd is large, a reflection of Broadbent's personal stature. The audience listens respectfully as he outlines his party's job-creation policy: planning agreements between government and industry; a government-operated fund into which companies must place a percentage of their profits for investments authorized or made directly by the federal government; an overhaul of the Department of Regional and Economic Expansion and government-financed capital works projects. The aim, Broadbent says, is to bring unemployment down to 6 per cent by 1982 and to 4 per cent by 1984.

Indeed, if Broadbent has made an intellectual contribution to the NDP, it consists in having focused the party's attention on the need to articulate an industrial strategy for Canada. Of course, the need to restructure the Canadian economy along more socialist lines has been central to CCF-NDP thinking since the Regina Manifesto, but none of Broadbent's predecessors as party leader put so much political emphasis on a government-directed, planned economy. His predecessors talked more about the inequities of capitalism, and they sometimes proposed sweeping reforms to free up more money for social programs such as pensions, family allowances, and unemployment insurance. Even the party's successful 1972 "Corporate Welfare Bums" campaign was an attack on the tax system, the reform of which would enable the federal government to pay more money to those in need.

Since winning the NDP leadership, Broadbent has faced an electorate increasingly concerned with the sins of government bureaucracy, growing budgetary deficits and a worsening current account deficit. If his predecessors ever talked about these problems, they usually did so in a cursory fashion. But Broadbent addresses these problems directly, tying them to Canada's need for a national industrial strategy, planning agreements between government and industry, and a more centrally planned economy. Whatever its economic merits, Broadbent's call for a national industrial strategy is probably too grandiose and too all-encompassing for many voters to understand. It smacks of so much idle talk, of pie-in-the-sky, although the NDP has made an effort to publish research papers supporting its arguments. It is a solution that appears one or even two steps removed from present-day reality. No matter how often Broadbent explains that unemployment is directly related to the decline in Canada's manufacturing sector, which is in turn tied to the control of the Canadian economy by multinational companies, he leaves his listeners feeling that NDP solutions are too long-term and are unlikely to offer much in the here and now.

Such is the legacy of a party that still considers itself a political reform movement with a mandate by history to educate the electorate into sharing its passion for social justice. There is a commendable intellectual honesty to the NDP campaign, but there is also a sense of moralizing about it that irritates a lot of voters.

The NDP stood no chance of winning Halifax, or any other seats on the Nova Scotia mainland; none of them was even considered for the party's "A" list.* Before the campaign, the NDP compiled "A" and "B" lists: "A" for ridings the party realistically hoped it might win, "B" for long shot bets and ridings where the party was trying to build for future elections. In drafting Broadbent's national tour, the NDP wanted him to visit all of the "A" ridings at least once and as many of the "B" ridings as possible. (The "A" ridings also received the most organizational help from party headquarters.) Every Sunday afternoon during the campaign, key NDP organizers met in Ottawa to plan, among other things, where Broadbent would go the week after next. In the days before the 1974 amendments to the Election Act, when NDP leaders chugged across the country in propeller-driven aircraft, the leader's itinerary was set weeks in advance. But the use of a chartered jet, made possible by the money the NDP receives under the act, gives the party more flexibility in designing the leader's tour.

There are always more requests for the leader's presence than the NDP can possibly accommodate in a campaign. Occasionally, the persistence of a local organizer in a hopeless riding persuaded the NDP national organizers to offer a slice of Broadbent's time. Broadbent would also visit hopeless ridings because the local organization had cobbled together an intriguing "media event":

---

*Below is a list of the NDP "A" ridings, with the "A" ridings won italicized: Humber-Port au Port-St. Barbe; Grand Falls-White Bay-Labrador; Cape Breton-East Richmond; Cape Breton-The Sydneys; Kenora; Thunder Bay-Atikokan; Thunder Bay-Nipigon; Timiskaming; Sault Ste. Marie; Nickel Belt; Cochrane; Timmins-Chapleau; Algoma; *Brant; Hamilton-Mountain*; Windsor-Walkerville; Essex-Windsor; *Beaches*; Etobicoke-Lakeshore; *Broadview-Greenwood*; York South-Weston; Scarborough West; *Oshawa*; Cambridge; *Churchill; Dauphin; Selkirk-Interlake; Winnipeg North; Winnipeg-North Centre; Winnipeg-Birds Hill; Winnipeg-St. James; Humboldt-Lake Centre; Mackenzie; Prince Albert; Regina East; Regina West; Saskatoon East; The Battlefords-Meadow Lake; Yorkton-Melville; Burnaby*; Cariboo-Chilcotin; *Comox-Powell River; Cowichan-Malahat-The Islands; Kamloops-Shuswap; Kootenay East-Revelstoke; Kootenay West; Mission-Port Moody; Nanaimo-Alberni; New Westminster-Coquitlam; Skeena*; Vancouver Centre; *Vancouver East; Vancouver Kingsway; Nunatsiaq*; Western Arctic.

hence the appearance of Broadbent in Simcoe North to participate in a torchlight parade at midnight. The visit did not do much for the voters of Simcoe North, but the sight of Broadbent sitting in a sleigh provided excellent fodder for television's insatiable appetite for the trivial.

In drafting Broadbent's itinerary, the members of the NDP strategy committee asked themselves three questions: (1) What will be the national impact? (2) What good will the visit do us in the riding? (3) Will the visit further the themes of our campaign? Using Halifax as an example, the answers were: (1) Speaking to a Board of Trade enhanced Broadbent's responsible, sober image; (2) Alexa McDonough, the NDP candidate in Halifax, was out-standing. Even though she could not win, she deserved showcas-ing. Halifax is also the most important city in Nova Scotia and the news centre of the Maritimes; (3) A speech on industrial policy highlighted one of the NDP's principal campaign themes.

Broadbent's itinerary was only one of several regular topics discussed at the Sunday strategy-committee meetings, which were attended by Robin Sears, the NDP federal secretary; Terry Grier, the national campaign chairman and a former MP; Marc Eliesen, NDP research director; Peter O'Malley, Broadbent's press secretary; Dick Proctor, Broadbent's executive assistant; Jo-Anne McNevin, NDP federal organizer, and Mary Ellen McQuay, the assistant federal secretary who worked on Broadbent's Oshawa campaigns in 1972 and 1974. At each session, Sears delivered a report on how the media covered the party that week. Everyone discussed Broadbent's speeches and compared notes on feedback from party organizers across the country.

Broadbent never attended these sessions. It was felt his presence would inhibit others from speaking freely, especially about his performance. Instead, Sears and Grier took the consen-sus of the meeting to him at 4 p.m. There were seldom many criticisms of his performances, although early in the campaign dozens of rank-and-file New Democrats were upset when Broad-bent called Clark a "fool" in a speech in Sudbury. It did not fit the NDP strategy to have Broadbent launching personal attacks against the other party leaders. Broadbent later regretted the remark; he always thought of Clark as a decent man. In fact, the Sunday after the remark, Sears and Grier were presenting the consensus of the strategy committee meeting when Broadbent interrupted: "Something's wrong. Don't tell me, I know. My mother phoned and gave me hell. I'm sorry. I won't do it again."

The NDP is without hope or prospects in Quebec, but as a party that sees itself as a national institution, it must at least give the appearance of trying to win support everywhere in Canada, including Quebec. There are also tiny groups of militants, who must be cheered and reassured that all of their now-hopeless work will prove eventually to have not been in vain.

Ever since the founding of the NDP's forerunner, the CCF, the party has been unable to penetrate the province of Quebec. In the early days of the party, it seldom stretched beyond an impressive but small group of English-speaking intellectuals and activists in Montreal such as Frank Scott, Eugene Forsey, and David Lewis. The Roman Catholic clergy cautioned its flock against succumbing to the evils of godless socialism. The union movement, a wellspring of intellectual and financial support for the party elsewhere in Canada, grew more slowly in Quebec than in English Canada, and when the movement gained strength in the 1950s, more than half of the movement was organized along the religious lines of several West European countries. When the Quiet Revolution arrived in the early 1960s, the political and cultural elite of Quebec turned towards state-encouraged manifestations of Quebec nationalism. As a pan-Canadian party with feeble roots in Quebec, the NDP was completely ignored by Quebeckers looking for political and economic reform. On economic issues, the NDP's natural ally was the Parti Québécois, but there could not be an accommodation between supporters of the two parties on the future shape of Quebec and Canada.

Some day Québécois may think of the NDP as other than a party of *les anglais*. The unions and the intellectuals may forsake the nationalist vision of independence and turn to the NDP. The industrial towns and their blue-collar inhabitants may see their hope for social justice in the NDP. But for now Broadbent must push himself through the Davey Shipyards in Lauzon near Quebec City, a politician speaking laboured French, trying to pierce the barrier of indifference separating Quebec from the NDP. As he makes his way through the shipyards, he chats jovially with the workers through a din of noise. Later he claims that some of the workers said that they would vote for the NDP. He adds happily that he understood all but one of those with whom he spoke, a sign of the progress he has made with his own French.

Broadbent lost his chance to speak fluent French after his re-election as an M.P. in 1972. He knew then that he wanted to become party leader. He was married to a francophone, and as an

M.P. he had access to the language courses offered by the House of Commons. But, like so many other busy people, he did not find sufficient time to apply himself to learning French. Once he became party leader it was too late, although he has since made enough progress to give simple answers in French.

Now he pays the price for his neglect. Gathered in the company cafeteria, the workers are alerted to his presence on the stage. Many have finished eating and so watch expressionless when he begins a short address. Others turn to their mates and resume interrupted conversations. Some keep their attention on their sausages, beans, and mashed potatoes. Two groups continue playing cards, oblivious to the commotion caused by the arrival of the media. Broadbent tells them earnestly about the NDP's commitment to a merchant marine, venturing occasionally from his prepared text. He struggles in his laboured French to establish a rapport, recalling that he represents an industrial town in Ontario (saying *"mon province"* instead of *"ma province"*), where politicians are expected to keep their promises (saying *"promises"* instead of *"promesses"*). It does not work; the barrier is too wide. There is perfunctory applause at the conclusion of his remarks and, mercifully, the event is over.

The campaign stretched over sixty-six days, but Broadbent spent only three of them in Quebec, a reflection of the NDP's overwhelming weakness in that province. In the 1979 election, the party won only 5.3 per cent of the votes in Quebec. Seventy-three of seventy-five NDP candidates in Quebec lost their deposits. In Metropolitan Montreal, even the farcical Rhinoceros Party had almost half as many votes as the NDP.

In 1980, the collapse of the Créditistes and Conservatives in Quebec, allowed the NDP to make marginal gains. The NDP won 8.8 per cent of the popular vote, compared with 5.3 per cent in 1979. The party's candidates finished second in thirty-five of Quebec's seventy-five ridings, a notable achievement except that the closest a New Democrat came to winning a seat was nearly 14,000 votes.

That candidate was René Matte, a former Créditiste M.P. from Champlain and a Parti Québécois sympathizer, who ran in his old riding for the NDP after losing as an Independent candidate in the 1979 election. Matte's candidacy symbolized a time bomb ticking away within the NDP. Matte was a more fervent Quebec nationalist than most of the party's candidates, but the Quebec wing of the NDP still has a more decentralized view of the future of Canadian federalism than do the vast majority of New Democrats in the rest of Canada. At the 1971 leadership convention, the issue of "special status" for Quebec split the delegates. The issue has since been held in check by the party leadership, but if the NDP gains strength in Quebec, especially by attracting *péquistes* or forging closer ties with nationalistically minded unions, the party will have to confront the explosive question of Quebec national-ism. And that will be agonizing for a party whose intellectual preference is for a strong central government that can direct the economy and redistribute income among regions and individuals.

The NDP has always expressed genuinely good intentions towards Quebec, but the party's membership is overwhelmingly drawn from English Canada. The NDP's political intelligence in Quebec is weak and the level of understanding of Quebec in the federal caucus is shaky.

That was amply demonstrated in the summer of 1976, when English-speaking air-traffic controllers, supported by airline pilots, went on strike against the use of both French and English in air-traffic control in selected parts of Canada. The strike soon became one of the most bitterly divisive issues for English and French Canadians since conscription, and the NDP caucus wrestled over its position. The party's membership in western Canada and Ontario saw, or chose to see, the issue as one of air safety; there was no one from Quebec in the caucus to argue that the issue was really one of language rights. Spurred on by hopelessly inadequate technical advice provided by Peter Sadler-Brown of the Machinists Union (and a former research director of the party), the NDP caucus accepted the issue as one of safety. Proudly, the NDP stood against the War Measures Act of 1970; sadly, it swallowed the conventional wisdom of English Canada, poisoned as it was by anti-French bigotry, in the controllers' dispute. If the NDP had supported the French-speaking controllers, several young Liberal M.P.s such as Serge Joyal and Pierre De Bané might have crossed the floor of the Commons. And then the NDP might have become a truly national political party.

The Chilean folk singers leave the stage of the union hall in Winnipeg to appreciative applause and expressions of solidarity for their struggle against the dictatorship clamped on their country by General Pinochet. Several minutes later, the NDP candidates from Manitoba stream down the centre aisle like a football team emerging for the game. They are introduced and asked to stand to acknowledge the cheers, the loudest being reserved for Stanley Knowles, the M.P. for Winnipeg-North

Centre, running for his thirteenth term in Parliament. He first sought election to the Commons in 1935, the year before Broadbent was born, and so astonishing is his knowledge of parliamentary procedure that newly appointed Speakers have been known to quake at the thought of ruling on one of his points of order or privilege. He has fought so tirelessly for improved pensions that any NDP candidate visiting a senior citizens home need only mention his name and await the flashes of recognition across the wrinkled faces of the audience. When death or incapacity finally snatches him from the Commons, he will be fondly remembered by Canadians everywhere, a testament offered only a tiny minority of those who served their country in Parliament. He is a pure coin in an age of debased political currency.

Broadbent, after a flowery introduction, opens with the same white lie about the NDP crowds being twice as large in this election as in 1979. "I want you to know that all across the country, we're going to make gains like we've never made in the history of the party." Tonight, he says he wants to talk about energy, and proceeds to do so with considerable vigour for about half an hour.

It turns out to be one of Broadbent's better speeches, delivered with an occasional modulation that softens the high-pitched intensity of his voice. His oratory will never transfix his audience—there is too much of the academic in him for that—but he has become a competent public performer from the trying days of his first campaign in Oshawa, when he could not restrain his intellectual predilection to smother his political points in nuance.

The fact that Broadbent successfully entered the House of Commons on his first try in 1968 was due in large measure to the Trudeau sweep of that year, which washed away other New Democrats across the country. He had been teaching political science at York University in Toronto, after having taught high school for a year in Oshawa and completed a doctorate in political philosophy at the London School of Economics, when he decided to run against Conservative incumbent Michael Starr in Oshawa. Starr had been a fixture in Oshawa since 1952, Minister of Labour in the Diefenbaker Government and a respected politician of Ukrainian descent revered by Oshawa's substantial Ukrainian population. Broadbent himself had impeccable Oshawa roots: he was born and raised in the city, where his father worked for General Motors and was a member of the United Autoworkers Union. But in 1968 the NDP organization in Oshawa was split by factionalism within the UAW local, and no one gave the earnest young professor much of a chance.

Starr, however, was vulnerable. He had grown complacent. Some of the younger Ukrainians were making the distinction their parents could not between communism and social democracy. Starr had run an embarrassingly bad campaign for the Conservative leadership in 1967, and he had not wielded a Cabinet minister's power for nearly six years. Most of all, Starr was the victim of Trudeaumania: many of his supporters defected to the Liberals. Broadbent, by uniting both factions of the UAW behind him and running an excellent door-to-door campaign, squeezed his way between Starr and the Liberals, winning by fifteen votes.

Three years later, Broadbent made the only serious mistake of his political career. He erred not so much in seeking the NDP leadership, although that was presumptuous enough for a freshman M.P. scarcely known outside of Ontario, but in running an ineffective campaign, which came apart at the convention when Broadbent waffled on the party's Quebec resolutions. He finished a humiliating fourth. He looked opportunistic and amateurish trying to avoid the crunching division of delegates between David Lewis, the winning candidate of the party establishment, and Jim Laxer, the leader of the Waffle and the darling of other anti-establishment groups within the NDP.

When he arrived in Oshawa for the 1972 election campaign, Broadbent was in political trouble. His run for the leadership had given him national exposure, at the price of keeping him away from his constituency. Starr was back as the Conservative candidate, with a Tory wind blowing across Ontario. The Liberals could not find a suitable local candidate, so they parachuted someone from Ottawa into Oshawa—a sure sign that the Liberal vote was about to slide. Broadbent's first campaign manager left in a disagreement, his replacement was ineffectual, and ten days into the campaign Broadbent looked like a loser.

The NDP, however, has one luxury that the major parties cannot afford. By fixing its sights on only a limited number of seats, it can appropriately deploy its resources to win them. Shortly after the campaign opened, alarm bells began ringing in the NDP organizational hierarchy in Ottawa: Broadbent, one of the party's brightest young M.P.s and the man whom David Lewis said privately would succeed him as NDP leader, was going to lose. Hence the arrival one morning of Jo-Anne McNevin, a veteran organizer from NDP campaigns in British Columbia. One of the smartest and toughest political organizers in Canada, McNevin studied the polling sheets pasted on the wall of Broadbent's committee rooms, asked a few questions, and declared: "This campaign is a disaster." Within seventy-two hours, she had stared down the chauvinist reaction to her arrival, issued instructions on every aspect of the campaign, reorganized the polling, and generally, by a combination of sweetness and sarcasm, galvanized the reluctant and shocked the complacent into a disciplined, inspired campaign team. Broadbent eventually won by 824 votes, a victory that cemented his hold on Oshawa. McNevin also organized his 1974 campaign, which he won by 10,230 votes. After he won the NDP leadership in July, 1975, Broadbent appointed McNevin the NDP's federal organizer, which means she now strikes the fear of the Almighty into the NDP faithful from Vancouver Island to Newfoundland, a scope that is at least commensurate with her talent.

Broadbent is now the NDP's most effective political weapon. In the 1980 election, the NDP's own polls showed him running ahead of the party. The same polls placed him ahead of Clark in Ontario, where the Conservatives' core vote is much higher than the NDP's, and ahead of both Clark and Trudeau in British Columbia. He was the centrepiece of the party's advertising in both the 1979 and 1980 elections. While the Conservatives and Liberals played down their own leaders, the NDP stuck Broadbent right in the viewers' faces. Everywhere he travelled, people said to him: "We'd like to vote for you, if only you weren't with the NDP," a refrain the party picked up in its advertising.

Broadbent's political appeal is quite straightforward. He is a direct and friendly man who gets on well with people. Although his tastes run to the finer things of life—good cigars, classical music, the *Manchester Guardian Weekly, Encounter, The New York Review of Books*, Sartre—he is untouched by intellectual snobbishness. He never forgets his union family—his brother still works for General Motors—or his childhood acquaintances who did not go as far as he has. He knows the union hall and the libraries of London. From each, he draws his passion for social democracy, so that when he discusses economic planning he is speaking as much from the heart as is Trudeau on Quebec. Broadbent imparts the impression that he believes what he is saying, rather than mouthing what someone else has told him to say for political gain. He does not lack for passions, but they are the intellectual formulations he has drawn from his reading and his youth in a working-class town, not the evangelical angers of his predecessors. His social democracy is pragmatic, almost comfortable, although no less bitterly opposed by many groups in Canada for that.

Broadbent has placed his stamp on every aspect of the federal NDP. He has succeeded in giving the national party an autonomy it lacked before his leadership, when the federal party was beholden to provincial associations for money, talent, and organization. He has put his own people—Sears, McNevin, and Grier—in places of authority within the party hierarchy. He has plucked from the wide stream of social democracy the issues on which he thinks the NDP should fight: a mixed economy, government planning, and a reformed tax system. He commands the loyalty and respect of the NDP caucus, leaning especially on Knowles and Bob Rae, M.P. for Broadview-Greenwood, who may succeed Broadbent as NDP leader. It is his party now, and when he enters a hall with the crowd chanting "We Want Ed," there is a warmth and an affection for him that would never have seemed possible in his early days in politics.

The NDP's 1980 election campaign was a rerun of the party's 1979 campaign effort. Like a late-night movie, it appealed to those who enjoyed the initial screening, but it did nothing for those unmoved the first time around.

The NDP campaign organizers understood the risks in trying the same kind of campaign in 1980. The decision to proceed along the same lines was taken at a twelve-hour election-planning-committee meeting in Room 301 of the House of Commons Centre Block on the day after the Government fell. By a fortuitous fluke, the meeting had actually been called for that day weeks before anyone knew that the Government would be defeated, and as a result, the party could start planning immediately for the campaign. (The same sort of miraculous coincidence occurred in 1979: an election-planning meeting had been scheduled for March 27, which turned out to be the day after Prime Minister Trudeau's decision to dissolve Parliament and call the May 22 election.) At the meeting, some of the senior members of the committee who had lived through the NDP campaigns of 1972 and 1974, warned their colleagues about boring the voters with a recycled campaign. They remembered the disappointing results in the 1974 campaign when the party ran lamely on a watered-down version of the 1972 "Corporate Welfare Bums" slogan. Everyone worried that the media would quickly label the NDP campaign a dud if not fed a steady diet of spicy, new fare.

Sears and members of Broadbent's personal staff, however, argued that insufficient time remained to develop new themes for the forthcoming campaign. They further maintained that in election campaigns parties can hope only to maximize existing advantages or to minimize liabilities; campaigns are too short to craft a new image for the leader or explain a batch of new policies. Finally, they reminded the committee of the party's general satisfaction with Broadbent's 1979 campaign. If, as the NDP suspected, the Liberals and Conservatives intended to crucify each other, why not pave the way to the New Jerusalem with a campaign of political virtue? To these arguments were added Broadbent's preference for the issues of the party's 1979 campaign. He felt most comfortable with them. They represented where he wanted to take the country and the party, and they had served the NDP well in the months leading to the election, especially the party's persistent critique of the Conservatives' muddled PetroCanada policy.

Discussion then turned to the NDP perennial strategic quandry: which of the other two parties posed the most serious political threat? As the third party in Canada, the NDP can seldom focus exclusively on one opponent; it must fight a national campaign on two fronts, an imperative made more pressing with each passing year as the Conservatives fade in Quebec and the Liberals decline in western Canada. Sears, among others, was convinced the Liberals were so far ahead that the NDP should make them the principal target. He was worried that the Liberals might unveil progressive policies during the campaign to create the impression of a leftward turn in Liberal thinking. (He turned out to be remarkably prescient.) That kind of Liberal shift would jeopardize marginally committed NDP voters on whom the party relied for making gains in Ontario. The NDP does best when the Liberals and Conservatives are evenly matched. If the Liberals were far ahead, the NDP must try to knock them down a peg, Sears reasoned.

Others, however, argued successfully that the NDP needed every Liberal vote it could get in western Canada, where the Conservatives were strong. Nor could the NDP ignore the Conservative Government, which fell after all on an NDP motion. The Conservatives were in power, and if the Liberals ran a poor campaign, the NDP could attract disaffected Conservatives who could not bring themselves to vote again for Trudeau. Finally, the strategy was set: the NDP would attack both parties in the national campaign, paying more attention to the Conservatives in western Canada and to the Liberals in Ontario.

In addition to myriad organizational headaches, the election planning committee also tackled several other tricky questions of strategy. The first was the decision about when to start the campaign. There was an underlying nervousness among those at the meeting about the public's reaction to the election call. A quick start would allow the NDP to explain immediately its reasons for defeating the Conservatives' budget. So rather than waiting until after the New Year to begin serious campaigning—as the Liberals did—Broadbent set off on a cross-country tour in the week before Christmas.

If Broadbent was to travel the high road while Clark and Trudeau scrapped in the gutter, the committee insisted that Broadbent avoid personal attacks on the other leaders. He followed this strategy throughout the campaign, apart from his lapse in calling Clark a fool in Sudbury. It would just not do for Broadbent— the man of integrity, sincerity, and intelligence in the NDP commercials—to be a political guttersnipe. Furthermore, the committee thought that the party, with its moralistic streak, would not stand for personal attacks, nor would the public like them. Personal attacks by one leader on another are devoured by the media, but the coverage of such attacks clouds a party's message on issues.

Finally, and most importantly, the party needed to settle on a media strategy. With funds provided by the Elections Act, the NDP spent vastly more money in the 1979 and 1980 campaigns than ever before on television and radio commercials. In 1979, the NDP spent $1.018 million on advertising, compared to $2.47 million for the Conservatives and $1.85 million for the Liberals. In 1980, the NDP had about $1.4 million to spend on radio and television. The NDP was still outgunned, but by selective concentration in key markets near the campaign's end, the NDP avoided in 1979 and 1980 the withering barrage of Conservative and Liberal commercials that used to hurt the NDP in campaigns before the latest amendments to the Elections Act. (In fact, the Conservatives insisted that the NDP spent more money on television advertising in Metropolitan Toronto in 1980 than did either of the other two parties.)

The NDP has also become extraordinarily professional in using television during campaigns. The NDP grasped the importance and vagaries of television later than the Conservatives and the Liberals did, but when the NDP awakened to the overwhelming importance of television in modern campaigning, it embraced the medium like a passionate lover. So television-oriented had the NDP become by 1979 that its campaign often appeared as little more than a string of "media events" featuring Broadbent at mines, mills, supermarkets, or senior citizen homes offering twenty-second snippets of NDP policy. It made for substantial exposure since the backdrops proved irresistible for television reporters, but the campaign looked lifeless to those following it on television. The election-planning committee opted for more traditional political rallies in 1980 to give the campaign the image of public enthusiasm it lacked in 1979.

For more than a year before the 1979 campaign, the party kept on staff a Montreal advertising professional, Mary Lynn Durrant, who prepared television material and a broadcast strategy for the campaign. She worked out of Broadbent's office, polishing his television technique, gathering film of him and assisting the party's advertising agency, Lawrence Wolf Advertising Limited.

Durrant and Wolf had fashioned commercials in 1979 that pleased the NDP election-planning committee. The commercials featured Broadbent unadorned, speaking directly into the camera. In that campaign, Broadbent was less well known than either Trudeau or Clark, so it made good sense to heighten his visibility. By the 1980 campaign, Broadbent's recognition factor was almost as high as those of Trudeau and Clark, and NDP polls showed that he was more favourably regarded by the electorate than his party was. The Conservatives and probably the Liberals were going to use negative advertising against each other, so the election-planning committee chose for 1980 the same kind of straightforward, serious commercials the party had used in 1979. The same format would also be a symbolic reminder that, while the other parties might be shifting their positions for partisan purposes, the steadfast NDP was not budging an inch.

Wolf, however, made his reputation in "competitive advertising," the art of direct comparison of your product to another. While accepting the need to concentrate on Broadbent, he wanted the leader to be more aggressive than in 1979, jabbing at Trudeau and Clark and their records. That clashed with the committee's desire to stay away from personal attacks. Wolf and Sears debated the strategy for ten days. What eventually emerged were advertisements featuring Broadbent talking about NDP issues with only brief criticisms of Trudeau and Clark, picking up his stump theme: "You've seen the Liberals. You've seen the Conservatives. Now, more than ever, it's time for the NDP."

One of the first batch of NDP commercials illustrated the technique of gently attacking both Trudeau and Clark while selling a positive NDP message. With only Broadbent on screen and the slogan "Ed Broadbent and the New Democrats" affixed to the end of the commercial, Broadbent's script read:

> Mr. Clark has been such a disappointment that it's easy to forget just how bad things were with Mr. Trudeau. For instance, Mr. Trudeau did almost nothing to make us self-sufficient in energy. It took the NDP to force Mr. Trudeau to create PetroCanada. Then, last fall, both he and Mr. Clark voted against our proposal that would have made PetroCanada number one in the industry. In this election, it's time to move forward, not backward.

Some of the NDP commercials were direct, upbeat explanations of party policy, again featuring only Broadbent.

> All of us want more for our children than we've had for ourselves. It makes me angry to see young Canadians unable to find jobs. Every Canadian should be able to work who wants to work. We've got to take the lead in developing our own economy. This can be done by transforming our resources into manufactured goods here at home. We should export finished products, not the resource. This is the way to create jobs for Canadians. Now, let's get on with it.

Broadbent's schedule was so arranged that he spent most of the time between Christmas and the new year working on the commercials. To get just the right shots of Broadbent, Wolf used long-range cameras and even knocked out the wall of a room during the hours of filming. The Toronto home of Stephen Lewis, former NDP leader in Ontario, was used for one location; the historic Grange House in Toronto for another. Poor Broadbent nearly melted filming a commercial in Grange House, where the central heating, television lights, and roaring fire in the fireplace combined to make the set unbearably hot. To ensure that the viewer focused on nothing but Broadbent in the five-minute, free-time commercials, Wolf blacked out everything else on the screen and shone a light only on Broadbent's face, while the leader talked earnestly about NDP policies in response to set-up questions asked by Wolf, sitting off-camera.

Wolf, a friendly, gregarious man, was delighted with the negative advertising produced for the Liberals by Red Leaf and for the Conservatives by Media Buying Services, whose offices are two throws of a stone from Wolf's in the sandblasted chic of Toronto's Yorkville district. Wolf may have built part of his reputation on "competitive advertising," but the ads he saw from the Liberals and Conservatives went too far. They had crossed the line from competitive advertising to negative advertising. As Wolf said one afternoon during the campaign:

> Most advertising people are full of shit. Most advertising has a certain contempt, a certain underestimation of the viewer that works to its detriment. There's this condescending attitude that you're talking to a moron, so, therefore, let's change the image all the time. Unless you have big pictures, little pictures, unless you're constantly shifting focus, you're going to lose the guy's attention. That's a lot of crap.
>
> What happens when you overproduce something? You've got too many things going on in a technical sense. You remember the technique, but you don't remember the content. The cleverness of the commercial overpowers the product. If you take Clark, who's a weak product anyway, and then overpower him, it doesn't enhance him, it buries him.
>
> Our strategy is really very simple. The other two parties are hiding their leaders. We're putting ours upfront. If you look at the Conservative and Liberal campaigns, it's the only advertising I've ever seen in the history of modern politics where the total focus of the advertising is on what's wrong with the other guy.
>
> Look at all the Liberal commercials, the subject is Clark. When you look at the Conservative commercials, the subject is Trudeau. That's really an assbackwards way to advertise. We're proud of our leader. We think he has something to say. He's a positive, rather than a negative option. We feel he's the best of three choices, rather than the worst of three evils.

Wolf's colourful denunciation of the tactics of the other parties was a trifle self-serving; the NDP themselves briefly joined their opponents in negative advertising. For part of the campaign, the NDP used what advertising people call "streeters," a collection of shots of ordinary people delivering the NDP message. It may take ten, or even twenty interviews to get a usable clip, and then the clips are run together to create the streeter. Any streeter must present the proper mix of people on the screen, so that viewers will be able to identify with the background, ethnic characteristics, or occupation of the faces on the screen. One NDP streeter ran this way:

> "Clark didn't keep one promise. Trudeau has the same characteristics as Clark. He reverses himself whenever he feels like it." "No, I don't trust Mr. Trudeau. It's clear to me that Trudeau hasn't known where he's going for about the last three or four years." "I think Trudeau could be a strong leader, but I think Trudeau is out of ideas." "I think Mr. Broadbent would be very responsive to the needs of Canadians." "Mr. Clark and Mr. Trudeau have both let us down actually."

Many rank-and-file New Democrats disliked the streeters. They found the commercials distasteful and contrary to the virtuous image the NDP was trying to achieve in the campaign. But their introduction gave a sharp edge to the NDP television strategy that both Sears and Wolf thought it needed.

In January 1980, on the eve of the party's television advertising campaign, Sears outlined the NDP's general strategy to party candidates and organizers in a confidential letter:

> After much discussion with the EPC [Election Planning Committee] and input from many provinces, we have come up with the following tactical approach:
> 1) Trust and integrity in leadership and government are assets for us this time, not only because of Ed's profile, but are also due to the party's reputation for keeping its promises.
> 2) We should deliver a positive message to voters, with a serious critique of the other two, but avoiding personal attack. While Clark and Trudeau are slanging away at each other, we will say, "Here is what the New Democrats pledge on the following issues, positively."
> 3) Both the old-line parties are competitors and our speeches, literature and advertising should take a balanced approach to them. Given Clark's unpopularity, it would be foolish to target the Tories alone. But, hammering the Liberal record exclusively may only solidify nervous Tory voters. . . .
> These are some of the general themes which will direct the national campaign and you will see them in the leader's tour and our media advertising.

The author of that letter, Robin Sears, was a most unlikely-looking member of the select group of backroom boys in Ottawa, whose advice shapes the warp and woof of politics. At twenty-nine, he was much the youngest of his breed, the son of a newspaperman, a disillusioned university student who wandered through Europe and North Africa for several years, an articulate young man with wire-rimmed glasses who could have passed for a university lecturer. He was born to social democracy: his grandfather Colin Cameron was a long-time NDP M.P. From his father, Val, one of the legendary wits of Canadian journalism, he developed an appreciation for the clever turn of phrase and a talent as an effective communicator. (In fact, the NDP put Sears up as their representative on television news specials during the campaign.) He is fascinated by political communication and knows the technology of modern politics, especially electronic gadgetry, as thoroughly as anyone in Ottawa. He joined the NDP in time for the 1974 election, working under federal secretary Cliff Scotton. When Scotton left to work in British Columbia, he recommended Sears as his replacement. At first, Sears' evident cockiness rankled older hands within the party who considered him a snotty upstart. But gradually his sheer competence at organization stilled the grumbling. He became one of Broadbent's closest advisors on matters of tactics and strategy, and was the daily link between the federal caucus and the party organization.

The NDP rank-and-file often treat party policy the way fundamentalist preachers approach the Scriptures: woe unto them who deviate from any chapter or verse. In addition, the NDP is a sprawling party, gathering together single-interest groups—gays, feminists, environmentalists—and union affiliates, university professors, farmers, practising politicians, and idealists (and ideologues) of every left-wing stripe. Keeping such disparate types content with the party leadership is a constant preoccupation of any NDP federal secretary. But Sears persevered with the tact he has developed on the job and the self-assurance he brought to it.

During the campaign, Sears occasionally joined Broadbent on his chartered plane (nicknamed FrigidAir by journalists), but mostly he remained in Ottawa at party headquarters. Only once did the NDP campaign get itself into trouble, and Sears played a crucial role in minimizing the negative consequences.

In mid-campaign, to the astonishment of the NDP (and the other parties, for that matter), foreign policy injected itself into the election. The Soviet Union had invaded Afghanistan, and in retaliation U.S. President Jimmy Carter proposed that nations boycott the Olympic Games in Moscow. Carter also urged other Western nations to join the United States in putting economic pressure on the Soviet Union. Broadbent immediately issued a tough anti-Soviet statement, the kind NDP leaders enjoy making to drive home the point that the NDP is not soft on communism. Broadbent condemned the invasion of Afghanistan, proposing that the Olympic Games be moved from Moscow. He said Carter deserved "100 per cent support" for his actions.

In British Columbia, Pauline Jewett, the M.P. for New Westminister-Coquitlam and the party's external-affairs critic, thought Broadbent had gone too far. "He's not speaking for me. We do not support military action or sabre-rattling," she said. Broadbent was not amused, nor were his advisors, who arranged for Broadbent and Jewett to patch the rift by telephone. But the real danger lay in the rank-and-file.

Political parties abhor divisions during election campaigns. The slightest crack can become an open breach, as Robert Stanfield learned to his chagrin in the Conservatives' 1974 campaign. Leading members of his party publicly questioned the party's call for wage-and-price controls. Many New Democrats thought Broadbent's "100 per cent support" comment was excessively fulsome. But Sears, sensing trouble, worked the telephone, contacting party members across the country to ensure that no further public statements were made by New Democrats restless with Broadbent's stance.

Sears also worried that foreign policy might begin motivating voters, especially after the mid-campaign revelation that officials at the Canadian embassy in Iran had successfully removed six American diplomats from the country after hiding them in the Canadian embassy. Foreign policy is a political nemesis for the NDP. Portions of the party's platform on foreign policy calling for a weaker commitment to NATO and NORAD are political liabilities. As a party that has never governed in Ottawa, the NDP is given little credibility on foreign affairs.

At the height of the interest in foreign affairs during the campaign, Broadbent postponed a scheduled press conference in northern Ontario because the media would have asked questions about foreign policy and the NDP wanted the issue to go away. At the same time, Sears asked the firm conducting the NDP polling to take a quick reading of the impact of foreign policy on the voters. The results came back within seventy-two hours: foreign policy was not swinging votes. With that grateful news the NDP returned to the issues of PetroCanada, energy policy, an industrial strategy, and Canadian nationalism—the pillars of the party's campaign—without political penalty.

The NDP polling firm, a fledgling company in Toronto called

Total Market Index, used a fascinating new technology to test voter reaction. The technology failed several times early in the campaign, to Sears' considerable annoyance, but when it worked properly, Sears could not have been more pleased. The technology eliminated a time-consuming step in the data-gathering process normally used by such firms. Instead of taking answers over the telephone, marking the answers on forms, and then collating the information for analysis, the TMI method allowed those taking the information over the telephone to put the results directly into a computer, where the results were analysed. This meant that the NDP could get back information to questions within forty-eight to seventy-two hours for a major survey.

The NDP restricted TMI's polling to Ontario, British Columbia, Saskatchewan, and Manitoba, because results from those provinces were all the party needed. The NDP pretends to be a national party, but it was not going anywhere in Quebec, New Brunswick, Prince Edward Island, mainland Nova Scotia, Alberta, and wide swaths of Ontario, and polling in those areas would only have confirmed the obvious. Polling is also exceedingly expensive, and despite the Elections Act, the NDP still has less money to spend on elections than the Conservatives or Liberals do. Until the final days of the campaign, the TMI surveys showed the Liberals holding their lead of nearly twenty points in Ontario. Only in the final week of the campaign did the Liberals begin to slip in Ontario. That trend consoled worried NDP organizers in that province, where the Liberals were the biggest obstacle to NDP success. In the west, the TMI data showed the NDP gaining in Manitoba, Saskatchewan, and British Columbia, a reading that was proven accurate on election night.

Some of those NDP gains in western Canada—especially in British Columbia—and some of the party's losses in Ontario pointed up the uneven success of the NDP's organizational link with the Canadian Labour Congress. The link grew from the NDP's frustration with the party's failure to do better in heavily unionized ridings. As a rule of thumb, the party gets about twenty-five per cent of the vote of organized labour. Similarly, NDP candidates from the union movement have an indifferent track record in federal politics. Across the country, the NDP would nominate union men and women, only to learn that the union rank-and-file did not always warm to one of their own. Six members of the NDP caucus are recent union members, but the rest are social workers, priests, small businessmen, professors, and lawyers: M.P.s who are sympathetic to but not themselves of the union movement.

Before the 1979 campaign, Broadbent encouraged the NDP-CLC link, believing in the western European model of aligning social democratic or socialist parties with the union movement. With much fanfare, the CLC leadership declared its fidelity to the NDP. In union towns, affiliated unions of the CLC set about trying to persuade the rank-and-file to support the NDP. There were telephone banks manned by union members, leaflets distributed everywhere, political seminars organized by the CLC, speeches by Broadbent to CLC conventions and, in the end, few political successes.

In 1980, the CLC was still working on the NDP campaign, but the CLC's tactics had changed. Instead of a fanfare of publicity, the CLC muted its public involvement. Union organizers tried to work directly in the plants through canvasses on the shop floor. The telephone banks were scrapped except in Windsor and Winnipeg. Again, however, the political results were indifferent. The NDP made gains in a handful of unionized ridings in the west, but the party lost five M.P.'s from Atlantic Canada and Ontario, and failed to crack Liberal strength in unionized cities such as Windsor, Sudbury, and Thunder Bay.

After the campaign, the CLC drafted a confidential report for its affiliates analysing the effectiveness of the CLC effort:

> The parallel campaign in the winter election was much better organized than the spring's. Both the CLC and affiliates learned from our first effort. Yet we are still only in the building stage. The majority of workers in Quebec and Alberta were *not* reached in any way. The majority of workers in other provinces were *not* reached by a true canvass. The majority were reached by a distribution. In absolute terms, then, the labour campaign did not succeed in its basic objective. However, in relative terms, it was a success.

Having switched from a telephone to a personal canvass in the plants, the CLC found itself with a shortage of qualified political organizers. The system required canvassers to follow up their initial contacts and to do more than just hand out leaflets—specially designed by the affiliated unions—encouraging workers to support the NDP.

The designation and training of a canvass organizer in

each local is where the system started to break down on a wide scale. (There were representatives and business agents who did little or nothing and thereby blocked the system. In some instances, this problem could be rectified by clear instructions from their officers and directors as to the priorities during an election. In other cases, it is more a question of the individual's incompetence or hostility.) The fault here can largely be laid at two causes: first, a lack of understanding of the importance of the role of the canvass organizer and, secondly, a shortage of time to identify and to train these people. Nevertheless, there was still an impressive list of people developed in this area. . . .

The weakness at the representative level for check-back were greatly increased by the absences of effective canvass organizers. The canvass organizers themselves were often guessing if a canvass, a distribution or nothing had been done. . . .

Nevertheless, the CLC remained committed after the election to more direct effort to help the NDP in future campaigns.

The 1980 election results were mildly disappointing for the NDP. With the Conservatives unpopular and the Liberals led by Trudeau, the NDP had hoped for more than thirty-two seats. Broadbent privately thought that the party could take forty. True, the NDP's 19.8 per cent of the popular vote brought the party tantalizingly close to the 20 per cent threshold the party has always sought. But in only two provinces did the NDP share of the popular vote rise significantly: by 4.2 per cent in British Columbia, where the increase paid off in three new seats, and by 3.7 per cent in Quebec, where the increase meant nothing. In Newfoundland, the NDP vote plummeted 14 per cent. Elsewhere, the gains and losses were marginal.

In western Canada, the NDP won all but four of its "A" ridings. That impressive showing was considerably aided in Saskatchewan and Manitoba by Liberals taking votes from entrenched Conservative incumbents. In Ontario, however, the NDP failed again to make an important breakthrough in the industrial centres, which hold the key to future national success for the NDP. With a leader from Ontario and a platform designed with Ontario's manufacturing industry in mind, the NDP still could not make gains. The party lost its three seats in northern Ontario, despite an increase in the popular vote, because the Conservatives collapsed in northern Ontario and many Conservatives bolted to the Liberals. The same movement occurred in Windsor: the NDP vote increased, but the Liberals held all three seats because so many Conservatives abandoned their party. The NDP's core vote in Ontario is just too small for the party to avoid being squashed when either of the larger parties has political momentum.

In Atlantic Canada, both NDP incumbents lost, leaving the NDP without a single M.P. in the five easternmost provinces— hardly a desirable state of affairs for a party that calls itself a national institution.

When the Conservatives won the 1979 election, New Democrats crowed about the irresistible decline of the Liberal Party. As the Liberals faded as a national party, so the NDP would rise until Canada possessed a two-party system of Conservatives and New Democrats. The return to power of the Liberals silenced that blather, and New Democrats were forced to devise a new myth in which to place their hopes. The fact remains that for all the party's efforts, the New Jerusalem is just a twinkle in the night.

~ 12 ~

The Desperation of Defeat

The exercise of power had not only taught the Conservatives many lessons, it forced them to run a campaign strikingly different from the one that brought them to power. In 1979, the Conservatives spoke with the rhetoric of an Opposition party but ran the final weeks of the campaign with the measured pace of a Government seeking re-election; in 1980, the Conservatives used the justificatory language of a Government but campaigned with the energy of an Opposition party trying to catch up.

Apart from the continuity of Clark's and Trudeau's attacks on each other, it often appeared in 1980 that the Conservatives and Liberals had traded scripts from the 1979 campaign. Clark, who spent the entire 1979 campaign telling Canadians to raise their expectations, entered the 1980 election warning of "tough times" and "hard decisions," the same sort of rhetoric Trudeau had used in the spring campaign to portray himself as the only leader with the strength required of a Prime Minister. Seven months later, it was Clark who depicted himself as the only leader with the political courage to make difficult decisions. Clark's speeches still exuded optimism that the nation's problems could be solved, but the solutions had been delayed until interest rates fell, the deficit was reduced, government spending curtailed, and the nation swallowed the higher energy prices needed to achieve self-sufficiency. Clark, having railed in 1979 against Trudeau's eleven years of broken promises, spent his 1980 campaign confronting accusations that he had not kept his word on economic and energy policies. Trudeau, who had spoken repeatedly about the crisis of national unity in 1979, avoided the subject for tactical reasons in 1980, leaving the subject to Clark, who insisted that his Government had done more to ease federal-provincial tensions in seven months than Trudeau in eleven years. Clark, often insulated from the media in 1979, was as approachable as a good book in the 1980 campaign. Instead, it was Trudeau who shunned the media until the final stages of his campaign, which was even more tightly controlled than Clark's in 1979.

Trudeau's campaign initially frustrated the Conservatives. They wanted a rerun of Trudeau's gunslinger approach of 1979 in which the Liberal leader deliberately drew as much attention to himself as possible. If Trudeau was not going to make himself an issue in the campaign, then the Conservatives would have to do the job for him, since antipathy to Trudeau's leadership was the Conservatives' best hope for re-election.

The Conservatives took less than a week to figure out the Liberals' game plan. On January 8, in Port Hawkesbury, Nova Scotia, and Alviston, Ontario, Clark began injecting mimickry of Trudeau and a string of jokes at Trudeau's expense into his standard campaign speech, knowing that the television networks (and the rest of the media, for that matter) would find in his animated attacks on Trudeau arresting film and good copy. In Alviston, he said:

> [Trudeau] is the only political leader in the history of this country, probably in the history of the world, whose slogan has been "Elect me and I will quit." Of course, you have to remember, he is the fellow who said in 1974 "Elect me and I will never introduce wage and price controls." . . . You know, one of the bills that they stopped from passing through the House of Commons was a bill that would have limited federal elections to forty-seven days. We know why they are against that. They can't get their platform together in forty-seven days. Instead of policy, what the Liberals have is a "peek-a-boo" campaign. They let Mr. Trudeau out for an hour a day and hope nobody sees him.
>
> Last year, you will remember he went around the country as the gunslinger. He was going to shoot anybody he could find, fight anybody in the House. Well, this year he has changed that. This year, he is the fugitive. And the whole theme of their campaign with the fugitive is to have him sneak in and out of town before anybody can notice.

Two days later in Toronto, Clark resumed his humorous attacks on the "peek-a-boo" campaign and the "fugitive."

> I hear, though, that they are changing their policy a little bit here in Metro, that they are planning another rally at the [Maple Leaf] Gardens. The doors are going to open at 6 p.m., the music will start at 7, the whole thing is going to be over by 10, then Pierre will speak at 11:30.

These sorts of attacks, delivered with Clark's improved sense of timing, attracted the media and amused his audiences everywhere except in Quebec. In Coaticook, Clark called Trudeau "*l'homme invisible*" and claimed that "*en mai dernier, le message libéral était très simple, c'était: Parle Fort, Pierre. Aujourd'hui c'est encore plus simple: Parle pas, Pierre.*" Several members of Clark's audience of about 450 persons tittered; the rest remained silent. What had worked for Clark in Nova Scotia and Ontario flopped in Quebec where voters did not appreciate the jests of an anglophone—and a Conservative to boot—against a native son adored by some and respected by most.

Clark struggled against Trudeau in Quebec like a heretic denouncing the Pope. So powerful was Trudeau's mystique and so entrenched was the Liberal Party in every corner of Quebec that Clark fared even worse than Stanfield had in attracting support. Under Stanfield, the Conservatives won 21.3 per cent of the votes in Quebec in the 1968 election, 17.4 per cent in the 1972 election, and 21.1 per cent in the 1974 election; under Clark, the Conservatives captured 13.4 per cent in the 1979 election and 12.4 per cent in the 1980 election.

On most Sundays throughout the campaign, Clark left Ottawa for a Quebec destination to begin his week of campaigning. He made more appearances in Quebec than in any province except Ontario, but he could not pick the Liberals' padlock on Quebec. He had certainly tried as Prime Minister to win favour for the Conservatives in Quebec and to demonstrate to Quebeckers that although the federal government was in the hands of a party with scanty support in Quebec, Ottawa could nonetheless take decisions to protect the French language and enhance the economic future of Quebec. When the Chouinard report was made public, recommending the introduction of bilingual air traffic control and disputing any notion that there were risks in the use of both English and French in air traffic control, Clark immediately accepted the recommendations, ending a sorry chapter of misinformation and bigotry that had grievously wounded Confederation. Clark withdrew a Liberal bill that would have given the federal government the authority to hold referendums on constitutional matters because he believed that the bill was an affront to Quebeckers. He had refused to engage in verbal feuds with the Parti Québécois Government, knowing that the Conservatives had neither the eminent spokesmen nor the resources to win a struggle for popularity with the PQ, and also feeling that a less hostile attitude in Ottawa towards the PQ would deprive the "yes" forces of a convenient target in the referendum on negotiating sovereignty-association. He had appointed a Quebecker as Clerk of the Privy Council and instructed all his ministers to hire at least one francophone for their personal staffs. He had tenaciously employed his imperfect but serviceable French. When he struggled for the right word in French he turned for help to his bilingual wife, Maureen McTeer, or smiled and inserted an English word into his French sentences. He had found a handful of attractive candidates to contest the 1980 election: de Cotret in Berthier-Maskinongé, Paul Arsenault in Gaspé, former Union Nationale Cabinet Minister Marcel Masse in LaBelle, Conservative Party president in Quebec Marcel Danis in Saint Hyacinthe, and two Union Nationale MLAs Fernand Grenier in Megantic-Compton-Stanstead, and Armand Russell in Shefford. All were defeated.

Clark was running against Trudeau and his own party's sorry history in Quebec. The prolonged estrangement between Quebec and the Conservative Party had been broken only in 1958 when Union Nationale Premier Maurice Duplessis' election machine, temporarily placed behind the Conservatives, won fifty Quebec seats for Diefenbaker. But the estrangement in every election since World War I had so enfeebled the Conservatives that they were forced to rely upon many Union Nationale organizers for their 1980 campaign, a sign of desperation since the Union Nationale was nearly extinct by 1980. Only in a few pockets of Quebec did a *bleu* tradition still linger with sufficient force to offer the Conservatives any hope of victory, but Trudeau's hold on the hearts and minds of Quebeckers rendered the Conservatives' effort fruitless even in those regions. Trudeau's reputation may often have been battered in English Canada since he became Liberal leader in 1968, but in the intervening years his reputation in Quebec had gone from strength to strength. In the curious ways of Quebec politics, Trudeau's electoral position in Quebec was solidified by the election of René Lévesque as Premier of Quebec, since Quebeckers had chosen their two most articulate political leaders for Ottawa and Quebec City, sensing that from the dialectical relationship between the two men and the points of view they represented would emerge a stronger Quebec. It was the reaction of a permanent minority group within Canada, entrusting its support to the two men who could best protect the minority's interests in their respective levels of government. In this politics of extended family, Clark was an outsider, handicapped by his party's anemic presence in Quebec, by the doleful legacy of Riel, by conscription, by Diefenbaker's shoddy treatment of French Canadian ministers, and by the rump within the party that voted against the Official Languages Act.* Quebec's stubborn fidelity to the Liberals prevented Stanfield from forming the Government in 1972 and Clark from winning a majority government in 1979. The province gave the Conservatives one of seventy-five seats in 1980, the Conservatives' worst performance in Quebec since 1945.

Quebeckers' perception of the role of government is different from that of English Canadians; and the Conservatives' long stretch in Opposition had hindered the party's understanding of that perception. Allan Gregg had outlined the problem in a December 1977 memorandum to Lowell Murray:

> When asked what in their view is the purpose of government, English Canadians tend to respond by stating: "to make laws" or "to represent my views" or "to provide for order." In Quebec, the response tends to be "to build roads" or "to provide jobs" or "to protect us." The difference then appears to be that English Canadians tend to view government from a leadership orientation while French Canadians view government as a distributive or allocative (ie. giving or providing things). . . . We [the Conservatives] are not the government and therefore cannot give tangible "things" . . . [and] there is a perception that our party has displayed a historical antipathy or misunderstanding of Quebec and therefore cannot give "concern" or protection. . . . In short, it would seem that even if voters understood and agreed with [our] propositions, they ignore their content because the very fact that Conservatives are articulating them undermines their credibility.

---

*For an excellent analysis of the Conservatives' troubled history in Quebec, see Marc La Terreur, *Les Tribulations des Conservateurs au Québec* (Presses de l'Université Laval, 1973).

Clark, like Stanfield, campaigned extensively in Quebec for two reasons. The first obviously was to win the handful of seats that might make the difference between victory and defeat, or between a majority and a minority government in the election. The second was to convince English Canadians that the Conservatives were a national party, capable of winning seats everywhere in Canada, including Quebec. The importance of campaigning in Quebec to influence English Canadian votes was outlined in a January 1978 memorandum on campaign strategy by Allan Gregg:

> Quebec, of course, creates particular problems for our party. While we know that we cannot win a large majority of the seats, I am convinced that creating the "impression" that we have a good chance of winning Quebec seats is vital to our winning seats in metropolitan English Canada. We are therefore caught between an all-out, and perhaps wasteful effort in Quebec, and waging a low-key campaign in Quebec and at the same time risking seats in English Canada.

Clark, therefore, plugged away in Quebec, although he dropped the mimickry and personal attacks on Trudeau. In all his Quebec appearances, Clark warned Quebeckers that their province was too dependent on foreign supplies of oil, but in Quebec, as elsewhere, voters did not see or accept the link between higher oil prices and self-sufficiency. Instead of focusing on self-sufficiency, the voters' attention was riveted on the more immediate higher prices. Those listening to Clark's call for "fundamental change" decided that if fundamental change meant sharply higher energy prices, they wanted none of it.

In this as in other matters Clark's misreading of his 1979 election mandate persisted in the 1980 campaign; he continued to believe that his government had been given a mandate for sweeping change, and his rhetoric reflected his conviction. At his first rally after the Christmas break, he told an Ottawa audience:

> Real changes are needed to protect our standard of living and to protect our quality of life. Real changes are needed to ensure the future prosperity of this country. . . . Only this government is prepared to make those real changes.

A week later, in Halifax, Clark put his case even more strongly.

> If we as a people are going to maintain the standard of living to which Canadians have become accustomed, if we

are going to improve the quality of life . . . then we are going to have to face some basic changes in the way we approach our national problems. . . . We are going to have to be prepared to face reality today in order to guarantee security tomorrow. That, in my judgement, was the mandate that my government received in May 1979. It was a mandate to bring some fundamental changes to the way that governments had approached the possibilities and potential of this nation.

In the last week of the campaign, the rhetoric had not changed. In a speech summarizing his campaign themes to the Canadian Club in Vancouver on February 12, Clark said:

I was elected because of a widespread sense that some very fundamental changes were needed in the conduct of the nation's business. As a government, we share that desire for change and, indeed, we have acted on that desire for change. . . . There is no question that while we made some mistakes, as a new government will, we also accepted that our fundamental mandate received May 22 was to bring a fundamental sense of change to the attitude the Ottawa government took to the economy, to energy, to the nature of the nation, to the role of individuals in this nation. We got those changes started. . . . We didn't try to hide anything. We put our changes up front. We spelled out the costs. We told Canadians what we were trying to do, why we were trying to do it. Fortunately, from a political point of view, events have helped to prove how right we were in some of the policies we put forward.

"Fundamental changes," "facing the hard realities," "tough decisions," "changing the direction of the country," "Real Change Deserves A Fair Chance": these phrases, while still emphasizing the need for change, were removed in spirit from the optimism of the Conservatives' 1979 campaign, when the election of a new Government was supposed to free the shackles imposed by the Liberals on Canada's potential. The theme of the nation's potential still ran through all of Clark's 1980 campaign speeches, but apparently the road to its achievement was going to be more tortuous than Clark had suggested in the 1979 campaign. The switch from Opposition to Government, which had shown the Conservatives the intractability of some problems and the constraints of power, forced Clark to set his achievements in the longer time-frame usually favoured by Governments, rather than to make promises of short-term improvement preferred by Opposition parties. In 1979, Trudeau argued that although Canada's economy had performed better than those of the other countries of the Western world, Canadians would still have to restrain their demands and lower their expectations to guarantee future prosperity. Voters, the majority of whom prefer benefits today to pleasures tomorrow, reacted as negatively to this unwelcome message from Trudeau as they did later to the same message from Clark.

The lessons of politics are easily forgotten. In the year and a half before the 1979 election, the Conservatives discovered from their polling that a deep sense of uncertainty about the future co-existed uneasily in the minds of many voters with an optimism that problems could be solved with strong political leadership. In the last half of the 1970s, Canadians worried that the unbroken prosperity of the post-war era was threatened by inflation, slow growth, and an increasingly unstable international economic order, especially in the energy field. This uncertainty was particularly acute among the affluent middle-class, who feared that the future would rob them of their prosperity and cloud their children's prospects. To these economic uncertainties was added the unsettled future of Confederation—the place of Quebec within the federal system and the shifting balance of power between the central and western Canadian provinces. There had been a surfeit of change in the late 1970s, and much of the nation's uncertainty flowed from the possibility, even the probability, that the future would bring even more dramatic changes than the recent past. In such a frame of mind, Canadians were unlikely to accept either Trudeau's call for lower expectations or Clark's summons to support "real change," since both evoked an unsettling vision of the immediate future that confirmed the nation's existing uncertainty.

In Clark's case, "real change" meant a continuation of Conservatives' policies such as higher energy prices that many voters rejected, especially those only marginally attached to the Conservative Party. These voters had not warmed to Trudeau's call for lower expectations in 1979, preferring instead the optimism of the Conservatives. Seven months later they found that Clark was also warning of "tough times" and "hard decisions" that required sacrifices many voters were unwilling to believe were necessary. They were prepared to see other oxen gored, but not their own. Those employed could support cutbacks in unemployment insurance; Ontarians favoured paying Albertans substantially less than the world price for crude oil; a majority of Canadians could countenance a reduction in the spending of the federal government, as long as the cuts did not affect programs that touched their lives. But if sacrifice meant higher taxes and more expensive gasoline for everyone, if that was what "real change" was about, then voters preferred the party offering a rosier vision of the future.

The call for sacrifice might have been successfully made by a leader who inspired confidence, but by 1979 Canadians had seen too many reversals of policy and had experienced too many disappointments with Trudeau to accept his entreaties. And Clark, beset by his reputation for breaking promises and plagued by his own public image, was a dubious personification of the leadership required to educe sacrifices from his fellow-countrymen.

Clark had barely begun his campaign when the question of broken promises was thrown in his face. From his first press conference on the day after his government collapsed to the end of the campaign, the image of broken promises haunted his campaign and diminished his credibility as a leader. In his first lengthy interview of the campaign, he was told by the interviewer: "A lot of people, sir, would agree that the things you did or didn't say during those six months [in office] don't entitle you to govern anymore. The embassy question for one. The change of direction on PetroCanada. The specifics of the budget." In his next interview, at a radio station in St. John's, the question arose again: "Getting back to the change in some of these policies that bear mention, does this not really destroy some of your credibility in this particular campaign? I mean, six months later you are on the road [and] you are saying something completely different." Two days later, he confronted the same allegation in an interview with the *London Free Press*: "But in preferring to emphasize the proposals that you started on, the public has the impression at least that your young administration was reversing itself on many issues." So it went throughout the campaign; the image of broken promises had assumed a life of its own.

In some fields, the image of broken promises was unfair to the Conservatives. They had attacked the deficit, increased spouses' allowances, begun to improve the grain transportation network, presented both freedom-of-information and parliamentary-reform proposals, offered a form of tax relief for homeowners, and designed an energy policy to move the country towards self-sufficiency in oil; all initiatives that flowed from promises of the

1979 campaign. But the Jerusalem embassy fiasco, the confusion over PetroCanada, the jettisoned $2-billion tax cut, high interest rates, and sharply increased energy prices created an image that Clark could not shake.

More damaging than the individual broken promises was the impression they imparted that the Conservatives, and Clark in particular, did not know how to govern the country. Such an impression would have been damaging for any government, but it was especially injurious to one so recently elected to office after a lengthy stretch in Opposition. This impression of incompetence was embodied in Clark's public image: a nice fellow, a bit out of his depth, and willing to make any promise or statement for political gain.

Inevitably, Clark was forced to confront himself, or rather the public's image of him, during the campaign. At first, he shrugged off the question of how he evaluated the political cost of his own image: "That is the most difficult question I have to face. And I guess I don't have one. I don't have a perception of it. . . . I don't hear all the jokes. I suppose I would not want to. But as a phenomenon, it's there. This is a highly cynical age." As the weeks wore on and the polls did not budge, he became frustrated and angered by the question: "If I'm beaten, that's all I'll be beaten by. We certainly won't be beaten by performance, because our performance is a good one," he said in Vancouver. The image problem was partly physical. The double chin, the awkward gait, the unnatural gestures of his hands, the nervous laugh, the mannerisms of a man affecting a more senior age—these were all captured and magnified by the relentless exposure of Clark on television. But the image also related to leadership, to controversial policies rejected or poorly understood and to the lack of intangible qualities of leadership which voters demand in those who ask for their support.

Ever since he became leader of the Conservative Party, Clark had struggled to convey an impression of inner strength to the electorate. Everything the Conservatives knew about the public's view of Clark from their intensive polling before the 1979 election and the reaction he generated when he travelled led to the conclusion that he was perceived as honest, diligent, and concerned, but also as weak, vacillating, and incapable of managing crisis situations. He had governed as Prime Minister with this image always in his mind, staking out firm positions and sticking to them even when they were wrong or politically costly, because he thought that nothing could be more damaging to him and to his Government than giving more credence to the public impression of his weakness. The call for "real change," "tough decisions," "facing the hard reality," was part of that four-year struggle to demonstrate the fortitude and vision that Canadians had never been persuaded he possessed. In the last three weeks of the campaign, he increasingly drew a comparison between his own leadership and Trudeau's, desperately hoping in the waning hours of his Government, he might yet be appreciated as a leader with the strength the country needed. He told a television interviewer:

> To the degree that leadership is an issue, leadership is not just a matter of appearing on camera, important as that is. Leadership is also a matter of being able to establish priorities and manage people. . . . Things that went wrong during the Trudeau years went wrong precisely because there had been a failure at the centre to be able to bring people together and point them in the direction where they could take the country. And I think we have been much more successful, not only in attracting good people but in keeping them and in getting them working together. That . . . is my definition of what leadership should be.

In Saskatoon, at one of his final rallies of the campaign, he invited Canadians to compare his leadership to Trudeau's: "Pierre Trudeau may want to be known for the Liberals he has driven away; I am quite happy to be known for the Conservatives I have brought together."

Clark made marginal headway with his image problem after fate handed the Conservatives an issue that they clutched with the desperation of a drowning man. The issue was foreign policy, an unlikely intruder into a Canadian election campaign. Foreign policy has seldom quickened the hearts of Canadian voters, and in the 1980 campaign the issue did not, according to polls by all three parties, win many votes for Clark, but it at least opened a few minds to what the Conservatives were saying on other issues.

None of the parties intended to talk about foreign policy when they plotted their early strategies for the 1980 campaign. But the Soviet Union's invasion of Afghanistan in December and U.S. President Jimmy Carter's retaliatory actions against the USSR, including a call for a boycott of the Olympic Games in Moscow, forced the other nations of the Western alliance to respond to Carter's initiatives. On January 10, Clark outlined a series of steps that Canada was prepared to take to express its displeasure with the Soviet invasion, including tightened controls on high technology exports, restrictions on scientific and cultural exchanges, and a halt to export credits and negotiations towards a consular agreement. Clark also pledged that Canada would not take advantage of Carter's ban on additional U.S. grain shipments to the Soviet Union by selling more Canadian grain to that country. On the Olympic Games, Clark said that Canada "questioned the appropriateness of holding the Olympic Games in Moscow." The next day, Clark told a press conference that he favoured moving the Games from Moscow, but he added: "We are not contemplating boycotting the Olympic Games." At his press conference a week later, held after the International Olympic Committee had reaffirmed its intention to hold the Games in Moscow, Clark repeated his earlier position: "My personal preference is not for a boycott. I have made that very clear. My personal preference is for a change in the site of the games. I intend to continue to impress that preference upon representatives of the Olympic Committee."

The Olympic boycott continued to receive considerable publicity since the United States kept pressing its allies and the Third World countries for support. Not only did the Conservatives believe that Canada should support the United States, but they thought it made good political sense to do so. The Conservatives' campaign on domestic affairs had not budged the polls since the beginning of the campaign; perhaps by injecting foreign policy into the campaign the Conservatives could gain ground on the Liberals. On January 22, External Affairs Minister Flora MacDonald ordered three Soviet diplomats to leave Canada for having used the Soviet embassy in Ottawa as a base for espionage against the United States. Although the announcement looked suspiciously as though it had been designed to influence the election, MacDonald insisted that the timing was coincidental, that the investigation had been going on for sixteen months. Three days later, on Friday, January 25, Clark began to hint that Canada might take a tougher stand on the Olympic boycott. "I am prepared to consider very seriously the question of a boycott if there is not a decision taken on the site, but I think at this stage that the site question is not dead. The possibility of moving the site is not a closed possibility." That afternoon, however, the Cabinet decided to support a Canadian boycott of the Games. The decision was taken knowing that Clark was to give a major speech on foreign policy about forty-eight hours later to a Ukrainian Independence Day rally at Massey Hall in Toronto. The Ukrainians, the majority of whom were bitterly anti-Soviet and staunch supporters of the Conservative Party, would provide the ideal audience for a hard-line speech on foreign policy. Clark's speech, full of the rhetoric of the Cold War, described the struggle between "two systems, one which reveres freedom, and the other which would stamp freedom out." After extolling his Government's commitment to increased military spending, Clark finally turned to the boycott. "In an ideal world, international sport should be separate from international politics, but the Soviet Union does not separate sport from politics. It was the same Soviet government that is inviting Canadian athletes to Moscow which sent Soviet troops to Afghanistan. They knew they had the games when they sent the troops. They expected the West to be weak. We shall not be weak."

The day after Clark's Cold War speech, Jean Pelletier, Washington correspondent for the Montreal newspaper *La Presse*, broke the story that the Canadian embassy in Tehran had spirited six U.S. diplomats out of Iran. A spasm of joyous reporting exploded in Canadian newspapers, and for several days thereafter newspapers recounted the details of the Canadian coup and the outpouring of American good-will towards Canada. Clark wisely refrained from trying to grab the credit for the coup; such an effort would have seemed indecently partisan and would have worked against him. But Canada's action in Iran kept foreign affairs in the headlines and provided tangible evidence, even to his sternest critics, that Clark had skilfully handled a subtle bit of diplomacy. If Clark could not take credit for the coup, he could at least use the coup to find a more sympathetic hearing on other issues. Believing that Canada's action in Iran had temporarily given the Conservatives more credibility, Clark redoubled his efforts to explain Conservative policies in other fields, arguing that in making hard and often unpopular decisions "events have proven that we were right."

Foreign policy helped the Conservatives, but it was not enough to overcome the enormous Liberal lead. If Clark had established a reputation for vision in foreign affairs, he might perhaps have sounded more plausible talking about the Soviet threat to world peace. But nothing that Clark had ever done led to the conclusion that he was raising foreign affairs for any other reason than its partisan appeal in a Canadian election campaign that he was losing. By the final week of the campaign, having exhausted the electorate's attention span with foreign affairs, Clark had returned to his original campaign themes, asking for a fair chance to continue making "real changes" in domestic policy.

Only eight days of campaigning remained before election day. Joe Clark sat in his room at the Hotel Vancouver, surrounded by his closest aides and the organizers of his tour: Neville and Gillies; press secretary Jock Osler; Ian Green, Clark's executive assistant; Peter Sharpe, Clark's tour co-ordinator; Brad Chapman and Art Lyon, Clark's wonderfully efficient co-ordinators of tour logistics (fondly nicknamed the Wagonmaster and the Assistant Wagonmaster by journalists). Others wandered in and out, looking as cheerless as the weather. A blanket of fog hung over the Lower Mainland. The window panes were streaked with rain. Everyone was tired, and a few were sick, victims of a flu that had struck about a third of those on Clark's plane.

The day had gone badly. In the morning, Clark had been driven to the airport for a flight to Campbell River on Vancouver Island. He had waited on board for forty-five minutes, hoping forlornly that the fog might lift. Finally, the pilot had conceded defeat to the elements, and Clark had been taken back to the hotel, where he had spoken by a telephone hook-up to his supporters gathered in Campbell River. The journalists who had crowded into the hotel room to hear his telephone speech had given him a standing ovation in jest when he had completed his remarks, the only dash of humour in an otherwise exasperating day.

While the fog continued to shroud the city, Clark and his staff pondered the remainder of the day. The original itinerary called for Clark to fly from Campbell River to Prince Rupert, about 850 kilometres north of Vancouver, for an evening rally. It was now 4:30 p.m., and the pilot reported that the plane could take off, but if the fog did not clear, the plane could not return to Vancouver after the rally in Prince Rupert. Even if he left immediately, Clark would still arrive an hour late in Prince Rupert, and the party had neither booked hotel accommodation in Prince Rupert nor made alternative arrangements to stay overnight in another city in case the fog persisted in Vancouver. Clark polled his staff; none of them wanted to go. Apart from logistical problems, everyone needed rest, including Clark, who had been campaigning at an exhausting pace since New Year's. The Prince Rupert rally would be held far too late to be reported on the national newscasts. Even the British Columbia television stations would not be able to get their film processed in time for an evening newscast. It was Saturday, and only a handful of newspapers published Sunday editions, so a rally in Prince Rupert would receive only a few scattered inches of coverage across Canada. Skeena riding, which included Prince Rupert, had been won by the NDP in 1979 and by the Liberals in

1974. The Conservatives had finished third in both elections and would probably do so again in 1980.

Joe Clark listened attentively to his advisors' counsel, then announced that he would take his chances on the weather and go to Prince Rupert. If there was any chance, however slim, that his presence might help the Conservatives capture Skeena, then he must go. The Conservatives had pledged financial help for the construction of a grain-handling terminal in Prince Rupert, and perhaps that promise could be parlayed into votes. An hour later, he was airborne, glancing down at the thick layers of clouds, pierced only by mountain peaks, their snow reflecting the soft purple of the twilight sky.

His advisors were correct. Only a handful of Canadians outside Prince Rupert heard about Clark's speech to about 500 Conservatives that Saturday night. The speech came too late for the deadlines of most of the journalists, and it did not prevent the Conservative candidate in Skeena from finishing a predictable third. Instead, the trip was for Joe Clark, who, for all the mistakes he made in office, could turn to his accusors at the end of the campaign and ask whether anyone else in the party could have campaigned with more furious intensity, doggedness, and even dignity for sixty-six backbreaking, mind-wrenching days to salvage a measure of respect for the Conservative Party.

It was not an easy campaign. Clark had everywhere battled his own image reflected in the cracked mirror of television. He had taken refuge in the strategy of leaders with an image problem; he had exposed himself to as many people as possible in the campaign, hoping that exposure would soften the negative image. He had campaigned for twelve to fourteen hours a day, shaking hands, speaking up to four times a day, appearing on local television programs and submitting himself to the uncertain mercies of radio hot-line shows. "Hello, it's Joe Clark here," he said brightly on a hot-line show in Niagara Falls. "I want to speak to the Prime Minister," replied the caller. "I am the Prime Minister," said Clark. "No, you're not," came the reply. He appeared before all kinds of audiences, including student crowds. He tried to read a button worn by a student at York University but could not make out the words. "It says, 'Save PetroCanada, Sell Clark'," shouted the student.

He had occasionally let his tongue run ahead of his thoughts, making statements that sounded portentous but were, in fact, ridiculous. Early in the campaign, he drew an indirect link between the dissolution of Parliament and the Soviet invasion of Afghanistan. Then he exulted in the energy potential of potatoes in

Charlottetown: "Oil, by its very nature, runs out. But, ladies and gentlemen, potatoes are forever."

Several times, he was forced to deal with mistakes made by other members of his party. An official at Conservative head-quarters inadvertently released details of the Conservatives' intention to double the tax credit for mortgage interest and property tax in the first year, since the election had prevented Parliament from enacting the measure in time for the 1979 taxa-tion. It was a minor slip, but it cost Clark an opportunity of making the announcement himself. Then Finance Minister John Crosbie hinted that if world oil prices moved up sharply, the federal government might have to raise domestic oil prices more rapidly than the schedule of increases in the Government's still-born agreement with Alberta. Clark met Newfoundland Premier Brian Peckford for what was supposed to be a headline-grabbing reaf-firmation of Clark's pledge to give coastal provinces control of offshore resources. Instead, Peckford turned to journalists after Clark had left and said he wanted the agreement in writing before the end of the campaign, an impossible demand.

The harder Clark campaigned, the more frequently a contrast was drawn between his own labours and the discouraging polls. It was frustrating enough to start a campaign twenty points behind, but when the public polls did not budge throughout the campaign and the final Gallup Poll, published on the Saturday before the vote, showed the Conservatives still trailing by twenty points, Clark was given an additional burden to carry. No matter how enthusiastic his audiences, no matter how effectively he delivered his speeches, the reporting of his campaign read like an obituary column. The polls may have contributed to the sympathy felt for him personally by non-partisan observers watching him struggle defiantly against the fate the polls foretold. But the polls tagged his campaign with a loser's image that disheartened his followers.

The wildly erroneous Gallup Poll on the last Saturday of the campaign, which showed the Liberals with a twenty-point lead (they won the election by ten points), threw Conservative head-quarters into a flap. To counter the depressing news, Conserva-tive campaign director Paul Curley took the unprecedented step of publishing a press release criticizing the Gallup Poll and providing information from the Conservatives' own polls which predicted a much closer election result than Gallup. Arriving in Toronto with Clark on Saturday night, chief-of-staff William Neville called Allan Gregg at home and implored him to come to Clark's hotel to explain the Conservatives' numbers to sceptical members of the media. Reluctantly, Gregg agreed and was immediately badgered for clarification by reporters at a late-evening press briefing, which ended when Curley, who was furious when he learned of Neville's request to Gregg, arrived at the briefing and cut off further questions, saying, "Come on, Gregg, since I pay your bills, can I see you for a few minutes." The briefing, hastily organized and ill-advised, was a final sign of the Conservatives' desperation. Sitting a block away at a Liberal party celebrating the end of their campaign, Keith Davey was shown a copy of Curley's press release. He shook his head, and his face broke into a sad smile; he, too, had known the despair of impending defeat in his long career.

In the final week, Clark campaigned with passion and dignity, nurturing hope within himself that he might still become the Harry Truman of Canadian politics. His audiences were large and exuberant, especially at his closing rallies of the campaign in Niagara Falls and the Toronto suburb of Etobicoke. More than 4,000 Conservatives greeted him in Etobicoke, a larger crowd than he had attracted in the same building in the last week of the 1979 campaign. "Think very deeply about which leader you can trust before voting Monday. More than ever before, Canada needs an honest government that will look to the future. . . . [The Liberals] want a blank cheque for policies they won't debate and priorities they won't discuss. . . . I ask you to think hard about energy and energy security. I ask you to think about deficits. We took tough decisions to face all these problems," he cried. He drove himself relentlessly: to Quebec for a day of campaigning for LaSalle and de Cotret, back to Toronto for a breakfast meeting with his candidates, and on to Thompson, Manitoba, for a rally squeezed into his schedule because at the last moment he thought it might make a difference in the riding.

He went home to Alberta to await the nation's verdict, his eyes red and his face puffy from fatigue. In Calgary, at his last rally of the campaign, he was joined by Alberta Premier Peter Lougheed, appearing with Clark for the first time in the campaign. With the election clearly lost, Lougheed praised Clark disingenuously as a "tough negotiator, who now, more than ever, has my respect and admiration."

On election night, Clark awaited the returns in a motel not far from the arena where he had heralded the birth of his Government on May 22, 1979. He had never allowed himself to become discouraged in the campaign, and he still hoped that if Atlantic Canada did not change, and if the Conservatives gained seats in the West to offset those lost in Ontario, the party might win a minority government.

He was handed the returns from Newfoundland, where the Conservatives thought that their promise of provincial control of offshore resources would win seats. The Conservatives were holding their two seats; elsewhere in the province the Liberals were piling up huge majorities. "They're not voting on issues down there," he remarked. Then, the returns were relayed to him from the Maritimes: Liberal gains and Conservative losses. He knew his dreams were shattered when Secretary of State David MacDonald conceded defeat in the Prince Edward Island riding of Egmont. "It's going to be a long night," Clark said simply.

~ 13 ~

The Second Coming

About 400 people had shuffled up the long hill, through the gently falling snow, towards the meeting hall at the curling club to warm themselves with chowder and the presence of Pierre Trudeau. Inside, they had stamped their feet, shaking the snow from their boots, unwrapped themselves, and found places at the long tables to await his arrival. Along both sides of the hall, groups of women attended to cauldrons of soup, ladling their contents into bowls carried to the tables by cheerful residents of Dalhousie, New Brunswick.

The hall was full now, and looking from the entrance down the hill, one could see Trudeau starting his ascent. He stopped to talk to a clutch of school children, whose fathers probably worked in the aging paper mill that loomed in the distance, shooting funnels of steam through its chimneys into the crisp, mid-January air. Perhaps Trudeau had even met some of their fathers when he toured the plant in the morning, a tour that had been more for the benefit of the television cameras than their fathers. The mayor of Dalhousie, the chain of office around his neck, was waiting in front of the city hall halfway up the hill, and Trudeau stopped to chat with him, too, and to sign Dalhousie's book of honour.

A rustle of anticipation gave way to applause when he finally entered the hall. He removed his fur hat and coat, waved in acknowledgement and started down the centre aisle, shaking hands along the way, until he sat at a table in the middle of the room, ate his chowder and made conversation with those around him. This was the Liberal campaign—a "people-oriented," concerned Trudeau, mingling with his fellow Canadians.

For the purposes of political packaging, Trudeau was now just another member of the Liberal "team." That meant not one but five speeches on this seventh day of the Trudeau campaign. Before Trudeau spoke, the good citizens of Dalhousie had to hear from Maurice Harquail, M.P. for Restigouche; Joe Daigle, Liberal leader in New Brunswick; Roméo LeBlanc, the former Liberal Fisheries Minister and the federal party's doyen in New Brunswick, and Newfoundland Liberal leader Don Jamieson. Just before Trudeau began his remarks, an aide propped a written text on the podium. For the first minute or two, while he thanked the women for the lunch and said how pleased he was to be in Dalhousie, Trudeau did not glance at the text. But when he lauded the town's paper mill for having been declared the safest paper mill in Canada in 1978, he read from the text and he never stopped consulting it for the next fifteen minutes. After five minutes, his voice was droning.

"My friends, when you look at the damage they [the Conservatives] did in six months, I think the people of Canada will thank God that we didn't give them more time to do more damage," he said with the intonation of a Gregorian chant.

"I tell you now that we won't promise to solve all your problems, nor to make you all rich overnight, but we will promise to do certain things and we'll do what we say we'll do, but more important, we'll do it well. Thank you very much."

For seven days, Trudeau's speeches had been like that: limp, passionless, recited from a text that listed the failures of the Clark Government. Not that his audiences seemed to object; they had come to see him, not to listen to every nuance of his speeches. His presence, rather than his words, seemed sufficient to satisfy their curiosity about the man who had been the central figure in the nation's politics for more than a decade.

Trudeau gave a similar speech the next day at the University of New Brunswick near Saint John. He ate in the students' cafeteria where the television cameras left him in peace after capturing the "event" on film. Then he walked into a jammed lecture hall, looked down at the text on the podium, and began reading about the Conservatives' regressive budget, the unfairness of the eighteen-cents-per-gallon excise tax on gasoline, high interest rates, the dangerous dismantling of PetroCanada, all policies which "are threatening the economic health of the Maritimes." He concluded, "The Conservatives have failed miserably in managing the economy, in creating jobs, in heading us towards energy security. The conclusion is very clear in many people's minds.

After six months of confusion, ineptitude, and abandoned promises, it's time to give Canada a chance." Having arrived at the end of his text, he said, "Thank you very much," smiled, waved, and left the hall.

Near the end of his remarks, Trudeau had said, "The budget and the policies that we will bring in, if we are elected on February 18, will tackle the serious issues in a far different way than I've shown Mr. Clark to have done." What did he mean? No one knew, and no one could find out, certainly not the members of the media who were kept away from Trudeau except for brief "scrums" at which he made short comments on carefully selected subjects. The night before in Moncton, he had carefully responded to Quebec Liberal leader Claude Ryan's "beige" paper on constitutional reform, but when a reporter pressed him for a clarification of his views on the Soviet invasion of Afghanistan, he had barked, "You ask me my ideas when I'm Prime Minister."

Indeed, he knew that he would again be Prime Minister of Canada. The Liberals' own polling and public opinion surveys gave the Liberals an insurmountable lead that could only disappear if the party made a memorable blunder in the campaign. To ensure his return to office, Trudeau had consented to Coutts' and Davey's strategy of keeping him and his party's policies from becoming issues in the campaign. That was why there were written texts and podiums, speeches from other members of the Liberal team, pleasing people-oriented opportunities for television cameras, and the same speech, altered slightly in every town with local references. Having watched the Conservatives trip themselves on their own promises, the Liberals were not about to make the same mistake. Nothing must be done by Trudeau or the party to dilute the focus of the Liberals' attacks on the Conservatives.

But there was another reason for the Liberals' sterility: the party was tired. For two years prior to their 1979 defeat the Liberals had governed without any purpose other than keeping themselves in power. After their defeat, by Trudeau's own admission, the party had lain low, bestirring itself to think about new policies only in the context of a leadership race. The party had used up its intellectual capital and had not had sufficient time before the election to rethink its priorities and consider new policies. Even if the Liberals had wanted to, they would have been hard-pressed to define a "blended price" for oil; such precision would have required an intellectual effort the Liberals had not expended. It did no good to ask the Liberals what their blended price was; they did not know, which was why three Liberal spokesmen gave three different answers in the campaign. The blended price was a slogan; woolly and reassuring, a bit like the Liberals themselves.

Trudeau offered several rationales for his campaign style when asked about it during the campaign. Most often, he explained that in 1979 the media had paid more attention to his gunslinger style than to what he had been saying. That was plausible enough as an explanation, because the media had been transfixed by every shout and gesticulation of his fiery performances. But that was what the Liberals had wanted in order to contrast Trudeau's strength with Clark's weakness. In 1980, Trudeau was uncomfortable with the new performing strategy. He often looked like a classical pianist forced to play ragtime for his keep. In Vancouver, he referred to British Columbians as "British Canadians," pronounced Jerusalem as "Jerasalem," and referred to Clark's policy of moving the Canadian embassy in Israel from "Tel Aviv to Tel Aviv." In Calgary, he forgot the name of a Liberal candidate, calling him "our friend from Bow River." In Kamloops, British Columbia, he got the name of the Liberal candidate wrong three times, and when he arrived at the closing line of his speech—"Joe Clark had his chance and he blew it; now it's time to give Canada a chance"—Trudeau must have realized how listless he had been because he carried on for another ten minutes with more passion than he had displayed throughout his basic campaign speech.

If it had been his first campaign, Canadians might have called him another Stanfield: dull, mechanical, lacking the spark and vision of leadership. But this was his fifth campaign as the leader of the Liberal Party. Canadians had already seen all his moods. They had felt his anger and heard his supplications. They had been quickened or repelled by his passions, but seldom left indifferent. They had observed him as a philosopher and as a man of action. They had listened to him in English and French, cajoling, pleading, lecturing, reasoning. They had watched him retire, saying he was not the one to lead the renewal of the Liberal Party ("I feel it is time for a new leader to take up this work") only to return from a sense of "duty" to his party and his country. Some Canadians were quite hostile towards him; their views would never change. Others believed he could do little wrong. But for the majority, he was a patchwork of contradictions, his strengths and weaknesses winding through the nation's political consciousness. Even when they rejected him in 1979, Canadians still remembered him as decisive, tough, and visionary. Whether the image corresponded to the reality was of less importance than the image's persistence even in defeat. Neither Trudeau nor the party needed to remind the electorate of those strengths in 1980; a vigorous campaign might have served only to recall his weaknesses.

For the first ten days of the campaign, Trudeau campaigned in a box of mirrors, each appearance resembling all the others. By design, there was no spontaneity, no life, not even an appreciable effort to reciprocate the affection of the audiences. This was the way the "strategy committee" had laid out Trudeau's campaign. He finally broke new ground in Toronto on January 12, outlining the "five major commitments" of the Liberal Party, each either a platitude or so qualified on all sides as to be unassailable. They were "to manage more rigorously the nation's finances in order to make more effective use of the taxpayers' money"; "to achieve energy security at a fair price for all Canadians"; "to develop industrial policies that will provide jobs, spur growth, and increase Canadian ownership and control of the economy"; "to build greater economic strength in each region of the country as the basis for overall Canadian prosperity"; and "to enhance the security of the individual by helping those who most need assistance." Trudeau's most specific commitment—to manage the nation's finances "which we must get back in order"—was an implicit admission of the unsatisfactory state of federal finances after sixteen years of Liberal rule. Trudeau promised to keep government expenditure growth below the increase in gross national product and to finance new programs by finding money in existing programs or by raising revenues. Now, that might have been a sharp point on which to hang the Liberal Party's credibility in power, but Trudeau immediately varnished the point with qualifications, "The deficit will be reduced in a phased and orderly fashion, but not at the expense of jobs, growth, and the attack on inflation." The Liberals, wiser perhaps and certainly more cynical than the Conservatives, were not about to make any specific commitments they might later regret. Did the Liberals favour an increase or a decrease in the deficit? "We are not dogmatic on that point," Trudeau said later in the campaign.

Three days later, Trudeau made one of his few detailed promises of the campaign. Speaking at Twenty-One McGill, Toronto's posh women's club, Trudeau pledged to increase the guaranteed income supplement for senior citizens by $35 per month. The program would cost $570 million, and Trudeau said the Liberals would finance the program by raising corporate income taxes. The promise was part of the Liberal principle to "first help those who need help most."

From Toronto, Trudeau flew to western Canada, where he made a promise that set off howls of laughter from Manitoba to British Columbia. In Estevan, Saskatchewan, Trudeau said, "It will be the policy of a new Liberal Government that the Canadian National Railways will double-track its entire line of 1,500 miles from Winnipeg to Vancouver. It will build a second parallel line by linking together all the sidings to form an extra track." It was the equivalent of Diefenbaker's magnificently vacuous promise to build a causeway from the mainland to Prince Edward Island. It was a poor excuse for a policy from a party ostensibly determined to recapture the favour of western Canada. Instead, farmers, businessmen, and editorial writers simply harpooned the promise as so much political blubbering. Canada had a serious grain transportation problem but no one who had studied the problem had ever recommended double-tracking as a solution. Instead, they proposed purchase of more hopper cars, improvement of west coast ports and freight-rate incentives.

The double-tracking promise perfectly symbolized the Liberals' problems in western Canada; they were hopelessly out of touch with the region. With only three M.P.s from western Canada after the 1979 election, the Liberals fell into a similar vicious circle of ignorance that trapped the Conservatives in Quebec: the lack of M.P.s from western Canada dulled the Liberals' sensitivity to western complaints, which in turn further enfeebled the Liberals' chances in that region of the country. In announcing his decision to lead the Liberals in the campaign, Trudeau had pledged to "make a special effort to gain supporters in western Canada. . . . I am troubled by the views of alienation and separation of any kind in this country. Westerners express their alienation from the national scene much as Quebeckers did a decade ago. I believe Quebeckers have found a new faith in Canada's future, and I want western Canadians to share the same dream and to become truly a part of a Liberal Government that I would have the honour and the responsibility to lead." These were laudable sentiments, and to demonstrate his renewed commitment to strengthening the party in the west, Trudeau opened his campaign in Winnipeg, where he said, "We will travel any distance, work however long, and commit whatever resources are necessary to ensure that western Canadians play a major role in a Liberal Government." He added that he would meet after his speech with "Liberals from across the prairies to develop a western platform." The meeting lasted about half an hour, and the platform reflected the brevity of the meeting and the Liberals' lack of resources in western Canada. In addition to double-tracking, Trudeau promised during the campaign to give more local autonomy to the port of Vancouver, to pour additional money into the development of the Trident aircraft in British Columbia, and to support a two-price system for wheat. This hodge-podge of policies lacked any coherent approach to the problems of western Canada. But, in scraping together a platform at the last minute, the Liberals could not count on advice from the region's most dynamic political leaders, since none of them was Liberal. At the provincial level, the party was dead in Alberta, moribund in British Columbia and Saskatchewan, and reduced to a single M.L.A. in Manitoba. The Liberals were a central Canadian party and were resented as such by westerners. In such circumstances, it was understandable that the Liberals' platform for western Canada was so insubstantial and, in the case of double-tracking, simply foolish.

Diefenbaker changed the political map of western Canada, breaking the Liberals' hold on Manitoba and Saskatchewan and the Social Credit Party's grip on Alberta. British Columbia remained as politically fickle towards Diefenbaker as it was later towards Trudeau, but Diefenbaker established the Conservatives as the strongest federal party in the three prairie provinces. His agricultural policies, his western roots, his ethnic origins, his vision of "One Canada" kept the prairies faithful to the Conservatives throughout his leadership. Even in Diefenbaker's losing campaigns of 1963 and 1965, the Conservatives decimated the Liberals on the prairies, winning forty-one seats to three for the Liberals in 1963, and forty-two seats to one for the Liberals in 1965. Trudeaumania assaulted but did not breach the Conservatives' western fiefdom in 1968; the Liberals won eleven seats on the Prairies—the party's best showing since 1953—compared with twenty-five for the Conservatives. But Trudeau's gains in the west could not be consolidated. Trudeau's bilingualism policies were widely resented. His western ministers carried less weight than their colleagues from Quebec and Ontario. Ron Basford of British Columbia and Otto Lang of Saskatchewan were the Liberals' best-known ministers from the west, but neither commanded a wide following. Lang's teutonic personality and insensitive handling of rail-line abandonment and other grain transportation matters turned most western farmers against him and the Liberals. After 1971, Trudeau confronted assertive provincial governments under Conservative Peter Lougheed in Alberta and

New Democrat Allan Blakeney in Saskatchewan, although Blakeney's Liberal predecessor, Premier Ross Thatcher, had also quarrelled incessantly with Trudeau. In the 1972 campaign, the Liberals lost almost all the ground captured in the 1968 campaign. The party won three seats on the prairies in the 1972 election, five seats in 1974, and two seats in 1979.

The mercurial British Columbia electorate, which had swung with the national trend against Diefenbaker in 1963 and 1965, embraced Trudeau enthusiastically in 1968, but began to sour on him shortly after giving the Liberals sixteen seats in that election. Bilingualism and the perceived central Canadian bias of his government were two of the factors that undermined Trudeau's support in British Columbia.

Although not as anemic as the Conservatives' presence in Quebec, the Liberals' condition in western Canada was certainly lamentable. In scattered ridings in 1980, the Liberals recruited excellent candidates: former provincial party leader Gordon Gibson and economist Peter Pearse in British Columbia, lawyer Clyne Harrandence and former M.P. Ralph Goodale in Saskatchewan, former M.L.A. and university professor Lloyd Axworthy in Manitoba. But elsewhere the Liberal candidates were invariably of second-rate quality, especially in Alberta where the Liberals had not won a seat since the 1968 election. It was little wonder, therefore, that the majority of western Liberals, who dreamed of a renaissance for their party in the west, had been so unenthusiastic about Trudeau's return as party leader. They knew that the party's chances were poor throughout the west with him as Liberal leader. In this, they were correct: the Liberals won two of seventy-five seats in the four western provinces in the 1980 election.

After spending nearly a week in western Canada, the Yukon, and the Northwest Territories, Trudeau flew to Sydney and then to Halifax, where he unveiled the party's deliberately vague energy policy. At each meeting, he continued to give the same tightly scripted performance, although he did begin to allow students to ask a few questions after his speeches at universities.

Trudeau was sticking meticulously to his standard speech criticizing the Conservatives and their budget when the subject of foreign affairs was injected into the campaign. He had planned to fly to Charlottetown for a rally, but Coutts and Davey thought he should say something about foreign policy, since the Conservatives seemed intent on pressing the issue in the campaign. As a result, the Liberals cancelled Trudeau's trip to Prince Edward Island, brought together 400 Liberals in Toronto and gave Trudeau's speech considerable advance billing. As it happened, the speech fell on the day the government confirmed that the Canadian embassy in Tehran had successfully smuggled six U.S. diplomats from Iran. The news of the successful mission forced Trudeau's speech-writers to insert a paragraph of praise into an otherwise damning indictment of the Conservatives' foreign policy performance:

> If it is true, as reported today, that Canadian external affairs officials in Tehran gave refuge to Americans in Iran during the hostage crisis, this is commendable action and all Canadians and myself applaud this brave work by external affairs officials and we commend the government for supporting it. It is in the long tradition of Canadians abroad acting to support those in danger and distress. This was true in Chile and elsewhere in the world in other crises, and if it's happened in Iran, we're proud of our Canadians there.

It was a shoddy paragraph of congratulations. Trudeau knew that the Canadian embassy had given sanctuary to the U.S. diplomats because Clark had informed him of Canada's actions several days after learning the news himself. The Liberals still persisted, however, in criticizing the Conservatives in the Commons for not helping the United States in its predicament in Iran. Seeking petty political gain, the Liberals portrayed the Conservative Government as weak and indecisive in the face of a provocation against an ally, although the Liberals knew that the Canadian government was doing more than any other western country to aid the United States. Trudeau kept insisting that Clark deserved blame for not having "picked up the phone" and rallied the other nations of the Western alliance to act in concert to help the United States, as if Canada had the power and the contacts to force the Japanese and Europeans into a common front. Significantly, Trudeau did nothing of the sort after the election, an indication of how hollow his criticisms of Clark had been.

In the same speech as he congratulated the Conservatives, Trudeau waffled on the question of boycotting the Olympic Games, saying, "I have doubts about the effectiveness of Canada deciding by itself, or only in concert with a few friendly nations, that we should boycott the Olympics." Trudeau, who wanted Canada to take the lead in forming a common front of nations against Iran, ironically thought Canada should await the decisions

of other nations before deciding whether to support an Olympic
boycott. "If a boycott could become the general policy of the
Western alliance, then of course our party would support that kind
of international action."

There was more irony yet to come. Shortly after his election
as Prime Minister in 1968, Trudeau had ordered a complete review
of Canada's foreign policy, believing that Pearson's "quiet diplomacy" was no longer appropriate for Canada in the 1970s. As a
result, Trudeau abandoned what he considered to be the fuzzy
internationalism of Pearson in favour of a foreign policy based on
the furtherance of Canada's own interests, especially economic, in
other countries. Now, in the heat of an election campaign, he laid
claim to his predecessor's mantle that he himself had thrown off
shortly after taking office. "There is little that Canada can do alone
to determine the course of events. What we can do, and this was
the secret of St. Laurent and Pearson and our Government, is to
lead the international community collectively towards a desired
course of action."

The next day, the shabby cynicism of his Toronto speech on
foreign policy was eclipsed by the kind of performance that had
made Pierre Trudeau the commanding presence in Canadian
politics for more than a decade. He showed the brilliant side of his
enigmatic personality, the one even his detractors were forced to
admit could not be rivalled in Canadian politics. The occasion was a
speech at Memorial University in St. John's which began, predictably enough, with a condemnation of the Clark Government. But
it was clear from the beginning of his remarks that his boisterous
audience of more than 800 wanted to hear about offshore
resources. Trudeau clearly wanted to talk about that subject too.
He hurried through his prepared text, telling hecklers who pestered
him about offshore resources, "I will talk about oil, and I'll answer
every question you want to ask me about oil."

In answering their questions, he inadvertently revealed the
palpable phoniness of the Liberal campaign in which Trudeau
talked incessantly about issues he neither cared much about nor
intended to press hard after the election, while he avoided, for
tactical reasons, the one issue that stirred the passions of his heart.
Trudeau had spoken repeatedly about national unity in the 1979
campaign, often in the context of energy negotiations between the
federal government and the producing provinces. He had even
spent two precious days in the final week of the campaign discussing patriation of the constitution, a subject without political

appeal, because he knew that he was losing the election and wanted to speak to history on a subject of abiding interest to him. He had done so against the wishes of his advisors, who knew how uninterested the electorate was in patriation and other subjects touching the constitution. After the election, Davey called national unity a "placard issue"; it was of cardinal importance to the country but of limited political appeal to voters preoccupied with safeguarding their own standard of living. In 1980, therefore, Trudeau had acquiesced to the wishes of Coutts and Davey and ignored national unity as much as possible. As a result the Liberal campaign became largely a spectacle of camouflage in which the leader talked about other issues in order to win the election, after which he would turn most of his attention to the one issue he didn't speak about, national unity. At the beginning of the campaign, Trudeau had sworn off talking about the Quebec referendum; he did not want either to open a rift between himself and Quebec Liberal leader Claude Ryan, whose views on Quebec's future role in Confederation he did not entirely share, or to divert attention from his attacks on the Conservatives. At his first Quebec rally of the campaign, he said, "Everybody knows how I feel about the future of Quebec. And there will be sufficient time after the 18th of February for saying what I have to say."

But the question of offshore resources was a different matter. Newfoundland was excited about the prospect of fabulous wealth from oil and natural gas lying off its coast within the 200-mile limit. It was impossible for a major politician, federal or provincial, to avoid the question of offshore resources when speaking to a Newfoundland audience, especially one as politically sensitive as students and faculty members at the province's university. Clark had agreed that coastal provinces should control offshore resources in the same way that all provinces had jurisdiction over resources within their land boundaries. Trudeau's argument was straight-forward: the ownership of offshore resources could be decided only by the Supreme Court. In the absence of a court ruling, the federal government could not give away a constitutional power that it might not possess. Even if it wanted to cede jurisdiction to the province, the federal government would need a constitutional amendment unanimously supported by all provinces. Rather than waiting for the jurisdictional question to be settled, Trudeau suggested that Ottawa retain jurisdiction but give Newfoundland "maximum benefits" from oil and natural gas until the province's per-capita income rose above the national average. But more revealing than the details of his proposal was the passion it summoned from him. For the first time in the campaign, his eyes flashed and his voice crackled with emotion; he was eloquent, *engagé*, and electric while he defended his conception of Canada:

> At this stage of my political career, I'm not going to change my tune. I want to offer you a larger vision and a grander dream. It's a vision where [Canadians] grow strong by helping each other. It's a dream of Newfoundland and Labrador whose people, having thrown off the last vestige of economic dependence, proudly reach out a helping hand to help other Canadians. And that's the choice that is perhaps offered to you at this historic time. . . . As a politician, the easiest thing for me would be to offer a future in which Newfoundland would be fabulously wealthy. . . . I could easily say that you could be fabulously wealthy and never have to share anything with anyone in Canada. . . . Well, that wouldn't be Canada. That wouldn't even be the kind of Newfoundland that your parents and grandparents wanted and dreamed about.

Then he related his hopes for Newfoundland to his vision of Quebec in Canada which, after so many struggles, still animated his spirit.

> And that's why the Liberal Party is not asking you to choose between Newfoundland and Canada. And in my province, in my whole career, I've been telling my people that they don't have to choose between Quebec and Canada. You choose the better of both worlds: a stronger Newfoundland in a stronger Canada.

He had spoken from the heart only fleetingly, but in those few minutes he had pulled the thread that ran through the Canadian dream from Macdonald and Laurier to all those who followed in their wake and defended a "larger vision" of Canada as a nation that was neither "*deux nations*" nor a compact of provinces nor a "community of communities." Those who have upheld such provincialist theses have invariably come to grief in federal politics because, for all the regional divisions in Canada, there exists the feeling, often submerged, across the country that Canada must be more than just the sum of its parts. Even if Trudeau had often provoked the parts to rub against each other with friction and anger, Canadians still believed that he possessed the strength and the "larger vision" to sustain the interests of the whole against the most powerful and fractious of its component parts.

After his sparkling performance in St. John's, Trudeau returned to his tightly controlled campaign. He flew to Quebec for rallies in Ascot Corners and Magog, where he delivered two listless speeches. The next day in Peterborough, his speech was so lifeless that even Coutts, whose strategy he was following, admitted that the speech was a "bit flat," which was as far as Coutts would ever go in criticizing his boss.

But even campaigning poorly in Peterborough, Trudeau still communicated a basic theme of the Liberals' campaign in Ontario: the Conservatives budget would do irreparable harm to the province. Everywhere Trudeau went in the campaign, he recited figures provided to him by the Liberal Party's research bureau in Ottawa showing the negative impact of the Conservatives' budget on the city, region, or province in which he was speaking. In Atlantic Canada, the figures estimated the financial burden of the excise tax on fishermen; in the west, the impact on farmers; in large cities, the additional costs for public transportation systems, and so on. The Liberals knew from their research how much damage the Ontario Conservative Government had done to Clark during the energy negotiations with Alberta. The Conservatives had captured power in 1979 by winning thirty-two more seats in Ontario than it had in the 1974 campaign. Thus, the Liberals expended the bulk of their campaign effort to undermine Clark's position in Ontario, quoting liberally from speeches by Ontario Premier William Davis and provincial treasurer Frank Miller that criticized the federal Conservatives' energy and budgetary policies. The Liberals also played upon Clark's western origins, subtly suggesting that Clark neither understood Ontario nor harboured good-will towards the province. Given Ontario's increasingly skittish reaction to changes in the balance of power in Confederation, especially the shift of influence towards western Canada, the Liberals wisely portrayed themselves as Ontario's only friend in federal politics. Trudeau put the point baldly in Peterborough:

> It's as though the budget was written without knowledge
> of the importance of energy costs to Ontario's economy
> and to Canada's, because Ontario counts for about half of
> all the manufacturing output in this country. . . . Canada,
> in order to be strong as a country, . . . needs a strong
> Ontario. It doesn't want a weakened shell. And I've often
> spoken in this campaign . . . about building up the differ-
> ent regions of Canada. Well, you can't at the same time

tear Ontario down. We have to use energy as a tool of our industrial strategy, not as a bludgeon to destroy the competitiveness of this particular province. . . . But by driving Canada's energy prices up to 85 per cent of world prices, that's what the Tories are doing to this province. They are weakening this province. And whether the Joe Clark Conservatives are doing it through ignorance, or policy, or weakness towards some other part of Canada, I can't say.

At least Trudeau had dropped the false accusation he made early in the campaign that the Conservatives wanted Canadian oil prices to reach world levels, but his inflammatory words—"tear down," "bludgeon," "weaken"—captured many headlines in Ontario during the campaign and reinforced the Liberals' message that Clark, the westerner, could not be trusted to protect the interests of Ontario.

After other Ontario rallies in Sudbury and Thunder Bay, Trudeau travelled to Alberta for his only visit of the campaign. Like Clark's and Broadbent's forays into Quebec, Trudeau's visits to Alberta were unproductive but obligatory; the party faithful in the province needed reassurance that their labours, although unrewarded by votes, were still appreciated by the national party. Even Jack Horner, his massive ego bruised but not shattered by his 1979 defeat as a Liberal in Crowfoot, was running again in Alberta, and such resolve as Horner and his fellow Liberal candidates demonstrated against insurmountable odds deserved the leader's acknowledgement. From Alberta, Trudeau flew across the country to Charlottetown, which he had passed up earlier in the campaign to deliver his speech on foreign policy in Toronto. Then, he returned to Ottawa to rest for the final week of campaigning.

Whatever lingering doubts may have persisted that the Liberals would win the election had been wiped away by the final week of the campaign. Goldfarb's numbers and the public polls continued to point to a Liberal victory, but there had always been a nagging suspicion among Liberals that some of their supporters, especially in southern Ontario, were "soft," capable of swinging at the last moment to the Conservatives or New Democrats. Both Clark and Broadbent were running vigorous campaigns, and there was still a reluctance, particularly among some marginally committed Liberals, to vote again for Trudeau. The enormous Liberal lead in public opinion might cause overconfidence among Liberal workers and keep some committed Liberals, who figured the outcome of the election was a foregone conclusion, from taking the

352 / Discipline of Power

trouble to vote. To forestall defections and overconfidence, either of which might deprive the Liberals of a majority, the strategy committee had decided at the beginning of the campaign that Trudeau should break out of his shell in the final week. Having nurtured the seeds of doubt about Clark for the first six weeks of the campaign, the Liberals reasoned that they needed to offer positive reinforcement at the end of the campaign to those who had turned away from the Conservatives but were still unhappy with the Liberal alternative.

A week before voting day, Trudeau removed the shackles from his public emotions. Before more than 2,000 Quebeckers in Lévis, he spoke "from the heart," dwelling for the first time in his campaign on the issue that had brought him into politics and sustained his attention throughout his political career. In his last Quebec speech of the campaign, he spoke, as he had so many times before, of Quebec's role in Canada.

> We have a country that was discovered, founded, explored, colonized by our ancestors [and] by our parents. And we have never lost sight of this Canada that can belong to all those who wish to build it together. And our role ... is not to dig ditches between people, not to differentiate between the French and the English, people from the west and people from the east ... our role, my fellow Quebeckers, is to build bridges towards others, to extend a hand to others.... What Quebeckers have never forgotten is that it is possible to be a Quebecker and a Canadian at the same time.

The next day in Toronto, he outlined the Liberals' mildly nationalistic industrial policy before returning to the theme of national unity in Winnipeg on February 13. There he sounded like the Trudeau of 1979, talking about the one subject of overriding importance to him.

> An increasing number of provinces are saying that we must buy provincial, whether it be eggs or food or manufactured products. We must not look to the Canadian market for our energy. We must not look to the Canadian market for our supplies. We must build ourselves into a little state separate from the others. Liberals say that's not Canada. Canada is one nation.... And we say to Mr. Clark and his party, Canada is not a community of communities where a lot of little feudal states try and get together to give some power to the national government.

The powers of the national government come to it under the constitution . . . and they come from the people of Canada. And the people of Canada want to vote in this election to say clearly that they want a government which will govern for the whole country, not for one province against the others, not for one part against the other.

As Prime Minister, Trudeau had tailored his policies to suit the drift of public opinion and the vagaries of circumstances. His economic policies had gyrated wildly while his Government attempted to tackle inflation and unemployment simultaneously, and his energy policies had pushed the country further away from self-sufficiency. His social policies had not appreciably closed the gap between rich and poor, and they had certainly not introduced a more "just" society in Canada. But he had remained constant and compelling in his view about the future of Canada, and for that he would be remembered long after he has passed from the Canadian political scene.

Throughout the 1980 campaign, Trudeau had consented to the arid scripts and the controlled campaign, but at the very end the approaching victory put joy into his campaign; he was alive again. As he returned again to issues that burst the constraints of partisanship and went to the core of the nation's existence, his speeches were animated, his rhetoric sharper. He was like a fighter ahead on points in the fifteenth round, dazzling the crowd with his unimpaired prowess. He would soon join Sir John A. Macdonald and Mackenzie King as the only Canadian Prime Ministers to have been voted back into office after losing an election. He had seized the improbable twist of circumstances that offered him a chance to affix an addendum to his record. Power, with which he had grown comfortable, would soon be his again. When Trudeau spoke to rapturous crowds in that final week, Coutts could be seen standing discreetly at the side of the hall, his eyes bright with the swelling ecstasy of imminent triumph.

As a fillip to his joy, Trudeau began competing with the members of the media in games of poetry identification in the final week. He inserted lines of poetry into his speeches, inviting the reporters to guess the poem. The reporters, in turn, tested him with quotations when he returned to his campaign plane. Seventy-two hours before the election returns were known, he broke free from his speech before a thousand Liberals in Scarborough, peered down at the members of the media in the front of the hall, and tossed off four lines of poetry, slightly amended:

> Turning and turning in the widening gyre
> The falcon cannot hear the falconer;
> Things fall apart; the centre cannot hold
> And mere anarchy is loosed upon the Tory Party.

He was paraphrasing William Butler Yeats' poem "The Second Coming."

Reflections

Within a month of the election, all had returned to normal in Ottawa; the Conservative interlude had passed like a dream and the capital awoke to the familiar faces and sounds of the Liberal Party. So short was the Conservative interlude and so paltry were its accomplishments that it seemed the Liberals had never been away, but rather had enjoyed an extended holiday, like a senior executive enjoying a sabbatical after long years of service. Trudeau shaved off the beard he had grown canoeing, reinstated Michael Pitfield as Clerk of the Privy Council, dismissed Grant Reuber and appointed Ian Stewart as deputy minister of finance, and carried on.

Trudeau enjoyed a freer hand after the election than any Prime Minister could imagine. Instead of seeking the leadership of his party, he had waited until his caucus and the Liberal national executive bade him to return, which made them beholden to him rather than the other way around. His victory elevated him to elder statesman within the party; his declared intention to resign before the next election liberated him from the usual worries of courting public opinion. He had offered few promises during the 1980 campaign, so there was little for which he could be held accountable by his party or his country. Canadians had given him the closest political equivalent to a blank cheque. He would not be asking them again for any favours, or so he said. He was like the Mexican President, ensconced in power, not seeking re-election, obligated to only a handful of colleagues, free to pursue the national interest as he alone saw fit, secure in the knowledge that history, not the voters at the next election, would judge his actions.

Trudeau had asked to see the obituary notices of his political career while sitting in Opposition, the dozens of articles written in that short interval between his announced intention to resign and his resurrection. They made for depressing reading. The media, which he despised, had largely written off his years as Prime Minister as ones of wasted opportunity for Canada, apart from historic and positive changes in bilingualism. The articles grated on his powerful pride; he could not be certain that historians would be kinder. He would use his final years in office to govern for them.

The post-election Cabinet both tipped his intentions and reflected the thinking of a handful of senior Liberals in their months in Opposition. Those who had committed *lèse-majesté* by opposing Trudeau's return as party leader—Robert Andras, Judd Buchanan, John Reid—either left politics or were banished from the Cabinet. Only his two trusted lieutenants were given the senior economic portfolios: Allan MacEachen at finance and Marc Lalonde at energy. The Ministry of State for Federal-Provincial Relations was abolished and a Cabinet neophyte, Mark MacGuigan, was appointed Minister of External Affairs. It was apparent from these appointments what Trudeau had in mind: MacEachen and Lalonde would implement the strategy worked out by a handful of Liberals in Opposition; he would concentrate on his own historical record through constitutional reforms and foreign policy.

The Liberals' restoration in the election of 1980 confirmed their belief that they were the nation's rightful governing party. Victory crushed the tentative grass-roots groping for answers to explain their 1979 defeat, which had been brought about by the party's lacklustre performance in office. From the beginning of 1978, election scares came about every four months—not all of them figments of the media's febrile imagination—as the Liberals desperately scoured their polls to find some way of restoring their popularity, waiting until the dying months of their five-year mandate for the political climate to change. During that eighteen-month period, Canada was governed by a party stripped of its last conviction, save the dearest one of all: clinging to power.

During the Conservative interlude, a small group of senior Liberals reflected upon what had gone awry. The group numbered fewer than a dozen and, as always, the most important men were Jim Coutts, his assistant Tom Axworthy (who later replaced Coutts as Trudeau's principal secretary), Marc Lalonde, Allan MacEachen, and Trudeau. Each of them always insisted that they were members of the party's "reformist" wing, and they may well have been in the early 1970s when that wing counted for something in the party. They had long since been compromised by the continuous holding of power so that their "reformism" had been gobbled up by an all-pervasive utilitarianism, which supporters called pragmatism and others called cynicism. They concluded that the Liberals had seriously erred in trying to "out-Tory the Tories," to use the group's catch-phrase. The Liberal Government, alarmed by the 1978–1979 decline in public opinion, had shifted to the political right. If given another chance, this small group resolved to be more progressive in social policy and nationalistic in economic policy.

For Trudeau and Lalonde especially, there was the added disappointment that, despite their efforts and deep personal convictions, both political power and financial resources had flowed from Ottawa to the provincial governments in the 1970s. In a last, desperate attempt to entice the provinces into a constitutional reform package in the last year of his 1974–1979 Government, Trudeau had offered them "Fourteen Points," the most radical transfer of power to the provinces he had ever contemplated. But the provincial governments, blinded by their rhetoric and their dislike for Trudeau, foolishly rejected the package almost out of hand. He would not make that mistake again. If he ever tackled constitutional reform, he would offer them next to nothing, insisting instead upon those principles of a charter of rights, patriation, a reassertion of federal authority, and improved fiscal arrangements for Ottawa in which he profoundly believed.

From these reflections sprang the constitutional reform initiative, the National Energy Policy of 1980 and the politically disastrous and economically inept MacEachen budget of November 1981. As Stephen Clarkson demonstrated in *Canada and the Reagan Challenge*,* the government retreated from many of its energy policies and altogether abandoned its nationalist economic policies in the face of furious American pressure, but these were the policies Trudeau, never himself terribly interested in either economics or promoting nationalism, delegated to Lalonde and MacEachen. The broad mass of the Liberal Party had been consulted only in a perfunctory way about these specific new policies. They had been dreamt up by only a small group of Liberals; they could be—and were—jettisoned by the same small group when the political going got too rough.

Having delegated the economic and energy fields to MacEachen and Lalonde, Trudeau left himself free to appeal to the judgement

---

*(Lorimer, 1982).

of history in the two fields dearest to him. He had ignored the question of national unity in the 1980 campaign, following Davey's and Coutts' advice to focus exclusively on Clark and economic issues. But when the electorate handed him his blank cheque, Trudeau wrote "Constitutional Reform" across it in capital letters. For two years, the Government of Canada was preoccupied by an intensely bitter fight with the provinces, the Supreme Court, the British Government, most of the media, and large sections of public opinion to bring the Constitution to Canada with a charter of rights. The details of that struggle have been related elsewhere,* but the battle represented the culmination of Trudeau's political career, a defiant toss of the head at his critics and the historians. Trudeau got much less from the eventual constitutional agreement than he had wanted, but that he got an agreement at all with patriation and a charter of rights testified to his fierce will and lifelong preoccupation with the role and rights of French-speaking Canadians.

He might not have cared that, when the hoopla surrounding patriation faded, neither he nor the Liberal Party received even temporary gratitude from the electorate, but the party surely did. For all the passion the constitutional reform debate generated among the political elite, it seldom touched ordinary voters; they remained stubbornly wedded in their political motivation to the most general of notions about national unity and the bread-and-butter concerns of their daily lives. With its arcane lexicon and endless repetition, the debate rolled on for months, even years, energizing some, boring most, so that when the Queen finally signed the new Canadian Constitution it was as if the whole country heaved a collective sigh of relief.

By the election of 1979, the Liberal Party had exhausted most of the compelling ideas it had developed during the 1960s and early 1970s. The Official Languages Act, new directions in foreign policy, expanded and often innovative social programs, hesitant moves to recapture control of the Canadian economy: these were all initiatives from the early years of Trudeau's Government. The second half of his 1974–1979 years in office had been less fertile, and the last two were positively barren. Not only was the party leadership intellectually tired, but the hemorrhaging of talented men and women from the front benches of the party exceeded the infusion of new blood. The National Energy Program and the MacEachen

---

*Robert Sheppard and Michael Valpy, *The National Deal* (Fleet Books, 1982).

budgets were the last gasps from the Trudeau men; the former a bold, even reckless, plan which foundered on the rocks of American opposition, world recession, and stable world energy prices; the latter so ill-considered that most of the controversial sections were humiliatingly withdrawn. By the mid-point of the government's term, MacEachen was relieved of the finance portfolio and replaced by Lalonde, the NEP and some of the Canadian oil companies it encouraged lay in bandages, and the brave talk about industrial strategy, expanding Canadian ownership, and toughening the Foreign Investment Review Agency had been banished from the Liberal vocabulary.

With the constitution patriated and the last spasms of the new energy and economic policies stilled, the Liberals found themselves where they had been from 1977 to 1979, drifting with events, waiting, wondering, hoping, speculating, in short, dying to know Pierre Trudeau's intentions. But he kept them guessing until the last possible moment, loving power and its trappings as much as ever, always finding one more compelling reason why he should stay on just a little bit longer.

For the longest time, it seemed plausible to await developments within the Conservative Party. Then, with Brian Mulroney elected as the new Conservative leader, it seemed prudent to use Trudeau's experience against the neophyte in the House of Commons. Then Trudeau launched his prolonged "peace initiative": four points to slow down the arms race and inject "political will" into disarmament negotiations, the selling of which took him to Europe, Japan, the United States, and elsewhere.

The international climate had deteriorated when Trudeau launched his initiative in the fall of 1983. The deployment of cruise and Pershing-2 missiles had both alarmed the Kremlin and upset public opinion in all five West European nations scheduled to receive them. The suspension by the Soviets of talks aimed at reducing intermediate-range nuclear weapons, the lack of progress at parallel talks on intercontinental nuclear weapons, the shooting down by the Soviets of a Korean Airlines plane, the arms build-ups by the United States and the Soviet Union, the rhetorical slanging matches between Washington and Moscow all contributed to a sharp increase in tension and uneasiness between the two camps.

Trudeau, genuinely alarmed at this deterioration and conscious that a disarmament initiative might provide a worthy conclusion to his historical record, postponed his day of reckoning about his political future by his initiative. The prospects for success were always small. Canada was a bit player in the disarmament game and there was little a country of Canada's size could do to move the super-powers from fixed positions. Trudeau's four points were vague and related only to long-term issues. But he could realistically argue that he had never promised a miracle and, if his initiative succeeded even marginally, he could depart having added an impressive foot-note to his career.

The longer he delayed, however, in the face of dismal, perhaps irredeemably dismal, public opinion surveys, the more likely it be-came that when he left, the Liberals would turn in desperation to the only possible successor with a scintilla of charisma, to the one man Trudeau least wished to succeed him: John Turner. Even Turner would confront the most daunting of prospects, restoring the abysmally poor Liberal standing. The Prime Minister continued to fascinate Canadians, for there was no one remotely like him in politics, but he had long overstayed his welcome. Indeed, the entire post-1976 period in Canadian politics can be read as a continuum of deepening annoyance with Trudeau and the Liberals, checked twice by events beyond their control from which they profited enor-mously: the election of the Parti Québécois in 1976 and the tragic fumbling of Joe Clark's Government. Not since the Ottomans had a dynasty so long forestalled the *fin de régime*.

In defeat, the Conservatives were again shackled by the Oppo-sition party mentality which, perhaps paradoxically, the election of a new leader and their resurgence in public opinion polls only strengthened. Shellshocked by their period in office, the Conserva-tives learned the wrong lessons from their defeat. In particular, they avoided all hard thinking about policies. Their policy confer-ence abounded in the vaguest generalities, as if specific commit-ments might conjure up the nightmare of all those ill-considered pre-1979 promises. In the House of Commons, Conservatives opposed without presenting alternative policies, fearing that any-thing specific might offer an inviting target for the hard-pressed Liberals. The higher the Conservatives rose in public opinion, the more reticent they became about telling anyone where they stood lest whatever they said might divert the public from its distaste for the Liberals. This might have made political sense; it would scarcely make for good government. A party needs policies and broad con-victions as sheet anchors against the buffetings of office, but no one watching the Conservatives under either Clark or Mulroney could predict which convictions might anchor a Conservative Gov-ernment.

The memories of those nine sad months of Conservative rule deepened their cynicism, gnawed at their political souls, made them hungrier for power. Even before Clark was dumped, the party had grown tougher, even nastier, in Opposition. Led by a combative house leader, Erik Nielsen, the Conservatives engaged in a series of obstructionist tactics in Parliament, keeping the bells ringing for fifteen days on one occasion rather than permitting a vote on a measure they opposed. Relations between the two major parties grew increasingly bitter in the Commons. Divided about their own leadership and uncertain of their own policies, the Conservatives could unite in fury only by attacking the Liberals more sharply than before.

Brian Mulroney, more shrewdly than any of the Conservative leadership candidates including Clark, appreciated this yearning for power. He was also best positioned, as an outsider, to exploit it because he had taken no part in the shambles that became the Conservative dreams of 1979. He could neither be held responsible, as could Clark and to a lesser extent Crosbie, nor be pinned down by any kind of record at all. He could—and did—suggest that he too shared the hurt of all those Conservatives denied a chance to experience the benefits of power: the patronage appointments, the invitations to public functions, the slush of government contracts, the ministerial phone calls, the prime-ministerial pats on the back. His promises to win seats in Quebec, then to use a majority government in a shamelessly partisan fashion, were the irresistibly tantalizing appeals that sealed his victory.

Defeat inevitably deepened the Conservatives' well-developed talents for braying, back-stabbing, and bitching. It exposed all the fissiparous tendencies of a party accustomed to opposition and added fresh ones. The Conservative worthies whose appointments lay unsigned on Clark's desk turned their drooling tongues to venomous chatter. Former ministers grumbled at the folly of their ministerial colleagues, of Clark's advisors, of Clark himself.

It took a few months for the party to collect its thoughts after the numbing defeat, but by the autumn parliamentary session of 1980 the cancerous cells of dissidence were forming. For two and a half years, the story of the Conservative Party was one of Joe Clark struggling like a harpooned whale to survive. He had first to persuade a massive majority to vote against holding a leadership review in a secret vote at the 1981 party convention. He faced the same challenge at the 1983 convention. Both times the results were the same: two-thirds against a review. The second vote persuaded him to fight for his leadership at an open convention.

The story of Clark's demise began in the half-light of intrigue: clusters of Conservatives in Ottawa and beyond, muttering, complaining, feeding upon each other's discontent, hardening that discontent into a conviction to act, searching for the appropriate actions to dispose of Clark. Some cells were composed of cranks whose activities were most energetically debunked by those who questioned the methods and timing, but not the ultimate objective, of dumping Clark.

Within the Conservative caucus, the cells grew fastest among those convinced that Clark could simply never win again. Of course, some of the dissidents felt slighted by his disregard for them during his time as Prime Minister, while others wanted to swing the party to the political right. However, the largest number considered Clark a liability, the only conceivable obstacle between the party and the honey pot of power. John Crosbie, who had pictured himself as a potential leader from his first day in Ottawa, began plotting his leadership campaign in the living room of his St. John's home on St. Patrick's Day, 1981, more than two years before that sweltering day in Ottawa when both Clark's and Crosbie's dreams were shattered. David Crombie, bearing justifiable grudges against Clark for having frozen him out of the Conservatives' inner Cabinet, also nursed leadership hopes.

Yet a majority of the caucus held fast for Clark through the final ballot in Ottawa. They represented, broadly speaking, the moderate Conservative MPs who either feared a sharp right turn for the party under a new leader or another Conservative bloodbath. It sickened the John Frasers, Jake Epps, Don Mazankowskis, and Flora MacDonalds to observe the intrigues unfolding, to hear the corrosive mutterings in the Conservative lobby. As the Liberals sank in public esteem, it seemed the height of folly to dump the leader. Nothing frightened them more than what they saw within their own party: the agitation of right-wingers for Thatcherite or Reaganite policies, the stridency of the Amway salesmen and young Conservative zealots with their simple nineteenth-century formulas, the hungering for political verities in a country of subtleties and compromises. They may not have agreed with everything Clark espoused, and they certainly had not agreed with everything he had done, but he was a moderate, considerate, humane individual whose brand of Conservatism most closely approximated their own.

For the longest time, Clark fought interminable rounds of

shadowboxing. He knew who his opponents were but he could not flush them out. They bided their time, believing the corrosive discontent would widen into a breach from which they could profit. The lion even lay down with the lamb when Brian Mulroney announced, with Clark at his side, that he supported the leader in the run-up to the 1983 Winnipeg convention. How many people remembered, listening to his lilting brogue, that his friends had kept several hundred anti-Clark delegates in a Hull motel until just prior to the 1981 leadership review vote, then herded them to the Ottawa Civic Centre to vote for review?

The 1983 Winnipeg convention staggered Clark's prospects. He had laboured mightily for months to secure a higher vote against a leadership review than he had received at the 1981 convention. He had tried calling in every political debt he had ever been owed to convince delegates to reject overwhelmingly a review. But there were too many grudges, too many dissidents, too many who considered Clark a loser. And among those who did vote against a review, there were undoubtedly many who did so from fear of a blood-bath rather than from a conviction that Clark was the best available Conservative leader. Two-thirds of the Winnipeg delegates voted against a review, but it was not enough to reaffirm the credibility of his leadership. The blood pouring from his political wounds would only have whetted appetites for more. He would staunch those wounds or lose his leadership by asking for a leadership convention; he would face his tormentors angrily, thoroughly, and with tragically misplaced confidence.

So Clark again set about proving himself to the party and the country. Indeed, it often appeared that Clark had seldom done anything else in his political career. Back to the coffee parties and Legion halls he went, scouring every constituency for votes, sounding defiant, as he often did when cornered, in case anyone thought him weak. "My way or the doorway," he told those who asked him about dissidents. Premier William Davis, who toyed with entering the race, would be a "regional" candidate, not exactly the kind of comment designed to entice members of the Big Blue Machine. Fighting with the bare knuckles of a political street fighter, he condoned his organizers' efforts to bus drunks and other befuddled individuals to delegate-selection meetings where they vied for space with similarly selected Mulroney supporters. Accused of unsavoury tactics, Clark bristled and told his critics that this was a political dogfight, not a tea party.

Clark fought with astonishing stamina, the apparent frailty of his physique belying one of the toughest political hides in Canada. He had been so mercilessly pilloried so many times before that nothing in this campaign could shake his dogged perseverance. Now his enemies were out in the open: Mulroney, his backroom tormentor without a day of parliamentary experience, supported by the dregs of the Conservative caucus and some of those right-wing groups who petrified Conservative moderates; John Crosbie, who had ached for the job for so long, a formidable campaigner outside Quebec; Michael Wilson, whom Clark had considered a trusted lieutenant; David Crombie, whose exaggerated ambitions Clark had always feared; and a straggle of others of little consequence save that none of them preferred Clark as their second choice. Indeed, that was Clark's most acute problem: having won the leadership in 1976 as the most acceptable second choice to the largest number of delegates, he was now nobody's second choice. None of the other candidates switched to him after dropping from the race. He possessed his own sizeable block of delegates, and no more. As Mulroney's and Crosbie's vote totals moved up, Clark's remained heartbreakingly steady until Mulroney pipped him on the final ballot. His face frozen in pain, Clark climbed to the podium, sang "O Canada" with the rest, congratulated the victor, and began picking up the pieces of his broken dreams.

Clark fought honourably and courageously for a moderate, tolerant Conservative Party, open to both French- and English-speaking Canadians, receptive to ethnic groups, women, and intellectuals. That he could not expand his sizeable block of delegates prevented him from winning; that the block remained solid to the end ensured that the party would not swing sharply to the political right. The new leader might make only a few bows in that direction, but Mulroney knew from years of observation—and Clark's block of delegates confirmed—that the Conservatives must remain near the centre of the political spectrum to prosper.

The enduring virtue of moderation, indeed the recognition of its political necessity in Canada, was among Clark's legacies to his party and the country. Another was his respect for French-speaking Canadians in a party not known for understanding their aspirations. Sure, they called him "Joe Beans" in crueller moments in Quebec, mocking his French. But he had made an effort; no, more than that, he had achieved admirable fluency in the language and struggled more than any Conservative leader to appreciate Quebec. Perhaps he deluded himself: applause from Quebec nationalists for a federal leader was an evanescent commodity, a shaky base upon which to build the party in the province, a chimera that had tempted Conservative leaders before. However, no fair person, let alone the most ardent *indépendantiste*, could claim that Clark wished to trample on Quebec, the French language, or the French culture. Praise, however faint, from Quebec Premier René Lévesque might not have helped Clark in English Canada or even in Quebec, but it represented one possible sign that the Conservatives and Quebec might reach an accommodation after so many decades of estrangement. Clark could not make the Conservatives a party Quebeckers could love, but he did make it a party they could no longer hate. And having gained for the party that measure of credibility, it was perhaps the cruellest cut of all that he should be beaten by a Quebecker who, through an accident of birth, spoke French like a native Quebecker and could rekindle the hope of winning those magical Quebec seats that would turn the Conservatives into a truly national party in Canada.

It must have seared Clark's soul to attend Conservative rallies in Quebec, peering over the podium at the aging and sad remnants of the *bleu* vote from rural Quebec transported to urban rallies, there to sit with the small-time insurance agents and other aspiring movers and shakers of Quebec society. So tightly did the Liberals control Quebec that a Conservative rally always looked like a joint convention of undertakers and their prospective clients. By defending provincial rights, especially during the constitutional debate, and by offering conciliation to provincial governments, Clark believed he could attract old-time nationalists as well as the new generation of Quebec-firsters. Other Conservative leaders as far back as Borden had tried variations on the same gambit. Clark's defeat ended the flirtation; Mulroney's view of Canada closely approximated Trudeau's. There would be no gestures of *bonne entente* towards the Parti Québécois Government, no hankering after the nationalists. He would appeal directly to the massive Liberal vote to support a native son, *un chef*. It would be a gamble as great as Clark's.

There was so much to admire in Joe Clark that in the natural outpouring of sympathy for him after the convention it was easy to lose sight of his shortcomings. He was honest, courageous, witty, and tenacious. He had the humility to admit error, a virtue his rival Trudeau never exhibited, and the innate graciousness to be steadfast to his principles and his party in defeat as much as in victory. He seldom debased the coin of politics: he never gave the finger to anyone, although, Lord knows, there were times when he must have wanted to. He worked prodigiously, to the limits of his abilities and energies. As time wore on, his knowledge of the country and of the world deepened so that if history had taken a different course—who knows?—he might have been an effective Prime Minister. All his personal virtues and political experience should not be lost either to the party or to the country.

Yet for someone who had spent so long in the backrooms of the party, Clark was an appallingly bad tactician. He had an uncertain strategic understanding, but his tactical sense was worse. He made so many miscalculations about short-term matters that he called into question his ability to lead. The willingness to allow his government's defeat in the Commons represented one of the monumental miscalculations in Canadian politics. But there were others: the imprudent promises, the platitudinous speech to the 1981 convention, the handling of other important Conservatives. He was stubborn to a fault because he could never stop fighting his public image as a wimp. And he never clearly conveyed either to the party or to the country a vision of where he wanted to take Canada. He tried hardest to articulate the idea of Canada as a "community of communities," but the idea itself, and his own uncertain definition of it, let him and the party down.

"Community of communities" was an intuition in search of a policy. It represented an intellectually defensible but politically dangerous way for a national party to view Canada, not as a country amounting to more than the sum of its parts but as a collection of parts in which Ottawa would be one, rather than first, among equals. It could have been the touchstone for a coherent alternative to Trudeau's brand of federalism had Clark been willing or able to define it, or explain how the country's institutions might be reformed to accommodate it, or offer some tangible evidence of its advantages from his own time in office. To the last days of his leadership, he could do none of these.

No one could gainsay Clark's passionate belief in "community of communities." He preached its putative virtues with more personal conviction and eloquence than any other idea, and there were occasions when he rendered the country a service in doing so. Against the conventional wisdom of the pundits and the gasps of apprehension from within the Conservative caucus, he bravely set himself against Trudeau's original constitutional package. His was a gut rejection of Trudeau's initiative supported by an Opposition leader's prudence in playing for time. Had he offered his party's general support, reserving judgement on the details, not only would he have faced rebellion from those Conservatives who thought Trudeau the Devil Incarnate, he would have allowed Trudeau to ram through a package that time revealed required substantial amendment.

This was Clark's bravest political decision, and history should judge him kindly for it. But, as ever, "community of communities" led up a blind alley. No one knew, least of all Clark, what alternative position the Conservatives should adopt. They had known for months that Trudeau intended to take an initiative, yet when it came the Conservatives were unprepared. Months of internal debate and interminable meetings ensued as the Conservatives searched for a detailed alternative that would do justice to "community of communities." But their first attempt was so palpably silly that it defied reasoned explanation: a constituent assembly and a national referendum to ratify its work. The ideas were laughed out of the national debate within days.

Gradually, the Conservatives coalesced around an attack on Trudeau's procedure for patriating the Constitution, an attack on procedure being easier to fit within the vague framework of "community of communities" than alternative policies. That was the enduring trouble with the idea: it was long on process but short on substance. Respect for process is important, even essential, in a federation, but ultimately debate must focus on ends as well as on means. "Community of communities" never offered a vision of what "ends" the Conservative Party under Clark had in mind. Never did the Conservatives convey the conviction that there were substantive positions for which as a federal government they would "fight, fight, and fight again." Of course, there were Conservative provincial governments, seldom in agreement among themselves, whose views the national Conservative leader must acknowledge. Wedges between him and the Conservative premiers would be cruelly exposed by the party's political foes. But those wedges would be the more painful because the federal Conservatives had bound themselves so tightly to their erstwhile provincial cousins.

Perhaps "community of communities" might have stood the test of political durability had Clark been able to demonstrate its merits from his months in office. But the whole country remembered, nowhere more ruefully than in the federal caucus, the bitter saga of his energy negotiations with Alberta. Or perhaps it might have been salvaged had Clark carried the idea to its logical conclusion and proposed reforms to give the provinces a stronger voice in federal institutions, as the Pepin-Robarts task force on national unity had recommended. At least that might have put some flesh on the skeleton of "community of communities." As it was, the idea floated across the country's political landscape, its shapelessness a further sign that its most eloquent exponent did not really know where to take the country.

Far from enhancing Joe Clark's stature as a national leader, "community of communities" undermined it. His idea furthered the impression of weakness by leaving him open to devastating attacks that he represented nothing more than a "handmaiden to the premiers," a "headwaiter," someone ready to "give away the shop." Clark was credited for "community of communities" in places where the Conservatives needed no help or among Quebec nationalists whose praise misled him into thinking that among them he could build a foundation for the Conservative Party in the province. He never did receive the thanks or support of the Conservative premiers, the very men whom "community of communities" ought to have attracted. Where were Peter Lougheed, William Davis, Richard Hatfield, Sterling Lyon, Brian Peckford, James Lee, Grant Devine, and John Buchanan at the Winnipeg convention? None of them were sitting in Joe Clark's box.

No sooner had the Conservatives tumbled from office than prominent voices within the Conservative caucus began muttering about "community of communities." They knew the federal party had been sandbagged in office by the Conservative premiers, and they resolved never to allow it to happen again. Indeed Clark himself delivered a speech at Spruce Grove, Alberta, in the opening days of the 1980 campaign that seemed to indicate that he, too, was having second thoughts. But he banished these from his mind, or at least from his future public pronouncements.

Brian Mulroney clearly disliked "community of communities" and set about early in his leadership to reorient the party towards a more resolutely national position on federal-provincial issues. No mileage could be gained, he believed, from being other than a national party defending national positions, even if these ran afoul of the view of some, or even all, of the Conservative premiers. Nowhere was this attitude more starkly demonstrated than in the party's support for the Liberal bill to penalize provinces which countenanced over-billing by doctors and user fees for medical services. One could scarcely have imagined the Conservatives under Clark supporting such a bill; too many Conservative provincial governments would have been offended.

So "community of communities" died with Joe Clark. But the

idea will some day be resurrected because it can represent a plausible way of trying to reconcile what Richard Simeon has called the
enduring Canadian tension between "nation-building" and "prov-
ince-building" or between what Northrop Frye has referred to as
the passion for "identity" and the yearning for "unity." When
"community of communities" resurfaces, undoubtedly with a new
catch phrase, it will have to reconcile these tensions by offering
provinces a more direct say in federal institutions. If, as never
happened under Joe Clark, the idea is carefully thought through, it
can offer a credible alternative for a federal party to the Ottawa-
always-knows-best centralism much favoured in recent years by
the Liberals.

The prospect of Conservative gains in Quebec under Mulroney
and the potential for Liberal gains under a new leader in the west
were the most encouraging developments of recent years. Certainly
the elections of 1979 and 1980 saddled Canada with a continuation
of one-party rule, the consequences of which have already distorted
the Canadian political system.

Ideally, political parties in a federation as diverse as Canada
should be strongly rooted in every region of the country so that all
regions will feel adequately represented in Ottawa whichever party
is in power. Since national parties are among the institutions that
bind together the often fractious parts of Canada, strength for
both parties in every region is a useful centripetal force in a country
with too many centrifugal forces. If the ideal can seldom be realized
because parties tend to be much stronger in one region than in
another, then a rotation of parties in power at least gives each
region the satisfaction of periodically seeing its political preference
in office. Prolonged one-party rule discourages regions opposed to
the dominant national party from feeling that their patience will be
rewarded by a change in government. The west, where alienation
had been growing apace, felt again after the 1980 election like an
outcast in Ottawa, the region's political preference overwhelmed
by the desires of the rest of the country.

That situation only served to increase western demands for
more provincial power, demands most insistently put by Premier
Peter Lougheed of Alberta in his energy negotiations with the
re-elected Liberals and by the western premiers in the constitutional
negotiations of 1981 and 1982. Having seen a Conservative Government they helped to elect in 1979 humbled less than a year later,
westerners could be forgiven for placing their trust in provincial
governments to protect western interests, believing that these

provincial governments could be more effective than Opposition parties in the Commons.

Quebec once again voted massively for the Liberals in 1980, giving the party seventy-four of seventy-five seats. The weakness of the two-party system in Quebec at the federal level continued to mean that when Quebeckers disagreed with the federal government, they would not find a haven for their discontent in Ottawa, where no Opposition from Quebec existed, but in the arena of provincial politics, where some party was likely to champion their cause. Without an alternative in Ottawa, Quebeckers would rally behind their provincial government, inducing the provincial government to interest itself in all matters properly federal and so increasing the strains on Confederation from Quebec.

The Liberal restoration of 1980, in addition to extending the negative influences of one-party rule, also deprived the civil service of an opportunity to work for a long period with another party. The civil service needed that opportunity, not because it was infested with card-carrying Liberals—although Liberal warhorses were scattered throughout the public service—but because the civil service had been approaching problems for too long from the perspective of the Liberal Party under Trudeau. The outlook and preferences of the Liberal Party became those of the civil service, and the civil service had difficulty conceiving new ways of tackling federal-provincial relations, social programs, or economic policy. There was nothing necessarily sinister or partisan in this affinity of perceptions; politicians simply felt comfortable with advice tailored to their own way of thinking and so favoured those who could provide them with such advice. The affinity was reciprocal: not only did the civil service see the country through a Liberal prism, but the Liberals accepted the assumptions of the civil service. The obsession with secrecy, the refusal to fetter the RCMP despite its transgressions, the belief that government can solve most, if not all, of the nation's problems: all of these beliefs of the senior mandarins became operating points of reference for the Liberal Party.

The marriage of outlook between the civil service and the Liberals under Trudeau was best exemplified by the expanded influence and power of both the Prime Minister's Office and that of the Clerk of the Privy Council under Michael Pitfield. There was an inevitability in the 1970s that power would grow at the nerve centre of government in relation to the so-called line departments, even the traditionally prestigious ones such as finance and external affairs. As the government sprawled into dozens of new policy areas and expanded its scope in existing ones, greater centralized monitoring was required to keep some semblance of order. But this centralization was carried to an unhealthy degree under Trudeau and his close friend Pitfield.

The weakness of most of Trudeau's later Cabinets abetted the trend. Apart from Lalonde, the post-1980 Trudeau Cabinets were lamentably short of talent; even MacEachen looked like a burnt-out case after his disastrous spell as finance minister. By mid-1983 the sapping of talent had been going on for the better part of a decade. John Turner, Donald Macdonald, Edgar Benson, Mitchell Sharp, Otto Lang, Ron Basford, Robert Andras, Alastair Gillespie, Barney Danson, Bud Drury, Gérard Pelletier, Jean Marchand, Jeanne Sauvé, and many lesser lights had retired or received big bites of the patronage cherry. Without strong ministers to defend line departments, the drift towards centralized power proceeded unchecked. The stream of departures also denuded the Liberal Party of potential leadership successors and contributed to its political decline.

Pitfield always insisted to anyone who cared to listen that his part in the centralization of power was apolitical, in keeping with the traditions of the Clerk's office. But so closely identified had he become with the Prime Minister, especially after his reinstatement as Clerk in 1980, that when Trudeau appointed him to the Senate the fig leaf fell from the apolitical argument. Nowhere was the dismay, even disgust, at that appointment more pronounced than in the upper reaches of the civil service, where mandarins who had struggled to maintain the political neutrality of the civil service felt their ideal profaned by the most powerful civil servant of all. They felt like senior army officers whose general had defected to the other side.*

The civil service served the Conservatives well, better than the party knew, for it was the civil service, among other groups, that warned against the consequences of moving the Canadian embassy in Israel, dismantling PetroCanada as a crown corporation, and introducing mortgage-interest and property-tax deductibility. Only towards the end of the Conservative interlude did the civil service understand and even appreciate the Conservatives. The civil service could have benefited from more exposure to the Conservatives, who would have challenged some existing procedures and ways of thinking, and given the civil service a healthy injection of talented men and women, Conservatives to be sure, from provincial governments or the private sector.

---

*For a brilliant analysis of Pitfield's role in Ottawa, see Christina McCall-Newman, *Grits*, part 4 (Macmillan, 1982).

The recent past tarnished the reputation of the entire political process and lowered public esteem for both major parties. Put crudely, Canadians were voting against someone rather than for something or someone in the elections of 1979 and 1980. Not since the last two elections involving John Diefenbaker in 1963 and 1965 had the level of political discourse in Canadian politics sunk so low. Bashing opponents is a necessary part of political life, but when negativism becomes the crowning objective of political strategy—as it was for both major parties in 1979 and 1980—then it is the body politic that suffers most. The political vacuity of both campaigns invited voters to share the cynicism of those seeking their support. The political abuse heaped by one leader on the other lowered the reputation of both when Canada needed sensitive, courageous, and even inspirational leadership to surmount the country's problems.

Important progress was made after 1980 in soothing part of the festering sore of constitutional reform, although only the most naive would suggest that the eternal Canadian question of the relations between English- and French-speaking Canadians and between Ottawa and the rest of the provinces had been resolved by the constitutional reform of 1982. In economic, energy, and cultural policy, Canada was still groping for policies that would lead to energy self-sufficiency, economic growth, and an affirmation of national identity. The government's margin for manoeuvre, always limited at the best of times, grew more slender when the deficit ballooned to $30 billion, nearly $20 billion more than when the Conservatives left office.

Canada entered the 1980s a more sorely divided nation than it had been on the eve of the 1970s. Not all the reasons for the souring of our national mood and the sapping of our confidence could be attributed to the failings of our politicians. Business, labour, and cultural leaders bore some responsibility for our inability to work together, and all of our important institutions felt the tremors of uncertainty and doubt afflicting the Western world's ability to sustain extraordinary affluence in the face of a changing world order. But the political area is ultimately where collective decisions about the future are made. Canadians have not been well served by their political parties in recent years, so it was with foreboding tempered by a measure of eternal optimism that we celebrated Trudeau's election-night cry: "Welcome to the 1980s." And it was with that same mixture of apprehension and optimism that Canadians awaited the political changes of the 1980s that might bring the purposeful and resourceful government the country needed.

Index